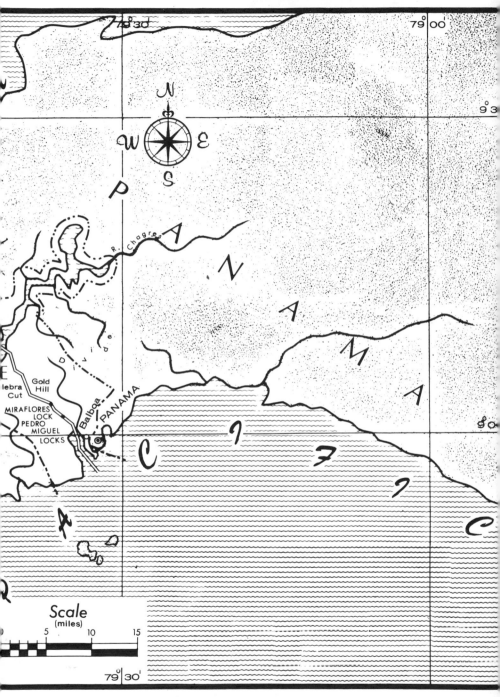

Philippe
Bunau-Varilla

Classical portrayal of Philippe Bunau-Varilla, part of the collection of Giselle Bunau-Varilla Rocco, Naiwasha, Kenya.

Philippe Bunau-Varilla

The Man behind The Panama Canal

Gustave Anguizola

Nelson–Hall nh Chicago

The author wishes to dedicate the first edition of this book to the Honorable William P. Clements, Jr., Governor of the State of Texas, who challenged the odds and was victorious in his quest for the highest State office.

Library of Congress Cataloging in Publication Data

Anguizola, G. A. 1927-
    Philippe Bunau-Varilla.

    Bibliography: p.
    Includes Index
    1. Panama Canal—History. 2. Bunau-Varilla, Philippe, 1895-1940. 3. Civil engineers—France—Biography.
TC774.A67   386'.444'09   79-13673
ISBN 0-88229-397-4

Manufactured in the United States of America

10   9   8   7   6   5   4   3   2   1

Contents

Foreword

Philippe Bunau-Varilla was not cast in any mold. He was original, inventive, dynamic, and highly intelligent. He had a warm and attractive personality. I was introduced to him in 1924 by the famous World War I correspondent Frank H. Simonds.

As a young man Philippe Bunau-Varilla was an engineer employed by Ferdinand de Lesseps, the builder of the Suez Canal. De Lesseps discovered that building a trans-isthmian canal in the American hemisphere was too much for any private company—the ground was much more difficult than at Suez and the man-killing yellow fever was an insuperable obstacle.

Bunau-Varilla, in an adventure reminiscent of the Arabian nights, persuaded the United States government to abandon its preference for putting a canal through Nicaragua and to commit itself to building one at Panama, where the French company had started its work. He sent a Nicaraguan postage stamp bearing a picture of Mt. Momotombo, a smoking volcano, to every senator to show that the Nicaraguans themselves admitted that their terrain was unstable.

When the northern provinces of Colombia seceded to form the Republic of Panama, Bunau-Varilla was there to write the constitution and to become the first Panamanian ambassador to Washington. He arranged with Theodore Roosevelt to have the U.S. Navy show the flag at the psychological moment.

World War I found Bunau-Varilla as Marshal Henri Philippe Petain's chief engineering officer at Verdun where, while in his sixties, he lost his leg in combat and, under fire, perfected a system of water purification which he was later to install throughout France.

When I met him he was old and I was in my early twenties. But there was something youthful about him which made him attractive to young people. He was a great individualist whose friendship meant much to me and whom I shall always remember.

Henry Cabot Lodge

Acknowledgments

Certainly this book could not have been possible without the help of the many persons whom I interviewed and corresponded with over many years, especially Madame Giselle Bunau-Varilla Rocco, Philippe Bunau-Varilla II, and Miss Florence Loomis, all of whom placed at my disposal the entire Varillana in their possession. Other generous people with whom I spoke and corresponded are given due credit in the end notes; however, there were others who provided encouragement and contributed information, such as engineers D.P. Schouwe and Dean M. Blanchard, Mr. and Mrs. Julius Ritter of Evansville, Indiana, Mr. and Mrs. Robert E. Long of Washington, D.C., Mr. Harry Damm and Drs. Daniel D. McGarry, Robert Quirk, O.O. Winther, and James E. Morlock, my academic mentors.

In an enterprise of this nature there has to be a plethora of corrigenda, and I am indebted to Ouilda Piner of Arlington, Texas, for her wise suggestions. Mrs. E.C. Barkasdale, novelist Benjamin Capps, Dr. Bob Perkins, and the Honorable Henry Cabot Lodge graciously consented to read chapters in their field of specialization. Many of my students enthusiastically, and without remuneration, helped in this task, especially Kenneth G. Tarrant and Thomas Tune.

For the drawings and part of the translation, I am grateful to the distinguished research scholar Orchard Lisle, and to Don Odell and Professor Leon B. Blair. Thanks are also due the junior typist, Michael Edwards, and the senior typist, Mrs. G. LaPlante. Various people in libraries and museums contributed to my efforts, especially Miss Patricia J. Palmer and her staff at the research library of Stanford University and Mrs. Mary Price of the library of the University of Texas at Arlington. Other librarians at the University of Chicago, the National Archives, the Archives of the Canal Company, the Library of Congress, and the Newberry Library deserve my gratitude. The Varillana in the Edward Price Bell manuscripts at the Newberry Library was very useful to me. For collecting oral and written information in Panama, I am indebted to Jose Cabezas, formerly with the Ministry of Education.

Few books are completed without financial help. I am grateful to Dr. Lee Taylor, former chairman of the research committee at the University of Texas in Arlington, and Dr. Lawrence L. Schkade, former dean of the University's graduate school, for their enthusiastic support which made possible a grant to defray travel and duplication expenses.

1

Early Dreams of a Canal and the Coming of a Railroad

Search for a Passage; Alexander von Humboldt; Early French Interest in an American Canal; American Interest; Building the Transcontinental Railroad at Panama.

Before his death on May 26, 1506, Columbus caused considerable confusion among learned geographers because of his own doubts that he had reached India. As early as 1497, the secretive admiral had begun to search for a hidden passage which may have led him to the South Sea. On reaching the mouth of the Orinoco River, Columbus declared that "your majesties have here a new world," and the idea of cutting the continent to realize the dream of an artificial passage was born.[1]

The arrival of Vasco Nunez de Balboa to the shores of the Pacific Ocean in the autumn of 1513 accelerated the drive to seek a westward route,[2] and there are some writers who affirm that this brief moment in the saga of the discoveries was the first act toward the construction of an interoceanic canal.[3] In 1517, one of Balboa's companions in his earlier journey from Santa Maria del Darien to the Ocean Sea, a relative of Hernan Cortez, named Alvaro de Ceron, sug-

1

gested a waterway at Panama. The course proposed by this adventurer, from Nombre de Dios to Panama City or from Uraba to the Gulf of San Miguel, was not unlike those drawn by later surveyors. However, Hernan Cortez was the first in an official capacity to consider cutting the continent in order to secure the union of the two oceans.

In a letter to Emperor Charles V, Cortez stated that the realization of such a project could be considered a greater glory than the conquest of New Spain.[4] Charles must have been highly impressed by the words of the conqueror because, in June 1523, he issued an imperial rescript "to seek the strait of which much is spoken,"[5] and the "Captain from Castille" quickly replied to his master with four letters saying that he was sending Diego de Hurtado to find the strait in Panama and to the north by the Floridas. Meanwhile Rodrigo de Albornoz, who had delivered the message for the Emperor to Cortez, wrote the king, on December 15, 1525, that "after arriving in these lands, I exerted myself with the Governor in order to give concrete expression to our efforts in seeking the passage which has been said and is believed to be in [the area of] the *especeria*."[6]

The subduer of the Aztecs needed no encouragement to continue the chase for an evanescent strait. Convinced that Montezuma's domains were not India, he questioned the unfortunate Mexican prince about the secret of the mysterious passage. Perhaps hoping to rid himself of the Spaniard the imperial hostage called upon his court painters to furnish Cortez with a "map of the coast,"[7] but Cortez was the first to give up the idea of a natural gateway to the Pacific when he began work to unite the rivers Chimalcas and Guazalcolco.[8] However, by 1528, he reverted to his earlier scheme of cutting the continent.[9]

The court in Spain was in no hurry to abandon the search for a passage, especially after an assembly of learned cartographers and experienced pilots approved a resolution in Badajoz supporting the belief that an all-water route would eventually be found between Newfoundland and Panama. But Cortez' advice was not lightly overlooked. In 1529, the new Governor of Panama, Don Pedro de los Rios, asked Captain Hernando de la Serna "to see if it is possible to use the waters of the Chagres River for the purpose of building a canal which will unite the two seas."[10]

Armed with these ideas and suggestions, the crown commissioned Antonio de la Gama, successor to de los Rios, "to proceed to find a better way between Panama and Nombre de Dios." At the same time the governor of Nicaragua, Diego Lopez de Salcedo, requested Captain Gabriel Rojas to look for the strait in the land of the two lakes.[11] The long rivalry between the two most rational choices for a canal was launched. It took four centuries of bitter confrontation and frustration before Panama emerged the winner, thanks to the genius of Philippe Bunau-Varilla.

The shifting of Pedro Arias Davila from the isthmus to Nicaragua, superseding Salcedo, interrupted the search for a passage in Central America; but in Panama, Antonio de la Gama took up his assignment with gusto. In a series of letters to the empress, dated February 22, May 15, and July 28, 1533, the enthusiastic official urged the government to compromise about the idea of an all-water passage by using part of the Chagres and then reaching Panama City through an artificial ditch.[12] Apparently without waiting for a reply, the notables of the isthmus went ahead with this plan as early as February 22, 1533.[13] Gaspar de Espinosa might not have been in complete agreement with this decision, because he wrote to Charles V on October 10, 1533, urging the monarch to adopt a route utilizing the waters of the Rio Grande.[14] The same day, and probably by the same courier, the group headed by de la Gama also wrote to the emperor, insisting on the Chagres route.[15]

A year later, on February 20, 1534, the colonists had a reply from Spain favoring the Chagres[16] route and asking the adelantado, Francisco de Barrionuevo, to settle once and for all the choice of a permanent trans-isthmian route,[17] but Barrionuevo sought to kill the all-water canal project. He wrote to the king as follows: "The opening of the canal would mean opening the doors of the Pacific to the Portuguese and to the French."[18] Nevertheless, Gaspar de Espinosa informéd the sovereign, on April 11, 1536, that Barrionuevo "did nothing yet because he had to resist Heredia."[19] (Pedro de Heredia, the conqueror of the coastal areas of present-day Colombia, was trying to move toward the isthmus.)

One can imagine Charles' reaction to such seemingly contradictory reports about an issue which the far-removed ruler must have deemed much less important than the Turks, the German princes, England, or France; yet he directed Adelantado Pascual de Andagoya, one of the promoters of the Chagres route, to conduct a new survey of this river. For entirely different reasons, Andagoya concurred with the Barrionuevo report that no canal should be built, because "no prince on earth, regardless of his power, is capable of forming a junction of both seas . . . nor of defraying the expenses required for such an undertaking."[20]

Andagoya was a realistic man. He urged the King to "clean the Chagres . . . there are only five leagues to Panama [from the end of the stream], and these can be built into a road . . . the royal command to see if the two oceans can be joined is the product of news lacking in knowledge."[21] But the idea of an isthmian canal persisted. Francisco Lopez de Gomara, in his *Historia de las Indias*, recommended the use of Peruvian Indians to dig the canal: ". . . if there is anyone who would like to build it [the canal], it can be done; enthusiasm is not lacking, money is not scarce, and the Indies, where it will be located, can furnish it all . . . for a King of Castille there is little that is impossible."[22]

The learned Italian engineer Juan Bautista Antonelli, who had a considerable reputation throughout Europe and enjoyed the favor of Philip II, advised the king against such a project and, soon afterwards, discussion of an interoceanic canal was discouraged in Spain.[23] But the Spaniards persisted in other investigations during the reigns of Philip III, IV and V. Diego Fernandez de Velazco was the first to survey the Atrato River, and it was surveyed at various times until 1719, when the sovereign, advised by the governor of Nueva Granada, signed a decree barring any further investigations of this route under penalty of death. The order was intended to protect the customhouse at Cartagena against smugglers.[24]

With the rise of the buccaneers, the British became aware of the importance of Panama.[25] William Patterson was the first Anglo-Saxon who tried to secure a permanent foothold in the umbilical cord of the Spanish Empire. For him, the possession of Panama was absolutely necessary in the struggle for world supremacy. Patterson prophesied that any nation able to control the Isthmus of Darien would hold the keys to the universe.[26]

The canal question remained in abeyance until late in the eighteenth century when Don Jose de Galvez, the visitador general de indias, recalling the early voyages in the Northwest, instructed Don Manuel de Galisteo to study anew the possibility of a canal somewhere between Tehuantepec and Panama. This search was never completed and interest died down with the beginning of the American Revolution, in which Spain became directly involved.[27]

Alexander von Humboldt's Stories and Prophesies about the Canal

The German geographer, Alexander von Humboldt, wrote of a priest in the land of the Choco River who, in 1788, persuaded the inhabitants of the region to cut through a hill in order to unite the waters of the rivers Quebdo and Atrato, thus creating a canal which first achieved interoceanic communication. Humboldt vividly described how canoes filled with cocoa and coffee succeeded in navigating the ditch, thanks to the help of a heavy rainfall. This famous naturalist and geographer also traveled in Mexico and became the most enthusiastic proponent of canals beyond the Rhine. He speculated about various canal routes including Tehuantepec and Nicaragua, but reached the conclusion that the undertaking of such a vast work should be left only to a nation dedicated to the highest interests of mankind.[28]

In his *Political Essay on the Kingdom of New Spain*, Humboldt listed nine different locations for an interoceanic canal; later, he reduced the number of possibilities to five: Tehuantepec,

Nicaragua, Panama, Darien, and Raspadura, all in the geographical center of the New World.[29] The German traveler left no doubt that his first choice was Panama, because the mountains of the isthmus are cut from each other by "valleys which [might] give a free course to the passage of waters."[30] Humboldt infected his countryman, Goethe, with his own enthusiasm for a canal at Panama under the suzerainty of the United States.[31] He also believed it would be necessary to create a separate and neutral state "dependent on the federation of the United States."[32] Nicaragua, he observed, is so reticulated with volcanoes that only madmen would think seriously of digging a canal there. Indeed, Bunau-Varilla later had to fight this insanity, and he used the same weapons suggested by von Humboldt—the tragic reality of devastating earthquakes such as that on December 23, 1972, which, like the violent tremors of 1931, had its epicentre inside what might have been the Nicaraguan Canal Zone.[33]

Native Spanish-Americans also visualized a canal at Panama. In April 1803, the English government received a secret memorandum from Don Francisco de Miranda listing several reasons why the isthmus might be the first spot in the vast empire of Spain that needed to be seized in order to harass the peninsular government, headed at the time by Don Manuel Godoy.[34] This *aide-memoire* was well received by William Pitt the younger, but the growing power of General Bonaparte had already made France a much stronger foe of England than Spain, and the prime minister, fearing a Franco-Spanish alliance, scuttled the plans of the Venezuelan conspirator.[35]

From his exile in Jamaica in 1815, Simon Bolivar also began to dream of a canal at Panama.[36] Later, as the leader of Gran Colombia (Greater Colombia), he proposed the construction of an interoceanic waterway to the Interamerican Congress of 1826, held in Panama City.[37] The congress authorized an immediate canal survey.[38]

Early French Interest in
an American Passage

French interest in an American canal can be traced to the

voyages of Giovanni da Verrazano, the Florentine navigator in the service of Francis I, who courageously tried to find a water passage during his two trips to the Americas.[39] Many schemes for a canal at Panama, Nicaragua, and Tehuantepec were discussed in France during the sixteenth and seventeenth centuries, when much of that country was being laced with a network of waterways.[40] An event in Asia—the signing of the Treaty of Nanking in late August 1842—caused the French to fix their attention more closely on an American canal. By this treaty, China was forced to open up to Western trade—including France—the cities of Canton, Shanghai, Amoy, Foochow, and Ningpo.[41]

The House of Napoleon, which had much to do with the promotion of a modern canal in Egypt, also gave much thought to the construction of a seaway in America. Louis Napoleon Bonaparte, while a political prisoner in the fortress of Hamm, planned a canal project through Nicaragua. (Its publication betrayed his dream of creating an empire in North America.) The prince referred to the sleepy town of Leon as a potential Western Constantinople which could "attain much prosperity and grandeur."[42]

Fourteen years later, at the height of his political power and fresh from victory in the Crimea, Napoleon III continued his alliance with England, forcing on China the Treaty of Tientsin of 1858.[43] Ironically, the aggressive posture of the two Western nations helped Russia become an Asian power. Posing as a friend and protector of the Celestial Empire, the czar received the vast territory between the rivers Amur and Usuri, creating the large maritime province of Siberia. Russia is the only country that has claimed, received, and retained to this date territory which was once part of China.

Without foregoing his opportunities in China, Napoleon III also began to pay attention, in 1859, to requests for intervention in Mexico. Perhaps in the knowledge that the emperor had, in his youth, dreamed of a canal in Central America, several entrepreneurs urged his government to seize Sonora and Tehuantepec and form a new corporation to replace the old Louisiana–Tehuantepec company.[44] The story of the Jecker claims, which motivated the French to create an empire in Mexico, and of the subsequent tragic demise of Maximilian of Austria, is well known.[45] However, the failure of the imperial design, prompted in part by United States' protests, left Panama the only logical spot on the continent for the canal. Later we shall see how quickly the French transferred their attention from Mexico to the mouth of the Chagres River.

American Interest in Trans-Isthmian Communication

A friend of Alexander Hamilton and John Knox, the Venezuelan Creole, Don Francisco de Miranda, might have been the first to alert the United States to the importance of securing the isthmus in perpetuity. He certainly spoke in these terms to both William Pitt the elder and Catherine of Russia.[46] A few years later, after the Monroe Declaration of December 23, 1822, the American government sent delegates to the Bolivarian Congress of 1826 at Panama, but it was not until 1846 that President James K. Polk's obsession with Manifest Destiny became a popular conviction. The question was not merely whether California should be acquired, but also the whole of Mexico.[47] Alarmed by Franco–British designs in North and Central America,[48] the United States accelerated a diplomatic offensive, for the first time evincing a serious official interest in canal construction. It led to a signed agreement with Nueva Granada by which its sovereignty was fully protected in exchange for the right of free transit.[49]

Obviously, the decade from 1840 to 1850 was an important one in our history. It witnessed the annexation of Texas, the acquisition of California and all the southwestern country from Mexico, and the final agreement with England for the northwestern boundary. The United States, having assumed a commanding position in the New World, had to interest itself in new and important trade routes, exactly as all other nations have done when they neared a period of commercial expansion and political maturity.

There was still no railroad to California, for the Union Pacific was not completed until 1869. The gold miners had to find another way to reach the west. Communication between the eastern part of the country and the vast territories recently acquired had become a political necessity. The United States had to be interested in any canal to be built between the two oceans. Should the work be successful, no European power must assume sole control of it. Consequently, interest in canal construction began to pervade the foreign policy of the new nation.

But the French, aware of these aims, kept a watchful eye on the movements of the American diplomatic agents traveling in Mexico and Central America. The political maneuvers, as well as the guessing game, duplicated what was going on between France and England over the Suez Canal. And in America, as in Egypt, railroad and canal building complemented each other. After the second half of the nineteenth century, in response to the pressure of many entrepreneurs interested in one or both of these methods of transportation through Panama, the Congress of Nueva Granada authorized negotiations for the establishment of an ocean-to-ocean railroad line.

Shortly after this law was passed, seizing as an excuse the duel of a local citizen with M. Russell, His Majesty's vice-consul at Panama City, an English naval squadron blockaded the mouth of the Chagres River and the harbor of Cartagena. Momentarily satisfied with official apologies and an indemnity, the war vessels flying the Union Jack retreated. But everyone in Panama and Washington feared that the British, using another excuse, might one day seize the isthmus. No doubt alarmed, and wishing to forestall such an unhappy occurrence, President Jackson commissioned Colonel Charles Biddle to travel to Panama and Bogota in 1836.[50]

This crisis with England, provoked in part by the Panamanians themselves, facilitated the work of the American agent in securing for his country a most-favored-nation treatment. After talking to the merchant princes and politicians in Panama, Colonel Biddle realized that the isthmians preferred that the Americans, rather than the British, be in possession of the strategic passage.[51] President

Jackson's emissary therefore began to drive hard to secure exclusive rights over the isthmus. Biddle's secret and successful negotiations bore positive results ten years later with the signing of the treaty of guarantees which placed the State of Panama under the protection of the United States. Simultaneously, Senator John Middleton Clayton introduced into the U.S. Senate a resolution proposing the construction of an American canal at Panama or other area of Central America.[52]

Like the English in Egypt, France became alarmed at hearing of the negotiations initiated by Colonel Biddle and continued by the accredited minister to Bogota, Benjamin A. Bidlack. The French Minister to Nueva Granada wrote to the Quai d'Orsay:

> Should New Granada summon the aid of the United States to suppress any threat of secession on the part of Panama or Veraguas, she will deliver to the Americans a position of military and commercial importance which will mean more to them than Gibraltar does to England. Should we not take the liberty of warning this government [New Granada] of the stupidity of this agreement that clearly compromises the very future [of New Granada]? The road that the United States will build at Panama will surely upset the present state of affairs. One day the public will no longer be indifferent and their interest in this matter might be hard to cope with.[53]

The clever diplomat needed no crystal ball to prophesy that, from the moment this treaty was signed, the isthmus was precariously attached to Nueva Granada.

Bogota was not a good place to keep diplomatic secrets. The terms of the convention were well known to the French. The treaty consisted of thirty-six general articles and one "additional article." However, the most important article is the thirty-fifth. Subdivided into six paragraphs, it dealt entirely with transisthmian communication, reading in part as follows:

> New Granada guarantees to the government of the United States of America, that the right of way or transit across the

Isthmus of Panama, upon any modes of communication that now exist, or that may be hereafter constructed, shall be open and free to the government and citizens of the United States of America . . . and the United States of America guarantees, positively and efficaciously to New Granada, by the present stipulation, the perfect neutrality of the before-mentioned Isthmus of Panama, with the view that the free transit from one to the other sea may not be interrupted or embarrassed; in consequence, the United States of America also guarantees, in the same manner, the rights of sovereignty and property which New Granada has and possesses over the said territory.[59]

The protection offered in this document was such a clear departure from traditional American foreign policy that President Polk apparently hesitated to send the treaty to the Senate. The explicit guarantees were so bluntly written that the chief executive believed they might create senatorial opposition to its ratification.[55] In his message to the Senate, he prudently inserted the following statement: " . . . the chargé d'affaires acted in this particular upon his own responsibility and without [my] instructions."[56]

This treaty, with its accompanying notes and correspondence, became an ace of spades in the hands of Philippe Bunau-Varilla a half-century later. After he talked with F.B. Loomis and J.B. Moore, these men convinced Theodore Roosevelt of the validity of United States' rights over the isthmus. The argument was so convincing that Secretary of State John Hay, who seemed sympathetic toward Nicaragua, endorsed Philippe's remote-control Panamanian revolution.[57]

But the English were determined, if not to spoil the American move, at least to share in the rewards of a transcontinental passage. In 1847, to forestall the unilateral success of the United States at Bogota, the British, acting in the name of his Mosquito majesty, seized the Mosquito territory from Nicaragua. Flushed by the diplomatic victories won at Bogota, President Polk retaliated, accepting the treaty signed by Nicaragua with his minister to Guatemala, Elijah Hise, on June 21, 1849.[58] The stage was set for the power confrontation that led to the signing of the Clayton-Bulwer Treaty of 1850. Simultaneously with these high-level moves, Nicaragua also granted exclusive rights for an interoceanic waterway to an American syndicate headed by the well-known entrepreneur Cornelius Vanderbilt. Lack of funds hindered the project, but it marks the beginning of a preference for the Nicaraguan route, a preference which only one man was able to change. That man was Bunau-Varilla.

Failing to raise capital to build his canal, Vanderbilt established a transit across Nicaragua for passengers and continued to operate it until unexpected opposition to the Vanderbilt interests from some of his Nicaraguan lieutenants broke up the transit. The next chapter describes the growth of anti-American feeling in Nicaragua and how the government of that nation began to take steps to annul the contract.[59]

In the meantime, E. George Squier replaced Elijah Hise in Central America, and he soon had to confront England's aggressive moves in the person of its consul in Managua, Frederick Chalfield. Squier had secured from Nicaragua another treaty guaranteeing the protection of the transportation company as well as a new canal convention. The jealousy and the exasperation of the British rose in proportion to the success of the Americans. Chalfield then contrived to seize Tigre Island from Honduras. Strategically located in the Gulf of Fonseca, Tigre Island could surely dominate the western terminus of any canal built through Central America.[60]

These maneuvers and counteractions of the American and British diplomats in Central America came out into the open at a moment when the aggressive foreign policy of President Polk was going down to defeat in the election of 1848. Defying the American claims in Central America, the British resorted to direct action by taking possession of San Juan de Nicaragua. The United States, still an adolescent giant with a leadership divided by the continuous bickerings of Whigs and Democrats, vacillated and worried. Perhaps in the knowledge of the terms of the Bidlack-Mallarino treaty, the terrified Nicaraguan minister to London, Don Juan Castrellon, requested of John Bancroft, his American counterpart in

England, that Nicaragua be admitted to the Union at once.[61]

The new chief executive, General Zachary Taylor, and his secretary of state, former Senator John Middleton Clayton, asked for negotiations and courteously told the British they could not recognize the Mosquito treaty.[62] The federal government insisted it sought no special privileges or unilateral concessions from the weak Latin-American republics, and conceded that the proposed maritime route should be open to all. After some exploratory talks in London between Lord Palmerston and Minister John Bancroft, the lordly foreign secretary accepted the suggestion, but only after Secretary Clayton declared that he "did not hold to President Monroe's no further colonization edict."[63]

Thus, without much vacillation, the British minister to Washington, Sir Henry Bulwer, and the U.S. secretary of state negotiated and signed in 1850 the treaty that bears their names. A step backward from President Polk's position toward Latin America, it applied to any canal project, whether at Panama or at Nicaragua, forcing the United States to accept a previously unwelcome party to any American waterway scheme. The canal was to be placed under joint patronage, it was to be neutral, no fortifications were to be allowed, and the principle of equality of treatment was to be enforced.

By the middle of the nineteenth century, an atmosphere of suspicion and rancor against England began to becloud the minds of most Americans. It was no secret that the United States had been opposed to the idea of any other power building a canal in this continent, Britain in particular. The suspicion turned to exasperation when, on the eve of ratification, Sir Henry Bulwer advised President Millard Fillmore that the treaty's limitation of fortifications did not apply to Belize and the Mosquito Islands.[64]

Contrary to many, I believe that the Clayton-Bulwer Treaty hindered canal construction. It retarded rather than stimulated interoceanic communication. Diplomatically, the treaty embodies a most difficult agreement, surely one of the most unpopular ever subscribed to by the United States.[65] From that moment, it became a prime American objective to cancel the most-favored-nation status granted to the British by this convention. Fifty years later, in 1901, thanks to the determination, sagacity, and realism of Senator Henry Cabot Lodge and President Theodore Roosevelt, this goal was achieved.[66]

The Building of the Transcontinental
Railroad at Panama

The geopolitical gyrations of small nations closely resemble geological cataclysms—they contract, expand, and again reduce their territorial boundaries until they reach their natural frontier or a political accommodation with another state which is believed to be enjoying at that moment greater economic stability. A case in point is provided by the new countries of Africa and the Near East.[67]

Because of parliamentary obstruction and revolution, Greater Colombia was first to feel the ax of disintegration. In no other country did "the refusal of quorum, dilatory motions, and time killing devices"[68] more successfully weaken the democratic structure than in the brainchild of Simon Bolivar. When ruinous parliamentary tactics were not at hand, the sons of Greater Colombia chose a quicker way to commit suicide—internecine warfare.[69]

As the frustrated and disappointed Bolivar withdrew to Santa Marta to await his day of reckoning with the Lord, Greater Colombia approached the doors of hell with a firm step and a derisive smile. Had it not been for the Napoleonic wars, which left Spain and Portugal as weak as an isthmian worker after malaria and France and England very tired, the Spanish-American colonies, and particularly the isthmus, would have fallen to either France or England. They might even now be struggling for secession, probably with the help of the United States.[70]

As Greater Colombia disintegrated, it sought stability by changing its name to Nueva Granada. However, French and British interest in Central and South America revived. Both countries tried to terminate the independent life of the River

Plata republics but, thanks to strongman Don Juan Manuel Rosas, they survived the attack.[71] In the United States, the need for an east-west route across Central America—any kind of quick route—was becoming more evident every day. It became urgent with the Forty-Niners. Shipping lines quickly connected New York with Colon and Panama with San Francisco. No road was more practical than the old Spanish *Camino Real*.

In the realm of transportation, no early modern invention was more captivating than the railroad. Since the arrival of the first operating locomotive in Wales, people had visualized both the shortening of distances and the saving of travel time.[72]

A few months before the ratification of the treaty of 1846 between Nueva Granada and the United States, impresario Mateo Klein, exhibiting a recommendation from the president of the State of Panama, Don Jose Maria Barriga, obtained from the acting head of state in Bogota, Don Rufino Cuervo, a railroad concession on behalf of a French group. This company, however, could not raise the necessary capital before 1848, when the treaty became effective.[73]

Panamanian writer M.M. Alba C., in his *Cronologia de los Gobernantes de Panama*, states:

> By this instrument [the Bidlack-Mallarino treaty of 1846], Nueva Granada, eager to insure the subjection of the Isthmus [to herself or to a foreign power?] for all practical purposes gave away to the other party, in exchange for an illusory guarantee of subjection and neutrality, the [entire] perimeter of this area of [our] national domain.[74]

We have already noted President Polk's apprehension about submitting this treaty to the Senate of the United States, but Senor Alba strongly suggests that the terms of this document, as well as the phraseology of the articles, were the work of the president of Nueva Granada, General Tomas Cipriano de Mosquera, and his foreign minister, Manuel M. Mallarino.[75] These charges are probably true. As minister to London in 1843, President Mosquera became alarmed by

British intrusions into Latin America, and he urged his American colleague in England to impress upon the secretary of state, John Calhoun, the necessity of building, at the earliest possible opportunity, a ship canal through the isthmus which was to be forever under the control of the United States.[75]

Alba's words make it clear that the charges of haste, sale, and treason directed against the man who successfully engineered the independence of the isthmus and the completion of the interoceanic canal through Panama—Bunau-Varilla— are not even remotely valid: "The [entire] perimeter of this area of the national domain," the isthmus, had already been ceded to the United States in 1846. It is ludicrous to think, and irrational to believe, that the United States, in 1903 or now, would forever abandon the reality of a dream of five centuries by surrendering the right to insure safe passage and neutrality at Panama.

The contract for building a railroad on the isthmus was signed while Jose Hilario Lopez was president of Nueva Granada and six months before Polk retired from office in Washington. The lucky entrepreneur was an American, William Aspinwall, who had acquired a copy of a railroad concession obtained ten years earlier by Manuel Salomon. The articles of Aspinwall's contract are identical to Salomon's. The Panama Railroad Company was to enjoy all transit profits for forty-nine years. The concessionaires received a virtual monopoly for overland transportation in Panama and, in 1867, when canal projects began to look serious enough to threaten the railroad, the contract was amended to stipulate that no canal grant should be considered valid without the consent of the Panama Railroad Company.[76] The contract was tenured at ninety-nine years.

The first ecological victim of the iron horse in the isthmus was a majestic palm tree pregnant with two dozen coconuts. In May 1850, in the presence of the president of the State of Panama, Don Jose Domingo de Obaldia, and about five hundred onlookers, railroad engineers James Baldwin and Charles Troutwine began to stab at the bark of the palm with

a silver ax. But the job was much too strenuous in the hot
sun, and it had to be finished by six Cuna aborigines from
San Blas in the pay of the contractors.[77]

When the first navigators touched land on the isthmus[78]
and northern South America, nature declared total war
against the white. When one endeavors to penetrate this
terra incognita, it is like entering a vast primeval forest, a
twilight jungle filled with strange forms and elusive shadows
peopling a wilderness through which there is no path except
that opened ahead of one's steps by the machete. The
vegetation cries aloud the pessimistic warnings of Claude
Levi-Strauss in *Tristes Tropiques*.[79] The soil, the branches, and
the streams are constantly traversed by armies of reptiles,
insects, and lower vertebrates in a state of perpetual hostility
to the intruder. The earth bitterly resents the tools that open
its wounds. Only the most persistent of humans can emerge
victorious.

In these thick jungles, few can survive without the machete. You must pick your way through, with ticks tumbling
off the branches onto your arms while reptiles and insects of
every species and size slowly retreat from your path or
immobilize you with a menacing stare. I have met, face-to-
face, some small-size replicas of the brontosaurus, such as the
fierce-looking water basilisk which, when annoyed, trans-
forms itself into a veritable Chimera of Arezzo.[80] But if you
consider yourself a nature lover, you will enjoy thrilling
moments of ecological splendor. Usually, when you arrive at
a clearing, you are treated to the sight of a flight of great
flocks of screeching parrots whose green color makes a deep
contrast across the bright blue sky—if it is not raining.

The fierce-looking iguana, the timid armadillo, as well as
the graceful egret might come to peer at you from the edge of
the swamp grass or from the tall mahogany trees; and the
multicolored howler monkeys fill the warm air with frighten-
ing roar. A witness to the building of the railroad writes:

> The luxuriance of the vegetation is beyond the powers of
> description. Now we pass impenetrable thickets of man-

groves, rising out of deep marshes, and sending from each branch down into the earth, and from each root into the air, offshoots which gather together into a matted growth, where the observer seeks in vain to unravel the mysterious involution of trunk, root, branch, and foliage. Now we come upon gigantic *espaves* and *coratos,* with girths of thirty feet, and statures of a hundred and thirty feet, out of a single trunk of which, without a plank or a seam, the natives build great vessels of twelve tons burden. . . . These giants of the forest seem, like Titans, offspring of heaven and earth, for they embrace with their mighty arms the one, and cling deep down into the bosom of the other; and the great twining plants which, rising from their roots, coil about their trunks, bind themselves in twisted fibre about their branches, and joining these great trees inseparably together, fasten them to the ground, remind us of the imprisonment which the Titans of old suffered from the cruelty of their father, Coelus.[81]

If the night catches you in the jungle, not even a bonfire will drive away the curious tenants of the forest whose rights you have violated by your trespass. No dose of tranquilizers or alcohol can shut out the nocturnal choir of the animal kingdom. One marvels at the conquistadores who, some- times herding hundreds of pigs, mules, and cattle, managed to walk thousands of miles in this living hell. One of these adventurers, Gil Gonzalez Davila, transported his ships from east to west and became the first European who sailed the "South Sea."[82]

The first railroad laborers had to toil under these terrifying conditions. Cutting through the caiman-infested swamps near the island of Manzanillo was a task reserved for heroes. The problem of recruiting, housing, feeding, and keeping the workers alive in this green hell became an almost insuperable undertaking for the Panama Railroad Company. The Irish came first, with broad smiles and characteristic charm, but those who managed to survive the apocalyptic scourge of yellow fever, malaria, and sun strokes departed with tears in their eyes and hardly any flesh on their bones. In despera- tion, the company recruited coolies. Asian labor had already been introduced into Mexico and Cuba. After the Treaty of

Nanking in 1842, legal trade in coolies through the ports of Amoy, Fuchow, Shanghai, and Canton became widespread.[83] Generally, the Chinese contracted to work for eight years for $4 a month. Food (mainly rice), clothing, and other necessities usually given to slaves were provided for them.[84] One thousand Chinese arrived to work for the railroad, but in a few weeks they too were riddled with disease and the government of the state surreptitiously permitted the company to distribute opium to the newcomers. The central authorities at Bogota frowned on this practice, however, and the Asians, deprived of the only form of relaxation possible to them, began to kill themselves at an alarming rate.

Twenty to thirty died every day. Some hanged themselves, using their own long hair as rope; others plunged from the nearest precipice; many more went to the beach, where they sat cross-legged and barefoot from dawn to dark, awaiting death. They meditated and prayed for the end of all personal desires and sensual obsessions. At times the silence was broken by a whispered yearning for a tranquil and abject surrender to the spirit of their long departed ancestors,[85] and then, as the night fell and the moon rose on the horizon, the high waves quietly engulfed the silhouettes and carried the bodies away.

Lack of physicians and a shortage of quinine contributed to the demise of the children of Cathay. Those who did not die booked passage for Veracruz or Habana. Others fled to Panama City, where, after weeks of hiding, they became laundrymen or lettuce and cabbage farmers.[86] (At the turn of the century, when the Republic of Panama was created and the canal had been finished, their descendants controlled the retail business of Colon and Panama City until 1940.)[87] In the absence of hands to cut the ties and nail the nails, it appeared as if work on the railroad had to surrender to the aggressive flora of the isthmus; however, a stream of immigrants to California came to the company's rescue. A human deluge arrived at the mouth of the Chagres. All kinds of men came— killers, gamblers, professional pickpockets, and quite a few company policemen, or "enforcers."

The company began to employ anyone who wished to work even for a few days, and thousands who were waiting for transportation to San Francisco were hired at minimum wages. On the short trips from the Atlantic Coast to the end of the line, only a few miles inland, the railroad made 2.5 million gold pesos packing human cargo[88] into the flat cars used to carry equipment and dirt. Those not able to book passage to the Golden Bay quickly gambled their savings away, died by the knife or the bullet, or were conquered by fever. Some of these travelers were not made for work of any kind. They formed gangs to rob merchants, workers, and other transients. *El Camino Real* became a living hell for everyone in its vicinity.

To aggravate matters, every political disturbance originating in Bogota rapidly spilled over onto the isthmus, where *liberales* and *conservadores* awaited a signal to butcher each other, protected by the shadows of the night.

From 1850 to 1855, when the railroad was being constructed, the State of Panama inaugurated twenty presidents, an average of four executives a year, while Nueva Granada elected, substituted, or deposed seven in Bogota. It is clear, then, that the Bidlack-Mallarino Treaty was worth signing—for Nueva Granada as well as for the United States. General Tomas Cipriano de Mosquera and his foreign minister knew their people well.[89] Added to these calamities was the general suffering of the population caused by the perennial scarcity of food and clothing, which always invites inflation.

The railroad was finished in 1855, but not before the arrival of a large number of Jamaicans and other blacks from Cartagena and the San Andres Islands. The distinguished scholar Don Ruben D. Carles says that as many as twenty-five thousand lives were lost in the building of the iron road,[90] but Emory Adams Allen states that only twenty-five hundred died.[91] Others exaggerate beyond belief and repeat the oft-told story that every tie in the railroad claimed a human life, but either of the more reliable figures is a great sacrifice to pay for the cause of progress, especially if one remembers that the railroad is only forty-five miles long.

The cost of the railroad far exceeded the company's expectations. A reporter for the *New York Tribune* estimated it at $7 million[92] but the chief engineer, Colonel Totten, declared that $6 million was the extent of the cost. These sums probably do not include the expenses of reconstructing parts of the road, replacing iron bridges, laying down lignum vitae ties, and procuring other material washed out by the incessant rains or considered necessary for the maintenance of the line. The aggregate receipts were estimated at $730,000, but again the chief engineer disputed this sum, which he considered less than the actual amount. However, $120,000 was received from the traffic in the single month of March 1855.[93]

Original estimates of the cost and revenues of the railroad, made in 1850, were as follows:[94]

Cost of the line $4,900,000
Gross receipts 860,000
Annual expense 344,000
Net revenue 516,000

It is clear, however, that by the day the iron road was dedicated, January 28, 1855, when coast-to-coast service—flat cars, freight cars, and regular passenger trains—was opened,[95] expenditures had risen to $8 million. Ten years later, in 1865, company books showed a net gain of $11.34 million.[96]

Despite this superavit the large capital investment was endangered from the very beginning. The terms of the contract with the government of Nueva Granada stated that:

> . . . at the expiration of twenty years, counted from the day on which the railroad shall have been completed and opened to public use, the government may redeem the privilege for the benefit of Nueva Granada, by the sum of five millions of dollars, to be paid as the whole amount of the indemnification. If the privilege should not be redeemed at that date, it shall continue in force ten years longer in favor of the Panama Railroad Company, and at the end of that time the government may redeem it by paying four millions of dollars; if it be not redeemed at the end of this latter period, it shall continue in

force ten years still longer, at the end of which the government may redeem it by paying two millions of dollars.[97]

But if the enfeebled government of Nueva Granada was too financially incapacitated to exert its option shortly after the completion of the railroad, it also, by its very weakness, created additional expense for the company. Bogota could not exert the slightest degree of authority to control vandalism, or prevent property damage and possible derailments of passenger and cargo trains. The line required the strictest surveillance twenty-four hours a day. Accordingly, the railroad officials took into their own hands the policing of the iron road and its vicinity, and it did not exercise this authority half-heartedly.

A private police force was organized. Heading it was an American emigré who took to his job with gusto. Short, slight, tough, and Texan, Ran Runnels, a former Ranger in his native state, had to his credit many deeds of daring. Because of his fierce determination he was considered the terror of evil-doers. His unimpressive appearance was deceiving. He quickly set himself to train and lead a constabulary of forty men of all heights and colors, a loose assortment of bravoes in a variety of dress. Negroes, mulattoes, white men, and yellow men mingled together in the ranks of his small police force. With Runnels as leader, they cleared the isthmus of robbers, incendiaries, and killers. In appreciation of their services, the company bestowed monthly upon Ran Runnels and his ragged regiment more than $4,000, but their lives were in danger every day.

They engaged liberally in whipping, imprisonment, and shooting down in an emergency, according to the powers delegated to the railroad by the government of Nueva Granada. Ran Runnels' praetorians could impose the death penalty on any desperado caught *in flagrante* at any hour of the day or night.[98] Despite all the difficulties, the tenacious company made the transcontinental railroad a reality. The railroad was the first concrete and gigantic step toward the centuries-old dream of joining the waters of the two oceans. Once incorporated into the Interoceanic Canal Company, the railroad became the invaluable right arm of the surveyors, engineers, laborers, and machines that were to make possible the canal at Panama.

2

DE LESSEPS COMES TO PANAMA

International Interest in a Canal Grows; Political Change in the Isthmus; The Reclus Brothers; De Lesseps and the Scientific Congress of 1879; Financing the Canal

The signing of the Clayton-Bulwer Treaty neutralized the United States and England in Panama. At the same time it was a providential omen to France. Although no party to this convention, France had no intention of relinquishing her canal ambitions. The position of the French in regard to canal politics in the 1850s closely resembled the strategy of the Fifth Republic a century later.[1] After 1850, and in the absence of any bilateral canal commitment to the parties involved in the Clayton-Bulwer Treaty, the French renewed their search for the best location in which to build a canal in America.

The Growing Interest in a Canal

In the United States, the two decades after 1850 were replete with international friction and internal turmoil. In fact, because of the slavery controversy, the country appeared to be navigating precariously, like New Granada, between Scylla and Charybdis. James Buchanan, the former

25

secretary of state who had conducted the final negotiations for the Bidlack-Mallarino Treaty,[2] found himself in the middle of a national debate which was about to plunge the Union into civil war. The leading Democrat was not the president but Stephen A. Douglas, whose posture in regard to slavery and the interoceanic canal was closely tied to his expansionist ideas.

The Napoleon-size Illinois senator was as aggressive oratorically as the French emperor was militarily. He had consistently advocated the building of a canal in Mexico, even if it became necessary to conquer Mexico for this purpose. His views on foreign policy, so well known at home and abroad, may have cost him the presidential nomination in 1856.[3] Buchanan himself told Douglas that he favored Douglas for president but realized that he himself was the better candidate.[4]

Because of continuous filibustering of United States' citizens against Nicaragua and the consequent anti-American feeling in that country, the subjects of Napoleon III were left alone in their pursuit of an unilateral canal policy. A French syndicate was able to conclude an agreement with Managua for the building of a waterway through the two lakes and the river San Juan, which is shared by neighboring Costa Rica, and the French agreed to keep a large fleet in Nicaraguan and Costa Rican waters for the protection of the two small nations. Despite the political and social agitation plaguing the United States at this time, and perhaps to please his influential supporter Stephen Douglas, President Buchanan moved quickly to scuttle the French contract. The erudite Texan, Mirabeau B. Lamar, was dispatched as special minister to Central America in September 1858.[5]

The American envoy was well aware of the reasons for the cancellation of an earlier American canal concession. In 1852, Colonel O. W. Childs and Commodore Cornelius Vanderbilt had acquired a Nicaraguan grant to build a waterway through that country. They subsequently formed the A. & P. Canal Company and tried to sell stock in it, but the scheme collapsed.[6] Some time later, the American Transportation Company was chartered and began operating steamers and

stagecoaches across Nicaragua. Early in 1855, two men associated with Vanderbilt in this later venture, Cornelius K.
Garrison and Charles Morgan (in an entrepreneurial grand-
stand steal), conspired to gain personal control of the transportation company.[7]

Garrison and Morgan found a willing front man in the
impetuous and power-hungry Tennessean William Walker.
This adventurer had led an unsuccessful filibustering expedition against Mexico and, by 1856,[8] aided by a small band of
followers, had assumed control of the land of the two lakes.
Backed by Vanderbilt's enemies, he consolidated his position
by becoming president of Nicaragua and receiving the official
recognition of the United States on July 12, 1856.[9] The new
head of state seized the disputed company and gave it to
Garrison and Morgan,[10] but the triumvirate's victory was
short-lived. Although Walker enjoyed the sympathy of the
slaveholding southern-American states, his actions collided
not only with the powerful Vanderbilt interests but with
those of the French and English.

Vanderbilt, offended, poured a fortune in arms and men
into the contest, managing to arouse the rest of the Central-
American states against Walker who, unable to maintain
himself after May 1, 1857, wisely surrendered to the United
States Navy. He was spirited away from his adopted country
and deposited back in Louisiana.[11] But Walker's ambition
remained unchecked, leading him to disaster. He twice went
back to Central America, in November 1857 and in June 1860,
the second time never to return to his native country.
Captured by the British, he was turned over to Honduras,
where he had landed, and was summarily executed.[12]

Irritated by Walker's activities, Nicaragua terminated the
agreement with Vanderbilt. But Lamar bluntly told Nicaragua
that the United States "would not tolerate the arbitrary
declaration of forfeiture of contracts made with American
citizens."[13] The minister knew he was on shaky ground, but
his diplomatic bluff produced the desired reaction. Official
support of the French scheme was withdrawn, even though
Vanderbilt's concession was not formally revalidated.

While the Americans were concerning themselves with the

French project in Nicaragua, the Russians sent the chief of staff of their imperial army to Panama to assess the possibility of entering the canal race. After a three-month sojourn spent mainly in the vicinity of Panama City, the Russian general and his assistants left the isthmus in the early summer of 1860. They were convinced that "the job of constructing a waterway in this hemisphere was a task reserved for demi-gods and Russia wanted no part of it."[14] Even so, the czar's interest in canal construction warned the Americans of the possibility of another unwelcome partner in the waterway stakes. The purchase of Alaska, negotiated by Secretary Seward eight years later, calmed such fears for the moment.

Political Change in the Isthmus

Meanwhile Nueva Granada was about to end another fratricidal conflict at the very moment when the United States was beginning its own. The net result of this "peace" was the birth of Gran Colombia (Greater Colombia) and the creation of the Estado Soberano de Panama. The isthmians were ecstatic about this sonorous name. The president of the Estado Soberano de Panamá, Don José Domingo de Obaldía, rushed a significant declaration through the state's assembly. Fearing the dislocation of transatlantic communication, the isthmus placed itself under the protection of the three most aggressive canal seekers—the United States, France, and England.[15]

The Panamanian scholar and cofounder of the University of Panama, Octavio Mendez Pereira, attaches enormous signifi-cance to this official statement. He says: "The Panamanians chose to break away from the slavery of arbitrary and revolutionary instability by placing their future and sov-ereignty under the protection of the three great powers."[16] Nothing in the resolution hides the naked wish of the Panamanians to forsake the instability of a permanent asso-ciation with Gran Colombia and their happiness in placing themselves and their country—not the future Canal Zone alone—"under the protection of the United States." It is worth noticing that, of the three powers under which they would have liked to live, they unequivocally preferred the United States of America.

The isthmians had reason for their preference. They remembered the American protests on the occasion of the "better-red-than-dead," peace-at-any-price pact of 1842, by which Bogota, under the leadership of President Pedro Alcantara Herran, granted the British the right of intervention in Panama.[17] What followed next was burlesque and a flagrant violation of sovereignty in the New World. Surely, in the second half of the nineteenth century, the inhabitants of Almirante must have retained some memory of the amusing extravaganza of August 16, 17, 18, and 19 of 1841.

Dressed in polychrome robes, "His Imperial Majesty the King of the Payas, Imperator of Mosquitia," Carlos Federico Roberto, a zambo from the San Andres Islands, appeared at Almirante Bay with an English naval escort to demand the return of his ancestral demesne—the isthmus, from Bocas del Toro to Darien. In the presence of court and counsellors, his majesty "annexed" this territory to his domains and named as resident proconsuls one Colonel Alejandro McDonald— who occupied the same position at Belize in Honduras—and H. D. C. Douglas, commander of the British squadron and the writer and producer of this charade.[18]

Three Nations Vie for a Canal Contract

England was in an imperialistic mood. With little to fear from France—for Paris had become her ally in the Near East as well as in Africa and Asia—England renewed her drive to become the chief beneficiary of a canal in this hemisphere. As the War between the States progressed, the British chose to ignore the contract between Nicaragua and the successors of Cornelius Vanderbilt. Behaving exactly as the French had earlier, Captain Bedford C. T. Pyn of the Royal Navy forced a bargain upon Managua in January 1864, acquiring sole rights to effect interoceanic communication through the two lakes. The English contrived to have the Nicaraguans create the impression that the "European [canal] equilibrium was being re-established [in Central America]."[19]

Perhaps in order to introduce a "true equilibrium" into canal politics, four years after the surrender of Appomattox,[20] H. W. Welk, a former associate of Commodore Vanderbilt in the A. & P. Canal Company, astutely exhibited a new covenant for a canal through Nicaragua which was an exact replica of the one signed earlier by Vanderbilt. The suggestion was clear: if the grant of 1852 had not been revalidated as a result of Mirabeau B. Lamar's visit to Nicaragua, this later document would supersede the English-inspired canal paper exacted from Managua by Captain Pyn in 1864.[21]

However, this was not to be. The French also became interested in "equilibrium" and suddenly found themselves in a position to retrieve the ground lost in 1858 when Nicaragua yielded to Lamar.[22] It was 1869: the Suez miracle was about to be dedicated and Napoleon III's as well as de Lesseps' dream of exporting the French canal-producing genius to the world was about to be realized. The weak Nicaraguan government, impressed by the colossal good fortune of the Gallic nation, repudiated the concession exhibited by Welk and signed one with Michel Chevalier, an emissary of the French emperor.[23] It appeared that France's tricolor might well be the flag to be hoisted in the land of the lakes. But again, this was not to be. The debacle of the French army and its surrender at Metz and Sedan, precipitating the end of the Second Empire,[24] impaired Chevalier's efforts to raise money for his canal. Nevertheless, Chevalier cherished the hope of realizing his engineering project until his death in 1879.[25]

In the 1870s, while the Third Republic was extricating itself from the financial pains of the war indemnity asked by the Second Reich, the United States was going through the throes of Reconstruction. At the same time, England, caught entirely by surprise by Prussia's victory over France, suddenly realized that there was a new power structure in the world. This fact not only dictated unusual tact in dealing with friends and foes alike but also, if possible, the acquisition of control of the Suez Canal Company.[26]

Gobierno Fuerte and the Birth of the
Republic of Colombia; An Obscure Canal Treaty

In spite of the endemic social turmoil that had plagued Gran Colombia since 1819, it suddenly began to experience some semblance of political maturity with a *gobierno fuerte*[27] under the presidency of the literateur Rafael Nunez. Like his contemporary, Tomas Cipriano de Mosquera, Nunez was the beneficiary of a long and salutary residency abroad, where he gained maturity and a deep understanding of his country. In nineteenth-century Colombia, no other politician-statesman except Bolivar held power longer and more often than he. Nunez promulgated a new constitution and changed the name of the nation for the third time in a century. The romantic idea of sovereignty, which had generated collective insanity among the unruly Panamanians, and caused thousands of deaths in sporadic *coup d'états* since 1860, came to a sudden end in 1885.[28] The new *centralista* charter decreed a departmental republic, the heads of which political subdivisions were to be appointed by the chief of state in Bogota. Article 201 of the new constitution stated that the Department of Panama was to be handled by "special legislation." Thus Gran Colombia disappeared, and the Republic of Colombia was born.[29]

The new order in Colombia brought about the first serious attempt to develop the country's economy in line with the current positivist trends.[30] A pioneer in these schemes, which were mainly concerned with the creation of a network of iron roads connecting the *sabana* of Bogota with several other cities such as Medellin and Cali, through the Magdalena River, was the Cuban-born American citizen, Francisco Xavier Cisneros. The constitution of 1860 had restricted railroad building, but by 1872 the legal objections were relaxed and official subsidies were authorized.

Except for the isthmian line, no other railroad had been built before Cisneros arrived from Cuba in 1868.[31] Many other adventurers came to Colombia with him, but he soon became the most influential entrepreneur in Bogota. He moved behind every government like a gray eminence: his railroad manual became a model, and no railroad deals could be initiated without his consent or participation. One of his most important projects was the completion of the Giradot railroad in 1888, which brought coffee to the plains of Bogota. Meanwhile, the Barranquilla railroad line prospered after a deep dock was built there to handle foreign trade.[32]

At the beginning of this rare age of economic prosperity in Colombia and a few months before the return of Rafael Nunez from Europe, a group of bankers from New York made the last attempt to secure private guarantees for the building of a waterway from ocean to ocean at Panama.[33] This maneuver produced the obscure Arosemena-Sanchez-Hulbert concession. Strangely, Panama's senatorial representatives in Congress opposed this arrangement, and the government withdrew its support. The agreement contained the following article:

> Once the canal is concluded, its possession, direction, handling, and inspection are totally in the hands of the United States of America and will be exercised by them without [any] intervention [by any party] but without jurisdiction over the territory [it occupies] or its inhabitants.[34]

Notwithstanding the importance given to this document by later generations of Panamanian intellectuals,[35] the agreement could not have survived a long debate in the Colombian Senate, where its authors had many enemies. The isthmian senator, Manuel de Jesus Quijano, commented bitterly in Bogota that the treaty was only the stepchild of three people, "a Jew, Jacobo Sanchez, an American [Hulbert], and Don Justo Arosemena."[36] The truth is that the Bidlack-Mallarino convention was still the official instrument controlling free transit from ocean to ocean. No American government would have rejected this covenant in favor of a dubious concession to individuals whose financial resources were considered too weak for an enterprise of this magnitude.

The failure of the Arosemena-Hulbert-Sanchez compact, like all other bizarre occurrences connected with the epic of the Panama Canal, was stored in the mind of Philippe Bunau-Varilla for later use. The treaty he signed on behalf of Panama in 1903 has elements of both the Bidlack-Mallarino Treaty and the rejected Arosemena-Hulbert-Sanchez agreement.[37] When the Hay–Bunau-Varilla Treaty was ratified in 1903, the canal engineer accomplished what all the others had failed to achieve.

After 1870, *Realpolitik* became the international political instrument with which Count Otto von Bismarck sought to maintain the *post-bellum* status quo in Europe. It could only be successfully accomplished by depriving France of allies. Hindered in this way from seeking revenge for the disaster of 1870, the Gallic nation sought to enhance its prestige in other continents by expanding its cultural and commercial ties with the rest of the world.

In the area of modern geographical and scientific exploration, the name of the Reclus brothers shines bright. These French geographers continued the work of Alexander von Humboldt, especially in America. Sensing the diplomatic and economic direction of France's foreign policy, Elisée and Onesime Reclus inspired the calling of two geographical congresses, in Antwerp in 1871, and in Paris in 1875.[38]

It is no surprise, then, that one of the central themes of these councils was the question of an American canal. Elisée Reclus had vivid memories of his sojourns in Nueva Granada between 1851 and 1857, when he traveled to Panama on three occasions. A republican exiled from France, he fell in love with the former Spanish colonies, where he observed at first hand the ecological and geographical wonders of the New World.[39]

Realizing that the topography of Panama was not accurately known, Onesime and Elisée Reclus turned the matter over to the Club of Commercial Geography, which later became the Society of Commercial Geography. Soon after, Ferdinand de Lesseps was made its president, and the move to raise money for a canal began, thanks to the presence of the experienced canal builder. Scientific inquiry became financial inquiry, which was then, as at Suez, turned into profit.

During his residence in Nueva Granada, Elisée Reclus had

familiarized himself with every canal study previously submitted to Bogota for consideration. One of these had been
made by the French engineer Napoleon Garella who, for the
first time in memory, wisely selected the Bay of Limon as an
appropriate spot for the Atlantic terminus of an isthmian
canal. This evaluation motivated the Italian general, Etienne
Turr, to seek and receive a firm canal concession from
Colombia in 1875. It is not clear how Turr managed to secure
this paper, but after 1875 those seriously interested in a canal
through Panama knew where to start.[40]

As on-the-spot investigation was necessary in order to win
public confidence in such an undertaking, the *Societé Civile
International du Canal Interoceanique de Darién* was created. This
group organized a survey of the various canal routes by the
third Reclus brother, Armand Elié Ebenezer, and the naval
lieutenant Lucien Napoleon Bonaparte Wyse. From the beginning the society attracted good and bad men, some of
whom were to plague Ferdinand de Lesseps and his collaborators. The most notorious were the Baron Jacques de
Reinach and the international swindler Cornelius Hertz.[41]

The two French surveyors were joined in America by the
Colombian engineer Pedro J. Sosa and, amid official rejoicing,
the explorers scouted and mapped the Gulf of San Blas, the
coast of Darien, and the Gulf of San Miguel. They also
navigated the rivers Tuira, Atrato, Grande, and Bayano. Not
wishing to arouse American suspicion, the scouting party at
no time trespassed on land already awarded to the Panama
Railroad Company.[42]

Correctly perceiving that the United States preferred a
canal through Nicaragua, Bonaparte Wyse and his in-law,
General Turr, obtained the necessary funds to undertake a
more accurate statistical and geodesic study in 1877. While
Armand Reclus was becoming acquainted with the forests of
Darien and the banks of the Chagres in the company of the
highest authorities of Panama, his companion, Bonaparte
Wyse, crystallized the goal of the French group by obtaining
a dubious and short-lived contract from the newly installed
regime of Julian Trujillo.[43]

On October 27, 1877, exhibiting the full powers granted to him by the *Societé Civile*, Lieutenant Wyse signed a document which became the law of the land in Colombia on May 18, 1878.[44] The *Contract Salgar-Wyse pour la concessión du canal interoceanique* (Former President Eustorgio Salgar, then secretary of the interior and foreign affairs, signed for Bogota) gave the French syndicate the exclusive right to build a canal.[45] It surrendered to the company all maritime and riparian rights in the area of the waterway and guaranteed to them land on both sides of its banks extending no less than two hundred meters in any direction. The concession was for ninety-nine years and provided for the completion of the work—if there were no unforeseen delays—in twelve years. The canal company also gained the right to build its own telegraph lines.[46]

Recognizing the Bidlack-Mallarino Treaty as the sole guarantee of order in the isthmus, the Salgar-Wyse covenant was silent about the protection of the installations of the projected canal. The French negotiators, for their part, ignored the many riots that had occurred in Panama since 1821[47] and chose to overlook the probability of new ones in the near future. Soon after it initiated the canal works, as we shall see in the next chapter, the canal company had to save itself by calling on the United States to end mob rule in the isthmus.[48]

De Lesseps and the Scientific Congress of 1879

As in Egypt, when Le Père's study of a canal route in 1803 became the basis for concrete discussions, the blueprints prepared by the Wyse-Reclus-Sosa group were closely examined by an international congress of savants which met in Paris from May 15 to 29, 1879. From the beginning of this meeting the cards were stacked in favor of a Panama route, although the polyglot experts were to consider eight possible locations within the geographical configuration of the isthmus and two outside of it. Ferdinand de Lesseps was only one of the delegates, but by the sheer magnetism of his personality and the glory of his name he quickly moved to center-stage.

The agenda for the congress contained the following canal possibilities:

1. Colombia, in the area of the Choco, using the waters of the Atrato and Truando rivers and profiting from the natural facilities of the Gulf of Uraba. A level canal, 210 kilometers long, two tunnels of 3 and 8 kilometers.
2. Colombia, in the area of the Choco, from the Bay of Chirichiri to the Gulf of Uraba, through the use of the rivers Atrato and Napipi; 290 kilometers long, 22 locks, and a tunnel of 6 kilometers. A locks canal.
3. Colombia, in the San Blas Archipelago, and using the waters of the Bayano River; 53 kilometers long and a tunnel of 15 kilometers. A sea-level canal.
4. Colombia, in the area of Darien, from Acandi to the Gulf of San Miguel; 125 kilometers long and a tunnel of 17 kilometers. A sea-level canal.
5. Colombia, in the area of Darien, from the Gulf of Uraba to the Gulf of San Miguel, using the entire length of the Atrato river; 235 kilometers long, 22 locks, and a tunnel of 2 kilometers. A locks canal.
6. Colombia, near Panama City, using the entire length of the Chagres River; 72 kilometers long and 25 locks. A locks canal.
7. Colombia, near Panama City, a sea-level canal, from Limon Bay to the Bay of Panama, using the entire length of the Chagres and Grande rivers; 73 kilometers long.
8. Colombia, near Panama City, 72 kilometers long, 11 locks, and a large artificial lake. A locks canal.
9. Mexico, at Tehuantepec; 280 kilometers long and 140 locks. A locks canal.
10. Nicaragua–Costa Rica, at Rivas, using the two lakes and the San Juan River; 292 kilometers long and 21 locks. A locks canal.[49]

Because of the two large bodies of water, the last route listed was deemed easiest to build. Any location in Panama was considered more expensive and difficult, but clearly shorter, as shown in the charts at the meeting.

There was still another problem to tackle. Should it be a sea-level passage or a locks waterway? Some leading person-alities in this assembly were in favor of a locks canal, among them the already renowned and future pioneer in steel towers, Gustave Eiffel.[50] De Lesseps wanted a sea-level canal and, undeterred by opposition, sought to convince the delegates with the slogan of an "oceanic Bosphorus." His efforts were rewarded when the scientists voted for a sea-level project by a margin of 78–12–8, "between the Gulf of Limon and the Bay of Panama."[51]

Of the 138 delegates, only 5—two of the Reclus brothers, Armand and Onesime; the engineer, Pedro J. Sosa, born in Panama; the Cuban Aniceto G. Menocal; and Bonaparte Wyse—had ever set foot in Mexico, Nicaragua, or Colombia. Much less had they ever imagined the massive problems involved in such an adventure. But the sound argument, backed up by a flawless presentation of the canal-at-any-price-at-Panama thesis by the Reclus-Wyse-Sosa triumvirate, plus de Lesseps' incomparable charm, won the day for the Panamanians.[52]

Little or no attention was paid by the delegates to financial details. The Sosa-Reclus budget was short by 10 percent of the ultimate cost of the canal. The congress conjectured that the expenditures for the waterway would be 1,174 million francs (approximately $425 million at that time). The engineering work was budgeted at 612 million francs (close to $303 million); administrative outlays at 38 million francs (nearly $22 million); miscellaneous expenditures 153 million francs (approximately $61 million); interest for twelve years at 241 million francs ($87 million); and maintenance at 130 million francs (around $52 million).[53]

De Lesseps and The Universal Interoceanic Canal Company

Shortly thereafter, The Universal Interoceanic Canal Company was chartered and the dynamic Ferdinand de Lesseps—

seventy-four years young—took command of his new destiny. Whether de Lesseps consulted or refused to consult the stars on this occasion is debatable. It was to be one of the last triumphs enjoyed by this remarkable man, whose fame and glory have risen steadily for the last twenty years.

Admiral de la Ronciere, the presiding chairman of the scientific congress, paid glowing tribute to de Lesseps at its close:

> Permit me, as we depart, to close this meeting by a wish which is already in your hearts. May that illustrious man, who has been the heart and soul of our deliberations, who has captivated us by charm, and who is the personification of these great enterprises, may he live long enough to see the end of this work which will bear his name forever. He has not been able to refuse to assume its command, and in so doing he continues to carry out the mission which has made him a citizen of the whole world.[54]

From this moment the life and deeds of Ferdinand de Lesseps belong to an Aeschylus,[55] for he was about to parallel the tragic fate of the Consul Atilius Regulus. With many victories to his credit and certain peace at hand, the Roman gambled his destiny and prolonged the war with Carthage, only to be captured and executed. In death Regulus became a living symbol to his countrymen, for he instilled in them, with this final sacrifice, an indomitable will to vindicate him which gained for Rome the ultimate triumph.[56] Just so did the sacrifice, humiliation, dishonor, and death of Ferdinand de Lesseps become, in the mind and spirit of Bunau-Varilla, a command which inspired him to justify de Lesseps' faith and realize the centuries-old dream of a canal in America.

However, it was not *hybris* that prompted Ferdinand de Lesseps to accept, in the twilight of his life and at the peak of his career, a task which might have deterred a younger man. It was a call to duty regardless of consequences. This is a recurrent phenomenon in civilization. In our own country, David K. Bruce was called out of retirement three times to smooth the diplomatic transition with Peking.[57] In France, Felix Fauré, former premier and cabinet minister, became president of the National Assembly in his old age, a post roughly comparable to speaker of the House of Representatives in the United States.[58]

Similar pressures were placed upon de Lesseps. The influential Leon Gambetta publicly glorified the canal builder and called him "the great Frenchman." Theoretically, the government of the Third Republic was committed to prove that it was capable of greater deeds than the fallen empire. The new breed of statesmen yearned for a spectacular industrial success which might make the world forget the military defeat of 1870. And in those years, gigantic projects were under way, especially in the realm of communication and trade. The Brooklyn Bridge[59]—about to be completed at the time—and France's International Exposition of 1879 were sure indications that technology was here to stay and that, if the Suez Canal was feasible under Napoleon III, the Panama Canal would not prove impossible during the presidency of Jules Grevy.[60]

One of the first acts of the canal company was to buy the Turr-Wyse concession on July 5, 1879, for 10 million francs. Recalling the Suez experience, de Lesseps appealed personally to the potential subscribers of the canal shares but, by August 7, only 50 million of the 400 million francs needed had been raised. After this setback, the president of the company decided to launch a publicity campaign. He created the *Bulletin of the Interoceanic Canal* and undertook a lecture tour of France which ended on December 8, 1879. On this date, de Lesseps boarded the steamship *Lafayette*, which had as its destination the far-away and little-known harbor of Colon.[61]

Probably to instill confidence in the forbidding isthmus, de Lesseps took with him his wife and children and a large group of engineering contractors, some of them veterans of the Suez campaign. One of these contractors, Abel Couvreux, was to exert a destructive and nefarious influence upon the canal builder, delivering the first blow in a chain of reverses. The timing of their arrival at the mouth of the Chagres, December 30, 1879, was probably arranged. The dry season, which begins around mid-December, lasts until late May. During these months the nights are cool and the winds are strong, especially in the north of the isthmus. However, had the canal builder counted among his thousands of acquaintances and admirers Dr. Carlos Finlay, he might not have traveled to Panama at this time. Precisely during these months, most of the females of the species of *Anopheles*, which spread malaria, hatch by the millions.[62] Dr. Finlay's hypothesis, universally rejected by medical scholars, was beginning to attract converts among lay persons. As will be shown later in this book, Dr. Finlay's proposition, like all good scientific theories, was easily proved correct or disproved entirely. It consisted of the usual three classical premises: (1) at least one case of yellow fever; (2) the presence of a body likely to become contaminated; and (3) a carrier which might transmit the disease from a sick to a healthy body undetected. This transmitting agent is the mosquito.[63]

Ferdinand de Lesseps arrived in Panama at a time when the happy-go-lucky departmental authorities were celebrating the arrival of the new year. Witness to their collective euphoria, he decided to symbolize the breaking of ground on January 1, 1880. But the ultimate fate of the First Interoceanic Canal Company suggests that the cabalistic Frenchman did not consult the stars. The first stroke of the pick—by his beautiful daughter, Ferdinande—was performed with the benefit of clergy and amid prayers, pomp, and carnival. The area in La Boca, where the ceremony took place, had been sprayed with holy water and blessed by the local bishop, while not too far away, in the absence of cannons, a rock was blown. The tremor and thunder of the explosion produced the calculated effect on the crowd of 4,000, who happily predicted another economic bonanza for the isthmus. Shortly after, they all went back to the city and continued a four-day-long celebration of what was to be a bountiful age.[64]

Financing the Canal

After spending six weeks inspecting the canal route and surviving dozens of balls, banquets, mosquitoes, and eager handshakes, de Lesseps and his party left for New York in mid-February 1880. Everywhere he went in the United States, he was received by an enthusiastic public.[65] The financial establishment, however, was reticent about backing his canal, because by this time sentiment favored Nicaragua. De Lesseps must have felt disappointed at not being able to form a Franco-American company—a major impediment to the ultimate success of the works—but he nevertheless returned to France in March 1880 proclaiming that "the security of the canal" was assured and that he had encountered much enthusiasm and "unanimous" backing for "our cause."[66]

While de Lesseps was still traveling, a technical commission created in Paris by the company had second thoughts about the outlay for engineering and other expenditures. Its new total budget exceeded 1,250 million francs—almost a million francs more than its earlier budget.[67]

On his way back to Europe, wishing to forestall any delay in raising capital—any amount of capital—de Lesseps lowered the total estimate by almost half—to a mere 658 million francs (close to $300 million).[68] This was not a financial estimate that could guarantee success for the project, and the canal builder has been excoriated ever since by the moguls of monetary affairs and pilloried by experts in accounting. But de Lesseps' past experience and the way he lined up his ducks before he started shooting indicates that this decision was probably not an act of folly but a calculated gamble. In the end, his gamble might have worked, had it not been for two insurmountable obstacles—disease and extortion. As if death were an unreal threat, the entrepreneurs of the First Interoceanic Canal Company refused to entertain the slightest thought of spending anything in search of an elusive and insignificant mosquito. They must be reproved for their thoughtlessness because, in the age of Louis Pasteur, such contempt for insects or bacteria was inexcusable.

De Lesseps' strategy, of revising the estimate downward, was the result of his keen observation and his anticipation of two future courses of action. If the money could not be raised

in toto, he could appeal later to the public or to the government as he had done during the under-financed days of
Suez. The Great Frenchman was not bereft of influence in the
Third Republic. On the contrary, his influence was greater
than during the reign of his cousin, Empress Eugénie. He
now needed no appointment to call on the Quai d'Orsay or
the Elysée. Everyone in France knew why his promising
diplomatic career had been unceremoniously cut short, and
few among the dispensers of power could ignore his well-
known democratic predilections. The important thing was for
the company to raise money quickly.

Portents of things to come were already in sight. Paris was
taking up where it had left off at the end of the Franco-
Prussian war. It was again becoming the effervescent cultural
capital of the world. Freedom of expression was again revered. The city was a magnet for artists, craftsmen, fashion
designers, writers, engineers, teachers, and scientists.
Creativity was given an opportunity to flow, and everyone
seemed eager to learn more about other people's talents. Paris
in the late nineteenth century was not just another city, but
something unique and precious.[69]

France, in 1881, was already trembling in anticipation of the
five-year celebration of the centennial of the Revolution of
1789. Vast sums of money had been earmarked for the
construction of the exposition which, as it took shape, began
to share the limelight with the far-away canal project. The
visual evidence of this psychological phenomenon was an
engineering miracle, Gustave Eiffel's imposing tower.

In response to this great public feeling and in the knowledge that no American capital was forthcoming, the French
legislature authorized only 300 million francs—less than a
fourth of the official budget—for the use of the canal company.[70] Unfazed by this not entirely unexpected reverse, de
Lesseps began to work full-time to raise money for the canal.
He staged banquets, conferences, publicity stunts, picnics,
and balloon advertisements. He paid an underwriting syndicate 32 million francs to secure the 300 million francs that had
been authorized for the canal. By October 1881, 600 million

francs had been raised. The entire subscription was carried out without foreign participation, and no shares of the stock were offered in the London or New York markets.[71] The company was reorganized and the experienced canal builder, Ferdinand de Lesseps, now seventy-six years old, appeared eager to begin digging.

Surely de Lesseps must have been aware of the risk involved in traversing the hazardous road ahead with only half the capital needed for the job. But he remained a true positivist, like Vicente Rocafuerte in Ecuador, Jose Ivo Limatour in Mexico,[75] and Xavier Cisneros in Colombia, and he firmly believed that progress is mankind's panacea; that, far from generating imperial ventures and breeding wars, it would eliminate conflict and bring about that elusive universal peace so eagerly sought for so many centuries. What could be better for the realization of this goal than interoceanic canals, open trade, and work for every man of good will? Under rosy skies, the First Interoceanic Canal Company began work in Panama. It was only when these romantic thoughts were exchanged for the realistic approach counseled by Bunau-Varilla that it became possible, at last, to vindicate the name of Ferdinand de Lesseps, and eventually, in 1978, with the ratification of a United States-Panama treaty, to hand over to the Panamanians a most enviable economic and international position among the peoples of the world.

3

The Canal Company and Political

Turmoil in Panama

The Interoceanic Canal Company at Work; The Period of the Contractors; Acquiring the Railroad; The Years of the Engineers; Arrival of Bunau-Varilla; His Engineering Survey; Insurrection and Mob Rule

From the very beginning of his association with the canal, Ferdinand de Lesseps rigidly attached himself to three plans which, as time passed, became fixed ideas: (1) the canal works were to follow the same pattern of acceleration as in Egypt— by the use of contractors; (2) money could always be raised for this canal provided the confidence of the French investors did not wane and the shares of Suez stock kept rising;[1] and (3) the waterway was to be a sea-level canal. He soon learned that each of these premises had to be abandoned for the sake of reality and, much too late, he witnessed the appearance of his two most unexpected and implacable enemies—financial plunder and disease.

In his late years, like other great people, Ferdinand de Lesseps withdrew to the company of trusted advisors. Some of them were veterans of the Egyptian campaign, whom he favored over engineers, servants, scholars, or financiers. He chose to call these friends "practical men."[2] To this elect group belongs the initial period of the Panama ordeal.

The Period of the Contractors

As we noted earlier, on his first voyage to the isthmus in 1880, de Lesseps took with him one of these companions, Abel Couvreux of Hersent-Couvreux, a contracting firm. From the moment this man boarded the steamship *Lafayette* for the trip to Panama, he began to exert a detrimental influence on the future of the canal. Bunau-Varilla calls him a man of "good faith but with an incredible naïveté."[3] Monsieur Couvreux extolled de Lesseps' courage in taking his family to Panama in order to prove that "the epithet of deadly climate used when speaking of the Panama Isthmus was nothing but an invention of his exasperated adversaries"; he figured that "the volume of earth and rock of all kinds to be excavated for the opening of the canal would not go beyond a maximum of 75 million cubic metres (about 100 million cubic yards). Also he persuaded de Lesseps to reduce the original budget to a mere $102.4 million. Let's hear Monsieur Couvreux speak again:

> This [is] why the estimates delivered at Panama on the fourteenth of February last, to M. de Lesseps by the Technical International Commission, reached the figure of $168 million. . . . All the documents which formed the basis of our calculations were brought back to Paris. . . . Their examination, and the details given by our fellow-workers who had returned to Paris convinced my father and M. Hersent that important reductions could be made on those estimates. . . . In consequence, after comparing these estimates with the cost of [the] work executed in Egypt they finally presented to M. de Lesseps these new estimates of $102.4 million.[4]

And with the same contempt with which he cavalierly dismissed the already discernible casualties inflicted by paludism,[5] yellow fever, blackwater fever, tick paralysis, equine encephalitis, dysentery, and beriberi, he continued:

> If it is possible to economize on the extraction of earth, why

would not the same thing be true of the rock? . . . We have
been obliged to admit a lateral inclination of four in the vertical
for one in the horizontal in the side slopes of the Culebra cut.
. . . Do we not see [in France] quarries—more than one
hundred eighty feet deep, the sides of which are vertical? . . .
Why should not such conditions exist there?[6]

Until the appearance of Bunau-Varilla, none of the canal
entrepreneurs paid the slightest attention to a stratigraphic
study of the water route, nor to the proven geological fact that
natural grassland offers stubborn resistance to digging, while
any soil of alluvial and diluvial origin, because of its moisture,
is hard to hold in check once enormous masses of the ground
have been opened into a trench. Both of these conditions exist
in the Isthmus of Panama. In time, and because of Bunau-
Varilla's personal study, it was proven—unfortunately much
too late for the First Interoceanic Canal Company—that,
without exception, the rock formations and the soil of Panama are of an entirely different origin than those of central
Europe. But the statements of Monsieur Couvreux were
pontificated like eternal truths spoken from an infallible
pulpit. Worse, this barrage of hallucinogenic words convinced de Lesseps that the construction of the canal was a
relatively easy task, and once the great man was satisfied in
this belief the same confidence filled the public mind.

This was the state of affairs when the contractors took over
the canal works on March 12, 1881,[7] a very bad time because
the torrential rains were only two months off. For a total of
over $110 million, Couvreux and Hersent undertook the
building of the canal, either at their own risk or on a cost-plus
basis, whichever was preferred. This, however, was a provisional arrangement, to become binding only after a trial
period not exceeding two years. Long before the trial period
expired, however, French participation in the construction of
the canal began to decline rapidly. The first force of European
engineers was totally ignorant of the real conditions on the
isthmus. None of them knew, even approximately, how many
cubic yards would have to be moved daily, monthly, or yearly.
No one had an idea of the nature of the earth beneath the

thick jungle. No one knew anything about the sanitary conditions and the prevalence of mass disease. Above all, not one of them, not even the contractors, had the slightest idea of the idiosyncrasies of the native workers. De Lesseps and the contractors had only seen—without observing them closely—part of the élite.

Little or no attention had been paid to a most vital problem, labor. No white could be recruited for peonage work at penurious rates. No white Colombians, or Chinese, for that matter, were available. All were busily forming their own syndicates to subcontract from the company or were entrenching themselves as shopkeepers, cooks, barmen, dairymen, morticians, bakers, or troubleshooters. Like locusts in season, hundreds of *leguleyos*[8] descended from Bogota ready to cross swords with the law in pursuit of a gold peso. The Indians were not to be had, because they came, saw, and departed.[9]

For a few weeks the contractors thought that they had found the solution to the labor problem. Why not bring the French-speaking cane-cutting blacks from the sugar plantations of Guadaloupe and Martinique? Had not the gods given these Negroes the strength of Achilles? But again the contractors forgot to do some research. The blacks from the French West Indies came mainly from the Cameroons and Gabon, and the *Asiento*[10] considered them a financial risk. They were the last to be sought and sold, and they cost less than any other slaves from West Africa.[11] Soon after these blacks arrived the canal contractors were to regret their move, for these workers proved to be "very poor, pretentious and always complaining."[12] However, by this time, disease itself was making liars of Monsieur Couvreux and Ferdinand de Lesseps. Mortality among the workers, particularly the whites, was frightfully high. Chief contracting engineer Louis Blanchet died at his post. Replacements for the dead and disabled were hard to find on short notice, and the contractors decided to throw in the towel on December 31, 1882. To soften the blow, they stated that they could not continue the work at their own risk but that they were willing to remain at the expense and risk of the company.

Acquiring the Railroad

Meanwhile, the company had to face another urgent problem—the acquisition of the railroad. Many influential people had already begun to claim—by cession or sale—most of the land adjacent to the line and in the neighborhood of the canal zone. On his trip back to Europe, Bonaparte Wyse had stopped in New York to discuss this matter, a fact that indicates that he had received preliminary assurances that the railroad would be sold to the Interoceanic Canal Company. Preoccupied with raising money, however, de Lesseps and his contractors[13] paid little attention to the railroad until the problem reached crisis proportions in 1882. Then, the interim government of Climaco Calderon delivered to the directorate of the company an ultimatum that might have signified the end of the works: its concession had no value unless an immediate agreement was reached with the Panama Railroad Company.[14]

With the first announcement that a canal was to be located near the railroad, hundreds of speculators had begun to acquire as much land as possible at the excavation sites and adjacent to the railroad. The government's warning increased this unrestricted acquisition of private property throughout the projected water route and made it imperative for the company to purchase the railroad shares. The nominal value of the railroad bonds in 1882 was $100, but their real worth was less than $50. Diminishing gold mining in California and the completion of the Union Pacific in 1870 had impaired railroad revenues in Panama. But it seemed certain that business would pick up as the canal works progressed. Suddenly, and without much bickering, de Lesseps paid $17.5 million for the seventy thousand railroad shares—$250 a share. The actual disbursement, considering commissions and under-the-counter deals for overdue coupons, was much higher, perhaps $20 million.[15] Ferdinand de Lesseps had suffered two serious setbacks; but for this man, as we have noted before, two lost battles meant only the beginning of a long war.

The Years of the Engineers

The dismal record of the contractors called for a complete overhauling of the company, not only its personnel but also its vertical organization, its day-to-day performance, and its budget. A distinguished engineer, Charles Dingler, was appointed general manager and chief engineer of canal works at Panama for the purpose of overhauling the entire interoceanic project. Theoretically he had authority over all workers, could sign or terminate contracts, could recommend to the company board structural changes, and was responsible for production. But, like the other chief engineers who succeeded him, he was embarrassed and assailed for conceiving and initiating policies which few in Panama, the United States, or France were familiar with or could understand.[16]

Dingler was a pioneer deeply in love with the canal idea but foolish enough to follow the example of the indomitable de Lesseps by taking his family to Panama with him. Under his energetic leadership, the grand ditch began to take shape. The moribund organization received a new lease on life by an injection of scientific and practical know-how—mainly because of his brilliant subordinate, Bunau-Varilla. During Monsieur Dingler's tenure as head of the canal works, adequate hospitals were built and, later, staffed with and supervised by European doctors and medical technicians. Comfortable wooden barracks were constructed in the newly dedicated town of Christopher Columbus on the Atlantic side. The commissary division which supplied goods or catered to the laborers near or at the excavation sites was placed in the hands of diligent contractors who saw to it that meals were adequate, served on time, and cooked by clean scullions.

Armadas of supply vessels arrived frequently at the Atlantic terminus of the railroad, with all necessary equipment—locomotives, dredges, iron mules, axes, cranes, tools, and spare parts. But the subcontractors more or less openly cheated the company when, in ignorance of local climatic conditions or in collusion with officials in the warehouses in New York and Paris, they shipped thousands of exotic items or extravagant orders to the isthmus.[17]

Dingler also attempted to solve the problem of performance within the Canal Zone by seeking workers in new labor markets.[18] Many contractors, some of them Chinese, were permitted to recruit men in Jamaica. They were discouraged from hiring workers from Tobago and Trinidad,[19] but those from Cartagena, the Islands of San Andres, and the lower Mississippi Valley were not rejected.[20] In spite of these directives and precautions, French-speaking blacks, more accessible to the canal, continued to arrive, but these "poor people, whose minds were still troubled by the confusion between slavery and manual labor, soon deserted the works and embraced [the] easier profession of sick workman. . . . The refusal of . . . physicians to admit to the hospital people who were perfectly sound was denounced as a crime against humanity [in the French Antilles]."[21]

Here was an old problem common to most people of the under-developed world—free-loading at a hospital or a sanitarium by the healthy of mind and body, and sometimes the well-to-do. Sanitary facilities attract most people, no matter what color the skin, and visual evidence of comforts never before experienced, such as adequate free food, comfortable beds free of bed-bugs, and clean showers, is as alluring as a garden of roses to the bees. No wonder the great humanitarian and savant, Dr. Albert Schweitzer, kept his sprawling hospital at Lambarene in Gabon, almost al fresco and devoid of any comforts except those that could be dispensed by clinical treatment or procured by empirical knowledge.[22]

Meanwhile, the general manager of the Interoceanic Canal Company and his immediate subordinates, the very able engineers, Hutin, Bunau-Varilla, Boyer, and Jacquier, could not cope with the increasing blackmail of the Colombian authorities. Everyone who had acquired land in the area of the Canal Zone within the last four years—and many lacked even a legal title—sought to amass shady profits by demanding an exorbitant price which the company was always compelled to pay.

No Colombian court of law dared invoke the right of eminent domain in order to set an equitable price for the land which had so suddenly passed from public to private hands. "Every leading citizen in Panama found that practicing law paid far better than running a revolution."[23] The company was hauled to court daily and within minutes adjudged guilty of the most bizarre "accidental claims" initiated by the workers and encouraged by the lawyers. With the "normal" cut of 20 percent of every adjudication in the courts—even for such ludicrous charges as trespassing on private property— dozens of law firms rapidly became wealthy.[24]

The chief engineer also spent considerable time and money entertaining visitors from Colombia, France, and the United States. Dr. Enrique Arce, with his never-exhausted sense of humor, called the guests "Bogota lizards." They came by the hundreds during the dry season. Fear of illness persuaded them to return to the *altiplano*[25] with the first raindrops, most likely immediately after Easter. A few venal politicians who remained too long contracted disease, and their final layover was rewarded with an untimely death.

The gentle and polite Monsieur Dingler was the most abused of all the general managers of the Interoceanic Canal Company, the favorite bête-noir of the Panamanians aside from Bunau-Varilla. In urgent need of an adequate mansion to entertain the seasonal flocks of visiting grafters, and in possession of a beautiful wife to grace the glittering receptions, he found no one willing to build his house for less than $100,000. He also needed a retreat where he could work in seclusion, but the cheapest for sale, a wooden cottage near the hospital, was not available for less than $50,000. These were enormous sums of money for those days, and these expenditures cannot be blamed on the executives of the company but on a kind of mass collusion, an activity in which the Colombians of those years excelled.

The Panamanians still talk about Dingler's luxurious car and per diem allowance of $50.[26] This is a fiction, for his "palace" car was only an office on wheels needed to inspect the works. It was of necessity, however, most often used to take visitors to the construction sites, and the daily allowance evaporated entertaining these unwelcome guests. Dingler's railroad car has been compared with those owned by the American tycoons Belmont, Vanderbilt, and Morgan, yet it was so modest that it lacked even a bed in which the tired chief engineer could take a siesta at a time when the rest of the forty thousand workers were enjoying this luxury.[27]

Dingler's supreme error was in his technical conception of the over-all engineering operation. His ideas about what machines were necessary were correct, and he ordered heavier digging equipment to be sent to the isthmus to coordinate the excavation works. But when he combined the digging derricks with the floating dredges of the Chagres Valley, he failed. He hoped to use pumps to transport the output of the dredges to the assigned dumping places, but the method was not successful. The error might have been easily corrected had he lived longer, for he might very well have adopted the plan suggested much later by Philippe.

At this time, any mechanical innovation was being vetoed by the contractors. In the end, the first general manager and chief engineer of the canal works at Panama paid for the mistakes of unchangeable minds, which are always the enemies of progress. He paid not only with his life but also with the lives of his family. Since history is influenced by beliefs that are often wrong, it is for errors that men have most nobly died, and so did Monsieur Dingler.

The Arrival of Philippe Bunau-Varilla

Jean Philippe Bunau-Varilla's interest in canals began early in his life. After a precocious but strictly supervised child-hood, Philippe was exposed at the young age of ten to the exhilarating miracle of Suez, which mesmerized all of France. Having studied the liberal arts, Philippe successfully completed the rigid years of preparatory school which opened the doors to the crack Ecole politechnique. Although this institution is a military school, it is exclusively devoted to the study of pure science, such as higher mathematics, physics, chemistry, geology, astronomy, and so on. Its aim is to provide the military and the civil services of the nation with scientifically educated officers. After completing these studies the cadets enter a professional school, but not before passing a series of examinations. Bunau-Varilla chose to become a member of the special school of the *ponts et chaussees* (bridges and highways).

Some years before entering the Ecole politechnique, Philippe had been impressed by his mother's words to an older youth who found himself dispirited because there were no more Suezes to conquer. When Madame Caroline Bunau-Varilla replied, "You still have the Panama Canal left," Philippe understood she was talking to him. It was in this way that the Renaissance idea of a canal in America entered and became permanent in the mind of the young genius. The day of decision arrived in the fall of 1880, when Ferdinand de Lesseps, on his return from America, came to speak at a convocation for the pupils of the Ecole. Seated in the front row, Philippe missed not a word or misunderstood a point during the hour-long dissertation. It was love at first sight.[28]

Official regulations requiring newly graduated engineers to serve the state prevented his joining the canal enterprise at once. After a series of overseas and at-home assignments, discouraged by his inability to get to America, Philippe sought the advice of his old mentor, the librarian of the School of Bridges and Highways, Monsieur Schwoebele. After attempting to dissuade him from such madness, the experienced friend reluctantly helped Bunau-Varilla to overcome the obstacles in his path.

A week later, Philippe was at sea, bound for Colon. He had as a companion the chief engineer and general manager of the Interoceanic Canal Company. It was October 6, 1884, and the happiest passenger on the steamship *Washington* was the exuberant Philippe.[29] This voyage was to be the first of nineteen transatlantic crossings for him, but for the unfortunate Monsieur Dingler, the next to last. Dingler was to return to France to die.

Emulating Ferdinand de Lesseps, who tried to anticipate every contingency and cover every detail before his return to

Egypt in 1856 at the request of Said Pasha, Bunau-Varilla became acquainted with every contrivance related to the canal project at Panama. He spent his twenty-one days at sea familiarizing himself with the problems confronting the builders of the grand ditch. On his arrival he was appointed head of the excavation works in the Pacific slope and placed in charge of cutting the cordillera at Culebra Hill. He soon realized that the canal route wove through a number of rivers and, at times, swollen streams that did not appear anywhere in the maps of Colombia or on the surveyors' blueprints. Some of these creeks emptied into the Chagres, but most did not. In theory and on paper, many miles of small streams were erroneously within the drainage radius of the Chagres River. Bunau-Varilla also became aware of the contractors' ignorance of diking, water conservation, and irrigation.

Taking into account such major factors as climatic conditions and the distribution of the flora, Bunau-Varilla discovered large uneven deposits of loess in the vicinity of the streams and much sagebrush in the hills and slopes, but a relative sparsity of arboreal species. Such botanical and geological distribution is unusual, because it was well known that under normal conditions there is little or no forestation in the loess. The young engineer also observed that the loess area had always been a steppe, but that most of the marshes within the radius of the projected canal lay in loess deposits. Puzzled by these findings, which clearly showed that the stratigraphy of the isthmus was entirely different from that of Europe, he reached the correct conclusion that the continent—at least in the area chosen for the canal—was geologically very young and that the large areas of loess were the result of windy storms rather than any other physical agent.[30] Another probability was that large-scale erosion of the higher ground had occurred during the ages of rain after the shaping of the land masses. Bunau-Varilla was close to presenting geology with a novel theory of a separate and independent formation of the continents. Today this theory—fantastic in the nineteenth century—is considered probably true.[31]

Each day, Bunau-Varilla became more convinced that the

contractors' lack of appreciation of the dissimilitude of soil and the variety of flora was responsible for the perplexing problems encountered in the excavation of the ditch. Culebra resisted all attacks and, once cutting began, the layer of loess extending saddle-back over the whole Culebra Hill began to drift, filling the trench, particularly after the arrival of the rains. In the lowlands, because of the incessant deluge and the sea currents, it was very hard to keep the water out. Obviously, the stratigraphic composition of the isthmus was not like that of the European continent, as Abel Couvreux had so persistently affirmed.

Patiently, Philippe began a tsunamic study of the bay. He found coastal currents, but noticed that, as a rule, the sea in this area was very smooth, thanks to protection from the ocean swells provided by the shape of the coastline. Now, if there were no swells, the sand and mud of the shore could not become mingled with the water. With the help of a giant marine dredge, he dared Poseidon to invade his trench. Months later, the cut opened by the mechanical monster was found to be exactly the same on the axis as in the depths. Philippe had solved the enigma of excavating the coastal slopes of the isthmus. But the monumental riddle at the middle of the cordillera was still two years away from solution. The young Bunau-Varilla had won his first battle, and his stature had grown in the eyes of his co-workers. Although he was not in charge of the divisional works in the two areas of excavation covering the Chagres Valley, Bunau-Varilla began to make daily notations in accordance with the studies he had made of the flora, soil, and waters of the entire region. He reasoned that the river by itself was not as important to the projected canal as the hundreds of streams that emptied into it; thus, the best source of water for the ditch probably had to be created—an artificial lake from which at any time of the year sufficient water could be drawn for the canal.[32]

Bunau-Varilla's Engineering Survey

Six months after his arrival in Panama, Bunau-Varilla found

himself in charge of the works of the first division at Colon, in addition to his already assigned third-divisional works.[33] Excavation in the Atlantic sector had been suddenly stopped by the very hard rock at the bottom of a part of the canal already opened. The French and American contracting firms were not in a hurry to solve a problem for which they had no responsibility. Stoppage of the dredging by such obstacles was well-compensated for by the company. Clearly, as Bunau-Varilla had already surmised by his own study of the geology of the isthmus, the lack of stratigraphic surveys was delaying the work.

Recalling an earlier experience in France, Philippe ordered holes to be drilled in the rocks a yard apart. In each artificial fissure, enough dynamite was placed to disintegrate the entire submerged quarry once it was blown. In five minutes the young engineer had solved a problem that had vexed his predecessors for months, and the dredges worked from that time onward without difficulty.[34]

The success of this experiment began to change the engineering conception calling for the construction of a sea-level canal at Panama or a locks canal at Nicaragua. The future of the Panama Canal had been assured by this unorthodox excavation. The cost of underwater excavation was reduced to open-air rock excavation—and it became clear that, with advanced methods of underwater demolition and better machines, the process had to be even cheaper.

As for Bunau-Varilla himself, he had seen and solved in his mind, in a lucid flash, the labyrinthine obstacle to a sea-level canal: "Construct," he said, "a [semi-rigid] locks canal first and [later, as transit increases], transform it [slowly] into a sea-level [strait], by dredging."[35] Had the Isthmian Canal Commission or the International Consulting Board, created in 1905 by the United States, adopted his suggestions—which Bunau-Varilla made available free of charge—the present dilemma of whether to build a new ditch or transform the present one into a strait would have been averted. At least he would have saved an astronomical sum of money, because mammoth works of this nature in the second half of the twentieth century can cost as much as the Vietnam War or the Apollo program.[36]

As the top leadership of the company in the isthmus became riddled with disease, additional responsibilities fell on Philippe's shoulders. By January 1885, he was placed in charge of another division of the works, leaving him scarcely more than three hours a day for rest. Of particular importance was the supervision of equipment and supplies being unloaded daily at Colon—without the benefit of docks—from an armada of chartered cargo vessels originating in France and New York. During my childhood, some of this hardware, such as the gigantic iron caldrons destined for the company's huge kitchens, could still be seen intact throughout the isthmus, being used as wash tubs or bathtubs.

Each of these cooking monsters could comfortably hold fifty chickens, two pigs, or half a steer, and all the condiments needed to prepare a *sancocho*, or a beef-stew.[37] The food cooked in each of these utensils normally fed one hundred workers. Rice and fish were not uncommon in the ration of the thousands of black workers, whose favorite dish was *bacalao* (stew) served with yucca, otoes, *name*, and hot peppers.[38] While touring the front line of the works, Bunau-Varilla often stopped at the large mess halls to eat this food.[39]

On January 31, 1885, Monsieur Dingler's wife died of the fever and, three months later, heartbroken and totally exhausted, the general manager and chief engineer sailed for France, where he died shortly after. His replacement, Maurice Hutin, also departed after narrowly escaping death from fever. Thus, the entire operation was left in Philippe's hands. For lack of an older substitute on the spot or a willing one elsewhere, the young man of twenty-six was appointed general manager and chief engineer of the Interoceanic Canal Company at Panama.[40]

Bunau-Varilla plunged enthusiastically into his new role, which he found a relief rather than a burden. The new responsibility made him uncontested head of more than fifty thousand workers and contractors. His decisions no longer required the approval of anyone else in the isthmus. He outlined a program calling for close contact with the workers; promotion of men regardless of nationality or color; rooting out of the crooks; increased supervision of the payrolls; daily visits to the hospitals, if possible; establishment of friendly relations with the American naval squadrons on both coasts of the isthmus; well-guided, but short excursions for official visitors to the excavating areas; and a goal of 1.4 million cubic yards per month.[41]

Insurrection in Panama

Some of the tasks confronting the young engineer were created by the company's directorate and its contractors. One, the attrition of his workers, was sown by nature. But Bunau-Varilla still had to face the problem of the savage political ambition of the trained zealots. As we observed earlier, the rise of Rafael Nunez brought an era of political peace to Colombia. However, the very anticipation of reform and order dismayed the professional troublemakers, particularly in Panama. These self-styled Jacobins were ready to depose, maim, and kill in the name of truth and at the expense of their fatherland. A serious insurrection began to take shape against Nunez in the summer of 1884.

During this chaotic state of affairs, and in the absence from Panama City of Departmental Chief Executive Damaso Cervera, and Chief Justice Ramon Valdes Lopez, a group of politicians conspired with the rest of the Supreme Court to depose the governor. They selected for the job Benjamin Ruiz, but the timely return of the two absent officials restored the appearance of normalcy for a few days, because the chief justice refused to participate in this chicanery. The usurper, Ruiz, raised an army, and only the intercession of the bishop of Panama, Dr. Jose T. Paul, prevented bloodshed. Bishop Paul's truce called for the resignation of both Cervera and Ruiz. The governor sacrificed his post on the altar of peace, yet as soon as this step was taken, Ruiz withdrew his resignation and claimed the governorship again.

One can imagine the impact of these events on the "law-and-order" mind of Rafael Nunez. He immediately ordered

Cervera restored to office and Ruiz disarmed and punished.[42] Philippe arrived in the isthmus just as this crisis was occurring, and he took note of the events. Later his new friend, Bishop Paul, filled in the details for his diary.[43]

Mob Rule

President Rafael Nunez, who had relatives and many close friends in Panama, decided to take a new look at Panamanian politics. Wishing to provide for a long period of peace and totally committed to the canal enterprise, he canceled a *personalismo*-style gubernatorial election in Panama in early 1884[44] and named a military commander, Ramon Santodomingo Vila, to take charge of and supervise the next election.[45] In line with his own convictions and his loyalty to his president, General Vila began to recruit a battalion of men to do battle with the enemies of the central government in other departments of Colombia. This move irritated the Panamanians, and the interim governor had to resort to force to end the politically inspired demonstrations against him. General Vila, in the meantime, altered his plan and sent to the battlefields the regular militia stationed at Colon, leaving one end of the strategic crossing devoid of military protection.

The military vacuum caused by this unwise maneuver opened the way for a revolt in Colon led by Pedro Prestán, Pautricell, and Cocobolo. The last two of these radicals claimed descent from Vincent Oge, Toussaint L'Overture, and Victor-Emmanuel Leclerc. The movement received considerable support from the foreign element in the city[46]— mostly British citizens and Antilleans—who hoped to establish a separate state in the isthmus that would eventually control the railroad and the canal. By the end of March 1885, the insurgents had in their hands what was left of the city which, in the first stages of the revolt, had been put to the torch.[47] Thanks to the courage and alertness of Bunau-Varilla, the mob failed to overrun the new settlement of Christopher Columbus, where the company had its headquarters. Disdaining personal peril, the young engineer spent most of the latter part of March organizing, training, and arming his workers for a last-ditch defense of the property and works entrusted to him.[48]

Shaken to its very foundations, the government stumbled into another blunder. To deal with the rebels in Colon, General Vila took with him most of the garrison quartered at Panama City, creating a new power vacuum in the Pacific side of the transcontinental route. Immediately after the departure of the soldiers for Colon, another self-styled redeemer appeared—a professional revolutionary named Carlos Aizpuru who had been waiting for this moment in the forests near Panama City. With more than 500 followers, he entered the defenseless town and began a purge of the inhabitants.

By April 1, 1885, both ends of the transisthmian road were involved in the smoke of battle. These bloody encounters were an experience from which Bunau-Varilla was to learn much. Many years later, he mentally reconstructed this violent episode in order to avoid a repetition of the tragedy of 1885 and bring peacefully to the Panamanians the canal for which they had yearned for centuries. By the evening of that fateful day in 1885, the situation had reversed itself completely. Panama City was in the hands of the Aizpuru irregulars and the governor and his troops were relatively safe in Colon.[49] At Panama City, the loss in lives and property was heavy. Several prominent citizens escaped death by donning nuns' habits and taking refuge in the convent.[50]

At Colon, which contained only wooden houses, 90 percent of the dwellings, the stores, and the wharves with all their contents were consumed by the flames kindled by Pautricell and Cocobolo. Thanks to Philippe, the conflagration was stopped at the very gates of the company. The American naval commander, R. Kane, watched the fire from his flagship *Galena* without raising a finger—conduct that caused his recall.[51] Vice-admiral James Edward Jouett superseded Kane, and later, after a conference with Bunau-Varilla and the accredited consuls at Colon, landed his marines and apprehended Pautricell and Cocobolo. Pedro Prestan, the intellectual leader of the mob, had been captured earlier by the forces of General Vila. But the turmoil was not yet over. Once in control of Panama City, Aizpuru seized the canal company's largest tug at La Boca and sent a committee of his partisans to Buenaventura, 360 miles to the south, in an attempt to win the recognition of the Bogota regime.

Meanwhile, the harassed commander-in-chief of the Colombian army, Eliseo Payan, fearing the spread of the rebellion from Panama to Buenaventura, decided to send one of his officers to settle the mutinies in both places. He designated for this task a bright young man named Rafael Reyes, whose timely arrival and meeting with Bunau-Varilla in the isthmus opened to him the doors of history. Marching alone under cover of night, Reyes found Buenaventura in chaos and most of the soldiers drunk. At the risk of his life, he managed to corral the armed mob and herd it into the hull of an abandoned ship which was towed away toward Panama by a tug sent earlier by Aizpuru. The rebel embassy had been disarmed and incarcerated.

With a madman in power at Panama City and a loyalist army navigating toward the isthmus, Admiral Jouett found himself in a very difficult position. He was able to cope with the problem, thanks to Philippe. Fearing more bloodshed, the admiral occupied all points on the strategic route and transferred his marines to the outskirts of Panama City. But, perhaps suspecting that he might have to face a united and combined native army, Jouett prohibited the landing of the Colombian contingent. Consumed by thirst and wearing a dirty uniform, General Reyes came ashore alone to parley with the Americans and to ask for water. But he looked more like a desperado than an official, and he was not received kindly. When he pretended not to speak English and asked for an interpreter, the admiral produced Bunau-Varilla.

General Reyes stated, through the interpreter, that he was there to restore order and offer guarantees to the inhabitants of Panama. While he awaited a reply, the Americans made sardonic comments and humiliating jokes about him. "His appearance was judged to be that of a savage whose military training and bearing could only be derided and ridiculed."[52]

The engineer was instructed to convey to Reyes the admiral's determination not to let the Colombian army land, but before translating these words the Frenchman cautioned the Americans about their personal remarks and expressed his opinion that this was a case "in which attire might very well hide a well mannered and civilized man." He confided to Admiral Jouett that the speech, words, manners, and delivery of this man were clues to his good breeding, fine education, and social standing.[53]

Without waiting for his "translation," General Reyes decided to make good the words of Bunau-Varilla. Speaking with an Oxford accent, the Colombian officer startled his audience by saying that he was there in accordance with the treaty of guarantees signed by the United States and Colombia in 1846 and that he considered Jouett's attitude a violation of this agreement. He added that under no circumstances would he return to Buenaventura without carrying out the orders of his superiors. Perplexed and deeply embarrassed, the American naval officer "turned to Philippe and smiled, quickly shook General Reyes' hand, congratulating him on his stand and agreeing to the landing of his troops . . . and when the soldiers disembarked, the American force rendered them military honors."[54]

Supported by the American marines, General Reyes refused to enter into any agreement with Aizpuru or to grant amnesty to him as requested. Soon after, the rebels surrendered unconditionally and the loyalist army occupied Panama City. Aizpuru was compelled to sign a statement which bound him to fight no more. All installations vital to the company were guarded by military police. But Bunau-Varilla sensed that the crisis had merely abated, and he confided his fears to Reyes and Jouett.

The next day, ten soldiers were quietly assassinated at headquarters and Reyes was informed that the city was about to be put to the torch. At Philippe's suggestion, Reyes disguised himself as a peon and began to visit all the towns and camps on the transisthmian route. In twelve days, the general gathered convincing evidence of a general uprising by the followers of Prestan, Cocobolo, and Pautricell. Without hesitation, Bogota granted Reyes authorization to execute the captive incendiaries. Pautricell and Cocobolo were condemned to the gallows by a military tribunal and were hanged next day on the ruins of the municipal building which they had burned. Prestan was executed two months later. The correspondents of the *New York Times* and the *New York Herald* cabled home, "Justice is done."[55]

The Weeks after the Rebellion

Throughout these months of mutiny and civil war, when the leadership of the isthmus so easily collapsed, when the inability of the government to control plunder, arson, and murder was so evident; when all the Panamanian politicians feared for their lives; when an American commander hesitated to enforce the terms of the Bidlack-Mallarino treaty; when Colon lay in ruins and Panama City half-destroyed; and when confidence in all social institutions had evaporated; the reputation of the general manager and chief engineer of the Interoceanic Canal Company rose.

With his characteristic genius for organization and quick decisions in the face of adversity, Bunau-Varilla ordered all the railroad cars and engines to the Pacific as soon as the Prestan mob began their incendiary acts. Later, on receiving the news that Aizpuru had revolted, he directed that all this mobile equipment be sent back to Colon. He confronted Aizpuru, sought an explanation for the seizure of the company's property, and when this man requested provisions for his followers, Bunau-Varilla calmly explained that the items demanded were in the commissaries at the town of Christopher Columbus. The railroad cars, added the chief engineer, were in the hands of the government in Colon. He explained that the six supply ships in the waters of Manzanillo Bay were unable to unload cargo because the wharves had been destroyed by Prestan. With consummate tact, and before the arrival of General Reyes, he offered his private railroad car to Aizpuru if he wished to initiate parleys with the governor, who was in Colon. Aizpuru declined.[56]

Placed in the epicentre of these crises, the chief engineer was not completely preoccupied with saving the company's property. Like Ferdinand de Lesseps during the plague in Egypt, Bunau-Varilla was greatly concerned with the fate of the canal employees, the Panamanian public, and the little people—children, women, Negroes, and Indians—as well as his influential acquaintances among the isthmian élite. At the first signs of trouble, Philippe transferred the women and children—black and white—who came to seek shelter at the company, to the flotilla of cargo ships in the Bay of Manzanillo.

Manuel Amador Guerrero, the future president of Panama, at this time a physician in the employ of the railroad, was trapped aboard one of the vessels at sea when the fires began. He had boarded the ship to examine a consignment of workers being sent by the contractors from Jamaica. Fearing for the doctor's safety, Bunau-Varilla sent a message by way of a canoe man asking that he remain where he was until the crisis abated. Another official of the company, the future head of the separatist junta in 1903, Jose Agustin Arango, was advised by Philippe, for the same reasons, to await developments at the camp of Gamboa.

After the capture of Prestan and his followers, Bunau-Varilla opened the stores of the company to the government soldiers, to the hungry, and to the destitute. Once Aizpuru's surrender was confirmed, he toured Panama City with still another member of the future secessionist committee of 1903, Federico Boyd. Visibly impressed by the damage inflicted on the town as well as by the number of casualties, Philippe sought to bolster the morale of the population by ordering that food and clothing from the stores of the company be distributed at the Plaza Santa Ana and at the atrium of the cathedral. A few days later, on July 4, in celebration of the new peace, Bunau-Varilla held a reception for the American officers at the Grand Hotel, to which all the local dignitaries were invited.[57]

4

Labor Troubles, Natural Disaster,

and Financial Crisis

Bunau-Varilla's Charisma; A Strike Is Averted; The Great Storm of 1885; Financial Crisis; "Long Live Death."

In a few weeks, Bunau-Varilla's name had become a household word throughout Panama and Colombia. Demands for his presence at public functions multiplied. Every official visitor or tourist demanded a meeting with *el gran Francés*—a sobriquet already given to Ferdinand de Lesseps.[1] July and December were the months in which most of the religious festivals and national holidays were scheduled. No event of this kind was considered a success unless it was graced with the departmental governor's presence, but after the arrival of the French, the company's executives shared the spotlight, as well as the expenses of the honor.

The most severe test of a man's physical and financial fitness was to become an *abanderado,* that is, a sponsor of a fiesta or a host of a *corrida de toros.*[2] In addition to the consumption of many quarts of strong spirits, this role also required the distribution of liquor to the mob, payment for the bulls as well as for the performance of the bullfighters and their troupe, and above all, *"un festin pantagruelique"* for the populace, in exchange for a few hundred *vivas*.[3] After 1880, the isthmians cleverly added Bastille Day to their long list of holidays, a celebration which lasted three days and at which time collective francophilia exploded in long cries of *viva el canal* (long live the canal) and *vivan los franceses* (long live the French).[4] But the anniversary of the Battle of Boyaca, the birth of Simon Bolivar, the *grito de Veraguas*, as well as Saint John's day, Assumption Day, and the feast of the Immaculata, also generated widespread euphoria.[5]

In spite of his heavy schedule, Philippe felt constrained to attend some of these functions for the sake of cultivating good relations. On at least one occasion he could not escape being named *abanderado*, but he frequently contrived to send someone else to represent the company.[6] It was at one of these diversions in 1885 that my paternal grandfather met Bunau-Varilla. Twenty-year-old Antonio Anguizola had arrived in Panama City from the distant region of Chiriqui with a shipload of cattle consigned by his elders to the pens of the company. The chief engineer, pleased by the size and weight of the animals, asked my grandfather to accompany him to the Atlantic Coast in his private railroad car. They talked about various subjects, and many years later after retiring from public and private life, Senor Anguizola reminisced about his youthful years and his indirect association with the canal.

> Bunau-Varilla's versatility was fantastic. He had the energy of ten horses. A devotée of progress, he considered it a positive force which one day would eliminate unnecessary wars. He sounded like a prophet of consummation. I spent two days at Colon and in our return trip we stopped to pick up Agustín.[7] Before bidding farewell to both [Arango and Bunau-Varilla], I invited them to come to Chiriqui and explore some huacas I had staked, huacas which were as old as Spain.[8]

Senor Anguizola was amazed at Philippe's knowledge of the flora, the fauna, the inhabitants of the isthmus, the canal workers, and the prevalent diseases. He was familiar with the many varieties of the most beautiful tree peculiar to the inner-tropical landscape, the palm, so much used in the manufac-ture of hats, and the royal palm, which grows to a height of 120 feet and is one of the most majestic productions of the earth. He also knew many species of trees, a most difficult accomplishment, for in the isthmus one is in the midst of a vast collection of flora from all points of the planet, thickly congregated, and differing widely in appearance.

Bunau-Varilla could point out with assurance the varieties of mahogany and cedar from which the natives usually make their canoes. Large boats called *bongoes*, forty to fifty feet long, were made from a single tree. These sea-going boats were in great demand by the company for quickly reaching the flotilla of ships in the bay. He knew the good qualities of the guachapali, found in abundance in Panama, a large tree which has something of the appearance of the oak and is very durable, and the *macano*, a crooked tree that does not readily decay under the ground or in the water. The author has seen stakes made of *macano* twenty-five years old, washed alter-nately by salt and fresh water, which showed no sign of deterioration.

The chief engineer could also identify on sight a large variety of isthmian cedars, and his analysis of the natives was most accurate for those days. He said:

> Nature has lavished upon them the most varied gifts, the climate is in a state of constant summer. [Nature also] has planted, reared, and ripened unaided, some of her best productions for their use. They are so well provided for, that they seem to be altogether free from any care for the future . . . [like] the spoiled children of a too-indulgent creator.[9]

After visiting some of the excavation sites, Bunau-Varilla, Senor Anguizola, and four other guests withdrew to the railroad car to get ready for dinner. The chief engineer had asked nine people, including grandfather, to sup with him that evening. They ate tapir, which is a solitary animal, intermediate between a hog and an elephant in appearance. Fully grown, it is about the size of a cow. One had been killed that afternoon near the workers' camp. (As a youngster I ate tapir several times; it has a delicious taste which approaches a mixture of roast pig, roast lamb, and fried chicken.)

As night fell, the guests in the railroad car became fascinated by the myriad luminous nocturnal insects such as the train worm, with its red "headlight" and rows of brilliant yellow lights. The firefly, which has two light-producing spots resembling twin headlights, and the lantern bugs, which are larger than the firefly and give out a constant phosphoric light from two points on their heads, are so brilliant that four of them, under a glass, will produce enough light to read by. That night the stewards serving the meal had placed at each corner of the dining car lights supplied by these fascinating creatures.

The subjects of conversation at the supper were the weather, the canal, geography, and the flora and fauna surrounding the railroad car. Not a word about politics. Unseasonal rains and cold winds had visited the isthmus the past two summers, and Bunau-Varilla wondered if this phenomenon had something to do with the eruption of Krakatoa, which had exploded in far-away Indonesia in late 1883. The thunder of the explosion and its immediate results had caught the scientific world by surprise. Bunau-Varilla believed, however, that the more far-reaching and delayed effects of the earthquake were beginning to be felt throughout a large area of the planet, especially in tropical America. He predicted that there would be torrential rainfalls during the next five years, and he worried about the effect of such rainfall on the excavation schedules. As we shall see later, he was anticipating the isthmian floods of late 1885 and 1888. In 1888, the Royal Society of England's report on the Krakatoa disaster confirmed Bunau-Varilla's apprehension this night in August 1885.[10]

Bunau-Varilla, Labor Arbitrator

By the end of July 1885, Bunau-Varilla had decided to begin a three-point program to improve labor performance. It called for: (1) intensification of the drive to enroll more Jamaican workers; (2) diminishing the tensions between Colombian and foreign workers; and (3) reducing absenteeism by half. Thousands of hours were being lost by drunkenness, overstaying in the city on week-ends, and injuries caused by carelessness. The hiring of Jamaicans had been considered earlier and rejected by the directors of the company, for Ferdinand de Lesseps still remembered his experience at Suez, where the British made trouble for him when he hired Egyptian *fellahs*. Most of the English-speaking blacks in the Caribbean came from the Ashanti, Fanti, Haussa, and Mandingo nations of West Africa. They were good people and highly coveted by the sugar planters in Cuba. The British, who had gained control of the *Asiento* in 1713, reserved the best slaves for their colonies. The Jamaicans were descendants of these tribes, which were considered superior in culture and intelligence.[11]

Because of the company's poor experience with French-speaking blacks, more than five hundred Jamaicans had been imported during the last months of the administration of Charles Dingler, the previous chief engineer and director of works. But to bring thousands of British subjects to the isthmus was a step that might well cause additional trouble for the company. Untrammeled by such fears, Philippe met with the departmental governor, Miguel Montoya, and later with the labor contractors, deciding on his own that the best policy would be a mass influx of Jamaicans. This calculated gamble elicited no objections from London or Bogota and, a month and a half later, thanks to this decision, the labor situation was considerably improved.[12]

England's silence about the recruiting of British subjects to work on the canal may have been caused by mounting preoccupations at home and abroad. In addition to the enmity between Benjamin Disraeli and William E. Gladstone, the British were troubled by the newly created German Empire; the *Alabama* claims; the Turko-Russian War of 1877, followed by the tedious negotiations of the Peace of Saint Stéfano; and the unwise policies of Viceroy Lord Lytton in India, which brought disaster in Afghanistan, the massacre of the army by the Zulus at Isandhlwana, and the defeat of C. G. Gordon at Khartoum.[13] It was perhaps clear to Bunau-Varilla that what England needed most at this moment was friends, and not enemies or new problems.

The second point in his program required more tact and elasticity. Discrimination exists even among the least of mortals. It is ever-present in men of every color, class, or rank. In general, the few hundreds of Spanish-speaking blacks from Cartagena, Buenaventura, Nicaragua, Mexico and Ecuador resented the presence of the Antilleans. In this large concentration of men, there were many who were hard to handle. The company's foremen were often startled by rebellious cries of *yo soy un hombre libre* (I am a free man), which signified a refusal to obey orders.[14]

When in better spirits, these men were good with the machete, and they carried this weapon with them constantly, even on their days off. For the slightest motive, such as *una mala mirado* (a bad look), and especially after a drinking bout with fermented corn beer or anisette, they vented their animosity by beating the English-speaking blacks with the side of the machete.[15] There was no way to disarm the Spanish-speaking trouble-makers, because the machete was the only tool capable of keeping the ever-embracing jungle away. A good machete man was also a valuable *trocha* worker,[16] and his sharp instrument was the quickest defense against formidable enemies and permanent residents of the forest—poisonous snakes. In self-defense the Jamaicans acquired guns, a move that created consternation among the foremen and fear in the hearts of the aggressors.

For an entire afternoon, Philippe heard both sides of this strange and serious dispute. One of the most successful labor contractors, the Dutch Marcus Junius Schouwe, sat by his side. He had been instrumental in bringing many of the Jamaican blacks to work in the canal, and a verdict against them could threaten the flow of this manpower. Even the excavation quotas could be seriously affected and, more important for Master Schouwe, profitable business could be ruined. Bunau-Varilla postponed the company's decision until the next day and, during the night, consulted with the departmental governor and other influential men such as Federico Boyd. Finally, he withdrew to the solitude of his studio. The liberal-arts curriculum had exposed Bunau-Varilla to such political and social theoreticians as Aristotle, Bodin, Locke, Montesquieu, Rousseau, and Hobbes. The problem seemed deeply rooted in the character of man within a political and social context. Clearly, Thomas Hobbes, in *Leviathan*, states that "laws of nature" are not commands, but "rules of reason."

> "A law of nature (*lex naturalis*), is a precept or general rule found out by reason, by which man is forbidden to do that which is destructive of his life, or taketh away the means of preserving the same, and to omit that by which he thinketh it may best be preserved." (CXIV, London, 1651).

Alfred Edward Taylor, in his biography of Hobbes, says that the meaning of Hobbes' statement "is simply that since every man desires to live, reflection shows us that it would be irrational to endanger our lives or to fail to protect them." Hobbes also refers to the first fundamental law of nature, which is to "seek peace and follow it." However, his second law dictates to all men the right of nature "to defend ourselves" (*Leviathan*, CXIV). This second law, as interpreted by Taylor, means "Do not to others what you are not prepared to allow them to do to you."[17] For Bunau-Varilla to disarm the Jamaicans would mean exposing them to the dangers of having done to them what the native Spanish-speaking blacks wanted to do "to others" but were not prepared to suffer themselves. Moreover, the chief engineer could not disarm the aggressors without jeopardizing the works, because their weapons were also valuable tools.[18]

After his usual three hours of sleep, Philippe woke with a solution that King Solomon would have applauded. As a child of revolutionary and slave-free France, he had not come to America to make slaves out of the English-speaking blacks at the hands of Spanish-speaking blacks. By mid-day, the company's judgment was definitely closer to Hobbes' thinking than to Rousseau's rule of the jungle for men in the jungle:[19] Both sides were to keep their weapons, for only fear of each other might keep the peace. Afterward, trouble subsided to a minimum.[20]

To reduce absenteeism among the Spanish-speaking blacks, pay day was rotated. The Jamaican laborers seldom went to the city, and when they did it was during daylight, for they did not drink alcoholic beverages or gamble. During the dry season there was a picnic every Sunday for the workers. Religious services of any kind were encouraged by the company, and the Jamaicans happily divided themselves into various congregations. Some stressed a strict interpretation of the Bible, others reveled in public testimonials of past experiences, still others practiced spirited singing, faith healing, or speaking in "divinely inspired tongues" (glossolalia). The French-speaking blacks opened up a clearing in the thick jungle and practiced the trances and rituals of voodoo.[21]

The Great Storm of December 1885

As if the evil forces in a Greek drama were joining hands to stop the attempt to unite the two oceans, the political near-disaster and the quarrels among the workers were soon followed by a natural calamity. Unexpectedly—because the "official" closing of the hurricane season in Panama is the last week in November—a storm of Homeric proportions fell upon the area of the canal on December 2, 1885.

"The ocean must have risen and fallen at once."[22] The velocity of the wind, calculated by Bunau-Varilla at more than one hundred miles an hour, increased in intensity during the night, at the very moment when the steamers were attempting to escape the severely burned docks at Colon harbor. The fragile vessels had no escape, and one by one they were knocked against the coastal reefs until they were all demolished. Fifty sailors drowned. Fortunately, two days earlier, the chief engineer had ordered that the flagship of the company, the steamer *Fournel*, as well as eleven other sailing ships, be brought inside the canal embarkment. These craft were to receive a coat of paint in anticipation of the arrival of very important visitors early in 1886.[23]

As the wind abated momentarily, the deluge increased. On the third day of the rains, it became evident that the embarkment in which the headquarters of the company was located, protected by a sea wall, was in danger of being carried away by the huge waves. It was possible that, after withstanding trial by fire the previous April, the work was in danger of being destroyed by nature's trial by water.

Bunau-Varilla reached Colon on the first day of the flood. He insisted that the engine pulling his car continue slowly over the tracks covered with water "as long as the water does not reach the fire."[24] Miraculously, the two elements were separated by three short inches. Had they joined forces in the furnace of the locomotive, the explosion would certainly have killed or severely injured the chief engineer, and the Panamanians might have witnessed the sudden disappearance of their canal dreams. Surely, when man is young, death seems far away.

Once he was in the Atlantic littoral, Bunau-Varilla's capacity for understanding a dangerous situation was again put to the test. The storm had regained its full strength and fury. This did not prevent Bunau-Varilla from organizing the rescue of those still alive amid the debris of sunken craft. Several vessels had been thrown upside down, and their polyglot crews of blacks, yellows, and whites, clinging to the sides like "human bunches of grapes,"[25] were clamoring in their native tongues for help. One of these ships was the English barque *Lyton*.

The captain of the company's flagship *Fournel*, already safe and out of the eye of the storm, sacrificed himself with two other sailors in a futile attempt to bring everyone ashore. Finally, Bunau-Varilla's efforts were rewarded when all those seemingly exposed to certain death—more than two hundred—were rescued. With characteristic fairness, the chief engineer gave the credit to others: "The hero of the day was [George] Espanet,"[26] a former naval officer who later continued to serve well the cause of the canal. However, the consular corps did not ignore Bunau-Varilla's spectacular rescue work. Two weeks later, the Quai d'Orsay received the following cable:

> The French Colony and [all] the foreigners have admired the generosity and devotion to a humanitarian duty of the employees of the Canal Company, at the head [of which] was Monsieur Bunau-Varilla.[27]

Bunau-Varilla was still worried about the fate of the workers stationed in camps within the inundated area. The water had risen in some places to fourteen feet above ground. As there was no thought this time of using locomotives for transportation, three *piraguas* (Indian canoes) were readied for the inspection trip. Philippe jumped in the front of the lead canoe. After two hours of paddling in waters infested with caimans and other species of the tropics the party reached dry land, the top of a hill. The boats had to be dragged to the other side of the crested promontory. One split into several pieces and the entire party embarked in the other two, a load that was much too heavy. The water reached to within two inches of the top of the canoes, and the slightest movement would have overturned them.

Several passengers whispered nervously that they did not know how to swim. But considering the other dangers in store, this handicap was actually an asset. The chief engineer calmed his companions by pointing to the not-too-distant trees. If they sank, he said, he could pull them to the safety of the branches. Yet it took steely composure to make the offer: The waters around those trees were as black as night, for the trunks of these giants of the forest, in marked contrast to the green foliage, were covered with millions of lethal black tarantulas.

Suddenly, the cries of one of the Jamaican paddlers diverted Bunau-Varilla's attention from tarantulas to an even closer enemy—coral snakes. Looking for shelter, a three-foot long reptile was swiftly swimming toward the lead canoe. In seconds, it joined the party aboard and pushed its head inside the chief engineer's right pocket. An ominous silence ensued. Then, calmly and without raising his voice, Bunau-Varilla asked one of his companions to gently lift a folded umbrella over which the body of the snake was resting. As if by command, the polychromatic creature coiled itself around the umbrella; then both were lowered to the waters and left behind.[28] After the disposal of such a dangerous guest, anything ahead would have been anticlimatic. Without further tribulations, the nervous explorers reached their destination a half-hour later.

On his return to Panama, Philippe ordered an accurate measurement of the flood, and methodical gauging was conducted by the various heads of the engineering sections. It was the first scientific measurement of this natural phenomenon in Latin America. Later, other great floods were measured according to the orders given at this time by Bunau-Varilla.[29] The study showed that more than one hundred five inches of rain had fallen within forty-eight hours on approximately ninety square miles.[30]

Pessimism and Financial Crisis

Despite the heavy toll of lives, livestock, supplies, ships, and equipment, the canal works emerged with only a few scars, still dominated by its exuberant young executive. A week after the flood, Bunau-Varilla sent a detailed report of the events and of the state of the engineering project to his superiors in Paris. He then turned his attention to minimizing the effect of the tragedy by accelerating the excavation.

By the end of January 1886, a record 1.424 million cubic yards had been excavated in twenty-nine days. Inspired by the enthusiasm of their boss, men of every color exerted themselves, their beasts, and their machines to a faster pace of work than in the years before. In February of 1886, 1.357 million cubic yards were dug; 1.385 million in March; 1.48 million in April[31]; 1.477 million in May, and 1.485 million in June.[32]

The workers were in a jubilant mood, and relations with the naval squadron of the United States were most cordial. But the losses due to the flood, in spite of Bunau-Varilla's honest report, had been greatly exaggerated abroad, and the usually reserved directorate of the company in France was beginning to doubt its own guidelines, which had assured the buyers of the public subscription of 1883 that the canal would be opened to traffic in 1888. Ferdinand de Lesseps himself had jeopardized his prestige by issuing an optimistic statement:

> We are certain to achieve the inauguration of the maritime Canal at Panama in 1888. We are confident of its very rapid construction and a quick opening. Not for one moment will we abandon our efforts to complete a work so impatiently awaited by the maritime and commercial interests of the entire world.[33]

At this time, those waiting in the sidelines for years, hoping to profit from the financial woes of the company and secretly expecting its collapse, began their move. It was generally expected that the enterprise would sooner or later need another infusion of money, and everyone associated with it knew that the quickest way to raise these funds was to appeal to the state. Confidence men, venal politicians, alert lawyers, unscrupulous newspapermen, and shady bankers sprang into action. The opportunity was much too good to miss.

Embezzlement, payroll padding, and nonexistent purchases could easily be hidden from scrutiny, especially when the press was venal. The situation offered these unscrupulous men, as well as the naïve directorate of the company—including de Lesseps—the chance they sought: to organize a lottery loan. Some of the bankers backing up the public subscription in 1883 had insisted on raising money this way and were ready to do so, among them the executives of the Credit Lyonnais in Paris.[34]

In late December 1885, after several small handouts to reporters and minor government agents, Baron Jacques de Reinach, one of the company's directors, opened up a Pandora's box which signaled the eventual death of the corporation. De Reinach, completely unaware of the unsavory reputation and spectacular financial manipulations of a confidence man named Cornelius Hertz, handed him $200,000 to publicize and advance the fortunes of the company, to buy influence, and dispense favors if need be.[35]

The more money Hertz received, the more favors he

promised and the more he spent, until he ruined de Reinach himself. It is said that in one of his weak moments the baron made this international swindler the sole financial agent of the company, without the authorization of de Lesseps or any of the other directors.[36] By 1890, Hertz had absconded with more than 10 million francs—over $4.775 million at the then-current rate.

Disturbed by these early signs of ruin due to political corruption and natural disaster, both Paris and Bogota decided to investigate. Colombia sent a technical delegation presided over by Juan Ponce de Leon, who sought an explanation for what was believed to be the company's desperate financial situation.[37] Bunau-Varilla spent considerable time traveling with the members of the delegation and entertained them without a show of ostentation. After two weeks of visiting the canal installations and the near islands, the Colombians had nothing but praise for the young engineer, whom their leader compared to Bonaparte:

> The only idea that I can give of my sentiments [said Ponce de Leon] is that you are of the blood of those who fought at Lodi, at Rivoli, at Marengo . . . of those who can win victory from the impossible.[38]

De Leon knew his French history well, but it was also evident that Philippe, with his charisma and logic, had exorcised another threat to the digging of a canal in Panama. There was always the risk that any regime in Colombia, alarmed by rumors of lack of money to finish the canal, might find an excuse to cancel the contract. In France, de Lesseps, like a man blinded by a mirage, accelerated his attempts to repeat the miracle of Suez in 1867, this time through a national lottery.

The French cabinet had considered a request for a lottery loan after the bloody isthmian uprisings of the spring of 1885.[39] The ministers, who feared to commit themselves to a position which might embarrass them in the future, turned the request over to a parliamentary committee. It was a wise move for the cabinet, but a delay for the canal enthusiasts, because committees are the most useless of all decision-making bodies.[40] If nothing is to be done and no decision is to be rendered, a committee must be appointed. True to its nature, this committee adjourned without a verdict. No wonder one of America's greatest historians, Walter Prescott Webb of Texas, said, "God so loved the world that he never created a committee."[41]

De Lesseps Returns to Panama

Early in the fall of 1885, alarmed by gossip aimed at discrediting the company, the French premier commissioned an able engineer, Armand Rousseau, to investigate the situation. De Lesseps, who had always wanted to raise foreign capital for his canal, conceived the idea of inviting as many chambers of commerce as possible to visit Panama and see the progress of the ditch at first hand. He sent his son Charles ahead to prepare the road for these guests and, very probably, to keep an eye on Monsieur Rousseau.

While Bunau-Varilla was routinely informing one after another distinguished official visitor about the progress of the excavations, employees of the company in Paris and New York were assembling an armada of ships and supplies to take care of the eminent guests invited by de Lesseps to Panama. Special care was taken to invite the chambers of commerce of New York, Germany, France, England, and Italy. The American delegation, which included many well-known political and financial figures, was organized by Cornelius N. Bliss, chairman of the executive committee of the chamber. He had been told by Count de Lesseps that all maritime corporations should be alerted to the nearness of the completion of the canal.[42]

On February 18, 1886, more than one hundred delegates arrived at Colon with "the Great Frenchman." In addition to the two de Lessepses, there were other officials of the corporation, including Theodore Motet, administrator of the assets of the company; Etienne Martin, general secretary; Gabriel Foresier, chief of transportation and maritime operations; Abbé Tiberi, chaplain of the hospital at Colon; Gabriel

Seleta, agent of the canal in New York; Louis Villars, member of the Paris municipality; Charles Bonnafous, chief engineer of roads and bridges; Dr. C. D'Nicolas, a naval surgeon; and Henry Cotter, stockholders' representative in charge of a committee to verify accounts.

From England came the duke of Sutherland, Admiral L. Carpenter, and Colonel Henry Talbot of the army. Engineer Leon Peschek headed a delegation sent by the German government, and the Marquis de Teano and a staff of five were observers from Italy. French municipalities were represented with large delegations from the chambers of commerce of such cities as Marseilles, Rouen, Saint Nazaire, and Bordeaux.[43] Several newspaper reporters also arrived, including the influential editor of the *Paris Economist*, Gabriel de Molinari, and A. Tissandier, editor of *La Nature*. Charles Stanhope, a well-known columnist for the *New York Herald*, represented the American press.

But the guest who proved to be an important link in the eventual acquisition of the canal works by the United States was the affable John Bigelow. President Lincoln's ambassador to the Tuilleries during the reign of Napoleon III met Philippe on this occasion, and it was a mutual and sincere friendship at first sight. The favorable impression that the young engineer made on the experienced American diplomat lasted. It was John Bigelow who made possible a liaison between Bunau-Varilla and another of Lincoln's former confidants, John Hay, a move which eventually paved the way for the final triumph of the canal idea at Panama.[44]

When the guests arrived, Ferdinand de Lesseps found he had to share the limelight with the indispensable Bunau-Varilla, who was the ideal type to bring off the extravaganza of publicity de Lesseps was seeking. Philippe exuded confidence, optimism, charm, and good cheer—the very antithesis of the gloomy feeling beginning to invade the minds of the stockholders in France. Philippe's words rang with a sense of destiny and purpose that influenced those around him, particularly the old canal builder, who seemed—once he set foot in Colon—to absorb the energy and enthusiasm of the young engineer. Bunau-Varilla was equally successful, whether giving a lecture tour of the installations or presiding at a reception or a banquet table.

There were several memorable social affairs, beginning with the reception and banquet at Colon on the day of the arrival. Admiral Jouett sent the band of his flagship to play for the more than three hundred guests.[45] The vice-president of the company, Charles de Lesseps, had brought with him several French and Italian chefs, and these gastronomic luminaries were joined in the kitchen by twenty-four other foreign and native cooks from the hotel and steamships in Manzanillo Bay.

Two receptions and two formal banquets were given on four different days. These huge affairs, which took place in the Grand Hotel, were graced by society belles, among them John Bigelow's daughter. Because of de Lesseps' love of dancing, local bands were in attendance and there was much dancing after dinner. At one of these immense receptions, attended by my grandfather, an impressive assortment of food was served buffet style: snails, beef bourguignon, *quiches et navarin* (lamb stew), *andouillettes* (chitterling sausages), *boudin* (blood sausage), breaded pig's feet, ham hocks, tripe in jelly, *rillettes* (pork paste) and pork liver, duck *pâté*, boiled shrimp in wine sauce, and broiled lobster with fresh pineapple. There was an abundance of French and Italian wines—Mouton Rothschild, Bordeaux, Burgundy, Beaujolais, Chianti Ruffino, Chianti Classico, and Frescobaldi.[46]

At a formal banquet given by the company, the following dishes were served: turtle soup with a dash of lime juice; *mousse de foie gras en aspic* (chicken livers blended with cream cheese, sherry, consommé, and Worcestershire sauce, in unflavored gelatin); *jambon d'Auvergne;* clam quiche; cold bass with *sauce gribiche;* lobster with pineapple in a cream made with Madeira; barbecue ribs bathed in Lafite; large shrimps warmed in coconut water and served with brandy sauce; and steamed *corbina* (a fish abundant in the Gulf of Panama) served with a pure sauce. The appetizer, medium-size pompano and sea bass tails, looked as though it would require an enormous amount of time and work to eat until the guests realized the meat had been puréed and shaped back into the original form. Pinot Noir, Chateau Gruaud-Larose, Gevrey-Chambertin, Chateau Greysac, and Chateau de Chenas were poured. There was plenty of Lafite and the toast was given with Charles Heidsieck champagne.

The governor's dinner for the foreign visitors was relatively modest: oyster bake, clam soup, roast pig, barbecued ribs, and *ceviche*. *Ceviche* is made with chopped raw fillets of *corbina*. In a deep glass or china dish, it is constantly beaten with a wooden spoon (a metal spoon cannot be used), while minced onions, lime or lemon juice, and hot yellow peppers are added. Prepared two days in advance and covered with lime juice at all times, it is served cold in cocktail glasses and eaten with crackers.[47] The dishes at this banquet were washed down with rum in coconut water, bourbon, and beer.[48]

True to the motto of *liberté, egalité et fraternité*, the people in the large plaza across from the Grand Hotel were not forgotten. For five *reales* (about twenty-five cents), anyone could buy a giant local tamale. This delicacy is prepared in the following manner: cook broken pieces of pork and meat in two cups of hot water, tomato sauce or tomatoes, an onion, salt, and pepper. Add a half-cup of water at a time until the meat is tender. The meat should have a large amount of sauce. In a separate vessel, stir a measured amount of *masa* (corn dough) after adding to it three-fourths of a cup of sauce. Simultaneously, prepare another sauce of sliced onion, tomato, shortening, and salt. Spread and grease a banana, plantain, or cabbage leaf dipped in hot water. In the center of the leaf, spread a portion of the *masa*. Add to it some of the meat, olives, and a little sauce. Fold the *masa* like a package, tie it with a string, and boil for twenty to forty-five minutes.[49]

Fried chicken and *corbina*, roast meat or suckling pig, rice with coconut and *gandules* (a small pea in season during the summer months in the isthmus), and *chicharrones* (pork cracklings) also constituted part of the popular diet. For less hungry stomachs there were *torrejas de maiz nuevo* (sweet corn fritters) prepared as follows: grate the corn and scrape the cobs with a knife, make a *masa* out of it; add eggs, salt, vanilla, cinnamon, and sugar. Mix all ingredients, beating for three minutes. Drop by the spoonful in hot oil to fry.[50] Sometimes the cook adds meat to this preparation, rolls it like a meat pie, and fries it in lard. There were also *carimañolas* (meat pies enveloped in ground yucca) prepared in the following manner: season ground meat with salt, Worcestershire sauce, vinegar, capers, onions, garlic, sugar, scallions, and parsley. Place the meat in the center of a portion of yucca dough, roll it to look like a small football, and fry it in hot oil over a low fire until it is soft.[51]

The children's favorites were the *panecillos*, hard biscuits in which the dough had been thoroughly mixed with either egg yolks or whites. Honey, sugar, salt, or cinnamon is added, and then the mixture is baked until hard. A good baker can sculpture these biscuits in many attractive shapes and forms for the small fry.

For those who wished a spirited post-celebration, there was plenty of cheap rum, whisky, and scotch. For the abstemious there were watermelon, papaya, ripe coconuts, *chicha de maiz* (an unfermented corn drink), milk, and coffee. The people walked around the park or danced al fresco to the tunes of local musical groups in which the guitar and the accordion predominated. Usually, the Olympian guests came down to the plaza seeking fresh air and socialized with the citizenry.[52]

Several other private and more informal social affairs were given by members of the consular corps or influential merchant princes. One was a candlelight reception and dinner under a full moon, given by the family of the entrepreneur Archibald Boardman Boyd, founder of the Panama *Star & Herald*.[53] The brothers Archibald Boyd II and Federico Boyd (the doyen of the consular corps) secured for this occasion the services of two Chinese and three Martinican cooks. For the first time in the memory of the guests, chefs mixed together dishes from the Caribbean and from the Gulf of Tonkin. The circular buffet tables were loaded with a variety of unique Afro-Asiatic culinary concoctions which were washed down with Pinot Noir, Charles Heidsieck,[54] and plenty of scotch diluted in coconut water. The dinner offered by the French consul listed, among other surprises, roast turkey Burgundy and duck cooked in wine sauce. Chateau Greysac, Burgundy Sparkling Rosé, and Lafite were generously poured.[55]

The local guests and hosts at these receptions would have been at ease at the Elysée or Buckingham Palace. There was already in Panama a financial and cultural set which was to increase in size and power upon the completion of the canal and upon the arrival of the republic that Bunau-Varilla helped create. There were the Obaldias, whose political and social connections throughout Colombia made them the undisputed first citizens; the Boyds, whose erudite father, Archibald Boardman, had emigrated from Ireland in the 1840s;[56] the Pinels and the Pizzas; the Arosemenas and the Arangos; the Arias and the Batistas; the Sosas and the Espinosas; the Fábregas and the Cazorlas and the Lastras; the Ehrmans; the Ycazas; the Meléndez and the Méndez; the Vallarinos; the Arjonas; the Valdés; and the Garays. All of them were well known to Philippe.

The activities were not confined to receptions and dinners. Bunau-Varilla awoke his foreign guests early. After a quick breakfast of fruit and coffee, milk or tea, the inspection tours scheduled daily by the company's staff departed—from the bay if travel was by sea or from the railroad station if it was by land or to the Atlantic Coast—not later than 7:30 A.M. The chief engineer led a different group every day, and his immediate assistants led others. After a light lunch at the camps at 1:00 P.M., followed by a short rest, the parties continued their excursions on horseback or by boat. By 6:00 P.M., everyone not staying overnight because of the distance was back in the city.[57] Trips by sea to the projected entrance of the canal and to such nearby islands as Taboga, Taboguilla, or Chame, or to the Archipelago of the Pearls required that the travelers remain away for the night.

On Thursdays and Saturdays, if there was a social affair scheduled, the parties returned an hour earlier. The tireless Bunau-Varilla, exhibiting no sign of fatigue, kept the visitors constantly on the move, which delighted the indefatigable de

Lesseps. Everyone, however, including the old count, was entitled to a short nap after returning from the field. It was the only extra rest Philippe allowed himself besides his regular sleep from 3:00 to 5:30 A.M. Immediately after dinner, and sometimes before the last guest had departed, Bunau-Varilla excused himself and withdrew to his office to work. He kept his immediate subordinates working with him until shortly after midnight.[59]

On free evenings the guests entertained themselves by riding a landau around the city or playing billiards or checkers. There were no card games. De Lesseps did not gamble in the ordinary way, and by this time he was hoping for a French lottery to save the canal. John Bigelow enjoyed the field trips and especially his conversations with Bunau-Varilla. He visited every camp, talked to the contractors, the workers, and the foremen, asked questions, wrote notes, and began to prepare his official report to the Chamber of Commerce of New York.[59]

Others were doing the same, including the newspaper reporters. Bunau-Varilla lost no opportunity to introduce to his guests—including Ferdinand de Lesseps—an indispensable arm of the company, the man most responsible for the scouting, selection, hiring, and transporting of black manpower to the isthmus: Marcus Junius Schouwe. Able, affable, punctual, and honest, this labor contractor with headquarters in Curaçao kept Jamaican workers joining the payroll of the canal. He was also prompt in rotating them when illness incapacitated them. The blacks affectionately called him "Master Jones," and the French executives called him "The Flying Dutchman" because of the speed with which he managed to fill labor quotas.[60] As we said earlier, the French wished to hire more Jamaicans and fewer workers from the French-speaking Caribbean possessions. Contractors like Schouwe made it possible.[61]

Every day something different and somewhat spectacular happened on the field trips. On one occasion, Philippe exploded a mine of twenty-five thousand cubic yards to blow a hill in the trajectory of the ditch. The observers, protected by distance, watched the mountain disintegrate before their eyes. That night, little cubes representing a thousandth part of one-millionth of the hill were presented to de Lesseps and each of the visiting embassies.[62] At another time, before Mardi Gras, de Lesseps, wearing a golden cape and riding a white stallion at the head of the entire party of guests—perhaps reminding himself of his gallop with Said Pasha in the Egyptian desert in the 1850s or unconsciously emulating Don Quixote—charged up the hillside at Culebra. From the very top of the mountain he raised his hands, waved at the multitude of workers far below, and surveyed his empire. He came down amid thunderous applause from a crowd which seemed to be truly impressed with the horsemanship of the eighty-one-year-old wonder. That night and the next, de Lesseps danced until the clock struck one.[63] Finally, on March 3, 1886, the steamer *Washington* raised anchor from Manzanillo Bay, taking away the two de Lessepses and all the delegates who had accompanied them.[64] Life became more normal for everyone connected with the canal works, especially for Bunau-Varilla.

It has been said many times that the receptions and banquets held during this round of visits to the canal were unnecessary expenditures. The critics of the company forget that it was imperative to court capital from sources outside France and that the foreign group was the best liaison for this purpose. The social affairs in Panama in 1886 left an indelible mark in the mind of the visitors, especially the Americans. Food was abundant and cheap in those bygone years, and the culinary experts who prepared the dishes were on leave from French hotels or on loan from the ships navigating the Panama route. Actually, the money spent on these functions was a good investment, if one considers that some very important members of the banking, commercial, and newspaper groups in the United States became aware of the progress achieved toward the excavation of an interoceanic canal in America. These people, particularly John Bigelow, were later to play decisive roles in the fate of the waterway through Panama. For this reason alone, what appears to many as a frivolous good time in the isthmus in the summer of 1886 proved to be, instead, a well-planned and successful public relations job.

"Long Live Death"[65]

It was common knowledge in France that a two-year tour of duty in Panama was enough for a white man if he wished to escape death from malaria or yellow fever. Bunau-Varilla's term was reaching that limit. Quite aside from this fact, however, the directors of the company in Paris, ignorant of what had been already achieved at the excavation site and still uneasy about having a youthful director and chief engineer, hired Leon Boyer to take over as head of the canal works. Older than Bunau-Varilla, Boyer was a distinguished alumnus of the *Corps des Ponts et Chaussées*, from which Bunau-Varilla had also graduated.

After his arrival in late January 1886, Monsieur Boyer, like the official investigator of the French cabinet, Armand Rousseau, had nothing but praise for the chief engineer. Their pessimism about the progress of the excavations, acquired in France, turned to exhilaration on learning firsthand that things were not only under Philippe's control but progressing so well that nobody else, considering the obstacles, could have done better. Their admiration for Philippe turned to astonishment at the sight of what had been achieved in Panama. On his return to France, Rousseau proposed the name of Bunau-Varilla for a rank in the Order of the Legion of Honor. Rousseau wrote to the chief engineer:

> I shall be happy to take any opportunity to bear further witness to the situation you had conquered on the Isthmus in the eyes of the foreigners as well as in those of the employees of the Canal, and of the honour which has resulted from it for our country and for the Corps to which we both belong.[66]

Leon Boyer, who was quietly learning his duties when de Lesseps and his entourage were in Panama, said to the chief engineer:

> I believed when I left France that nothing had been done

here, but I find you have done all that could possibly be done. I believed there were no employees here worthy of the name. I brought sixty new engineers with me. They are picked men, men I knew personally, men I had tried and found to be first-class men in France. What service do they render here (when you have done everything)? None at all. They are sick, dead, or gone. I find of value here only the men I met here on my arrival and who I thought were valueless. What an intense surprise for me is that![67]

Monsieur Boyer became increasingly attached to his young mentor. Because of Bunau-Varilla's unusual talent for public relations and Boyer's own limitations in this field, Boyer asked that before Philippe turn over the responsibilities of building the canal to him, he should handle another impending crisis. The company's directorate, without consulting the engineers, had just decided to substitute large contracting firms for the small companies and entrepreneurs who had, up to that moment, shared the excavation work. So sudden a decision posed problems as grave as those generated the previous winter by the confrontation between Spanish-speaking and English-speaking blacks. The tedious discussions necessary to reach an equitable understanding required considerable diplomacy.[68] Only Bunau-Varilla could generate enough charm to effect a final agreement.

Perhaps frightened by a premonition of early death, Boyer feared remaining in Panama. A few days after de Lesseps' departure at the end of the carnival season on March 10, 1886, casualties due to disease rose tenfold. Sensing the nearness of disease and death, many workers took to heavy drinking. It was commonly believed that alcohol could prevent or forestall an early end to life, if the disease were malaria or yellow fever. Fortified with a few drinks or totally intoxicated, these unfortunate young men found temporary escape from their thoughts in sad songs which permeated the chilly and cold air of the night. Invariably, their mournful melodies ended with the cry, "Long live death."[69]

Very soon, as though nature were determined to scuttle the canal, the plague was to attempt success where revolution,

trial by fire, trial by water, and conflict among the workers
had failed. Philippe, Boyer, and the entire high echelon of the
Interoceanic Canal Company in Panama were about to be
knocked down, like bowling pins, with disease. Few among
them would rise again. Luckily for Panama, one of those who
survived was Bunau-Varilla.

5

DISEASE

Long-distance Effects of the Krakatoa Explosion; Bunau-Varilla Prepares to Turn Over the Reins to Leon Boyer; Diseases of the Canal Area; Malaria and Quina; Medical Research; Bunau-Varilla Contracts Yellow Fever; He Recovers and Leaves the Field to His Successor

Unseasonal rain fell throughout March and April 1886, becoming continuous in May, when winter arrives in Panama. But excavation did not diminish, as Bunau-Varilla had feared, nor did the rains directly hamper his work. Little was it suspected that the accelerated tempo was to become one of the causes of the intensification of disease. Unwittingly, the company was digging its own grave; the more it dug, the larger and better were the reservoirs conducive to the breeding of mosquitoes.

Without the slightest doubt, as proved by the report of the Royal Society of England,[1] the far-away explosion of Krakatoa eventually influenced the progress of the canal at Panama. Krakatoa was a volcanic islet located in the strait of Sunda, between Sumatra and Java, Indonesia. Most of the material ejected was andesiatic glass (pitchstone).[2]

The submerged peak began to give clues of the coming event on May 20, 1883. After a month of alerting everyone in the vicinity of the archipelago, the volcano accelerated its warnings through August 15, increased its daily intensity thereafter, and reached a paroxysm on August 26. The climax came between 10:00 A.M. and 3:00 P.M. on August 27. Explosions of decreasing power continued during September and October. By the end of October 1883, the first part of this extraordinary event—the cataclysm proper—had come to an end.[3]

Estimates of the casualties vary. Some say 36,000 is a good figure,[4] others place the toll at 36,880.[5] Indonesian and Chinese estimates are 150,000. Ichthyological and environmental damage to the South Pacific and the neighboring lands was incalculable.[6] Giant tidal waves were recorded as far away as Hawaii and the entire western coast of North, Central, and South America. But during the three months in which Krakatoa was gradually preparing for its stellar performance, people exhibited only curiosity.

Pleasant excursions were organized from Batavia, and a steamer full of happy revelers attempted to reach the vicinity of the eruption.[7] As the intensity of the salvos increased, the Batavians, 96 miles away, became mildly concerned, perhaps because the thunder of the volcano "sounded like the discharges of artillery at their very doors" and they were unable to sleep. This infernal noise and the debris sent high into the stratosphere marked the second phase of the seismic shock. As the climax neared, Krakatoa could be heard 2,968 miles away in the Indian Ocean and on the island of Martin Garcia, 2,267 miles from the center of the noise.[8]

Yet, one of the most remarkable facts concerning the inundation remains to be told. Reverend Philip Neale, British chaplain at Batavia, walked in the countryside the day after the earthquake and found

> . . . great masses of white coral lying at the side of our path in every direction. Some of these were of immense size, and had been cast up more than two or three miles from the seashore. It was evident as they were of coral formation, that these immense blocks of solid rock had been torn up from their ocean bed in the midst of the Sunda Straits, borne inland

by the gigantic wave, and finally left on the land several miles from the shore.[9]

Reverend Neale states that had he not seen it, he would not have believed that these great masses of rock could have been carried so far inland. "Many of these rocks were from twenty to thirty tons in weight, and some of the largest must have been nearly double." This witness and his companions figured the size of the largest block of coral rock "as weighing no less than fifty tons."[10]

During the second stage of the explosion, celestial phenomena generated by Krakatoa manifested themselves in strange sunsets all over the world. The sun and the moon kept changing color continuously, from red to yellow to green to blue to purple, and there were other "unbelievable features in the sky from Tierra del Fuego to Lake Superior; from China to Guinea; from Panama to Australia." For several years after 1883, the earth experienced very cold summers and icy winters. The Isthmus was also affected.[11]

The mighty eruption produced a giant air wave of cosmic dimensions and importance, affecting every particle of the atmosphere. The dust revolved with the velocity of an "express train," leaving behind a lofty haze of extensive cirro-stratus clouds (a very long cloud formation stratified like an endless skyscraper, the first floors being of filamentous structure). The cirro-stratus mass of clouds changed to darker and more awesome colors as they approached the Equator and the Isthmus of Panama, where they became an atmospheric fixture for many months afterwards.[12]

For a better understanding of the great Krakatoa disaster and its aftermath, visualize a pebble thrown into a pond of calm water. Circular waves are formed immediately and continue outward. One might visualize a small globe of approximately eight to ten thousand miles in diameter falling in the quiet air. Its sudden thrust will at once initiate a series of circular atmospheric waves which will race away from the center of activity like the waves caused by the pebble thrown into the calm pond. As the centrifugal waves of air race away, the circle grows larger and its radius increases—first by hundreds of miles, then by thousands—eventually reaching the Isthmus of Panama and the Equator. Once in the opposite hemisphere, centripetal forces are set in motion, inverting the direction of the air waves toward their origin. The process recurs many times until calm has been restored to the skies.

At the end of this turbulence, the debris-loaded atmosphere was ready to commence the third and last stage of the Krakatoa explosion, directly affecting the future of the canal by delaying the excavation program. The return of the contaminated volcanic material back to earth from the atmosphere produced rains bearing the colors of the spectrum. To many superstitious people, it appeared as if the isthmus was being punished for violating geography, for cutting what God had united.[13]

Bunau-Varilla Prepares to Turn Over the Reins as Disease Decimates the Corps of Engineers

As the summer rains of 1885 and 1886 continued, sickness intensified everywhere. Bunau-Varilla began to concentrate on the administrative details relating to the transfer of command to the new director general-designate, Leon Boyer. Having successfully coped with the problem of replacing small contractors with larger firms, the chief engineer found himself with a more relaxed schedule. He had been able to persuade some of the little companies to form larger ones, fulfilling the requirements dictated by the canal lords in Paris. In so doing, he had avoided much of the asperity and frustration usually generated in negotiations of this kind.

Philippe also had to meet and extend hospitality to the distinguished visitors who were now coming to Panama in great numbers to glimpse the engineering marvel-to-be. Every one of them wished to talk with the director general, whose name was beginning to be known in Europe as well as in America. Some of these acquaintances were useful to Bunau-Varilla later, particularly when his role changed to that of canal impresario.[14] The herculean responsibility carried for so long on Philippe's shoulders began to be transferred to Leon Boyer's. However, an overworked body, from which the chief engineer had exacted the impossible, now appeared about to collapse.

By March 18, 1886, the two top engineers had agreed that Bunau-Varilla would work only sixty more days, time deemed necessary to inform Boyer of all the details of the gigantic organization. But as the days went by, Philippe had to spend considerable time at hospitals, bidding farewell from this world to Boyer's crew. Of more than sixty young engineers brought over by Boyer two months earlier, only seven had not yet shown the obvious signs of yellow fever.[15]

It is necessary to realize Boyer's state of mind during the last of Bunau-Varilla's days in the isthmus. Boyer was better known for the lucidity of his methods than for any original ideas or quick reactions in a crisis, in contrast to Philippe. Boyer was also wondering about the wisdom of learning to run the canal works when men were dying everywhere and death was staring even at him. Within a month, his premonition was to be realized, but luckily for the canal and for Panama, his young mentor, Bunau-Varilla, had miraculously escaped.

Other Killer Maladies of the Isthmus: Beriberi

The sporadic summer rains caused by Krakatoa provided sufficient stagnant water to make the mosquitoes comfortable in their quarters. Every housekeeper had a domestic breeding place, if only a flower pot in which a little too much water had been used. There were cans filled with water into which the legs of the tables and beds had been placed as protection against ants in, of all places, the hospital. Broken beer and wine bottles, cisterns, water barrels, and roof gutters were later found to be the most general breeding places for mosquitoes. Numerous other attacks on the workers' physical constitution frequently brought them to the hospitals, only to be finished off by a more pernicious disease.

One of these destructive maladies was beriberi, an ailment of the peripheral nerves caused by a deficiency of vitamin B_1, thiamine, characterized by pains in and paralysis of the extremities and severe emaciation or swelling of the body. It produces great muscular debility, a distressful rigidity of the limbs, and cachexia (a condition of general indisposition, with malnutrition and wasting of the body due to chronic constitutional infection such as tuberculosis or cancer). Some medical authorities diagnose the ailment as the result of eating polished rice exclusively. It sometimes degenerates into dropsy.[16]

Beriberi particularly affected the Chinese population of the isthmus. As we explained earlier, the Chinese sought security and health away from the inclement weather and its harmful effects; most withdrew to the shelter of a laundry shop or a small store. The humidity and lack of fresh air, worsened sometimes by a deep sniff from an opium pipe, aggravated their condition. Some afflicted people cured themselves by spending time near a dry beach, burying themselves in the hot sand, eating an abundance of fresh food, and drinking a few cups of wine from a felled corozo palm tree every morning and evening.[17]

Niguas, Snakebite, and Alacrán: Remedies

Another calamity affecting the workers was the nigua. H. Cermoise says:

> It is an imperceptible insect which penetrates the foot and toes. Its presence is revealed by an inflammation which causes gangrene. . . . The niguas are one of the most common pests of the country and there are natives who have lost all their toes [to the niguas]. (Translation by the author.)[18]

Within a week a person can lose toes, a foot, even a leg to the niguas. Treatment consists of lancing the swelling and extracting the insect and its eggs, then thoroughly cleaning the opening with hot water and alcohol. The wound is then packed with wet, mashed tobacco.[19]

Lethal snakebites were very common. If a bitten human or animal did not receive immediate aid, death came in less than two hours. The local antidote was *cimaruba cedrón*. The seeds of this plant are first scraped and then macerated in the alcohol or brandy with which the reptile's incision is to be washed. The scrapings are then bound onto the incision. A better way to use this wonderful cure is to refine the seeds into a dry powder which is sprinkled into the wound after it is cleaned with hot water.[20] Philippe Bunau-Varilla always carried a match box filled with this magic powder, a gift from my grandfather.[21] During the sojourn of the distinguished guests of the company in February and March 1886, at the request of Bunau-Varilla, every visitor was provided by Dr. Amador Guerrero with this powder as well as with quinine tablets.[22]

Another calamity facing the workers, perhaps more often than snakebite, was the sting of the scorpion commonly known as *alacrán (Centruroides suffusus)*. There are many species and colors of *alacráns*—black, red, brown, and green-ish-yellow—the last the most difficult to detect during the day. If prompt aid is not given, the sting of a scorpion can be fatal. Native herbalists recommend rubbing the entrails of the dead *alacrán*, along with alcohol or lemon juice, on the washed and dried wound—provided the scorpion had been captured. Trapping the deadly creature is very difficult. In most cases, it attacks its victims while they are at rest or asleep and, as soon as it discharges its venom, it runs away. Many do-it-yourself pharmacists always had several smashed specimens soaked in alcohol and ready for an emergency. Philippe carried some of these cures back to France. Today, says Philippe Bunau-Varilla II, there is a laboratory in Paris which specializes in the preparation of a serum using the entrails of *alacráns*, which is sold throughout the world as an antidote for the sting of the much-feared scorpion.

Tick Paralysis and Encephalitis

Another frequent ailment among the canal workers was tick paralysis. The jungle was literally covered with many varieties of ticks of different colors. As the malady has the same symptoms as a viral illness, it passed almost undetected among the heavy casualties caused by yellow fever and malaria. Dog ticks and wood ticks can produce paralysis by injecting a toxin into the host, but there is another tick which carries a germ. The exact toxic substance varies from tick to tick. The toxin is transmitted by the saliva of the insect.[23]

Somewhat less prevalent, but also a killer that claimed many canal employees, was the dread encephalitis. It is a mortal form of sleeping sickness which, like yellow fever and malaria, is transmitted by a flying carrier like the mosquito.[24] Bunau-Varilla suspected that one of his private secretaries died of this disorder, and not of yellow fever.[25] Thus, if you died—and many Frenchmen brought their coffins with them—you might still have avoided the two heavyweights, malaria and yellow fever. There was plenty of dysentery, *tabardillo* (sun stroke), fatal liver ailments caused by a parasite symbiotic with a river snail, and the agonizing blackwater fever.

Sunstroke, Fevers, and Blackwater Fever

Sunstroke affected a large number of canal workers, some of whom never returned to work or survived. I also contracted it once, in my childhood. My maternal grandmother, gifted in the art of the *curandero* (a naturopathic doctor or artful amateur medical practitioner), owned an extensive pharmacopoeia. When she observed that my temperature had climbed over 101°F, she sent for some plants and herbs growing on the bank of a creek. These she cut and boiled. The concoction was then chilled, and my head bathed with it three times an hour. By next morning, when the physician arrived, I was ready to resume my kite flying under the blazing March sun but, this time, sporting an enormous sombrero.

Ever since humanity began to suffer the ravages of disease, a rise in body temperature has been associated with many kinds of disorders. The generally accepted normal temperature is 98.6°F (mouth) and 99.6°F (rectum). It rarely exceeds 106°F by rectum, but some persons have survived brief levels of up to 113°F.[26]

People with malaria and yellow fever are often, but not always, aware of the growing sensation of warmth. As the internal temperature rises, the skin may feel very cold and there may be shaking chills. Most fevers bring a host of other symptoms, such as headache, muscle pains, nausea, vomiting, sweating, and flushing. G. Pickering, writing on the regulation of body temperature in healthy and sick people states:

> The primary mechanism of fever appears to be [a] disturbed function of those centers in the brain (hypothalamus and midbrain) which control mechanisms for heat production and loss. These affect particularly the activity of voluntary muscle fibers and the flow of blood to the surface of the body.

It is believed that thermoregulation is upset by injured tissue which, in turn, affects the function of the cerebral centers.[27]

One of the most consuming and vexing of ailments was blackwater fever, believed to have paludal origins. It was also believed that in order to acquire this malady, the victim must have resided in the contaminated area for at least six months and have survived four bouts of malaria.[28]

The distressing symptoms of blackwater fever, malaria, and yellow fever are conspicuous in the writings of antiquity. Hippocrates made an approximate prognosis of malaria and possibly of yellow fever twenty-four hundred years ago.[29] These diseases are characterized by prostrating chills, anemia, rapid pulse, vomiting, passage of dark-red to black urine, and temperatures from 102°F to 105°F. Unlike yellow fever, in which recovery means immunity, one attack of malaria predisposes one to another. Once recovered, the patient must abandon the endemic area as soon as possible.[30]

Etymologically, the term *blackwater fever* suggests the discharge of black waters through the urethral canal, which might have been the origin of its name. In Spanish it means a high temperature, which is the result of *aguas negras* (black waters). During rains, outhouses overflowed and the excreta that had accumulated in the *retretes* changed into a black liquescent fluid of high toxicity which, once out of its dam, contaminated streams, soil, and environment with its pestilential bacteria. Long before the mosquito was discovered to be the carrier of this and other diseases, it was believed that such intolerable hygienic conditions were a passport to eternity. Much later, when the anopheles was identified, laymen and physicians suspected that insects contaminated by black waters could transmit the illness and finish off animal or human in three days.[31] The hypothesis suggested earlier, namely that malarial attacks are a precondition of blackwater fever, cannot be considered valid. Many people, during and after the construction days of the canal, acquired the disease without previously suffering from or adjusting to endemic paludal attacks.[32]

There were many more perils to the lives of the workers which, when not detected in time, predisposed hundreds of them to more serious illnesses. As the digging of the ditch intensified, the canal bed expanded, drawing to it many of the streams that before had flowed freely. The flow of these waters, especially the Chagres River, had kept in check a snail carrying microscopic parasites responsible for a liver ailment in humans. With its access to the ocean inhibited, the snail thrived near the workers' camps.[33] A similar situation has recently been created in Egypt. Interruption of the spring floods of the Nile by the Russian-built Aswan Dam entrenched this same organic disorder in the land of the Pharaohs, and it reached epidemic proportions.[34]

Bunau-Varilla Visits the Dying

Too little gratitude has been expressed to the canal workers who, in the face of so many calamities, played Russian roulette with their lives, exposing themselves each minute of the day to hidden tropical enemies. Philippe Bunau-Varilla understood this. Promptly at 9:00 A.M. the chief engineer arrived at the hospital for his first visits of the day. Tense greetings and emotional farewells were exchanged between him and his workers. With poise and assurance, Bunau-Varilla shook hands, touched their arms and heads, and patted their cheeks, always with a shining and hopeful smile on his lips. Later in the night, in the solitude of his studio, with time to himself, the young engineer wondered if death was saving him only to preside over the liquidation of his courageous army.[35]

As the white crosses in the French cemetery multiplied, it was difficult to say which of the many prevalent diseases had killed the last man. The general belief was that there were only two main culprits—malaria and yellow fever. Philippe kept close score of this unfinished game with death. He prophesied to Leon Boyer that only 15 percent of the working force brought by him in January would live to see Europe again. "The rest will die,"[36] he said. This revelation no doubt had a traumatic effect on his already scared successor-to-be.

The Wind-Dried, Fever-Chasing Powder of the American World: Quina

In addition to the coveted gold bullion that the Spaniards found in the New World, they also encountered many dangers; perhaps the most pervasive was malaria.[37] Early in their adventure, the Iberians observed that the Incas had developed some immunity against this disorder, but apparently the surviving Peruvians could not be dispossessed of their secret as easily as they had been of their gold. For a hundred years after the beginning of the conquest, the white man was exposed to the ravages of malaria in America. In 1621, a kind Jesuit was restored to health by a native *curandero*, and the secret of cascarilla, as the Indians named the bark of certain trees, was revealed. Almost simultaneously, Ana de Osorio, widow of Don Luís de Velasco, married the grandee Luis Jeronimo Fernandez de Cabrera y Bobadilla, marquis de Chinchon.[38]

In 1628, the marquis became the viceroy of New Toledo (Peru), but the following year his wife became ill, and the symptoms pointed toward malaria. The viceroy, who had heard of the friar's good fortune years earlier, ordered a search for the mysterious bark. One of his *correjidores* (rural mayors), Juan Lopez de Canizares, sent the medical potion from Loja. The marchioness was cured, and in gratitude for the "miracle" she distributed refined cascara and wine to the poor. The substance was immediately named by the populace "marchioness powder". Later, the tree of the quina became known as *Chinchon*, or Cinchona.[38]

Juan de la Vega, the viceroy's physician, was the first

millionaire to owe his fortune to the new discovery. He transported shiploads of the bark to Spain and sold it wholesale in Seville for seven hundred gold reales a pound (over $100), a fabulous price in 1640. The general of the Society of Jesus, Cardinal de Lugo, imported the cascara to Italy, refined it, and distributed it free to the people of Rome; thus the substance became "Jesuit's powder." From Rome, the miracle wood passed to France, where the influential Cardinal Giulio Mazarin administered it to his young king, Louis XIV, who had contracted the illness. But it was Jean-Jacques Chifflet, physician to the governor-general of the Netherlands, Archduque Leopold of Austria, who was the first to publish a comprehensive treatise on the mysterious finding: *Pulvis febrifugus Orbis americani ventilatus* (Brussels, 1653), which means "Wind-dried, fever-chasing powder of the American world." Chifflet's work caused a sensation in the learned circles of the Old World.[40]

In England, although the medical secret was known during the last years of Oliver Cromwell's rule (1651-1659), it was Robert Talbor, of Cambridge, who made quina known to the élite of Britain after having restored the health of King Charles II in 1678.[41] Rumors had persisted earlier that Cromwell died of malaria after refusing to take quina because he wished no favors from the Jesuits. Talbor went to Versailles, where he administered the medicine to the dauphin (designated Louis XV), who bought the secret from him at a high price on the condition that it could not be divulged until Talbor's death. After the demise of the royal physician, another consultant to the court, Nicolas Blegny, wrote a popularized version of the miracle drug, *Le remede anglais pour la guerison des fievres, publie par ordre du roi* (The English remedy for the treatment of the fever, published by royal command).[42] However, the job of preventing malaria was left for the Spanish savant Jose Celestino Mutis and the Panamanian J. L. Ruiz.

Jose Celestino Mutis

Doctor Mutis was born in Cadiz of an élite family and, after

studying at Seville and Madrid, left Spain for New Granada
in 1760. Early in his academic career he became an admirer of
Carolus Linnaeus, the Swedish naturalist. Once established
in Bogota, he devoted much time to sanitary problems,
including the planning of cemeteries, prevention of small-
pox, and combatting malaria. Mutis was an earlier version of
Philippe Bunau-Varilla, restless in the pursuit of the ultimate
truth, curious about the unknown, and possessing a store-
house of versatility and energy. Mutis popularized in Europe
many South-American plants and herbs, such as ipecac
(Ipecacuanha), tolu balsam (*Myrospermum tolniferum*), Peruvian balsam (*Myrospermum peraiferum*), and the cinnamon
laurel of the Andes. But his preoccupation was quina. He sent
Linnaeus a sample of the bark and drawings of the tree.[43]

An attempt by two of Dr. Mutis' contemporaries to capital-
ize on his discoveries failed. Dr. Ruiz Lopez and Jose Pavon,
claiming that they had discovered quina, later wrote a series
of treatises on the flora of South America, such as *Quinologia*
(Madrid, 1792), *Letter about the Quina* (Madrid, 1794), and *Flora
Peruviana et Chilensis* (Peruvian and Chilean Flora) (Madrid,
1802). In frustration, Dr. Ruiz Lopez sued Mutis, but lost his
case against Mutis. Afterwards, he printed a brochure: *Defense and Demonstration of the true discoverer of the Quina in the
kingdom of Santa Fe* (Madrid, 1802).[44] Ruiz Lopez returned to
Colombia, where he died in 1822. Mutis' perseverance and
scholarship convinced both America and Europe, particularly
after his meeting with Alexander von Humboldt. The German geographer stopped in Bogota late in the eighteenth
century solely to visit with Mutis. A few years earlier, the
king had commanded Mutis to launch an expedition through
the jungles of the continent in search of new species of flora
and fauna. He was accompanied by eighteen of his students
and, at his death in 1808, had arranged for the printing of the
monumental work *Flora de Bogota o de Nueva Granada* (Flora of
Bogota or New Granada), which was completed by his
nephew. His erudite treatise *El Arcano de la Quina* (The secret
of the Quina; Bogotá, 1793) placed the burden of alleviating
the scourge of malaria on the bark of the Cinchona.[45] In

deference to Mutis' tireless work in the field of natural science, Linnaeus the younger named the beautiful genus Mutisia of the family Compositae, which comprises fifty species of plants found in tropical and semitropical America.[46]

Very few men have been so devoted to medical efforts to cure disease, prolong life, and relieve suffering as the good doctor Mutis. Yet it might well be that the efforts of the Spanish sage, so well-publicized by his better known friends—Linnaeus and Humboldt—created dangers perhaps more serious than those they tried to eradicate. He spread his talent thin. A versatile genius, Mutis engaged in myriad activities not closely connected with malaria or quina, such as collecting and editing a grammar of the Indian languages of the Chibchas, Mosca, and Achanguas, as well as initiating efforts which led to the erection of the astronomical observatory at Bogota (the highest in the world). Mutis was also concerned with the day-and-night barometric variations in the altiplano of the Colombian capital. Naturally, these activities took much time from his prime scientific love, the Cinchona.[47]

Like the Clayton-Bulwer Treaty of which mention is made elsewhere in this book, the popularization and crowning of quina as the key drug in the eradication of paludal suffering—thanks to Jose Celestino Mutis—inhibited, rather than advanced, the fight against the disease. Most medical authorities concentrated their efforts on curing the malady rather than seeking its true origin. As we know, the world had to wait another hundred years, until the appearance of such pioneers as Carlos Finlay, William Gorgas, and Walter Reed, in order to launch a frontal attack in our ongoing war with paludal distemper and its consanguineous relative, the dread yellow fever.[48]

Dr. Carlos Finlay and Other Medical Research Workers

In 1880, the year canal excavations began, Charles Louis Lavern found and described the malaria parasite in Algeria. And in 1886, when Bunau-Varilla fell critically ill in Panama,

the Italian scientist Camillo Golzi pointed out that the parox-
ysms of the fever are coincidental with the segmentation of
the blood parasites. (Dr. Golzi had previously acquired world
renown because of his investigations into the structure of the
nervous system.)[49] When the First Interoceanic Canal Company was about to die and the second was being created by
Philippe, 1889 to 1893, Theobald Smith and F. L. Kilborne,
demonstrated that the tick is the carrier of the piroplasm-
producing Texas fever in cattle and thus laid the basis for the
detection of the role not only of ticks, but also of other
arthropods, such as mites, crustacea, and especially insects,
in the transmission of diseases to animals as well as humans.
Dr. Carlos Finlay's theory was gaining momentum.

Dr. Carlos Finlay was a distinguished Cuban physician of
Scotch-French ancestry. Educated in France and the United
States, he demonstrated his idealism early by rejecting lucra-
tive offers to practice in New York's Spanish colony in the
1850s. Having survived full-scale attacks of cholera and typhoid, he was physically well-qualified to undertake the
investigation of these and other diseases such as yellow fever
and malaria.

Dr. Finlay acquired great popularity in 1867 when he
became convinced that the epidemic of cholera afflicting
Cuba was caused by infested waters. But the scientific world
laughed at him. As early as 1871, he turned his attention to
the mosquito as the possible cause of yellow fever and
malaria. Ten years later, in 1881, Finlay formulated his mosquito theory and correctly zeroed in on a carrier of yellow
fever organisms and named the species—*Aedes aegypti*.

Dr. Finlay observed that in order for an epidemic to begin,
there had to be at least one previous case of the fever. He
expressed the belief, later proved correct, that the survivors of
yellow fever were immune to further attacks. He suggested
that a mild form of the disease might in some cases not be
fatal to the indigenous population and still be deadly to
immigrants.

As we observed elsewhere in this book, Dr. Finlay affirmed
that the transmitting agent was an "innocent" carrier, inde-

pendent of patient and malady, and that the outbreak of widespread malaria and yellow fever coincided with the arrival of the mosquito season. But the medical world ignored his research and ignored his dissertations for thirty years. Ordinary people in Cuba and the rest of Latin America were among his first converts.[50]

When Bunau-Varilla arrived in Panama, thanks to the work of Mutis and his disciples, pharmacologies already listed more than nineteen types of Cinchona. The populace bought and drank these other *jarabes* (syrups) as often as many in our time buy and take vitamin C to prevent and cure the common cold and, if possible, to escape the flu.[51] They also believed that it could save them from yellow fever.

But the inhabitants of tropical America, where the marvelous plant thrives, could boast of stronger potions and more certain preventives and cures. Philippe Bunau-Varilla was not ignorant of these panaceas. Long before the bark of the Cinchona was refined into powder, Peruvian natives soaked the cascara in water. In other areas of tropical and subtropical America, they soaked the quina bark in the juice collected from a felled corozo palm tree. This mixture was taken twice a day, preferably before breakfast and at bedtime. Later, the élite soaked the wood in wine or brandy and boiled it with eucalyptus, orange, or lemon leaves; the result was a less bitter tea with the same good outcome. (Both my grandfathers always kept full wine and brandy bottles in which the bark of the Cinchona could be seen.) Tradition and experience had spread the belief that the potion distilled out of the cascara, the branches, and the leaves of the Cinchona in wine or brandy was a much better preventive and a quicker cure against malaria than the powder and tablets of quina or the many brands of *jarabes* produced in Europe and consumed everywhere.[52]

The chief engineer used to remind those around him never to forget their daily doses of the medicine, liquid, or tablets. Most Frenchmen, for whom wine was a substitute for water back home, found the liquid formula less distasteful. The combination of juice from the grape and the wonder wood may have been responsible for saving many from the ravages of malaria, including Bunau-Varilla. Wine contains almost 400 constituents which provide considerable amounts of iron and a great number of vitamins. "It also helps fight germs, relieves tensions, and helps the heart." Studies conducted by the Wine Institute show that wine can "lower the blood level of cholesterol, a fatty substance closely linked to heart trouble and clogged arteries. Wine also helps dilate small blood vessels and [for] many is not only a preventive but also a treatment for stroke."[53]

It is interesting to know that all the early civilizations, particularly in the Western world, relied heavily on wine as a source of food and body heat. Wine does have calming properties, and perhaps it is true that it lowers high blood pressure. During the building of the canal, dry table wine and *tinto* (dark red) were recommended by the experts as the best to mix with the bark of the Cinchona. Most of the Panamanian élite, as well as the French, drank a glass of dry table wine with the meal.[54] Today, the experts say that such a healthy custom can keep sugar levels in the blood low, preventing diabetes.[55] Yet the imbibing of the potion—wine and quina—was an ordeal, because it tastes like hemlock. Most of the canal workers, seeking a more delectable flavor while taking their doses of quina, diluted the potion by increasing the amount of wine in the dose, diminishing their chances of success.

The physicians in the canal zone, the white workers, and the Panamanian élite knew how to prepare or where to secure the highly recommended potions. My maternal grandmother had a formula which she called "valerian quina." At Easter and Christmas, she freely distributed to family and friends her antipaludal juice. Her recipe was as follows: Small pieces of ground Cinchona were immersed in distilled or boiled water for twenty-four hours. This combination was cooked for two hours and, as it cooled, valerian was added. Once it was cold, a small portion of alcoholized sulphuric acid was poured in. Mixed well, it was filtered an hour later, at which time close to 100 cc. of juice from the bark of a citrus tree joined the mixture. Once more it was filtered, and the product was poured into half-filled sixteen-ounce bottles of a good cognac or wine, preferably Courvoisier, Jerez de la Frontera, or Lafite.

My oft-quoted sources, Drs. Americo Valero and Enrique Arce, always fearing contamination of any kind, occasionally imbibed a potion similar to the one my grandmother used to prepare. They assured me that the daily doses of concentrated quina and wine taken by Bunau-Varilla helped him escape death from yellow fever.[56] Certainly the chief engineer had read about the symptoms of his possible killers in Panama and also about medical progress in taming these diseases. He kept in his studio C. M. de la Condamine's *Relation abregés d'un voyage fait dans l'interieur de l'Amérique meriodinale* (Paris, 1745), the memoirs of the marchioness of Chinchón, and H. Triana's *Nouvelles etudes sur les Quinquinas*.[57] Like Napoleon during the Egyptian campaign of 1799, Philippe made his subordinates read all the available literature about malaria and yellow fever.[58]

Bunau-Varilla Prevents a Second "Watermelon Massacre"

Besides coping with potentially fatal diseases and natural enemies, Philippe had to handle emergencies arising from human frailties. And as part of his training for the job of new canal chief, Leon Boyer needed to learn how to manage public relations, especially in times of crises. Since the company patrolled the areas where the workers congregated on pay day, Bunau-Varilla decided to take Boyer with him on one of the routine patrols. It was Saturday, March 20, 1886, at 8:00 P.M., that the chief engineer and Boyer, both in immaculate white uniforms, and a cluster of ten guards, arrived at a *cantina* (a bar) in *El Camino Real*. The place was filled with men, most of them canal employees, black and white, plus American sailors and travelers. Some time before the arrival of the patrol, a young American had generously bought drinks for the customers. After he had purchased and paid for several rounds of booze for himself and everyone present, certain patrons of the establishment began to plot to rob him. The barmaid, in collusion with the ruffians, suddenly demanded immediate payment for the American's last drink. She insisted he had not paid for that one drink. As the argument became heated and tempers were about to explode, Bunau-Varilla and his group made their appearance.

Once more, the chief engineer was the man at the right time and place. It was inconceivable that the sailor could have failed to pay for one shot of bourbon, when payment for all the liquor he had ordered had been collected. Bunau-Varilla realized that the rowdy element wanted an excuse to rob and kill the happy visitor who had given the impression, true or false, that he was carrying a large sum of money. The timely intrusion of the enforcers of the law and the two impressively dressed canal officials separated the unruly crowd into two groups. Most of them stood near the new arrivals while the evildoers knotted together at the other end of the *cantina*.

Calmly, Bunau-Varilla identified himself and his followers, paid the four reales demanded of the young customer, asked the canal workers first and everyone else afterwards, to leave the premises, and took the American with him under protective custody. A few among the bad element reached for their machetes, refused to move away, and began to yell *"Yo soy muy macho"* (I am a he-man); but the sight of the company's pistols and pointed rifles scattered them. The charged atmosphere cleared. Bunau-Varilla had prevented another "watermelon massacre" (the riot of 1855, described earlier, in which many Americans died). The next day, the *cantina* was closed forever, and its owners, with their retinue of bootleggers, whores, and pimps, were on their way to Tehuantepec.[59] In the early morning hours of March 22, 1886, three separate messages arrived at the chief engineer's railroad car. They bore congratulations for the way Philippe had handled a situation which had all the ingredients of another racial crisis. They were from Admiral Jouett, the French consul-general (La Vielle), and the governor of Panama, Santodomingo Vila.[60]

The History of Yellow Fever

Bunau-Varilla had read extensively about the history of yellow fever and other tropical illnesses. He had also observed at first hand, the quick progress of the disease and the speedy demise of many of his subordinates. Two of his immediate assistants, G. Petit and P. Sordoillet, both division chiefs, died within the time prognosticated for victims of yellow fever.[61] Philippe also knew that like malaria, yellow fever was well known in antiquity. He knew the symptoms as reported by all authorities from Hippocrates to his own time. It was clear to him that the disease had not changed its strategy of attack in two millennia.

This malady had been assigned to the class of diseases known as *xymotic* (fear of *xyma*, the Greek word for yeast). It was also known as *febris typhus icterodes* (typhoid jaundice fever), *febris cum nigro vomito* (fever with black vomit), the *fievre jaunde* of the French (yellow fever), and the *vomito negro* of the Spaniards (black vomit). It was known to the Caribs in America as early as 1655, when the French called it *coup de barre* (expressive of the muscular pains of the illness, as if produced by blows from a stick.)[62] Homer opened his great epic poem the *Iliad* with an allusion to a fever epidemic that in a few days caused havoc among the Hellenes at the siege of Troy, and the brilliant historian Thucydides also made reference to a destructive fever in Athens in 429 B.C. He himself might have been sidelined and escaped death, but the statesman Pericles did not.[63]

In the middle of the Peloponnesian War, this Athenian disaster was brought under control by Hippocrates, who introduced some innovations in hygiene which have since become routine in every civilized community. He ordered the washing and scrubbing of every house and street, the draining of every pool of water, the burning of all objects handled by the diseased, and the cleaning of the sewer lines. The sewer systems of the classical Greek city states were no more than septic tanks which overflowed when much rain fell. It was not until the early republic of Rome that aqueducts and sewers of monumental dimensions appeared. The engineer Sextus Julius Frontinus left a wealth of information on the construction and maintenance of these two necessities in the preservation of public health.[64] Had the French initiated their works by first constructing sanitary facilities of this kind, the final story of the canal would have been different.

The measures Hippocrates took in Athens to eliminate urban fever must have killed most of the mosquitoes' breeding places, because the plague stopped. Walter Reed in Cuba and William Gorgas in Panama did the same in the twentieth century in order to begin their battle against yellow fever and malaria.[65]

Bunau-Varilla was familiar with the diagnosis of yellow fever given by Hippocrates, "the Prince of Medicine." "And whereas the signs of death are innumerable, there are no signs of health being secure." The chief engineer was particularly concerned with what had been described by Hippocrates as the symptoms of approaching death, especially "excessively slow pulse,"[66] which he had often felt and tested during his daily visits to the hospitals. It was obvious to him that the illness had not changed through the ages, although there were some clear signs that in many cases it was strongly individual in its characteristics. In some instances, the patient lasted a fortnight; in others two or three days more.

Bunau-Varilla Survives Yellow Fever

Despite all his precautions, medical and otherwise, the chief engineer and director general of canal works at Panama finally experienced the agony of the fever. Surely, he came closer this time than on any previous occasion to rendering the ultimate sacrifice for the cause of the canal at Panama.

A nonsmoker and an abstemious drinker, Bunau-Varilla had also learned that a good method to chase away the insects—mosquitoes or other species—was to build a curtain of smoke near or around himself. What better way to keep the annoying creatures at bay than to take up smoking? Many of his Panamanian friends practiced this custom, if not for the pleasure of inhalation, at least for the insulation provided against the ever-present pests. Philippe, too, followed this custom, building around him a veritable wall of nicotine fumes as his primary defensive barrier, particularly during the evening.[67]

Nevertheless, Philippe's case exemplified the classic course of the disease. On March 30, 1886, he ate lunch in the company of a group of distinguished persons who had come to view the progress of the canal, among them Guy Patrenotre, a foreign-service officer in the Quai d'Orsay and brother of the French minister to Peking. Arrangements were made to meet the next morning at 8:00, when Bunau-Varilla was to take them on a tour of the installation. The meeting never took place. After his daily hospital inspection in the late afternoon, the chief engineer withdrew to his studio, ate his supper at 7:00, took his bath and went to bed at 11:00. At 1:15 A.M. on March 31, his valet, George Octave, who slept in an adjacent room, woke to the noise of an earthquake-like commotion centered in the springs of his boss's bed. With great trepidation, Octave ran to the nearest cottage, where various technicians slept, yelling: "The *calentura*! Master Philippe has the *calentura* [fever]." In half an hour, a physician and a retinue of attendants arrived.

Having witnessed very few recoveries from the fever in his many hospital visits, Bunau-Varilla had prepared Octave and the other servants in the house for the eventuality of his being stricken with disease. They were not to move him from his quarters. Furthermore, the treatment prescribed by the local *curanderos* was to be followed if possible. His servants followed his instructions. After the paroxysmal stage was over, exudation was not achieved until the end of the third day.[68] Showing the lucidity of mind characteristic of most patients with yellow fever, Philippe joked with his physician who, with a confident air, assured the bedridden engineer that things were under control and that his ordeal soon would be over. Little did he know that the chief engineer was an even greater expert in tropical maladies than he. With a weak smile, the patient replied, "I am [really] doing as well as a man can do when approaching the cemetery." "Why do you say that, monsieur le directeur?" asked the surprised doctor. The reply was astonishingly brutal and to the point. "[Because] at the start [of the paroxysm], my pulse was sixty per minute, the following day it had fallen to fifty, yesterday to forty . . . and today it is thirty. In three more days I will not be here to make any more observations about myself."[69]

Bunau-Varilla's doctor probably did not trust the brandy and quina potion prescribed by the herbalists, or, deceived by the apparent progress of the victim, did not believe it was needed at this moment. Now, however, the situation was different. It was a question of time, and there was not much left. He had to recognize that the chief engineer was knowledgeable about yellow fever, and he could not let him die just for the sake of protecting the medical profession. After taking the patient's pulse, the physician withdrew for a few minutes, only to reappear with the "wonderful remedy," already poured in an ewer from which it was transferred into a glass. The potion was administered in obedience to the *curandero's* instructions, and the weakened man slept soundly that night.[70] By the following morning, the falling of the pulse had been reversed. On the sixth day, after additional doses of "brandy," as Bunau-Varilla called it, recovery was in sight and death had been cheated.[71]

On April 11, 1886, Philippe was well enough to be led on board a steamer bound for New York City. It was not until the hour of departure that Leon Boyer—knowing that Philippe was out of danger—confided "a secret." He had been ill with yellow fever. The chief engineer smiled and said nothing. From the first chill of his early paroxysm, Bunau-Varilla had known what had struck him, and it was this recognition that saved him.

While bidding goodbye to the many friends who came aboard, he felt as if he was leaving a piece of his body and soul in the land to which he had devoted so many efforts, where he had fought so many struggles and endured so many sorrows—all for the sake of the canal.[72]

On April 17, 1886, the ex-chief engineer left New York and sailed for Le Havre on the *Labrador*, where he was the center of a happy surprise. Bunau-Varilla had disappointed his guests on the projected tour of the canal the day he became ill. While Bunau-Varilla was locked in mortal combat with death, Guy Patrenotre, the French diplomat in that group, was on his way to France by way of New York. By coincidence, Patrenotre also booked passage on the *Labrador*. Having received a letter on the morning of his departure announcing Philippe's demise and then seeing the name Bunau-Varilla on the passenger list, the polite Patrenotre rushed to Philippe and asked in a sorrowful voice: "Are you related to the Bunau-Varilla who just died in Panama? I suppose you are. I offer to you, sir, my deep condolences." The solicitous Patrenotre was surprised when Philippe responded, "I am very glad, sir, to accept for myself your gracious sympathy."[72]

Two weeks after Philippe's departure, Leon Boyer, the new director of canal works, was struck down with yellow fever while leaving a funeral. So virulent was the venom injected by the mosquito in Boyer's blood that the new chief engineer lasted only four days.[73] He awoke from his comatose state only long enough to write for everyone to see, "Do not abandon Panama,"[74] a message that Bunau-Varilla took to heart.

There is little doubt, despite his detractors, that the former chief engineer and director of canal works had left his mark in Panama during his first tour of duty.[75] As a contractor, he would surpass that record in the next few years, becoming the prime mover behind the company. After 1900, he would chisel a more indelible *epistemon*[76] in the broad and very difficult field of diplomacy and international relations by maneuvering the creation of a new state.

When Philippe left Panama in 1886, he had at work in the isthmus dredging and excavating machines far more powerful and efficient than ever used on the Suez Canal or anywhere else. One of these machines, the "New York," was excavating sixty-five hundred cubic yards every twenty-four hours. In all, seven large dredges were at work at the moment of Philippe's departure. Eleven kilometers of the main canal w :re completed, from Colon to Caimito.

Eight new dredges, thirty-four new excavators, and 110 locomotives were about to begin work in May 1886. The excavation quotas had been raised far above previous estimates and performances beginning in November 1885, and there was harmony among the various ethnic groups digging the grand ditch. Thanks to Philippe's prodding, the Dutch company which had contracted to cut Culebra Hill ordered a new type of machine from Glons, near Liege, in Belgium.[77] And Philippe was already working on the blueprints for his hydraulic dredge, which revolutionized the technique of large-scale excavations.

Bunau-Varilla suspected that he had rendered great service to the centuries-old dream of constructing a waterway through the American isthmus. Enormous strides had been made, and his personal services, which were confirmed years later, had been fruitful.

Clearly, Philippe's presence in Panama and his boundless energy and dedication to his job had assured the eventual success of the canal.

6

Financial and Political Ruin

The Geology of the Canal Area and Its Effect on Excavation; Bunau-Varilla Becomes a Contractor; Political Scandal in France; The Canal Company Fails; Philippe Tries Politics; Charles de Lesseps Tells All; Bunau-Varilla Is Investigated

Although icebergs are present when there is a mild winter, late April is not a bad time to navigate the north Atlantic. Probably because of the unseasonable frigid weather generated throughout the world by the eruption of Krakatoa, 1886 was almost devoid of the seasonal presence of the ice mountains in the northern sea route.[1] Except for the rumors on board ship of the impending failure of the Interoceanic Canal Company, Philippe's crossing of the ocean was a quiet and richly deserved sojourn across the solitary dark waters.

These rumors of bankruptcy tended to stampede the general public and stockholders into losing confidence in the company, and many passengers, American and French alike, anticipated the collapse of de Lesseps' empire. Philippe decided to pay little attention to this talk. He was still very young and on his way to a full recovery from yellow fever; still, his experiences in Panama had made him wiser by at least twenty years—an asset which was not to be wasted in the decades ahead of him.

During and immediately after the crossing, Philippe was preoccupied with devising ways to overcome the geographical difficulties involved in the completion of the waterway. Above all, he was concerned with the insoluble problem of the cordillera at Culebra Hill. Little had been accomplished at Culebra because of the blindness of the company's directors, the stubborn opposition of the contractors, the incessant rains, and disease. The contractors, as well as the company's executives in Paris, seemed to enjoy changing the strategy worked out by the engineers in the field.

Despite his near death from yellow fever, Bunau-Varilla seemed at this time, to many of his critics, oblivious to the problem of the endemic plagues of the isthmus and its influence on the canal.[2] This apparent ignoring of the ever-present evidence of disease may have been, in the end, a contributing factor to his ultimate success. Had Bunau-Varilla mobilized his tremendous energy in an attempt to bring about a quick eradication of the malaises plaguing his working force, he might have missed his great opportunity, and today he would be only a footnote in the history of progress. For Panama as well as for the backers of the canal, it was a blessing that he let others tackle this problem while he concentrated on the technological, financial, political, and diplomatic difficulties facing the waterway. As he overcame these obstacles, one by one, the dream of a canal at Panama became a stronger possibility. So, knowing the recent advances in the medical field, Bunau-Varilla continued to express confidence that the plagues of the isthmus would be conquered sooner rather than later.[3]

The Problem of Culebra Hill

Culebra Hill was the highest point of the cordillera at the crossroads of the isthmus. It was a mile long, according to Bunau-Varilla's calculations. Its high point was 300 feet above the sea, and the high point on the axis of a sea-level canal was 330 feet. In four years, the average altitude, something like 307 feet, had been only reduced 12 feet. It was still 295 feet above the bottom of the hill and 265 feet above sea level.[4] A technical reassessment of the situation was imperative because it was possible that the canal could be finished on both sides of the sierra long before the mass of the rock in the middle was cut. Philippe had already solved the problem of cutting the rocks by the use of dredges. He also conveyed to Ferdinand de Lesseps during de Lesseps' second visit to Panama in 1886 what he thought of the idea of a locks canal first, later to be made into a sea-level waterway.[5]

Not being an engineer by profession, de Lesseps did not take enthusiastically to this suggestion. Besides he was already totally committed to a sea-level passage at any cost. But Bunau-Varilla knew that even if his plan were accepted, the rate of excavation—something like three feet a year—was much too slow for the already heralded century of mechanical wonders. Figures like these would have been well-received by the engineers plotting to cut Suez in 2000 B.C. Count de Lesseps had unwisely alerted all maritime companies to ready themselves to cross the continent through his canal in 1888.[6]

Every one of the canal technicians hoped to increase the rate of excavation during the rainless summer months, but in the last two years winter and estivo-autumnal conditions had been the same.

In his quiet and solitary nights at sea, Philippe nursed a plan to attack the mountain at Culebra with speed and determination—that is, to excavate it faster than the slides caused by the cuts could fill it in. The cut-out earth had to be eliminated as quickly as possible, and the dump had to be made stable at all times, now that the rains seemed destined to continue forever. The former chief engineer had made this suggestion to the Anglo-Dutch contractors before he left Panama, but they chose to continue at a leisurely pace.

The contractors, aware that nothing short of a complete takeover by the new canal corporation could force them to speed up, worked, from the very beginning of their tenure, at a snail's pace. This baffling behavior was a challenge to

Bunau-Varilla. Wise in the stratigraphy of the region, he advanced several premises, each one of which later proved to be correct.

Philippe's Geological Study of the Area of the Canal

The geological formation of the isthmus, so different from that found in Suez and Corinth, fascinated Philippe and confirmed what he suspected. The entire mass of land was structured by three different kinds of stone—sedimentary, volcanic, and intrusive igneous rocks. If he could lay the bed of his ditch over the comparatively soft marl (clayey limestone), there would be no problem in scheduling the opening of the waterway for 1891.[7] Was it possible, he wondered, that geology itself, millions of years ago, had set the stage for the cutting of the continent only at Panama?[8] Most likely, the canal—whether locks or sea level—would have to avoid a cut through intrusive igneous material. Still, to escape the sharp turns of the cordillera and follow a semistraight line, it would have to touch a little of the hard volcanic area.[9]

Philippe's survey bore fruit when he learned that it was not necessary to dig through the hard igneous mass and that the volcanic crest at Culebra was the very end of the mass of geological rocks. He needed only to cut through it and find marl again, almost within reach of the sea of Balboa.[10] Convinced of his findings, he set out to conquer Culebra, the obstacle barring his path to success. Figure 6–1 shows not only the geological formation in the area of the canal, but Bunau-Varilla's ingenuity in avoiding the harder volcanic stone in order to build the water route through softer limestone.[11]

Philippe Reassesses the Excavation Strategy

Philippe recognized that at Culebra and elsewhere throughout the excavation sites certain dumps of the spoil banks remained relatively stable in spite of the rains. Why? Obviously, the answer was because of the nature of the clay. The loads of earth, when dumped, remained separated from each other as if they were pieces of rock. Therefore, the spoil banks, he reasoned, must contain about 40 percent hollow space equally distributed in their mass. He ordered the dumps at Culebra built as follows: first a railroad line was established from inside the cut, where the excavator was working, to the side of a convenient valley. Then the side of the adjacent hill was excavated so as to allow the creation of a railroad line following the horizontal section of the hill. Trains were then brought along this line, and their contents dumped on the hillside below. The hill under the railroad line was thus progressively covered by the dumped soil.

Once the new mass was thick enough, a new track was built parallel to the first one so as to get nearer the crest of the dump. This operation was repeated many times. When the dump was formed, it resembled a large mesa, the sides of which plunged into the valley below. Above it, virgin forest covered the top of the hill. But as soon as the rains set in, the dumped mass suddenly collapsed and slid away, enveloping rails, ties, cars and men.[12]

Clearly, the water, flowing in broad streams from the top of the hill, had weakened the soapy clay, transforming it into a lake of mud. In a desperate attempt to solve this problem, Bunau-Varilla had bridges built perpendicular to the hillside, to support the first line and to enable the workers to dump the loads off these bridges into the valley. Later, a series of wooden bridges across the valleys was built from which the earth was dumped. Unloading the trains in this manner filled up the space below the first track and, in this way, a large stable embankment was erected, on both sides of which trains could be emptied without fear of slides.

However, there was another urgent problem. In the interior of the cut there were still masses of slippery mud which became thinner as the rains intensified; yet the subsoil under this artificial marsh had been shown by soundings to be compact and firm. The real difficulty was to remove the coat of semifluid clay that was, in some places, thirty to sixty feet thick.[13] A long, hot summer would harden the liquid mud. And, after that, the giant machines might be able to scoop the solid mass of brown earth as if it were chocolate ice-cream. But this was not to be. The far-away eruption of Krakatoa and its worldwide repercussions put an end to dry summers in the canal area for a period of five years.

Bunau-Varilla Becomes a Canal Contractor

Philippe's arrival in France in late April 1886 was destined to change his career beyond the scope of his imagination. After a five-week vacation in Normandy and in Vichy, where he stopped to enjoy the waters, the former chief engineer began to feel healthy again. The deficit in sleep incurred during his tenure in Panama had been corrected. Before his five-month leave ended, he was once more obsessed by the canal.[14]

Although the news of the near collapse of the Anglo-Dutch contractors could not be ignored and the fact was no secret to Philippe, the directorate of the company sought to conceal the gravity of the crisis from the stockholders. On July 28, 1886, when Philippe returned to Paris, he received a message from Charles de Lesseps. He was asked to come to headquarters for "routine" consultations on the thirtieth of the month.

Sensing the urgency of the summons, Philippe replied that he would be happy to see Monsieur de Lesseps the next day. Their meeting lasted a week. At these sessions with de Lesseps, Bunau-Varilla laid down his plans and his terms. If the canal were to be saved, all experimentation must end at once. If Culebra were to be attacked successfully, "Let me do away with the contractors and carry out the task directly with the employees of the company."[15] And, in exchange for saving the company, Philippe demanded full power to choose his collaborators and the right to reward them for services rendered. He promised to surrender all powers once the battle had been won, at which time, if the directorate of the company desired, "I shall again be able to assume the general management of the works."[16]

Bunau-Varilla convinced the young de Lesseps of the soundness of his advice and the validity of his plans for overcoming the baffling Culebra cut. But the canal board, among whom was Baron de Reinach, later to be revealed as a master parliamentary manipulator, completely scuttled the plan.[17]

Undaunted by this setback, Charles de Lesseps returned to Bunau-Varilla two days later and said to him:

> Could not this group of men, full of energy, ready to carry out your ideas, be found among the small contractors instead of among the engineers employed by the company? Why should you not put yourself at the head of a contracting company, the elements of which you would select according to your judgment? You would then be able to employ the full liberty of action which the strictness of the regulations of a great company like ours will never allow you. Act, at the Panama Canal, the part of Borel and Lavalley at Suez. It is the greatest service you can render to the Panama undertaking.[18]

The suggestion was clear: save the canal works at any cost. Young de Lesseps' proposition upset all Bunau-Varilla's plans for his future. He was still a member of the *Corps des Ponts et Chaussées*—namely, a civil servant. To leave this highly regarded professional organization to become a contractor would mean beginning a new life.[19] Little did Bunau-Varilla suspect that by taking charge of a nonexistent contracting firm he was to open the way to complete mastery of the canal's destiny. Strange as it seems, the investigator for the Colombian regime in 1885, Ponce de Leon, had eulogized Philippe as a man whose destiny was about to explode in deeds comparable with Napoleon's battle laurels in Italy.[20]

Bunau-Varilla Tames Culebra Hill

Bunau-Varilla knew his history, and he remembered the praises of the Colombian diplomat on this occasion. He resigned from the élite engineering corps supported by the government, and also from the Interoceanic canal company. By September 1, 1886, his contracting organization was ready for action. Two other engineers, veterans of the Panama campaign, and his brother Maurice completed the firm. By the end of October 1886, Philippe was again on his way to Colon.[21]

The news of Philippe's return to the isthmus had preceded him, and there was a large contingent of citizens and canal workers waiting for him on shore. Among them was the state governor, General Alejandro Posada, who brought with him a warm word from President Rafael Nunez, now in total control of Colombia. The law-and-order rule of Dr. Nunez was to be complemented by Bunau-Varilla's engineering marvels in his second attempt to finish the canal. Without doubt, the brilliant administrations of two of Nunez' surrogates, generals Posada and Juan V. Ayscardi, contributed to the enormous progress made in the excavation of the canal between 1886 and 1888.[22]

Corruption disappeared and honesty returned to canal and country, thanks to the new French contractor, Bunau-Varilla, and to the two able Colombian administrators. The critical Panamanian historian, M. M. Alba C., states:

> A moderate man and very competent administrator, General Posada was the personification of goodness in the midst of so much evil. He conducted his duties with such discretion and skill that for the first time since the old Province of Castilla del Oro seceded from Spain, the departmental chest showed a surplus. Such an extraordinary performance [never equaled again] furnished the treasury with the great sum of 125,000 gold pesos.[23]

Providence seems to have smiled upon the contractor and the isthmus in general. The rains subsided somewhat during the summers of 1887 and 1888. Immune to yellow fever and wise about all the other local plagues, Philippe plunged into action. The new methods for establishing the dumps and containing the slides succeeded admirably. There were no more slides at the spoil banks at Culebra. Bunau-Varilla's struggle against so great a natural obstacle produced the result he foresaw: at no point did they have to withdraw before the landslides, but the victory was dearly purchased. At certain points, the cost of one cubic yard of excavation rose from $1.06 to $22.[24] Such financial sacrifices could not have been asked of self-serving contractors who wanted to prolong the work indefinitely.

Aided by the political calm in what had been the world

center of discontent and revolutionary activity, Bunau-Varilla was able to travel throughout Colombia and visit Cartagena twice. He met President Rafael Nunez and Dr. M. A. Sanclemente.[25] To keep in touch with his ground crews and to miss some of the plagues of the isthmus, Philippe spent several weeks in Curaçao, Guadeloupe, Tobago, and Martinique.

By February 1887, for the first time since work had begun, the rains were no longer able to stop the trains or the excavating machines. And wherever he traveled, Philippe kept planning the acceleration of the excavations. As explained earlier, his method of submarine blasting made all rocks dredgeable. An enterprising contractor adopted it. Instead of excavating with trains and steam shovels, he decided to do the job by dredging to the required depth of thirty feet. The infiltrations of water were pumped away to keep the cut dry below sea level. The new principle was equal to open-air excavation, and more economical.

Observing this contractor at work, Bunau-Varilla realized that if he built a locks canal it no longer needed to become permanent. It could be, instead, a step toward the ideal sea-level ditch. The end, instead of being infinitely far off, seemed almost within reach, and the building of the sea-level waterway could be started as soon as interoceanic transit through the locks canal began.[26]

Moreover, the company's fears of bankruptcy could now be allayed, for it might not be necessary to wait for the last cubic yard to be dug before collecting the first tolls. Philippe knew that his plan had to be presented to the canal's board of directors adroitly. Ferdinand de Lesseps had already told him in no uncertain terms that he wanted no part of a locks canal scheme—even a temporary one. The old count had to be convinced that his design was not going to be abandoned.

In preparation for his next engineering coup and before he sailed for France in February 1887, Bunau-Varilla dug two artificial lagoons on each side of the saddle and at both extremities of the sections at Culebra Hill.[27]

A New Engineering Strategy

Back in Paris, Philippe spent much time traveling through

the city's industrial complex, and sometimes out to Lyons, Marseilles, and Alsace, in search of the equipment necessary for his job. He also made three trips to Belgium and one to Germany. Every night he thought about a locks canal and searched for a way to convince the company. He read Demosthenes, Aristotle, and other of the peripatetic philosophers. He could hardly call on the directors of the company and say, "I want a locks canal." He could foresee their frantic objections to such a revolutionary suggestion.[28]

But on a rainy night in May 1887, after reading Heraclitus of Pontus, the solution came to him. Heraclitus was the Greek metaphysicist who demonstrated movement by walking. He also advanced the theory that change is the most dynamic force in the universe. Like Archimedes, Bunau-Varilla jumped out of bed and began to yell, "I have it, I have it."[29] The commotion awoke his mother and the servants, and for a moment there was much consternation. The consensus was that Philippe had again caught, if not yellow fever, another deadly disease in faraway Panama. Oblivious to the presence of the entire household, he began to write on the dining table. When he had finished, he lifted his eyes and smiled. The collective tension was relieved, but his mother's fear did not abate until Philippe said: "Open a bottle of champagne, a few bottles mother, we will celebrate for a few minutes. I have found the secret of my success. Tomorrow, I am sure, the company will accept my plans."[30]

It took three days for Charles de Lesseps to assemble the canal lords to hear what their rising star had to say. Bunau-Varilla began by informing them of the latest progress in the excavation schedules and of the machinery he had bought to be used in Panama. Then he continued:

> As you can surmise by my report and that of the present chief engineer in Panama, we have reached the proper method of excavations, which is the dredging method. It makes us impervious to the rains and the landslides. Let's now generalize my system. Let me subdivide the canal route into a series of pools. When we unite these pools by locks, we shall have continuous water communication in which dredges, tugs, and

scows will float. Let me make these locks wide enough for sea vessels. Continuation of the work will in no way interfere with the passage of these vessels. You will not have thus built a lock canal. You will simply have utilized your works in order to open up the navigation of the isthmus. The company will be in a position to levy tolls. You will be master of the future.[31]

Like a doctoral candidate waiting for the final decision of an academic committee, Bunau-Varilla was respectfully asked to leave the room. He went to the coffee shop, but in five minutes a messenger paged him. The smiling urchin, who looked to Philippe like a messenger from the gods, handed him an envelope and stood silently waiting. The short note read: "Write down, please, Monsieur Bunau-Varilla, when you propose to finish the canal." Without hesitation Philippe wrote, on a separate sheet: "In the autumn of 1891, Messieurs."[32]

Twenty minutes later, Charles de Lesseps, led by the *petit bleu*,[33] arrived to accompany Bunau-Varilla back to the meeting room. After some token opposition from Ferdinand de Lesseps, who still wanted a sea-level ditch, the directors of the Interoceanic Canal Company unanimously endorsed the new strategy.[34] The canal moguls, who only a few months earlier, after the destructive floods of December 1885, had considered Bunau-Varilla much too green for the post of chief engineer, had totally surrendered to him.

The New Strategy at Work

Happy as the dolphins that escorted the steamer *Lafayette* as it entered the Caribbean, and still undeterred by rumors of an imminent financial scandal involving executives of the company, Bunau-Varilla returned to Colon in mid-summer, 1887. Again a crowd of more than 200 came to welcome him. This time, with the taste of victory in his mouth, Philippe's smile was contagious.[35]

For all practical purposes, Bunau-Varilla's efforts were channeled toward the building of a locks canal. Making it into a sea-level waterway was to be done later, without bringing navigation to a halt. Even the engineers assembled for the

project were unable to conceive how this might be accomplished. Indeed, they were aghast at the potential effect upon
a lock of lowering the level above it. Manifestly impossible,
they maintained—and they were not totally incorrect, in the
light of conventional construction of locks.

But to Bunau-Varilla, the solution to the problem was
simple, so simple that it escaped the stereotyped thinking of
these well-disciplined minds. Let us review the basic
engineering factors of the summit level of a canal with locks at
its two ends. The paired lock gates have respective heights
proportionate to the maximum depth of water they are
required to hold back. In conventional practice, the height of
the upstream gates will be equal to the depth of the canal
only, whereas the height of the downstream gates of the very
same lock will be equal to the depth of the canal plus the fall
between the summit level and the lateral channel below, with
which it is connected.

The upper gates are positioned at the top of this giant
staircase, so to speak, which makes it evident that it would be
necessary, in order to lower the level of water above the lock,
to bring all navigation to a halt in order to excavate the canal
bed and dredge it down to a level equal to the depth of the
canal plus the fall of the lock. (See Fig. 6–2.)

But, as Bunau-Varilla pointed out, the difficulty vanishes if
gates of identical height are incorporated into the design of
the lock, equating the total depth of the canal plus the fall
(whether at the downstream or upstream end of the locks),
and if, at its two extremities, the bed of the summit level canal
segment is dug down to the altitude of the bottom of the
lower adjoining laterals for a distance of, say, nine hundred
feet from the lock entrance. (See Fig. 6–3.) With these minor
modifications, Philippe affirmed, "the whole difficulty of
transforming a lock canal into a sea-level canal, without
hampering navigation, is entirely solved."

> One may deepen three feet, for instance, by dredging the
> summit level without touching the lock and without troubling
> the navigation, if half the width of the summit level is reserved
> for the works and the rest for navigation. As in the case of the

The Completed Trans-Isthmus Lock Canal Across Panama

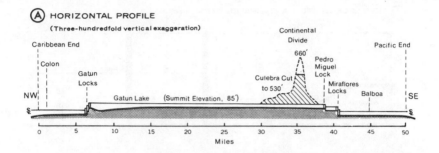

Ⓐ HORIZONTAL PROFILE
(Three-hundredfold vertical exaggeration)

Continental
Divide

Caribbean End

Colon

Gatun
Locks

660'

Pedro
Miguel
Lock

Pacific End

Culebra Cut
to 530'

Miraflores
Locks

Balboa

NW

Gatun Lake   (Summit Elevation, 85')

SE

0   5   10   15   20   25   30   35   40   45   50
Miles

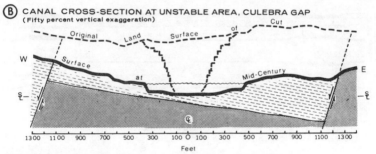

Ⓑ CANAL CROSS-SECTION AT UNSTABLE AREA, CULEBRA GAP
(Fifty percent vertical exaggeration)

Cut

Original   Land   Surface   of

W

Surface   at   Mid-Century   E

1300 1100   900   700   500   300   100 0 100   300   500   700   900   1100 1300
Feet

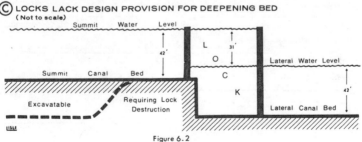

Ⓒ LOCKS LACK DESIGN PROVISION FOR DEEPENING BED
(Not to scale)

Summit   Water   Level

42'

L

31'

O

Lateral Water Level

Summit   Canal   Bed

C

K

42'

Excavatable

Requiring Lock
Destruction

Lateral Canal Bed

LISLE

Figure 6.2

Bunau-Varilla's Transformation, Locks To Sea-Level Waterway

(Not to scale)

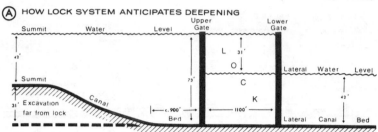

(A) HOW LOCK SYSTEM ANTICIPATES DEEPENING

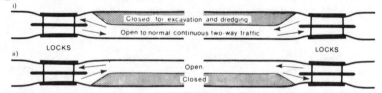

(B) DEEPENING NEVER HALTS TRAFFIC

i)

ii)

(C) PROGRESSIVE EXCAVATION FROM LOCKS
TO SEA-LEVEL CANAL

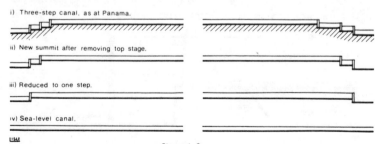

i) Three-step canal, as at Panama.

ii) New summit after removing top stage.

iii) Reduced to one step.

iv) Sea-level canal.

Figure 6.3

transformation the final bottom width would be 500 ft., there will always remain during the dredging works a minimum width of 250 ft. unhampered for the circulation of shipping.

This deepening of three feet once made, the depth of the canal in the summit level is, therefore, brought beyond the standard dimension. The level of the water can be lowered by three feet without hampering in the least the operation of the locks or the circulation of ships.

The two same successive operations, dredging the bottom and lowering the water level can be repeated until the water surface in the summit level is brought down to the altitude of the water surface in the adjoining level.

At this moment the lock gates can be removed and the new summit level is formed of the old summit level and of the two adjoining ones.

The masonry of the locks will simply form masses of artificial rock which will be removed like any other mass of rock on the side of the canal.[36]

Although Bunau-Varilla sketched out his proposal as a single-step, or two-stage, lock-canal system in this example, he pointed out that two, three, or more steps would facilitate the ultimate removal of the locks without stopping navigation during the long process of cutting the canal down to sea level.

Once Philippe's ideas had been sketched out, he began to organize another corporation, modeled after his own Culebra Company, to lighten the burden on the locks contractor he had designated, the eminent Gustave Eiffel. Bunau-Varilla was absolutely convinced of the validity of his plans and of the methods to be followed. He had solved the Interoceanic Canal Company's most difficult engineering problem. Unfortunately, he was unable to extricate the corporation from its financial woes, produced by its own directors.[37]

Besides working on his drawings, Philippe chose the location of the locks and the quality of the stone to be used in the canal. He had scheduled the opening of the canal for 1891, although he expected to achieve this goal earlier. The amount of earth to be excavated was 56 million cubic yards, and he knew his powerful machines could excavate more than 16 million cubic yards a year, and lower the cut not to the

140-foot level but to a 110-foot level. The canal was to be opened with five locks of a 28-foot fall at each side of the mountain divide.

By January 1888, it appeared that all obstacles in the way of the successful completion of the works had been meticulously anticipated and that canal users throughout the world could look happily forward to the inauguration of the seaway before December 1891. The progress of the works and their cost were based on existing conditions and figures. There was no further risk to be run. The arrival of the mechanical apparatus requested by Bunau-Varilla made it possible to dispense with thousands of laborers. Even the weather began to improve, and the proportion of wet to dry-season excavation rose from 52 percent to 73 percent.[38] Moreover, the exodus of the unneeded workers probably contributed to the diminution of serious illness.[39]

The most difficult part of the remaining task was not the cutting of Culebra, but the construction of the locks, and this work was already more than six months ahead of schedule. When the work was stopped, Bunau-Varilla's Culebra Company had reached an average depth of 235 feet above sea level. All the hard ground had been removed. By 1888, only 15 feet of excavation remained. Philippe had proved that the cordillera could be cut through at the altitude of 140 feet above sea level and that it would correspond to a lock canal with a summit of 170 feet above sea level.[40] In two years, the average level of the axis at Culebra Hill had been lowered by thirty feet; at the previous rate, it would have been only 6 feet. On the day the work stood still, only 6.5 million cubic yards of excavation were needed to conquer the continent and join the oceans![41]

The progress in the canal works generated by the dynamic personality of Bunau-Varilla and the reign of peace insured by the arrival of Dr. Rafael Nunez on the political scene of Colombia were complemented by the reforms inaugurated in Panama by the departmental governor, Alejandro Posada. Encouraged by the prospect of a soon-to-be-open canal and applauded by Philippe, General Posada reorganized the police force, placing at its head honest and dedicated officers such as the prefect of the corps, Tomas Herrera. Strict hygienic regulations were enforced in order to control the endemic plagues and prevent epidemics. And most important, as noted elsewhere, fiscal responsibility was achieved.[42]

This proficiency, unknown before in Panama, extended throughout the administration of Posada's successor, Governor Juan V. Aycardi (March 8, 1888–August 31, 1893). With the aid of some of the French technicians secured by Bunau-Varilla, Panama became the first department of Colombia to enjoy intercity telephone lines. They were strung between Panama City and Colon, and to other towns north of the capital. Both cities were also among the first in the Western Hemisphere to own a system of public lights.[43] A new upper-level school, modeled after the French lycées, was opened in Panama City during these years.[44]

Political Turmoil and Financial Trouble

Soon after Philippe's return to France in May 1887 to buy new machinery, the company made public the fact that Colombia, late in 1886, had granted it another hundred thousand hectares of land. The implication was clear: Bogota had confidence in the success of the canal. All that was required was the support of a friendly ministry in France to back up the projected lottery loan.

But in July 1887, France woke to the first salvos of a long political, financial, and racial crisis. *Les affaires Boulangisme, Panamisme et Dreyfusisme* had arrived.[45] The son-in-law of Jules Grevy, head of the French state, had been exposed a trafficker in honors. Every rank in the coveted order of the Legion of Honor was for sale, and the man behind the counter was Daniel Wilson. Among those suspected of having bought the much-sought distinction was financier Cornelius Hertz, whose association with the company was no secret.[46]

In the confusion following Daniel Wilson's revelations, hope for a lottery loan to save the canal was momentarily shattered. Unable to gain a vote of confidence, the French ministry fell. The new government, perhaps already sensing the company's troubles, wanted no part of a bill authorizing a lottery. Ferdinand de Lesseps and his son appealed to the public, blaming the reversal on the enemies of the corporation.[47] Still, the directors felt that all might turn out well in the end: they thought that Grevy would be followed by General Boulanger, who would prove to be an even better friend of the canal.

Puzzled by the parliamentary intrigues, Philippe sailed again for Panama in the autumn of 1887. A few weeks after his landing, his brother Etienne wrote to him the unpublished details of the president's resignation. Etienne Bunau-Varilla's letter also contained information about the latest political developments.

Notwithstanding his removal to a military command far from Alsace-Lorraine, the image of General Boulanger and his handsome face continued to mesmerize the French. *Boulangerisme* was in full swing. Philippe described this idol of the French to his friends in Panama:

> Dressed in brilliantly colored military tunics and riding a superb stallion, except for his moustache, he could be the model for a Napoleon if seen by David, Steuben, Gerard, or Swebach. He is already well known in every corner of the French empire, in Africa as well as in Asia . . . however I have advised [the directorate of the company], much caution [in dealing with Boulanger or the politicians promoting him].[48]

The behind-the-stage parliamentary maneuvers designed to choose a successor to Jules Grevy ended December 1887, with the selection of Francois Marie Sadi Carnot.[49]

The selection of Carnot as president was not a good omen for the company. Fresh ideas were badly needed by the canal directors. Count de Lesseps and his partners knew little of the uncanny ability already shown in the isthmus by Bunau-Varilla, the ability to discern the reality beneath the fustian of politics and statesmanship. But perhaps it was fortunate for him not to have been consulted about these political and financial decisions. It left him unscathed for the long battles ahead. Yet, through his brother, Philippe managed to caution Charles de Lesseps against making alliances with the parties or personalities in open contest for political power.[50]

His advice was not followed. Ferdinand de Lesseps, acting as if he had all the time in the world, began a new tour of France, called for a meeting of the stockholders, and directed his colleagues to find new allies within the Chamber of Deputies. By the first week of March 1888, ten deputies from many shades of the political spectrum, including partisans of Boulanger, sponsored a bill authorizing the issue of a lottery. The scheme, which promised quick redemption, did not bring enough revenue, and it became imperative, as it had been in Suez, to receive permission for a lottery loan.[51] A lottery loan, it should be explained, is one which would authorize the corporation to borrow money to finish the project and delay payment on the interest accruing to the bonds. The government could also guarantee the bonds if it chose to.

The New Bond Issue

While these maneuvers to save the canal were taking place, *l'affaire Boulanger* gained momentum. In the spring love flourishes, and the company began to turn its eyes towards the handsome general. Could he be a new Napoleon III? (Emperor Napoleon III had saved Suez in 1866.) Such thoughts dominated the minds of the stockholders and directors in May 1887. The ill-fated courtship between the military officer and the company was about to begin. It was destined to be a fatal friendship for both.

For the moment, the directorate of the corporation continued to work overtime on the deputies and senators. The job paid off on June 5, 1888, when both chambers yielded to de Lesseps' charm and approved a lottery loan. Soon after the passing of the bill, the company succeeded in negotiating a short-term advance of $900,000 with the *Credit Lyonnais*.[52]

In order to strengthen his political future, General Boulanger absented himself from his army post several times, and the government cancelled his commission. Undaunted by this reverse, the general demanded the revision of the constitution[53] and was overwhelmingly elected to the Chamber of Deputies as representative of two departments. His victory was not without the support of the six hundred thousand canal stockholders, by this time his open partisans. Boulanger's victory and the constitutional question posed by his followers brought down one of the canal bête noires. Pierre-Emmanuel Tirard and his cabinet fell and the regime of Charles Floquet took over.[54]

News of these developments was communicated to Philippe in Panama, and the isthmus celebrated.[55] The new law authorized the issuance of bonds for $144 million, of which $24 million was to be withdrawn for lottery prizes and reimbursement of the bonds. One hundred and twenty million dollars would remain with which to pay for completion of the works and for interest due up to the day of the opening of the canal—according to the company, within three-and-one-half years.

Previous experience had demonstrated that the bond subscribers had furnished an average of $30 million yearly. The company expected the lottery to bring in an average of $55 million annually. Even the respected *Credit Lyonnais* predicted this bonanza.[56] However, the canal moguls and their financial sages overlooked the enormous expenditures of France's centennial celebration in 1889 and of the associated international exposition. Millions of francs had been spent beautifying Paris alone. The government's credit at this time was not as good as that of Napoleon III in 1866, and it refused to back the lottery loan with an official guarantee. Moreover, the public was worried, distracted, and politically divided, and the individual's pocketbook was not as full as in the late 1860s.

Needless to say, the directors of the corporation had done a superb job of public relations and arm twisting. It was now time for the financiers to take over and create the complicated apparatus of the lottery loan in order to harvest the money needed for the canal. But from the very moment they began to plan these moves, there was confusion, disagreement, and disorganization. Baron de Reinach wisely proposed setting up several lotteries, to keep the public's interest high while the pockets of the would-be buyers and shareholders were replenished with cash. However, it also would have prevented the creation of the big prizes that might have been an attraction to the would-be subscribers.[57]

Probably in an attempt to quickly recoup the sums they lent the company, the bankers, led by Charles Marie Germain of the *Credit Lyonnais*, demanded that the entire bond issue, $144 million, be offered at once and in one package. Had Bunau-Varilla been in France at this moment, he would have certainly challenged the judgment of the financiers and perhaps been able to reverse the fortunes of the company. But the decision of the *Credit Lyonnais* and its executives was considered final. This respected banking institution had the power of the Chase Manhattan Bank in America in the twentieth century, and its agents' words were as authoritative as those of the Rockefeller family in the United States. So, with the utmost reluctance, Charles de Lesseps surrendered to the banker's ukase, a move which amounted to accepting a death sentence.

The sick corporation stumbled into its last agony on June 26, 1888. On this date it offered to the public 2,000,000 bonds in denominations of $72 each. Payment was to be made on seven dates—the last one November 10, 1889. Four dollars per bond were to be paid on the day of the subscription, and some of the lottery prizes were as high as $125,000. As soon as this step was announced, the enemies of the canal began to work overtime to wreck the subscription, especially the press, which backed up its campaign with plain lies. On the day the bonds were issued, the press "killed" Ferdinand de Lesseps. The false news of his demise was telegraphed all over the world.

These lies had their effect. Prices were depressed, the shares falling from $72 to $53 in a few days. Only eight hundred thousand tickets were sold, and fewer than three hundred and fifty thousand subscribers applied for the bonds. The bankers' methods proved to be disastrous. Perhaps if they had issued the bonds every six months for a year and a half—something like six hundred and sixty thousand each time—the money could have been raised despite the tight money market and the existence of other attractive investments in the new overseas colonies. The dumping of the whole bundle of securities in one package was a heavy burden on the shoulders and pockets of the not too enthusiastic investors.

Four dollars a share was received from each subscriber on the first day and $8 four days later. This amounted to approximately $9.6 million of the $58 million subscribed. But the lottery multiplied the company's troubles. The company had to invest for each ticket close to $8, not only for the eight hundred thousand bonds subscribed, but also for each of the 2 mil-certificates offered for sale. The funds for the drawing had to be complete, and the lots could not be subdivided. The outcome was that the corporation had to give away $16 million when it was receiving only $9.6 million. Compounding the problem were the traditional hand-outs and give-aways for which the company was famous.[58] The first millions received were earmarked to pay for "publicity" ($1.82 million), to Baron de Reinach for "patronage" ($750,000), and for the idea of having "suggested" the lottery (to the German banker Hugo Oberndoerffer, $500,000).[59]

To all this, the company added an insane financing plan of its own. The single subscription was cancelled, and the earlier method suggested by Baron de Reinach—small issues—was adopted. But it was much too late. Public confidence in the company began to fall, while the intensity of the Boulanger affair, presaging political instability, scared money away from all investments. In panic, the directors decided to reduce the price of the unsold bonds—to $18, to $17, and, by December 1888, to $16.50. Count de Lesseps and his son undertook another trip throughout the country asking for public support. The old entrepreneur assured his listeners that the canal was about to be opened for navigation.[60] Surely before 1891.

The Company Tries to Show the Canal "In Operation"

Impressed by the voice of de Lesseps and the optimistic

reports coming from Panama, Baron de Reinach (very probably at Cornelius Hertz's suggestion) proposed a spectacular publicity stunt—an idea that might mislead the nation but could stampede the public into buying the entire subscription in a matter of days. Why not produce drawings or daguerrotypes showing several ships navigating the waterway? Wasn't Bunau-Varilla digging small lakes later to be connected to form the canal bed? So why not place on them the small yachts waiting for the inauguration of the ditch, take their picture, and pay the press to issue extra editions announcing the miracle?

Nature seemed willing to cooperate. Heavy rain had returned to the isthmus beginning in July 1888, causing another flood like the deluge of 1885. Philippe had taken to Panama a wet-plate camera made in London by Thomas Ross. He took several pictures of the excavation sites and also of the flood. Some of the yachts bought by the company for the inauguration of the canal floated freely in their moorings during and after the heavy rains. Their graceful silhouettes had been recorded by the camera, and the photos were sent to Etienne Bunau-Varilla in Paris. Aware of the existence of these shots, Hertz approached Etienne about the matter of their publication, but the alert Bunau-Varilla, sensing that such deception might hurt his brother, asked for time to consult Philippe.

The two brothers had been secretly using an edition of a French dictionary and C. M. de la Condamine's *Relation abreqes d'un voyage fait dans l'interieur de l'Amerique meridionale* (Paris, 1745), a work already cited in this book and a favorite of Philippe, for digital code-writing. They used it for emergency cables or when messengers seemed unreliable. In a few days, Philippe replied: "Impress upon Charles de Lesseps what is at hand. Under no circumstances is this scheme to be implemented. Pictures are not to be released. The company will be sued by every one of the stockholders if plan succeeds." Baron de Reinach withdrew his proposal.[61]

"Stop All Works on December 31"

While the company was agonizing, General Boulanger's erratic star zigzagged all over the French skies. On his return to Paris after his smashing electoral triumph, the general was received like a conqueror, and President Carnot felt a chill through the corridors of the Elysée. But the political turmoil ended in a duel between Boulanger and Premier Floquet. In this encounter, the general was severely wounded in the neck, necessitating a long recovery, and a majority of the deputies expelled him from the legislature.

Undeterred by this setback, Boulanger's partisans nominated him for another seat in the assembly and, on August 19, 1888, with the help of the supporters of the canal, the charismatic candidate was once more elected to represent the districts of Charenta Inferior, the Somme, and Nord. In January of 1889, Boulanger's name was again entered in an election to represent part of the city of Paris. The result was the same. He was openly supported by the canal stockholders, and the voters elected him by a two-to-one margin. Since by this time the entire official machinery was against him, it was Boulanger's finest hour.

Between August 1888 and February 1889, the Boulanger movement reached dizzy heights and the hopes of the company rose. Had the general given the word or consented, the multitude of his partisans, the canal bondholders, the police, and various units of the army would have carried him on their shoulders to the Elysée and forcibly installed him in office. But Boulanger hesitated while his enemies grew in strength and number and the company agonized.

One of the last drastic moves of the interoceanic corporation was to try metamorphosis. This project called for transforming the association into a new one which, in turn, was to breathe air into the inert structure of the old and refloat it. A clever suggestion, but much too late. Another strategy involved the sale of a new bond issue through a second-class bank. It did not work, and the enterprise sank lower and lower, until, on December 14, 1888, the telegraph carried to Panama the terse message, "Stop all works on December 31."[62] Aware of the company's backing of his cause, General Boulanger conveyed his sympathy to Ferdinand de Lesseps.[63]

With little else to lose now, Count de Lesseps and his

associates publicly endorsed the political fortunes of the general, who expressed his faith in the canal by buying twenty-five shares.[64] De Lesseps reciprocated by giving a splendid dinner for Boulanger and his advisors.[65] Destiny seems to have played a sardonic joke on both the general and the company, for both their lives were to end shortly thereafter. As far as the saga of the canal is concerned, the martial figure of Boulanger is of interest because he openly sympathized with the canal and, had he been elevated to the highest office in the land, he probably would have duplicated Napoleon III's generosity towards de Lesseps in 1866 and saved the waterway. Now, Panamanian schoolchildren are taught early to deprecate the names of Boulanger and Bunau-Varilla. The general is depicted as a maniacal would-be dictator eager to smother the "glorious" Third Republic, which to them is the epitome of democracy and freedom. "It was *Boulangerisme* which ruined the canal."[66] In reality, it was the Third Republic and its legions of venal politicians and corrupt parliamentary committees that contributed heavily to the demise of the First Interoceanic Canal Company.[67]

On February 5, 1889, the Civil Court of the Seine (district of Paris) dissolved the *Compagnie Universalle du Canal Interoceanique*.[68] The formerly powerful corporation that had controlled an empire on two continents and had promised so much progress to the world was dead. The mourners numbered thousands on both sides of the ocean. Besides the de Lessepses, none was more pathetic than Philippe, whose tears had to be added to the sweat and blood he had shed before. Little did he suspect on that day that Fortune was only trying his patience and testing his power. Exactly twenty-five years later, when the canal was opened, the tears he shed into the Chagres River were tears of joy.

Philippe Is Unlucky in Politics, but Lucky in Love

While awaiting the arrival of his brother Etienne from France, Philippe conferred daily with canal and government officials in Panama, trying to bolster their sagging hopes and lighten their depression. Etienne was bringing statistics considered necessary for Philippe's next step—seeking a seat in the Chamber of Deputies. The news from France was not too discouraging, and Philippe decided to return to Paris after a *tour d'horizon* (vacation) in Nicaragua.

During his last sojourn in France, Bunau-Varilla had sought and received the advice of one of the leading geologists of the century, the Irish sage Sir John Griffith, who encouraged Philippe to make a thorough study of the Nicaraguan route. At this very early date, Bunau-Varilla was already considering means and ways by which, if need be, he could scuttle the revived idea of a canal through the land of the two lakes. A rival canal to the north of Panama would be a bad business proposition for his own ditch. And now, with ruin facing the isthmian enterprise, it was imperative to reassess the competition. He had reason to consider the Nicaraguan route Panama's worst threat.

In Central America, he navigated the lakes, rivers, and waters on both coasts, taking soundings every few miles. After two weeks of this unusual vacation, Philippe left for the United States carrying with him a box filled with rocks and sediment he had collected at different spots through the proposed canal route and within the blueprinted Nicaraguan canal zone. After arriving in New York in the middle of March 1889, Bunau-Varilla had two meetings with the company's staff, and he later visited John Bigelow.

The American diplomat encouraged the Frenchman to try for a seat in the Chamber and, at the same time, raised the young man's spirits by pointing out that before any negotiations for a canal through Nicaragua could commence, Britain's position on this issue would need clarification and, if possible, neutralization by treaty. Bunau-Varilla landed in France deeply absorbed by these thoughts, but he soon became interested in the patriotic celebrations commemorating the centennial of the Revolution and the plans for his own electoral campaign.[69]

With public attention concentrated on the festivities and many politicians actively seeking the limelight, the rumors about the directors of the company did not become public in

1889. But as the congressional races approached, the word *Panama* and the epithet *"Panamiste"* (thief) became political dynamite. By the end of October, Philippe had lost his race for a constituency in the provinces by six hundred votes. He was not known politically, and he had campaigned on the strength of the company and the promise of good government. He was much too late. A year earlier, amidst the hysteria of *Boulangerisme*, he might have won by six thousand.

Bidding momentary farewell to the world of politics, Bunau-Varilla turned his thoughts to a very personal business—love. Not sure if he was immune to yellow fever or susceptible to the attacks of other tropical diseases, Philippe had postponed his marriage. By 1890, his immunity had stood the test of time, and he and his brother decided to begin raising families. In the spring of that year, they married the Brunhoff sisters—Ida and Sonia, sisters of Maurice Brunhoff, a famous art editor who had retouched some of the pictures brought back to Paris by Philippe. The Bunau-Varillas and Maurice Brunhoff had been classmates in school. Philippe's marriage to Ida Brunhoff did not cool his passion for the canal, nor did his wife attempt to interfere. She accepted the fact that her husband was a "bigamist" at heart. She must have understood this before her betrothal, for she never showed jealousy of Philippe's other love—Panama.[70]

The Directors Under Attack

The fading away of Boulanger's star and Bunau-Varilla's unsuccessful attempt to enter the world of politics left the stockholders of the company without clout, and most of the press and the deputies were eager to dispose of the company's directors with the excuse that they had supported a quasi-revolutionary attempt to destroy the Republic. In truth, they were resentful that the company had not given away more money before its demise, and they feared exposure for their acceptance of past gratuities.

For months, while the assets of the corporation were being liquidated, the steam within the scandal-loaded caldron was gaining the force with which to blow off the lid. The fearful predictions of those apprehensive souls who had occupied heights of power or held authority in the past were realized when the French right, left, and center began to blame each other for the failure of the canal. The howlings of the press, the consternation of the security holders, and the ambition of certain Young Turks in politics brought about the publication of a book exposing the company and vilifying Ferdinand de Lesseps:

> This scoundrel, walks about like a triumphant hero. The poor devil who has broken a window to steal a loaf of bread is paraded under the guard of a police officer. . . . Nobody will ever open a judicial inquiry into the affair wherein $300 million of savings of the Nation were engulfed. This man will never once be asked: What have you done with that money? The Senate, which de Lesseps has loaded with presents, hastily voted the Bankruptcy Law so that this criminal might not be branded.[71]

This was a reckless innuendo, because the law dealing with commercial companies in those days was not applicable to the canal corporation.

The excoriation of Count de Lesseps continued:

> The consecration of Ferdinand de Lesseps as a great Frenchman is a joke. . . . With the exception of [Leon] Gambetta and Jules Ferry, it may be asserted that no contemporary Frenchman was ever more systematically hostile to French interests nor ever did more damage to his country.[72]

Under such attacks, the walls of the fortress-like and secret-loaded corporation began to crack wide open. Little by little, these hysterical denunciations permeated the people's minds. Some sensation-seeking newspapermen opened a campaign against corruption—a move that everyone knew was directed at the thief-infested Chamber of Deputies. But there was still an even chance of putting out the fire before ruining the more than six hundred thousand stockholders. Aware of the danger and in fear that the scandal might reach even higher than the banking circles and the National Assembly, President Carnot, Prime Minister Emile Loubet, and the attorney general hesitated. Later, when the conflagration seemed beyond control, they were either powerless to do anything or joined the incendiaries to save their own political lives.[73]

On June 11, 1891, fearing the outraged citizenry, the grand committees in the Chamber of Deputies introduced a resolution ordering an investigation of the affairs of the defunct corporation. Every member of the Chamber voted for it. The judge of the Paris court was charged with setting up the apparatus for judiciary proceedings, which began a week later. Government corruption became the talk of France, and Parisians were discussing what the press reported daily in a cascade of extra editions. Innocent as well as guilty wished to see the end of it and demanded that if there had been any grafters or blackmailers, they should be sent to Devil's Island.[74]

Fearful of detection or eager to destroy personal and political enemies, the deputies who had taken money from the company sought places on the investigating committees. Parliamentary figures and their staffs planted stories in the press or leaked information to the public about alleged misdeeds of colleagues, financial figures, company directors, and even President Carnot. As in the Watergate revelations, politically important persons were involved in the scandal or tainted with it, even if they could not be implicated—and anyone who came forward with accusations, true or false, was promised immunity from prosecution.

Shortly it was discovered that the deputies in one of these self-appointed witch-hunting groups had requested and accepted gratuities from the company in the past. One audacious reporter asked what the difference was between their "grant" or "endowment" and the crimes of which they were accusing their enemies and the canal directors. One of the press's targets was ex-Premier Maurice Rouvier, considered by all a friend of the corporation's lobbyists. One of the committeemen responded to a reporter: "Quiet, sir. I am only an accident, but Count de Lesseps and Premier Rouvier are great men. They are two stars in the blue sky of France."[75]

Meanwhile, Louis Ricard, a maverick politician who years before, as mayor of Rouen, had extolled de Lesseps' genius, became minister of justice and, with the always-eager prosecutor Jules Quesnay de Beaurepaire, set about destroying the directors of the dead company. As soon as Beaurepaire received the report of the judicial inquiry, his delusions of grandeur quickened. He had here in a net the biggest fish of the century, bigger than General Boulanger, Ferdinand de Lesseps and his crew. What an opportunity to crash the gates of history.

The prospect of a spectacular suit against a corporation which a few months back had inspired awe, and the possibility of ruining forever the name and lives of men who were universally revered, were powerful temptations to the publicity-starved attorney general. He proposed that the government bring all the canal directors to trial, a few at a time. First he proposed to prosecute the two de Lessepses, directors Henri Cottu and Marius Fontana, and Gustave Eiffel. In the letter recommending this step, Beaurepaire maligned these men the same way he had maligned Boulanger and with the same intensity he was to direct against the innocent and unfortunate Alfred Dreyfus a few years later.

The attorney general was well aware that the charges might not stand up in court, but he was willing to interrogate these men to "enlighten public opinion." A paragraph of this letter reads:

> The possible result, the dangers of prosecution, are as follows: An acquittal is possible. But what of that? The prosecuting magistrate will have done his duty, and if he is not successful in convincing the courts he will have at least enlightened public opinion.[76]

These men were not involved in any criminal transaction. There was no trace of kickbacks, and no payments to contractors beyond what was due for excavations made and for contractual obligations duly stipulated. There was no record of misappropriation of funds by members of the directorate. Thus, President Carnot was not impressed by Beaurepaire's document and decided to have Minister Ricard reprimand the reckless attorney general who, pulling in his horns, wrote another opinion that was the exact opposite of his earlier one:

> The prosecuting attorney would be unable to show fraudulent intent, which is an essential element of any crime or misdemeanor. Nothing has been neglected and all accusations have been gathered and collected together. The whole history of the company has been searched and probed. . . . In the presence of the magistrates, when witnesses had to make precise statements, those who had not vanished entirely presented simple hypotheses or suffered from total lapse of memory. . . . I think that in this affair, as in all others, the magistrate must as a primary duty be inspired only by that which is prescribed by law.[77]

The Trial

It seemed that the final word had been said. The pronouncement of the procurator general had been heard, and the clouds which had been about to envelop everyone seemed to thin. But the directorate of the company was destined to pay for its blunders. Eduoard Drumont, who had so bitterly "documented" his accusations against de Lesseps in his book *The Last Battle*, renewed his attacks after Beaurepaire's second opinion in a memorandum which he considered *de minimus* (without judicial value). At the same time, a new generation of reporters, sensing corruption in the establishment, kept asking for a thorough investigation.

Terrified by the maneuvers of the press corps and Drumont, Minister Ricard and his clique in the Chamber decided to outdo them and cut down de Lesseps and his associates. On January 10, 1892, there began one of the strangest trials in history—against the two de Lessepses, Henry Cottu, Gustave Eiffel, and Marius Fontana. The true rascals were hiding behind the pompous attorney general or in the spectators' gallery. Bunau-Varilla sought to testify on behalf of the accused, but his pleadings were ignored.[78]

The recriminations and accusations eventually enveloped the whole Third Republic, with the exception of the military. By February 1893, ten deputies, including the influential Charles Francois Sains-Leroy and former finance minister, Charles Baihaut, were under indictment. Ex-Prime Minister Rouvier miraculously escaped trial. All the dirty linen was washed in public. The entire Chamber of Deputies and most of the Senate had solicited bribes from the very beginning of the company's existence. Charles de Lesseps, who in an act of self-sacrifice assumed all responsibility for the supposed misdeeds of his father, told the whole story.

The faceless bureaucracy was satisfied by one of three "bag-men," Emile Anton, who worked with the lobbies and the grand committees. And the hidden hierarchy was placated by the other two—Baron de Reinach and his alter ego, Cornelius Hertz. The former moved within the parliamentary circles pledged to the Rouvier party, the latter around and through the congressmen committed to Georges Clemenceau. It was revealed and quickly acknowledged that Minister Charles Baihaut had solicited and accepted $90,000 from the younger de Lesseps in exchange for his support of the bond issue in 1885.[79] The respected Senator Albert Grevy, brother of the former chief of state, and their brother-in-law, Representative Gustave Gabron, had happily boarded the gravy train.[80]

The babble of recriminations and exposures began to abate when Baron de Reinach, broken in spirit, committed suicide. His amanuensis, Cornelius Hertz, and Emile Arton had conveniently fled the country at the first tip that they faced arrest. Afterwards, the Chamber's committees and the courts of justice showed no interest whatsoever in forcing the return of the recalcitrant witnesses.[81] It may have been just as well; they could have implicated the tribunal, too. The defendants were admirably represented by the forensic academician (member of the French Academy) Daniel Barboux. But no rhetorical or rational argument could save the accused except at the risk of blaming the National Assembly for the scandal.

Throughout this ordeal, Charles de Lesseps stole the show from the prosecutors. With directness and simplicity, he made a statement, roughly paraphrased as "The company had met its enemies and it was us."[82] In a government blindly committed to a policy of inaction and benign neglect, a little corruption at the beginning had multiplied like cancer cells. The company's early pernicious habits of silently rewarding extortionists and making advance pay-offs for possible future favors (as in the case of Minister Baihaut) multiplied the outstretched hands.

Within ten years, Charles de Lesseps testified, the directorate's largesse had created an army of parasites. The evidence at hand leads us to believe that Baron de Reinach and his staff of bag-men attempted to leave no discontented bribe-taker in the land. In compromising the establishment, they might have hoped to avoid jealousy and discontent among the bribed and the extortionists who escaped detection and exposure. It simply did not work.

The scandal generated by the failure of the company abated with the flight of Hertz and Arton, and Baron de Reinach's suicide on November 10, 1892. It was widely rumored that Hertz and Arton might have dragged down other "stars in the blue sky of France," such as Georges Clemenceau and Emile Loubet. So intense were the attacks on Clemenceau that he risked a duel to clear his name. Nevertheless, the rumors connecting him with the canal scandal caused "the tiger" to lose his seat in the legislature, and he endured a decade of political eclipse.[83]

Finally, Samuel Perivier, the presiding judge, tried to end the trial. The scientific congress of 1879 provided the magistrate with the "proof" and "rationale" he needed to pronounce sentence on Ferdinand de Lesseps. That symposium of savants had predicted the canal traffic at 7.25 million tons. Later, after the company found itself in trouble, a government commission had arbitrarily lowered this figure to 4.1 million tons. Perivier solemnly proclaimed that, in these figures, anyone could see ample proof of fraudulent intent. How could anyone not feloniously inclined speak of a traffic of 7.25 million tons for a faraway ditch in[84] the middle of a jungle populated by savages?

On September 12, 1893, all those on trial with the two de Lessepses were convicted, but only Charles Baihaut served most of his sentence. The rest of the condemned were incarcerated for a short term or had the verdict set aside on appeal to the Supreme Court. Gustave Eiffel demanded total vindication. He was tried again by his peers in the Legion of Honor, and this time he was acquitted. Count de Lesseps survived for one more year. He died on December 7, 1894.[85]

The Scandal Crosses the Ocean

In his testimony, Charles de Lesseps mentioned that over $4 million had been paid to an American group, a statement that triggered an investigation by a congressional committee in Washington. In addition to the heavy sums the company spent in the United States for food and equipment—in some cases for totally unnecessary material such as snow shovels, thousands of lanterns, and barrels of ink—the canal directors had several bankers and government officials on this side of the Atlantic on their payroll.

Congressman Josiah Patterson found several prominent Americans among those who were taking money, supposedly for lending their respected names to the company. These were Jesse Seligman, a senior partner in the firm of Drexel, Morgan and Co.; Charles Winslow, of Winslow, Lanier and Co.; and the secretary of the navy in President Rutherford B. Hayes' administration, Richard W. Thompson. Seligman stated that each of these firms, and Thompson, had received close to $2 million in eight years, not counting the more than $40 million secured by these agencies to make purchases on behalf of the company.[86] Secretary Thompson probably would not have been asked to lend his name to the enterprise had he not been in the Cabinet. There were other rumors in Paris, Bogota, and Panama connecting various influential officials in the isthmus, Colombia, and the United States with the splendid generosity of the interoceanic corporation.[87]

Bunau-Varilla under Investigation

On the advice of John Bigelow, Philippe wrote a book in

1892 delineating the rosy prospect of finishing the canal in three more years. It was not only an effort to save the idea of the waterway at Panama, but also an attempt to shore up the sagging fortunes of the company's directors, then on trial. The first part of Philippe's treatise aimed at exorcising forever the question of Culebra, which was the basis for many of the attacks against the canal.

Philippe recommended raising $112 million to complete operations, $35 million by the issue of new shares and $77 million through the sale of bonds. The second phase of the proposal was the liquidation of the first corporation and the creation of a new one with the assets left over. Philippe initiated a move to seek support from members of Parliament not yet tainted by the scandal.[88] This was perhaps the most difficult part of the package, for it meant finding an honest deputy.

Philippe's activities on behalf of the canal attracted immediate attention from the wrong people. The enemies of the waterway, especially the legislature and the judiciary, turned on him. Egged on or bribed by the anti-de Lesseps forces, an obscure accountant, D. John Flory, came before the Paris court to declare that he was being crushed by his conscience. Grievous rumors, said Flory, compelled him to resign his job, rumors which had to do with a supposed commission of $0.21 per cubic yard for 27 million cubic yards, paid to Baron de Reinach for the handling of the Culebra contract with Bunau-Varilla's corporation in Panama.

The alleged "criminal" fee amounted to more than $5.5 million. Instead of chastising the rumor bearer, Magistrate Perivier exclaimed: "Allons, Allons, Monsieur l'ecrivain . . . tres bon, tres bon, continuez vouz. . . ." (Go on, go on, Sir . . . very good, very good, continue.) Encouraged by the bench and coached by the prosecutor, the "witness" expanded his story and inflated his figures.[89]

It was no longer $0.21 per cubic yard. Perhaps thinking of the rampant inflationary spiral in France at the time, the ex-accountant escalated the cost to $0.45 per cubic yard, and finally reached the staggering sum of $0.85 per cubic yard. Moreover, he said, the new contractors had received $1.25 per cubic yard excavated. In the end, the $5.5 million commission paid Baron de Reinach reached more than $12 million.

This was to be the first serious charge against Bunau-Varilla's character and test of his temper and patience, but it was not to be the last. As this charade proceeded, threatening to involve more innocent people, Charles de Lesseps felt obliged to come forward once more and state the facts. Composed and dignified, the young de Lesseps denied the allegations with precise and irrefutable figures. In the knowledge that Baron de Reinach could not testify in his own defense, the judge exclaimed, "But the Baron did give away six million dollars!" His statement awakened the interest of an investigating committee of the Chamber of Deputies. The contractors were called on the carpet.

Artige, Sonderegger and Co., subcontractors, was represented at the inquiry by Bunau-Varilla. It was a memorable encounter, in which the investigative committee found out that this witness was not to be cowed, entrapped, or silenced. Philippe was kept waiting for more than a half-hour in a room adjacent to the committee's quarters, where he was able to hear the insidious remarks of the deputies about the company. The last legislator to enter the room announced the latest fabrication: "Gentlemen, I have just heard an interesting piece of news. There were on the high staff of the canal company at Panama more than thirty escaped or liberated convicts."[90]

Aware of what to expect at this judicial examination, Bunau-Varilla repeated to the deputies precisely what Charles de Lesseps had explained to the court earlier. Prices per cubic yard of excavation were not uniform. It depended on the altitude, hardness, and accessibility of the terrain. For lower areas, the excavation prices per cubic yard were minimal. The average excavation cost was $1.20, with adjustments made from time to time to encourage speed and for the extra cost of pumping. The contract with the new corporation was even lower, $1.17 per cubic yard, but the French contractors undertook to pay 12.75¢ to the Anglo-Dutch concern. The net price received by the new contracting group was almost identical to the amount paid the old.

Furthermore, Philippe had never met with Baron de Reinach about this transaction, and the story of a commission paid to the dead director was "a stupid and malicious fabrication."[91] To reach an understanding with the Anglo-Dutch company, the new contractors gave it $350,000 in severance pay. This arrangement amounted to a tacit understanding that the first corporation was actually selling the contract to the second.

A committeeman asked, "Why pay an indemnity to an engineering group which did not accomplish its task?" "Yes, a good question," answered Philippe, "but we are not in France. We all worked under the laws of Colombia." Colombian laws made no distinction between a contractor and a person holding a lease, and a lawsuit would have been needed to eject the Anglo-Dutch group from the isthmus. That action, in the hands of Colombian lawyers and judges in Bogota, would have required years and incalculable expenditures. The canal works would have been paralyzed and delayed, and the original lease for the construction of the canal would have expired.

The questioner was not convinced. "Could not a satisfactory judicial decision have been obtained against the Anglo-Dutch company for a much smaller sum?" Philippe replied:

> I am not as well-informed as you appear to be about such a shameful transaction as that to which you allude. I never saw nor heard of any such thing being done either in Panama or France. I do not know what it would have cost. If you want such information, you must ask it from someone else.

The legislators pretended to be embarrassed, but another interrogator continued: "What was the moral character of the agents of the canal company?"

> Gentlemen . . . the echoes of your vaulted lobbies have informed me in advance of your reasons for asking these questions. . . . Calumny, gentlemen, is like rabies when transmitted from rabbit to rabbit. . . . At each transaction it becomes more virulent. That story of the thirty convicts is calumny in its most virulent form, due to the number of times it has been transmitted from man to man.

The representative who had re-told the story earlier confessed: "I am the culprit," to which Bunau-Varilla retorted:

> Not the culprit, sir, but the victim; you are the victim of an absurd invention. Not only the upper staff, but the small employees, were carefully examined before being hired. At the outset, less care was taken, any man asking for work was recruited . . . a legal certificate was made obligatory a few months later.

As Philippe began a learned and technical lecture on the difficulties encountered by the company in the isthmus in addition to the unhealthful climate and the many diseases, the panel of inquirers decided it was not competent to hear these technical and scientific considerations. On the contrary, answered Bunau-Varilla:

> Your mission requires you to obtain information as to the reasons why and how money was spent. You have to discover whether it was rational or not. How can I tell you that if I am muzzled as soon as I speak of a technical question? How can you judge the Panama work if you close your ears as soon as the difficulties of its execution and the solutions they entailed are described before you? . . . The deputies discuss and vote on railways, harbors, excavations, public works. I never heard that you refused to be enlightened on these matters because you are not technical men. Hear me for a moment. You will see if what I say is beyond your power of comprehension or not. It seems incredible to me that you should ask for light and refuse it when it is presented to you.[92]

But the inquiring commission had already closed its ears. It heard no more testimony from Bunau-Varilla. The investigation was officially closed.

After a few months of conversations and much gossip among the committeemen, they decided to file a report in which Monsieur Flory's "rumors" were to be inserted as truth. What about Philippe's appearance before the congressmen? It was to be edited in such a way as to give the impression that he had caved in under the avalanche of questions put to him by the committee. Bunau-Varilla's friends warned him of what to expect, and he returned to Paris from a trip to Germany and went immediately to the Chamber of Deputies. The legislator in charge of putting the report together was out of the city, but Philippe had him back at his office within three days.

Bunau-Varilla thundered in the hall of the committee:

> Sir, the whole thing is a shameful and mendacious invention. Let me restate the truth. I have come, Mr. Deputy, to ask you to register my protest against the [publication] in this report [of charges] concerning that supposed bribe to Baron de Reinach.[93]

The congressman replied that he had airtight proof that what was to be published was the truth. In a firm voice, Philippe said:

> Monsieur, I am speaking to a lawyer, to a legislator, therefore to a man who knows what is requisite to constitute judicial proof. We are here . . . on the third floor of the building. You may well believe I have no intention whatever of committing suicide. Now, if you produce the proof you speak of, and if you remain satisfied that it is really a proof, I undertake to leave this room by the window instead of the door. Now go back inside and look at your supposed proof and examine it carefully. I will give you all the time you require, and in the meanwhile I will light a cigar and await you.

Sixty minutes later the deputy was back, looking haggard. He apologized:

> Indeed, sir, I am very sorry; I regret very much what has happened. How can I repair such an error? I shall immediately go to the government printing office to see what can be done. Sir, [I beg you] to believe I am greatly embarrassed. I am going to do all I can.

The assemblyman could not suppress the libelous paragraph because the report was printed, bound, and ready for distribution; however, he managed to come close to fulfilling his promise. He postponed publication of the information until an additional page was inserted at the beginning and at the end titled *errata*. In this page the congressman published, in his own name and that of the other committeemen, a statement that the only basis for mentioning the supposed commission to Baron de Reinach was a rumor heard by a former employee of the company.[94]

Ahead lay the ordeals awaiting Philippe on the road to presenting the Panamanians with a gift for kings—an interoceanic canal. At the moment, Panama's destiny looked as blighted as the hopes of conquering the malaises plaguing her towns and forests. The possibility of finishing the canal was as remote as the likelihood of seeing one of her citizens walk over the waters of the Chagres. If Philippe could only anticipate the imponderables, he might one day see the opening of the canal at Panama.

By now the picture was clear. Human greed was the real culprit. The company's directors and their tormentors were only actors, accidents, falling meteorites in the drama of attempting to join the two oceans. In order to avoid their pitfalls and rescue Panama from its present ruin, he had to become the only director, the only entrepreneurial force. With these thoughts in mind, Bunau-Varilla set himself to infuse new life into the enterprise.

7

The United States Prepares to Build

a Canal—in Nicaragua

Bunau-Varilla Wins Important American Political Friends; He Becomes a Publisher; He Seeks New Supporters; The Dreyfus Affair; Revolution and Depression in Cuba and Colombia; The United States Favors Nicaragua; Philippe Uses His Political Influence; A Turnaround

With the death of the French canal company, the projected Nicaraguan route gained momentum. In order for the Panama route to win, Nicaragua had to lose. Philippe understood this better than anyone else and, sooner than expected, two influential supporters arrived to help him—Francis B. Loomis and Whitelaw Reid.

Reid had been a correspondent for several newspapers, including the *Cleveland Herald* and the *Cincinnati Gazette*, during the Civil War in America.[1] Traveling through the South with Chief Justice Salmon P. Chase, Reid had recorded his observations in newspaper letters later published under the title *After the War* (1866). One of the most celebrated publicists of the nineteenth century, he became well acquainted with such leaders as Salmon P. Chase, Charles Summers, Henry Winter Davis, James Garfield, James G. Blaine, John Milton Hay, and Horace Greeley, who in 1869 named him editor of the *New York Tribune*. At his invitation,

Mark Twain, Richard Henry Stoddard, Bret Harte, and Hay became contributors or joined the editorial staff of the *Tribune*.[2] After Greeley's death, with the help of William Walter Phelps and John Bigelow, Reid won a battle with powerful financial interests for the control of the *Tribune*. At thirty-five, he became the head of the mightiest newspaper in America, and fifteen years later the *Tribune* was strong and prosperous.[3]

Reid played a masterful role in the contested Rutherford Hayes–Samuel Tilden election of 1876, unraveling the famous "cipher dispatches," and established himself as a kingmaker. After a severe trauma in 1881 because of the assassination of his close friend, James Garfield, whom he had groomed for the presidency, Reid supported Garfield's successor, Chester Arthur,[4] and engineered the election of Benjamin Harrison in 1888. By then, Reid was ready to surrender to the pleas of his friends and accept public office, becoming minister to France in 1889.

Reid arrived in Paris when *Boulangerisme* was limping away, *Panamisme* was at its height, and *Dreyfusisme* was about to erupt. His demeanor, attractive personality, and fluent French opened every door in the Gallic nation. He was at home at the Elysée and at the official game preserve at Rambouillet,[5] but more important for the history of the canal at Panama, he was soon to meet Philippe Bunau-Varilla.

The meeting between Philippe and the American diplomat came about in 1890 through Reid's confidant and friend, Francis B. Loomis, a member of one of America's most illustrious families. His "ancestors just missed the *Mayflower*."[6] Graduated from Marietta College, Loomis joined the staff of the *New York Tribune* in 1883, shortly after resigning as the official librarian of his home state. In 1885, he became Washington correspondent for several Midwestern newspapers and met the members of the House and Senate. Charming, handsome, and erudite, Loomis soon gained the confidence of the rest of the "Ohio gang" that ran the country in those days,[7] and particularly Whitelaw Reid's.

With such a powerful mentor, Francis B. Loomis was to play an important role in the history of his country. In 1890, through the influence of the minister to France, Reid, Loomis was appointed consul at Saint Etienne. Like Reid, he did not leave America without first seeing the elder statesman Bigelow, who took the opportunity to send a confidential message to Philippe about the status of the company's office in the United States.[8] Shortly after his arrival in France, Loomis and Bunau-Varilla met for the first time, and it was friendship at first sight, terminated only by Philippe's death in 1940. A month after their meeting, Philippe met the American minister and became his friend also. As we shall see, Loomis' behind-the-scenes maneuvers to change public opinion in America in favor of Panama, in the revolution which created a new state, and in the signing of the canal treaty of 1903, was second only to that of the French engineer.

Philippe Becomes a Newspaper Publisher

John Bigelow's word of encouragement to Philippe by way of Loomis, and Loomis' and Reid's optimism lent new hope to the canal idea. In 1892, urged by Loomis and Reid, Philippe took the long-meditated step of buying part of a newspaper in which he could defend the canal against the attacks of Drumont's *La Libre Parole* [Free Speech] and other sheets. Philippe and his brother Maurice first tried to buy *Le Temps* and then *Figaro*. Unsuccessful, they settled for a share of *Le Matin*.[9] This move proved to be one of the most practical steps towards the achievement of the Panama route.

Soon after this transaction, news of the near-opening of the Corinth Canal was received. The cutting of the isthmus at Corinth was an age-old dream.[10] Work on this canal proceeded on schedule, and its inauguration in the spring of 1893 excited Philippe. Nicaragua could be hosting the next ceremony, especially in view of reawakened American interest in that route. To advance the fortunes of the ditch at Panama, its supporters had to gather concrete evidence of the liabilities of the Nicaraguan route. Therefore, in the summer of 1893, Philippe traveled to Italy with the geologist J. Griffith, who was preoccupied with the probability of another large-scale earthquake in the eastern Mediterranean.[11]

Bunau-Varilla and Griffith were mindful of the various

earthquakes that had plagued southern Italy since 79 A.D., and particularly the violent tremors at Ischia in 1883, when many lives were lost.[12] Philippe and Dr. Griffith decided to explore this area in search of samples with which to make a stratigraphical comparison with the rocks brought from Nicaragua. The island of Ischia became an open laboratory for the two researchers.

> Before the earthquake, which brought so much damage in this beautiful island on July 28, 1883, there had been some indications of unusual subterranean activity; some of the springs had shown abnormal variations of temperature . . . there had been many slight earthquake-shocks in different parts of the island, and the instruments in the seismological observatories at Naples and Rome were in increased motion.[13]

The abundance of volcanic debris left by the seismic occurrence ten years earlier verified their hunch. Comparative measurements convinced Bunau-Varilla and Griffith of the late formation of the mountain range in Nicaragua, evidence which indicated an unstable terrain.

As if these findings were not adequate, the Nicaraguans themselves offered positive evidence of Bunau-Varilla's suspicion. Beginning in 1862, Managua began to issue a series of stamps engraved and printed by the American Bank Note Company of New York City, all in vivid yellow, deep blue, and black, extolling the many volcanoes that dotted the country. The stamps attracted so much attention in the philatelic world that biennial reissues were commissioned in 1869–1871, 1877–1878, and 1878–1880.[14] Simultaneously with the last group of stamps, Colombia placed on sale a series advertising the canal at Panama: a five-cent stamp in green, blue-green, and dull green; a ten-cent blue; a twenty-cent red; and a fifty-cent yellow-ochre stamp. Each of these stamps carried the picture of a ship and the isthmus, with a line marking the projected canal cut.[15]

On his return to Paris in the summer of 1893, Philippe found a letter from a friend in Nicaragua. The envelope was covered with stamps glorifying the dreadful volcanoes. Managua had issued a new series commemorating Columbus' epic voyage on the fourth centennial of the discovery. And, not satisfied with this philatelic coup, Nicaragua reissued the 1862 series which showed four pregnant volcanoes about to erupt.[16] Philippe stored away the information.

Bunau-Varilla Attempts to Reawaken Interest in His Canal in France and Russia

From 1892 to 1899, French politics were immersed in intrigue and permeated with anti-Semitism because of *l'affaire Dreyfus*. In need of allies in the government and armed with his book, published in March 1892, Philippe began to look for a man not connected with the Panama experience who could function as a publicist for a resurrected canal. The attempt was not without risk. From the secure barricade of his newspaper *La Libre Parole*, Edouard Drumont, the author of *The Last Battle* (a diatribe against de Lesseps), continued his vendetta against the Panama route. The attacks were phrased like warnings. The "gigantic swindle" was not to be revived. In order to keep it buried, Drumont promised to keep everyone informed of its possible resurrection—by Bunau-Varilla or anyone else.[17]

Meanwhile, Philippe found an enthusiastic admirer and supporter in Henri Burdeau, a much-respected career technocrat with considerable influence and wide experience in financial circles. To aid the cause of the canal, Burdeau needed the approval of the old canal enthusiast Maurice Rouvier, then minister of finance. The former premier was appalled by the very word *canal*.[18] It must be remembered that Rouvier had narrowly escaped indictment because of his close association with the defunct French company. Various other efforts to secure another sponsor who could rally support for the canal failed. Since financial backing within France seemed unlikely, the resourceful Philippe sought allies abroad.

The system of alliances with which Prince Bismarck had encircled France after 1870 began to crack after 1890. The first moves toward the Entente Cordiale between France and Russia had been signaled by the glittering reception tendered to a French naval squadron at Kronstadt in 1891. Alexander III pursued this alliance by a military concord between the general staffs of the two nations in July 1892. Encouraged by these high-level moves, Philippe went to St. Petersburg.

Through the influence of a Russian acquaintance, Prince Vasilev Tatischeff, Philippe was able to reach the inner sanctum of the Czar's headquarters and was presented to the powerful Sergei Y. Witte in the spring of 1894. After explaining to the minister how the Panama undertaking, once virtually completed, had been halted by financial blunders, Philippe sought to whet the imperialistic appetites of the Russian bear in Asia. By helping to finish the canal, Russia not only could give evidence of its desire to cement the entente, but could also advance its interests in the Far East, at that time reaching concrete expression with the construction of the Trans-Siberian railroad. Russia would reap the glory of having united Europe and Asia by land, and the two oceans at Panama. Bunau-Varilla felt that the Franco-Russian canal could be finished in four years at an additional cost of $140 million.[19]

On his return to France, Philippe reported his conversations in Russia and the emperor's friendly reception of his idea. Premier Jean Casimir Perier, very much under the influence of Bunau-Varilla's friend, Henri Burdeau, reacted favorably to the proposal and worked out a project by which, if bonds worth $30 million were floated, the government would guarantee the interest on them. However, the receiver of the company's assets vetoed the scheme: he was satisfied with a company that capitalized its shares at only $12 million. On May 22, 1894, while this stalemate was being discussed within French political circles, the government fell.

In fact, every one of these mentors was removed by death or from power in rapid succession. On June 25, 1894, France was plunged into another national crisis by the death of Sadi Carnot, mortally wounded in Lyons by anarchist bullets. On November 1, Alexander III suffered the same fate. Bunau-Varilla's loyal friend, Henri Burdeau, died on December 12, 1894.[20]

The fabulously wealthy Jean Casimir Perier succeeded Carnot on June 25, 1894. But the political scene was complicated by the rising turmoil of the Dreyfus case and by uncontrollable inflation, and Perier was forced to resign on January 15, 1895. With his political eclipse, the hopes for a canal at Panama collapsed again.

President Perier was succeeded by the handsome Felix Fauré, who was what is known in America as a "rivers and harbors" politician, a man credited with promoting riparian public works but with no appetite for international projects such as the Franco-Russian canal partnership suggested by Bunau-Varilla.

Philippe Finds Proof of Dreyfus' Innocence

Bunau-Varilla decided to wait for a change in the political and social makeup of his country. Comforted by the knowledge that he was immune to yellow fever, he decided to see for himself the hydroelectric and mining potentialities of Equatorial Africa and the Congo, to which he sailed in December 1894. Alfred Dreyfus had been one of Bunau-Varilla's classmates and, years later, both had attended symposia at Saint Cyr, France's highest military college. Weeks before Dreyfus' trial began, he learned of Philippe's projected expedition and wrote him a letter outlining the character of the country and telling him how best to go about his mission.[21]

The evidence which sent Dreyfus to Devil's Island was the infamous *bordereau*, a folio with data attributed to Dreyfus, containing evidence of his betrayal of military information to Germany.[22] By serendipity, Philippe was able to prove Dreyfus' innocence. On the evening of November 8, 1896, at an officer's party, a subaltern was passing around a copy of the *bordereau* which had been used as evidence against Dreyfus. Philippe politely asked if he could read the folio at home. Would they let him take it with him until the next day?

He carried the *bordereau* to his office and compared it with the letter he had received from Dreyfus before his African journey. As he had guessed, there was not the least similarity in handwriting. He took the document to his brother Maurice, and the two became convinced that Dreyfus had been framed.[23]

A facsimile of the *bordereau* was reproduced in *Le Matin*, Bunau-Varilla's daily, on November 10, 1896. The editor, Maurice, asked if there were any readers who could identify the author of the document, as it evidently was not written by Dreyfus. In response, a Parisian stockbroker appeared at the office of the newspaper with a number of letters written by Major C. F. Walsin-Esterhazy. A comparison of these epistles with the *bordereau* showed that Esterhazy was its author. Doubts began to arise in the minds of General R. F. C. Le Mouton de Boideffre, chief of staff, and Lieutenant Georges Piquart, head of the statistical section.

Wishing to keep the case closed, the prosecution stated that Dreyfus had been convicted on other secret evidence, and not the *bordereau* published by *Le Matin*. What evidence was this? Evidence so secret that only the judges and the prosecuting attorney could see it, but not the defense. That statement brought about a universal outcry against the judiciary and the military and caused the fall of the government. Even President Felix Fauré, who considered Dreyfus guilty, was shaken. Fauré's timely death and the elevation of Emile Loubet, who believed in Dreyfus' innocence, eventually brought about the total vindication of the officer[24] whose guilt was first questioned, at great risk, by Bunau-Varilla.

A New French Company

During the political unheaval in France, a new Panama company was formed. This corporation, founded in the autumn of 1894, followed the outline in Philippe's book of 1892, but instead of proposing to raise $35 million for the first phase of the works, it was satisfied with $12 million. The new directors of the organization chose to call themselves "technical commissioners." These technicians were abysmally ignorant of the Panama situation and, indeed, the new company seemed content simply to sap what was left of the old company and then disappear. C. Hersent, who had

committed gross errors during the life of the previous corporation, was named one of its technicians. Certainly he was
ready to become one of its executioners.[25]

The new company ignored everyone who had engineering
experience at Panama, especially Philippe, yet it followed his
advice and named a law firm—Sullivan and Cromwell—to
represent it and, if possible, advance its interests in the
United States. The directorate of the new company appointed
an international technical commission in February 1896, to
"re-discover" the isthmus and make a report which would be
palatable to the American power structure. Fourteen engineers from Germany, the United States, Russia, Belgium,
Colombia, and France were selected, but the most enthusiastic of them all, Bunau-Varilla, was left out. The commission
speedily prepared a report which was nothing but a confirmation of the features of the canal project described by
Philippe in 1892. It was ready on November 16, 1896, but
William Nelson Cromwell, the lawyer representing the new
company, overplayed his hand. The head of the technical
commission and Cromwell secured an appointment with
President McKinley on December 2, 1896,[26] but rumors of
Colombian displeasure at these activities alerted Senator John
T. Morgan, who charged in the Senate that interests friendly
to Panama were endangering the American choice of Nic-
aragua.[27] McKinley dropped the matter.

A few months later, the head of the technical commission,
A. Robaglia, wrote to Philippe:

> I have been personally struck by the comparison you have
> drawn between the Panama Canal and the Nicaraguan Canal.
> Your demonstrations seemed to me luminous. I can explain
> only by other than technical consideration the persistence of a
> portion of American opinion in favor of Nicaragua.[28]

Revolution in Colombia

Meanwhile, Panama's situation remained desperate.
"There is no good faith in America," wrote Simón Bolivar in
1829, "nor among the nations of America. Treaties are scraps
of paper; constitutions, printed matter; elections, battles;

freedom, anarchy; and life, a torment."[29] The Liberator's farewell address was echoed by Francisco Bilbao in 1862, when he warned of the chaotic nature of "constitutional" governments in Latin America.[30]

Certainly the former Spanish Empire, especially Colombia, had not been a paragon of law and order. What Salvador de Madariaga examined as "absolute passion" without "self control"[31] was more common in Colombia than in any other former Spanish colony.

The *Latin American Research Review* published a critical bibliography of "Violence in Colombia" listing 119 works dealing with violence and printed in Colombia from the early nineteenth century to 1973.[32] Among the authors are some of the best Spanish-speaking writers, such as German Arciniegas, Leon J. Helguera, Ernesto Restrepo Tirado, Manuel Restrepo, and the sociologist Orlando Fals Borda.[33] Although President Rafael Nunez, ruling through surrogates in Bogota, brought subversion under control from his ranch in Cartagena, violence did not disappear from the land during his administrations; it only took a leave of absence, and when it returned on his death in 1894, it returned with all the fury of a Caribbean hurricane.

While civil strife was traversing the valleys of the Magdalena and Cauca rivers on its way to the isthmus, Panama was in the midst of an economic depression which did not diminish with the official announcement in 1895 that the new canal company was ready to continue excavations. The good news, spread by the mysterious communication system of the wireless and roadless jungle, brought back increasing numbers of former black workers who hoped for employment, and once more the endemic plagues seized upon their prey. To make life more intolerable, a conflagration of unknown origin destroyed half of Panama City the same year. The feeble attempt to continue the interrupted work did not bring prosperity to the beleaguered Panamanians.[34]

Revolution in Cuba

The American minister to France, Whitelaw Reid, returned

to the United States as a peacemaker for his own Republican party, which was at this time threatened from within by the rising power of the New York politician Thomas C. Platt and from without by the resurrected Democrats led by Grover Cleveland. Despite Platt's opposition, Reid received the Republican vice-presidential nomination in the summer of 1892 at Minneapolis, setting the stage for a feud between himself and Platt, one of the most bitter struggles in American politics. Benjamin Harrison and Reid went down to defeat in the autumn elections, but the setback did not reduce Reid's influence. Reid supported President Cleveland in his chief policies—defense of the gold standard and conciliatory overtures toward a peaceful solution of the Cuban imbroglio.

After traveling in Greece, the Near East, and North Africa, Reid returned to his ranch in Arizona ready to enter the political wars once more.[35] Meanwhile, his friend Loomis had temporarily abandoned diplomacy to become editor-in-chief of the *Cincinnati Daily Tribune*. In 1896, while the Cuban situation worsened, Reid was playing his role of kingmaker with gusto. Refusing second place, he endorsed William McKinley for the presidential nomination on the Republican ticket. On April 8, 1896, Reid wrote to Loomis, at this time the voice of the Ohio gang, that he had "no desire to become vice-president."[36]

Candidate William McKinley threw himself into the arms of his friend Reid once the campaign began. McKinley wrote to Reid in 1896:

> Canton, Ohio, June 24, 1896
> My Dear Mr. Reid: In making acknowledgement of your kind telegram I wish also to thank you for all you have done, both personally and through the powerful influence of the *Tribune*. I also want you to feel perfectly free to communicate to me any suggestions that may occur to you as to the management of the campaign.
>
> Very sincerely,
> Wm. McKinley[37]

And just before his electoral victory, Reid visited McKinley in Canton, Ohio. The Cuban question was very much on the candidate's mind. Reid had in mind the ministry to England for himself.[38]

In selecting his cabinet, McKinley, like every other Republican president since Hayes, sought Reid's opinion. Reid answered:

> I utterly reject the theory that Cabinet appointments can be wisely used for placating enemies or conciliating factions. Patronage may perhaps be so used, but a homogeneous and efficient administration, devoted solely to you and your purposes, is impossible if Cabinet places are not held above that level.[39]

In the beginning, Reid's close ally, John Milton Hay, supported him, but Boss Thomas Platt of New York was ready to block Reid's appointment. Eventually, McKinley persuaded Hay to take the job himself, while Loomis, through Reid and Hay, received the ministry at Caracas.

Although Reid favored a peaceful solution of the Cuban question, he was an imperialist at heart. "Some day we will have Cuba, as well as the Sandwich Islands. To that extent I believe in Manifest Destiny," he wrote McKinley in the autumn of 1896.[40] Meanwhile, the American financial crisis of 1895 had increased mass unemployment throughout Cuba. Spain's attempt to solve these problems took the form of a military expedition charged with ending rebellion against the mother country. The new challenge was met by revolutionaries such as Maximo Gomez, Jose Marti, Antonio Maceo, and Calixto Garcia. The rebels drew up a constitution and demanded independence.[41]

Military operations against the Cubans were intensified under the command of the able Valeriano Weyler Nicolau, but his methods of dealing with the insurgents brought about international criticism of Spain. At a time when Weyler's measures were about to quell the resistance, the ministry of Praxedes Mateo Sagasta recalled the general in exchange for an American promise not to help the rebels.[42] At this moment, President McKinley, advised by Reid, requested Spain's consent for the United States to mediate the conflict. In February 1898, while this offer was being considered in

Madrid, the battleship *Maine* was blown up in Havana Harbor.[43]

Public opinion in the United States was becoming inflamed by the cry for war. Reid, who was named special ambassador to England to attend the jubilee festivities honoring Queen Victoria, was asked by McKinley to undertake a side trip to Spain as minister plenipotentiary with instructions to arrange the purchase of Cuba. Reid approached his former Paris colleague, the Duque de Sotomayor, who assured the American of the futility of his mission.[44]

The Treaty of Paris of 1898

"The fleet under my command offers the nation, as a Fourth of July present, the whole of Cervera's fleet." With this message on July 4, 1898, Admiral William T. Sampson signaled the end of the Spanish-American war, of Spain as a colonial power, and the rising of a new colossus—the United States.[45] Surely, the dream of an interoceanic canal was becoming closer to fulfillment. McKinley, who liked Reid's ideas about the acquisition of an island empire, named his friend a member of the peace commission. Reid's views had not been well received by the French press, nor had the pro-Spanish Paris newspapers helped the cause of the canal at Panama. Public sentiment in America became anti-French, venting its animosity against any promotion by French interests. Thus, at the insistence of John Bigelow, Cromwell's lobbying for the new Panama canal company came to a halt. Bigelow and his friends then began silent moves and oral persuasion to promote a canal in Panama, such as the distribution of Philippe's 1892 book among such members of America's powerful intellectual élite as the Hays, the Pinchots, the Bancrofts, Henry Adams, and Wayne Parker.

Reid's spirits rose, however, upon receipt of Ambassador Horace Porter's confidential letter assuring him that the hostility of the press in Paris did not extend to the public or to the government. In anticipation of his voyage to the peace conference, Reid made use of Bunau-Varilla's newspaper to soothe the feelings of his French hosts.

Reid took the position that his country was "threatened" by

the command to acquire an empire. By October, 15, 1898, he was comfortably installed in Paris, ready to begin talks about the peace terms. In addition to Reid, there were four other negotiators and a secretary to the commission, Professor John Bassett Moore of Columbia University.[46]

The choice of Paris as the seat of the peace conference proved advantageous to both Reid and Bunau-Varilla. Because of Reid's earlier sojourn in France, his fluency in the language, and his unbending stand on the matter of the Cuban debt, raised by the Spaniards, he soon became the leading treaty maker among the Americans.[47] It is not necessary to delve into the terms of the Treaty of Paris of 1898, but the acquisition of Puerto Rico and the setting up of a protectorate over Cuba by the United States revived the issue of a canal, a subject much discussed in France because of the initiative of Bunau-Varilla.

Bunau-Varilla was cognizant of the adroit maneuvering in the United States for the building of a Nicaraguan canal. Daily reports came to him from a legion of new acquaintances he had entertained in Paris, thanks to introductions from John Bigelow and the personal intervention of Percy Peixotto, an American insurance representative with headquarters near the Place de la Concorde. Among these new friends was the invaluable Asher Baker, a naval officer well aware of the canal problems, who had influential friends in Congress. Philippe had little trouble convincing him of the advantages of the Panama route, and the convert promised to devote his spare time to convincing everyone back home.[48]

Encouraged by the new developments, relentless in his determination, and inflexible in his aim, Philippe pressed the issue of the Panama canal at two meetings with Reid, and the sage politician was impressed. Reid understood that this young man had the courage of his convictions, unsurpassed knowledge of the facts, and the willingness to defy public opinion in France and America in order to change the well-publicized plans for the Nicaraguan scheme. These were qualities that a newsman and newsmaker like Reid admired. He promised to help.[49]

Revolution in Colombia

When Rafael Nunez declared, "Gentlemen: The constitution of 1863 has ceased to exist . . .," Colombia entered upon a period of managed peace. Three plans for a new constitution were presented in December 1885: one by Dr. J. D. Ospina Camacho; another, a copy of the Argentine constitution, by Dr. Jose Maria Samper; and a third by General Rafael Reyes. The constitutional council and Nunez were not pleased with any of these drafts, and writer Miguel Antonio Caro was appointed to draw a new document which became the ruling instrument of Colombia on August 4, 1886.[50]

The new constitution was conservative in character, but even the liberals, tired of subversion, accepted it because it "recognizes or consecrates in principle all the great liberties of modern law . . . many of them defined with Anglo-Saxon precision, to which ours was not equal." The Panamanians did not like this legal instrument at first because it placed the isthmus under direct control of Bogota, yet it did not name Panama as an integral part of the republic. Fourteen departments and their capitals were recognized, but Panama was omitted.[51] Panama was to have an entirely different charter.

A year later, in December 1887, this apparently strong constitution received a severe jolt with the signing of a concordat with the Vatican, a seemingly harmless move which was to be the main ideological excuse for the political conflagration that followed Nunez's death. The president had previously declared that:

> . . . the press should be a torch and not a firebrand, a messenger of truth and not of calumny. The unrestricted commerce in firearms and ammunition is a constant stimulus to civil war, and religious tolerance does not exclude the acknowledgement of the Catholic Church as that of the great majority of the people of Colombia.[52]

Very few realized the extent and ramifications of the concordat, which in reality was the brainchild of two of Nunez's conservative backers, Carlos Holguin and his brother-in-law, Miguel Antonio Caro.[53]

The country was partitioned by new conquerors, the religious orders. But unlike the captains of the conquest, they
arrived to fish for souls.[54] The mass immigration of the friars
began with the naming in 1885 of one of Bunau-Varilla's
acquaintances, Monsegnor Jose Talesforo Paul, archbishop of
Colombia. The Jesuits returned, followed by the Salesians,
the Christian Brothers, the Congregation of the Immaculate
Heart of Mary, the Lazarists, the Sisters of Charity of Tours,
the Augustinian Recollects, the Capuchins, the Society of
Mary, and the Mission of the Magdalena.[55] Doubtless these
orders performed great service to the rural population and
conducted themselves within the canons of Christian piety;
however, many among the liberal élite resented their numbers and, in particular, their control of the schools. Some
writers insisted that even the common people reacted against
the men and women of the robe and that the Indians saw the
return of the "caste spirit," if not the caste system itself.[56]

Hoping that his country could be ruled by Constitution
rather than by men, Nunez withdrew to the seclusion of his
estate in Cartagena to watch the political show now in the
hands of his lieutenants in Bogota. Carlos Holguin and
Miguel Antonio Caro held office under his watchful eye,[57] but
when the time for new elections arrived in 1891, Nunez did
not know whom to choose for vice-president. Two prospects
appeared, General Marcelino Velez and Caro. At the beginning Nunez encouraged Velez, but finally settled for Caro,
who again became vice-president, in charge of the executive
power in Bogota. The president's indecision signaled the
fragmentation of his party between nationalists and historical
conservatives, but the real winners were the moribund liberals.[58]

Liberal agitation, particularly in the press, resulted in
government suspension of various newspapers. In an attempt to reunite his followers and display his already well-
known altruism, Nunez refused his salary as president and
reimbursed the state all the monies paid to him as chief
executive since 1888. Shortly thereafter, attempting to re-
spond to the call of his followers to return to Bogota and take

command of the political situation, he died. Dr. Nunez collapsed at the very moment of his departure from Cartagena.[59] His demise ended attempts at national conciliation, and politics in Colombia took a sharp turn toward direct action and confrontation. On the night of January 22, 1895, the country was once more immersed in subversion. Notwithstanding the government's control of this rebellion, Colombia remained in a precarious state of alert prompted by *levantamientos* (rebellions) in various sections.[60]

Reopening the Canal Works

By Law No. 91 of December 6, 1892, the Colombian Congress authorized the president to negotiate the extension of the canal concession requested by the French in 1889. In accordance with this law, the Suarez-Mange agreement was signed on April 4, 1893, and the contract was extended to October 31, 1904, with the understanding that the waterway should be finished by that time. Two million dollars were paid to the government by the new company. President Caro then requested the discharge of four thousand soldiers to save 2.7 million gold pesos annually—the administration hoped to find employment for these men in Panama or in other projects created by the revival of the economy by the canal.[61] However, the new canal company did not have enough liquid capital to restore Panama, much less Colombia, to its previous prosperity. Meanwhile, it was time for elections.

The conservatives supported a ticket whose combined ages were more than 165 years. On the day of the Battle of Santiago Bay in Cuba, the electoral council declared that Drs. Manuel Antonio Sanclemente and Jose Manuel Marroquin had been elected president and vice-president for a six-year term. But, plagued by illness and suffering because of the altitude of Bogota, Sanclemente left his duties to the vice-president and removed himself to a provincial town, from which he attempted to conduct affairs. In 1898, the new company requested another ten-year extension. In 1899, talks between Nicolas Esguerra and the corporation began in Paris, but just as the Colombian Congress was about to give its consent to the extension, the nation was shaken by a rebellion. The Nunez constitution of 1886 had given the executive "extraordinary powers" under such conditions and, advised by his Cabinet and without a Congress in session, President Sanclemente authorized the signing of the Calderon-Mancini document on April 25, 1900. It extended the canal concession until October 31, 1910.[62] Another $2 million was paid for this extension.

Thus, at the very time that Whitelaw Reid and the Spaniards were negotiating peace terms in Paris, the Colombian chief of state was both physically and politically incapacitated, the government was near bankruptcy, insurrection was everywhere, and the giant ditch at Panama was breeding billions of mosquitoes. Only Bunau-Varilla and his small army of collaborators were optimistic. Pessimism increased when the revolution reached the area of the canal. Beginning in June 1900, conservatives and liberals killed each other with gusto in several battles.[63] To expedite the offensive against the insurgents, a clique of incumbent politicians, led by the future canal negotiator Carlos Martinez Silva, engineered a *coup d'état* on the last day of July 1900 and elevated Dr. Marroquin to the presidency. Removed from office, the octogenarian Sanclemente was placed under house arrest.

A New Canal Commission in the United States

By the autumn of 1898, the new French canal company was ready to abandon its project. Following Bunau-Varilla's meetings with Reid, the directors took Philippe's advice and again offered the canal to President McKinley. Privately, the French engineer urged Asher Baker and Bigelow to distribute his book in America, and its widespread circulation within political circles in Washington began to change the minds of the powers-that-be in the United States.[64] Meanwhile, the activities of Senator John T. Morgan in favor of Nicaragua were mirrored in the House of Representatives by Republican Congressman William Peters Hepburn. Although born in Ohio, Hepburn was not directly tied to the Ohio gang. His home was Iowa, a state which he had represented in Congress for many years. Morgan and Hepburn each hoped that the glory of having promoted the canal would redound on each alone and that the prestige of its legalization by Congress would fall to their respective parties. Both politicians were demanding that the government take a firm stand on the Nicaraguan route on the basis of a report rendered in 1897 by a commission named to study Nicaragua. Their personal rivalry was to benefit the persistent Bunau-Varilla.[65]

To counter their moves, Philippe went into high gear. He was already known in America and in Europe as "Mr. Canal," and at this time Francis B. Loomis coined the palindrome: "A man, a plan, a canal—Panama!" meaning Bunau-Varilla.[66] The first step in Philippe's plan was to forestall any official commitment to the Nicaraguan route without a prior investigation of Panama. Accordingly, Bigelow wrote to the secretary of state asking that this suggestion be included in the president's message to the Congress in 1899.[67] On his return from France, Whiteland Reid asked the same favor of the president.[68]

To increase pressure for the Panama route and improve the prospects of Bunau-Varilla's victory, Bigelow, now in his eighty-second year, moved to Washington. Lieutenant Asher Baker joined him and they both began to prepare the ground for the arrival of Bunau-Varilla. But Philippe, aware of the intensity of turmoil in Colombia and fearing that his presence in the United States at this time might unite Hepburn and Morgan,[69] decided to investigate the situation in Colombia from neighboring Venezuela. He accepted an invitation from Loomis, the American envoy to Caracas, to visit that country.

The appointment of newly married Francis B. Loomis as envoy extraordinary and minister plenipotentiary to Venezuela was not only a wedding present from Hay and McKinley, but also an expression of the American desire to observe at first hand the activities of England in that area.[70] Loomis' keen observations of Venezuela were highly regarded in Washington. When Bunau-Varilla arrived in Caracas, the country appeared calm; the capital city was a sleepy town where a customer could buy his milk still warm from the udder of a cow brought to his door. There was not the slightest sight or smell of oil in Lake Maracaibo. But Loomis apprehensively watched the spread of violence near the canal and the strange naval moves on the coast by England and Germany, who were also observing the turmoil.[71]

At this time, acting mostly on intuition, Loomis began a close association with an obscure under secretary of the navy, named Theodore Roosevelt. Although Loomis corresponded with Hay and Reid, he did not ignore Roosevelt. He dutifully reported England's sea moves to the navy under secretary, eliciting this response from Roosevelt in January 1898:

> Received your letter and shall present it to the Secretary immediately upon his return. . . . I quite understand the force of what you say, and I shall urge the Secretary to do as you desire.[72]

For months before Loomis and Bunau-Varilla met in Caracas, it was known that several Colombian departments were contemplating secession. The areas under suspicion were Cauca, Magdalena, Bolivar, and Panama.[73] Insurrection was said to be supported from abroad, making possible the continuation of guerrilla warfare even after a district had been pacified.[74] Would it be feasible to dramatize the canal idea by proclaiming a new nation composed of dissident states? It was in Caracas that Loomis and Philippe first plotted the revolution that cut Panama's umbilical cord with Colombia. Even if the canal were finished, it would always be endangered by civil war, said Philippe. Only if the United States took a direct interest could we succeed in this dream, thought Loomis.[75]

Loomis knew that Colombia was not ready to sell Panama.[76] Slowly but firmly, Loomis and Bunau-Varilla combined their efforts to publish, in South-American dailies, every newsworthy activity of the treatymaker Reid in Paris, particularly his ideas about the Cuban debt. The plight of Panama was indirectly but cleverly compared with that of Cuba in regard to Spain. All the interviews given by Reid in Paris to Le Matin were translated and headlined in the Venezuelan press.[77] A less-beleaguered nation than Colombia or a more intelligent public would have taken the hint at this time. But public and private warnings of this nature only exasperated Bogota.[78]

During this trip to Venezuela, Philippe met the influential Colombian citizen Pedro Nel Ospina, to whom he confided the idea that a canal owned and operated by the United States might not be a bad thing for Colombia. Ospina was not enthusiastic about this move, nor were his conservative friends or liberal enemies. The Spanish-American War had generated a traumatic reaction throughout Colombian society, and there was much anti-American feeling in Bogota as well as Panama.[79] Philippe sensed that he should not approach his Panamanian friends at this time. Besides, he agreed with Loomis that Panama's secession could not be managed by Panama alone. He therefore bypassed the isthmus on his return voyage to New York, going by way of Trinidad and Saint Lucia.[80]

In order for Philippe to succeed with his canal dream, the canal had to be transferred to the United States. Colombia had to ratify such an agreement and grant a concession to the United States. But if Colombia refused, Philippe, with the aid of Hay, Loomis, and McKinley, must emancipate Panama and any other states of Colombia willing to secede, then negotiate with the new state. He realized that the first and last steps would be the most difficult and controversial because of international opposition and the Nicaraguan party in Congress. But Loomis told him not to worry, for McKinley's re-election was a foregone conclusion. Enthusiastically, Philippe set to work on the first step.

Bunau-Varilla knew that the basis of a successful negotiation was knowing as much as possible about the people involved. For Philippe, the study of people was vital to his work. He knew all the potential Panamanian revolutionaries, but very little about his American opponents. Aware that his attack on the Nicaraguan route had to be totally pragmatic, Philippe was ready to negotiate realities and problems rather than make demands. The plight of the new company should be the last issue to be brought out in the upcoming debate.

Philippe realized that his presentations had to be not only forceful but knowledgeable. He must make the American government understand the situation and must present it as an advantage. In this way and in this frame of mind, Bunau-Varilla began his campaign to destroy the enviable Nicaraguan position. No Panamanian or Colombian could have been better qualified for the job. At this moment, Philippe was expressing not only his own ideas and the interests of the proponents of the canal, but also the hopes of the isthmians whose agonies he very well knew. But before putting his plans into effect, he quietly returned to France.

A New Canal Commission

The influence of Bunau-Varilla's friends and the circulation of his book in Congress resulted in the passage of a House resolution providing for a new canal commission to study both routes—as Philippe had suggested. Disregarding the protests of William Nelson Cromwell, who objected to the naming of any man previously associated with studies of the Nicaragua route, McKinley reappointed the board that had made the earlier survey and added three new members: George Morison, Alfred Noble, and William Burr, all civil engineers. As reconstituted in June 1899, the commission was bound to demonstrate again the superiority of Nicaragua. Consequently, there was no objection from Morgan or Hepburn about the size or nature of this group. Admiral John G. Walker chaired the sessions again.[81]

John Bigelow and Asher Baker canvassed the commissioners and found that six of them were already committed to Nicaragua; the other three, believing that Panama was an impossibility, were supposed to be open-minded, but in the end would vote with the others. Under these unfavorable circumstances, the battle for a canal at Panama entered its penultimate stage. Very few Panamanians were aware of these events, for they too were concerned with questions of life and death.

The commission split up into various committees, and the

three engineers—at the prodding of Bigelow and Reid—were placed in one of these units and sent to Europe to study the maritime canals of Manchester and Kiel and the archives of the old canal company in Paris. Philippe was eagerly waiting for them, with introductions from Bigelow and the lawyer Frank Pavey. He lost no time in bringing them over to his side, but he was not sure that they could turn the tide.

Knowing of the impending negotiations between the United States and England regarding canal rights in America, Philippe sailed for Egypt in the autumn of 1899, ostensibly to attend the ceremonies of the inauguration of a monument to de Lesseps but with the secret aim of interesting the shipping world in his canal. Among his new converts were several bankers and the influential Englishman, Sir John Wolfe Barry, who carried Bunau-Varilla's project to London. But the Boer War,[82] then one of Britain's most immediate problems, diverted interest from this matter. He returned to France at the urgent call of his brother Etienne.[83]

Financial Chicanery

The new company's directors were about to effectuate a secret plan to form a canal company in America with a liquid capital of $5,000. On paper, the corporation owned $30 million. The mastermind of this speculative venture was William Nelson Cromwell. The American company was to purchase:

> . . . the maritime ship canal of the *Compagnie nouvelle du canal de Panama* and the railway across the Isthmus of Panama . . . to issue shares, bonds, debenture stock . . . to vary the investments of the Company; to mortgage, pledge, or charge all or any part of the property, concessions, rights, and franchises of the Company acquired or to be acquired: to make advances upon, hold in trust, sell or dispose of, and otherwise deal with any of the investments or securities aforementioned.[84]

Obviously, the directors of the new company and Cromwell intended to sell all the equipment in Panama to the United States if the isthmian route was adopted. Surely, with the well-publicized understanding that a canal through Nicaragua or any other place was to be constructed under the authority, administration, and control of the federal government, Cromwell did not expect to sell shares to the public. It was clear that the stockholders of the old and new companies were unaware of these machinations, for it seemed certain they would lose their investments in this transaction. The new American corporation, registered in Trenton, New Jersey, on December 27, 1899, was the first of two serious attempts by Cromwell to supersede Bunau-Varilla. Alerted by Philippe, the receiver of the old company and the representative of the shareholders appealed to the judiciary, who forced the company's board to resign. The tribunal appointed an administrator to manage affairs until the election of a new board. The carbon copy of the new French canal company disappeared as quickly as it had been formed.[85]

American Politics and Diplomacy Help the Canal

Even before the presidential campaign began, the two traditional parties had decided that the two gladiators in the election of 1896 were good enough in 1900. The stage was set for another battle between William Jennings Bryan and William McKinley. Loomis returned to the United States from Venezuela in June 1900, while Reid and the *New York Tribune* extolled McKinley's virtues. Meanwhile the political star of Marcus Alonzo Hanna continued to shine.

Hanna, like Reid and Loomis, belonged to the Ohio gang. His wealth and influence were as great as Reid's, and his financial contributions to Garfield's election had been decisive in the 1880 campaign. At one time, Hanna promoted the fortunes of John Sherman, senator from Ohio, but, encountering opposition to his choice, he settled for McKinley, whom he began to groom as possible presidential timber. Hanna's money and Reid's newspapers elected McKinley the first time. Hanna refused the public office offered him by McKinley, the job of postmaster general. Soon, however, the president rewarded his friend by making John Sherman the secretary of state in 1897. Thus the door was open to Hanna, who received a senatorial appointment which was later narrowly confirmed by the Ohio legislature.[86] By a stroke of the pen, McKinley had placed in the Senate of the United States another soon-to-be apostle of Bunau-Varilla's ideas.

As chairman of the national committee of his party, Hanna moved early to secure McKinley's unanimous renomination. Simultaneously, Hay and Loomis began polling the delegates to the Republican convention about their vice-presidential choice and again, as in 1898, Reid's name was prominently mentioned. Reid, however, rejected the idea, thereby denying himself the presidency, which would have fallen to him at McKinley's death. Theodore Roosevelt himself was not too eager for the honor, but his nomination was strengthened by the election of Senator Lodge as permanent chairman of the convention. At the same time, the hopes for Panama were enhanced when the party, in its platform, endorsed "an Isthmian canal," protected, owned, and controlled by the government of the United States.[87] This paragraph was suggested by Lodge.[88]

Reid's *Tribune* had not supported all of Roosevelt's policies as governor of New York, but the two men were on cordial terms. After his nomination as vice president, Roosevelt asked to see Reid; thenceforth their association was steady and their views complemented each other.[89]

The Republicans won the election of 1900 by a million votes. Months later, Henry Cabot Lodge went to England to attempt to persuade the British to give up their objections to an American canal.[90] Tired of Boss Platt's impertinences, McKinley named Andrew White of Cornell University minister to Germany. Horace Porter had already been named ambassador to France. An appointment for Reid could not get past Senator Platt's veto, but McKinley made him special ambassador to England on the occasion of the Jubilee of Queen Victoria, a selection which needed no senatorial confirmation. Francis B. Loomis went from Venezuela to Lisbon with the same rank[91], and Hanna began consolidating his post on the Senate's Committee on Interoceanic Canals, to which he had been appointed at McKinley's insistence.[92] And in France, while the Colombian minister attended the première of Gustave Clayentieu's opera *Louise*, Bunau-Varilla worked into the early hours of the morning enlisting supporters for his canal. No prominent American left France without visiting Philippe's splendid residence and without hearing his well-documented sales talk on behalf of Panama. Every one of these visitors, including the powerful Henry Cabot Lodge, left converted to the new creed.

Lodge was at this time the junior senator from Massachusetts. He was a man of retentive memory and solid intellect, endowed with political adroitness and literary skill. His conversation was a model of diction and elegance and, by 1900, he was the most erudite speaker in Congress. After a slow start at Harvard and studies in Italy, where he fell in love with classicism, Lodge was elected to the House at thirty-seven and to the Senate at forty-three. His close political association with Theodore Roosevelt began at the Republican Convention of 1884, which nominated James G. Blaine. While in Congress, he championed civil-service reform and, on his recommendation, Roosevelt became a member of the Civil Service Commission.[93]

Lodge, an expansionist like Reid, believed the time had come to build an interoceanic canal in America under the management of the United States, but, more important for Bunau-Varilla, the senator was convinced that the canal should be built through Panama. Philippe's documentation and his experience in Panama impressed the influential senator whose own star was to shine continuously over the American political scene until his death in November of 1924.[94]

England Cedes Canal Rights to the United States

American efforts to scuttle the Clayton-Bulwer Treaty began with Hay's ministry to England and progressed with Whitelaw Reid's special ambassadorship on the occasion of Queen Victoria's Jubilee. In December 1898, when the negotiations for the Treaty of Paris were almost complete, Ambassador Henry White opened formal negotiations in London.[95]

This round of talks led to the first Hay-Pauncefote Treaty. The document neutralized the waterway in war and peace, but it was so amended by the Senate that it failed of ratification in England. After McKinley's re-election, Hay pressed for an understanding with the British. In the spring of 1901, White wrote to Hay: "I spent last night with Teddy [Roosevelt] who was in capital form and in a very friendly mood to the treaty favorable to the Panama route. . . ."[96] And on September 19, 1901, while Lord Pauncefote was returning to Washington as England's envoy, Lodge wrote Roosevelt that he had strong hopes for a treaty that could be "laid before Congress in December, and which we can promptly ratify."[97]

As Lodge had predicted, the new treaty was ready for ratification in December 1901. It abrogated the Clayton-Bulwer Treaty of 1850 and gave the United States sole rights to build and operate a canal which was to be used by all nations without discrimination. Its neutrality was left to the United States to enforce. The much-discussed problem of fortifications was omitted, but any policing necessary to keep the canal open to world traffic was implicitly sanctioned.[98] Strongly supported by Lodge and Hanna, the treaty was ratified on December 16, 1901, by a vote of seventy-two to six.[99]

It was clear to Britain that the conditions under which the Clayton-Bulwer Treaty had been negotiated no longer existed. The strength of the two contracting states had been reversed. England's interest in the Caribbean had decreased, while that of the United States had doubled as a result of the Treaty of Paris of 1898. The way was open for the United States to build the canal—through Nicaragua or Panama.

Bunau-Varilla in the United States

While the Hay-Pauncefote Treaty was being renegotiated, Philippe launched a crusade designed to convert the power élite. He arrived in New York in January 1901, and by the sixteenth of the month was addressing the Commercial Club of Cincinnati, where he made a profound impression on the leaders of the Midwest. So successful was his speech that the

Society of Civil Engineers asked him to speak and, immediately thereafter, through the friendly offices of many of the
new converts, including a Catholic priest, Monsignor
Schmitz Didier, and Watts Taylor, he was able to meet Colonel
Myron T. Herrick, Senator Hanna's friend. Herrick arranged
for Philippe to speak to a cluster of influential entrepreneurs,
all of them closely allied with Hanna. A few days later, when
the senator returned to Cleveland, his friends had changed
their minds about a canal in Nicaragua.

Herrick and Hanna arranged for Philippe to speak in
Boston at the invitation of Lucius Tuttle, president of the
Boston and Maine Railroad. From Massachusetts, Philippe
traveled to Chicago at the invitation of James Deering of the
National Business League, and he eventually went to New
York to speak before its Chamber of Commerce, thanks to
John Bigelow.[100] Philadelphia, Pittsburgh, and New Orleans
were later added to his itinerary. An opera star could not have
fared better. Everywhere, the cold reasoning, the amiable
persuasion, and the adroit persistence of Bunau-Varilla
opened doors for him.[101]

Philippe decided to print a flier which he hoped to distribute personally to members of the government in Washington. He titled his brochure *Panama or Nicaragua?* He chose
to have Nicaragua destroy herself with the evidence of her
many volcanos:

> If the experience of four centuries is not a mere byword, if
> the indisputable proofs, written in letters of fire on the surface
> of the soil, of the continuous, violent, and increasing volcanic
> activity in Nicaragua, are not a mere dream, the route over that
> Isthmus is not only eventually exposed to, but certain, sooner
> or later, to be the prey of that uncontrollable power of Nature,
> before which flight is the only resource.
>
> To prefer the Nicaragua route to the Panama route, the
> unstable route to the stable one, would mean preferring the
> stability of a pyramid on its point to the stability of a pyramid
> on its base, when to that stability is attached the prosperity
> and welfare of a whole continent.
>
> The Panama route, having no winds, no currents (except

on rare occasions), no sharp curves, no sediments, no bad harbours, no volcanoes, enjoys to the highest degree the three essential qualities totally lacking to the Nicaragua solution—

Continuity of Operation

Security of Transit

Stability of Structure

Besides that, it is three times shorter, will cost much less than the Nicaragua route, and is easily transformable into a Bosphorus, the only form that will definitively answer to the world-wide interests to be served by the route, and allow of a passage from ocean to ocean in five hours.

The brochure was graced with many diagrams and statistics which Philippe had prepared in his spare time between journeys and lectures. Each page illustrated the dangers of Nicaragua. He demonstrated that, at an eruption in 1835 of *Cosequina*, a minor volcano, lasting forty-four hours, the volume of volcanic matter was equal to the total volume of the prism of the projected canal.[102]

While Philippe waited for an appointment with Senator Hanna, Myron T. Herrick and the senator came to New York, where Bunau-Varilla was informally introduced to the Ohio politician. The same day, Philippe met McKinley's friend, Comptroller of the Currency Charles Dawes, to whom he had a letter of introduction from an Englishman he met in Egypt, Sir Edwyin Dawes. Dawes arranged a visit to the White House and, through the efforts of his own lawyer, Frank Pavey, Philippe met his nemesis, Senator John T. Morgan.

Hanna was impressed by what he had heard, read, and seen:

My friends at Cleveland had told me what an echo your words had had in their minds. You have already provoked an intense movement in favor of Panama. . . . I thought, formerly, that Panama was a demonstrated impossibility. . . . The most qualified engineers asserted it. . . . But I supposed Nicaragua to be a relatively easy work. The only information I ever saw about Panama was a kind of prospectus distributed some time ago by the lawyers of The Company, but I did not attach much importance to it. Today I grasp clearly the whole question. . . .

> I am an old mining operator. If two mines are offered to me, I
> prefer the one which I know to be good.[103]

The senator, however, alerted Bunau-Varilla to the fact that he
had to take the word of the canal commission, implying that
these men also had to be converted. On April 7, 1901, when
Bunau-Varilla was received by McKinley, he left his documented prospectus with the president. The next day he
visited Morgan, and the old senator tried to turn the tables on
Philippe by convincing him of the virtues of Nicaragua.
When Bunau-Varilla mentioned the volcanoes, Morgan
retorted, "Volcanoes will never impress the Senate. . . . The
volcano argument is dead; with it you will not win a single
vote." As Philippe rose to leave, saying, "We shall see about
that," Morgan charged that Bunau-Varilla knew what a rotten
project Panama was and that he would not dare to invest one
dollar in that absurd scheme.[104] On April 9, 1901, the
mouthpiece of the Nicaraguan partisans, the *New York American*, published an account of Philippe's first invasion of the
inner sanctum of Nicaragua's bastion.[105]

During his lecture tour, Philippe took every precaution not
to offend the members of the canal commission. He suspected that in spite of Cromwell's enthusiasm for the project,
the lawyer might have made more enemies than friends. Had
not Senator Hanna stated that he paid little attention to a
prospectus distributed by the lawyers of the new company?
Before departing for Le Havre, Philippe again entertained the
three engineers on the commission—Burr, Morison, and
Ernst. Strange as it appeared to Philippe, the only difference
of opinion Morison had with him was over the issue of
volcanoes. Morison thought the possibility of volcanic disturbance too remote to deserve serious consideration.

Politely, Philippe addressed himself to Morison and made a
striking comparison between man-made and natural calamities. "Do not France, Germany, England and Russia spend
immense sums of money yearly to insulate themselves
against the danger of war?" This danger nobody can deny,
and nobody can calculate. "Would it not be a shame, if
Nicaragua is chosen that, in spite of these assurances, a great

price has to be paid in the end because the seismic possibility has been ignored?"

Morison realized that no matter how remote the probability might appear, Philippe wished to emphasize the seismic possibility because it was a strong point against Nicaragua. Finally Bunau-Varilla wrote to Morison:

> To those who think I am exaggerating this capital point I may say: Open any dictionary of geography, any encyclopedia, and read the article entitled "Nicaragua"; look at the Nicaraguan postage stamps. Youthful nations like to put on their coat of arms what best symbolizes their moral domain or characterizes their native soil. What have the Nicaraguans chosen to characterize their country on their coat of arms, on their postage stamps? Volcanoes.[106]

In the face of such evidence, Morison capitulated and accepted the theory of temblors. In three months of lecturing and lobbying, Philippe was about to reverse the anti-Panamanian feeling in America. For the first time, the Nicaraguan partisans became alarmed.[107] On April 11, 1901, Philippe sailed for France in a state of euphoria. But once more, this was to be only a round in the next-to-last battle. While Bunau-Varilla was in the United States, the new company dismissed Cromwell as counsel.

Theodore Roosevelt Becomes President

Philippe's brother Maurice went to Cuba and Central America as a reporter to investigate the progress of the fight against malaria and yellow fever, and Bunau-Varilla spent much of that summer of 1901 digesting secret correspondence from his friends in Panama. He was becoming convinced that only a miracle could prevent Panama's secession. It was obvious that, after the end of the long civil war plaguing Colombia, it would be much too weak to prevent a coup, especially one supported by Washington. Philippe's association with the new company was not cordial, but the chairman of the board, Maurice Hutin, kept him informed of developments. Philippe's relations with the Americans were excellent, and his hopes were enhanced when he saw his friend

Loomis in late August. The two exchanged views about the future of Panama and again found themselves in complete agreement. As to the canal, there were only two things that mattered at this time: the conclusion of the treaty with England and the decision of the stockholders about the price at which they would sell if the United States canal commission made the request.[108] But, as had happened many times before, a catastrophe was to place the canal in jeopardy.

On September 6, 1901, McKinley fell mortally wounded in Buffalo; he died on the fourteenth. The fifth head of state who had been receptive to Bunau-Varilla's personal pleadings in favor of his canal had disappeared.[109] Perhaps the canal itself was destined to follow them and die quietly. Had it not been for the determined Frenchman, it would have. The tragedy at Buffalo generated a momentary crisis within American bureaucracy and political circles. Whitelaw Reid and John Hay were in despair. It was the second time they had lost a president who was an intimate friend, the first having been Garfield. The weight of the shock was accentuated by the recent demise of other close associates—James G. Blaine, John Sherman, William Evars, and Benjamin Harrison. The tragedy intensified Hay's personal grief—his son Adelbert had died a few days earlier. Preparing for his return to his post from his estate in New Hampshire, Hay wrote to Reid:

> I shall be packing my paper cases next week, to go back to Washington after a summer of misery and disaster such as my life has never before experienced.[110]

Plagued by arthritis and confronted by negotiations for several treaties and conventions, the least of which was the one with Colombia, Hay entertained the thought of resigning while Roosevelt toyed with the idea of replacing him with Elihu Root. Reid, however, pressed Hay to stay:

> There is always certain comfort when one can feel that fate has done its worst! Don't worry about the aches and pains. They come to all men! I haven't been old before, either; and I don't feel so, very often, even now.[111]

Senator Lodge, for his part, expressed pleasure at Hay's decision to remain in the Cabinet. Communicating his feelings to Roosevelt from Paris, he congratulated the president on being so fortunate as to have both Root and Hay.[112] Although Hay was staying, he needed able, loyal, and confidential assistance in order to fulfill his duties as secretary of state. Bunau-Varilla's friend Francis B. Loomis was Hay's choice for the newly created post of first assistant secretary of state.[113] And, after two meetings with Bunau-Varilla in Paris, Lodge became an open partisan of the Panama route. Writing to the president only two days after taking office he said, "We must not tie you down to Nicaragua for I am strongly inclined to think that Panama is the best." The political chips were finally falling into place.

Philippe Makes a Last Appeal to the French

As soon as Philippe landed on his native soil, he decided to make a last appeal to the French to keep the canal. Although he was at odds with the directors of the new company, he enjoyed the support of most of the stockholders. They knew him well, and many of them had voted for him when he had run for the Assembly in 1889. His call to the French to save the canal for France took the form of paid advertisements in all the leading newspapers. The ad, handled by Lagrance & Cerf Co., appeared twice, on April 25 and May 10. In his appeal to the public, Bunau-Varilla wrote:

> To the small investors I say: Give the example, because it is in the depths of the masses of the nation that the heart beats. To those of big fortunes I say: Remember that the only justification of riches in a democracy is to be useful to all when the nation needs her resources. Do not fear slander. Enlist in the solidarity of courage, have the courage of solidarity for the public welfare.[114]

Philippe offered to contribute $400,000 of his personal fortune to back the canal. He also wrote to prominent bankers and to Emile Loubet, the chief of state. Bunau-Varilla's appeals were partially reproduced as news items in the press of Europe, where they received favorable comments. From Helsinki to Peking, and from London to Panama, Philippe received congratulatory messages, but no concrete offers. His partners in *Le Matin*, in which Bunau-Varilla had made investments since 1892 and was soon to own, were sympathetic but not overjoyed. Philippe's tormentor, *La Libre Parole*, controlled by Drumont, bestirred itself to sarcasm:

> It is a very pretty page, a page traced by an artistic hand, as Goncourd would have said, that Monsieur Bunau-Varilla offered for our perusal last week on the final sheet of the newspapers. . . . I confess myself to making a bow before the phantom that Monsieur Bunau-Varilla has thought fit to bring on to the stage from the wings.[115]

Philippe's appeals did not fall on deaf ears but on empty pockets. Colonial ventures, the exodus of thousands of middle-class citizens to the new possessions, industrial investments, and the recent Twentieth Century International Exposition of Paris had taken much money out of circulation. Moreover, French financial circles and the regime in power were aware of the fight between Nicaragua and Panama. Investment in a problematic waterway did not seem a wise proposition to the bankers. Bunau-Varilla perceived these handicaps, but he wished to ascertain for himself that there was no interest in France in finishing the canal. Canvassing his countrymen in this fashion cost him more than $40,000,[116] a sum which Colombia and the Panamanians never remotely considered spending to promote their own prosperity.

A Turnaround

After Roosevelt's installation and Bunau-Varilla's interview with Loomis, Philippe urged Maurice Hutin to answer the canal commission. Admiral John Walker had sounded out the directorate of the new company about their intentions with this laconic message: "Are you willing to sell? Are you able to sell? How much would you sell for?"[117] Up to the time of Philippe's return to France in April 1901, the directors had reason to delay their answer. According to the Salgar-Wyse concession of 1878, the assets of the corporation and the contract were not to be transferred to any foreign government.[118] Before departing, on April 11, 1901, Philippe visited Carlos Martinez Silva, the new Colombian envoy, who months before had installed Manuel Marroquin as president in Bogota. The obsequious Senor Silva promised Philippe to intercede with Marroquin to waive the prohibition. And by the end of the month, the new company was given a free hand to sell.[119] Admiral Walker renewed his request.

As soon as this obstacle was overcome, the directors of the new company began to play a coy game. Hutin, in the name of his colleagues, initiated a lengthy correspondence with Admiral Walker filled with a lot of empty terminology. This inexplicable attitude annoyed the commission, leading to a vote which favored Nicaragua by 8 to 1. Yet, because of Morison's pleadings, they decided to wait a few more weeks. On October 17, 1901, Maurice Hutin crossed the ocean with what the commission interpreted as the final reply. Hutin informed the commission that the assets of the corporation were worth $109,141,500 and that he was willing to accept arbitration to reach a sales price.[120] Experts in Colombia, Panama, France, and the United States agreed that, had Hutin asked $90 million at this time, he would have received no less than $80 million.[121] Philippe would have accepted that without consulting the stockholders or the directors, but Hutin remained uncommitted.

Exactly a month later, on November 16, 1901, the commission recommended Nicaragua. The merits of both proposals were compared. Although Nicaragua would cost $189,864,062 and Panama $144,233,358, the estimate for Panama was not final until the purchase price of the new company's assets was added. The irritated commission estimated the value of those assets at a mere $40 million.[122] The vote for Nicaragua was unanimous, but the report was to be kept secret. There were rumors, however, and Asher Baker communicated them to Philippe,[123] who decided to return to America on November 13, 1901. On landing, the mouthpiece of Nicaragua—the *New*

York Journal—received Bunau-Varilla with headlines confirming the suspected bad news. One of the commission's junior assistants had been bribed by the newspaper, and the secret was out.[124] There was only one encouraging ray of hope. The *Journal* also published a minority report signed by Morison recommending Panama; however, this disagreement had occurred at the first balloting of the commission in August, not during its final session in November.

Another man would have returned to France, but not Philippe. He had seen and heard so much wavering, pulling, pushing, and rumors about the canal that he was certain this was not the last word. He took the train for Washington and went directly to see Myron T. Herrick, Senator Hanna's friend. The rejection of Panama coincided with the signing of the Hay-Pauncefote Treaty, and Herrick as well as Hanna had grasped the gravity of the situation. Bunau-Varilla underscored the fact that scientific considerations had to take priority over moral guidelines when dealing with the canal. The senator understood the point and promised action in the Senate.[125]

Meanwhile, on November 29, 1901, Philippe sent a long cable to *Le Matin* in which he appealed to the dilatory directorate of the new company to make a decision. Eight days later, on December 6, while the parsimonious directors argued about what to do, Congressman Hepburn introduced a measure in the House asking for $180 million to build the Nicaraguan waterway. The bill, slated for discussion on the floor January 7, 1902, provided for an immediate appropriation of $10 million to begin work.[126] There was no time to waste. Bunau-Varilla left New York on December 12, 1901, and on his arrival in Paris, he took control of the destinies of the new company exactly as he had done with the old company during its last years of existence. He addressed a meeting of the stockholders and chastised the do-nothing directors, giving them an ultimatum to sell for $40 million or lose all. Simultaneously, *Le Matin* demanded immediate action.[127] The shareholders removed Hutin, named Marius Bo in his place, and authorized him to make an offer to the United States.[128]

Marius Bo cabled Admiral Walker the new company's surrender on January 4, 1902. Edouard Lampre was dispatched to effect the sale, but debate on the Hepburn Bill began on January 7, and by January 9, with two dissenting votes, it was approved by the House. An attempt to leave the final decision to the president was rejected, 170 to 120.[129] Once more Nicaragua was victorious, but Bunau-Varilla was not ready to quit. He cabled Whitelaw Reid, Loomis, Asher Baker, and Bigelow, and the *New York Tribune* took the initiative in trying to deflect the public mind from Nicaragua. Soon other newspapers followed suit, including the *New York Times* and the *Chicago Evening Post*.[130] The *New York Herald* was intoxicated with joy, yet it implied that the Nicaraguan project was an American romance which was not to be cut short because of adverse scientific evidence. The paper added that if a referendum were conducted, the decision would be for Nicaragua.[131] Roosevelt was ready to begin the digging in Nicaragua, but Lodge and Reid asked him to give the new company a last opportunity.[132] In compliance with this request, Roosevelt ordered Admiral Walker to see Lampre. On January 16, led by Commissioner Morison, the canal commission reversed itself:

> After considering the changed conditions that now exist and all the facts and circumstances upon which its present judgment must be based, the Commission is of the opinion that "the most practicable and feasible route" for an Isthmian canal is that known as the Panama route.[133]

President Roosevelt sent this message to the Congress, where the senator from Wisconsin, John Coit Spooner, on January 28, 1902, proposed a modification to the Hepburn Bill. Spooner was a good lawyer and needed little help in drafting the amendment. He was a Midwest politician who worked well with the Ohio gang. Because of his parliamentary expertise he was selected to open the fight for Panama in the Senate. Hay, Hanna, and Bigelow were in complete agreement with this strategy. Senator Lodge persistently supported the isthmian route among the Eastern senators.[134]

But Roosevelt was still not willing to risk a fight with the powerful Nicaraguan lobby.

The amendment by Spooner authorized Roosevelt to buy the new company's property for $40 million if valid title could be secured to build an interoceanic passage, and to acquire in perpetuity from Colombia no less than six miles of land for the purpose of operating and defending the canal.[135] William N. Cromwell, who had been reinstated as lawyer for the new company at the intercession of Philippe, claimed later that he prepared the amendment, and he wrote to the directors in Paris to this effect. The new resolution warned Colombia that if, within a certain period of time, no agreement was reached with Bogota, the president was at liberty to proceed with the Nicaraguan project.[136]

Negotiations with Colombia

By 1901, the regime of Dr. Manuel Marroquin was harassed on every side by subversion, and Panama was in fratricidal combat. Under these conditions, Colombians and isthmians alike had little time for canal politics. For months there had not been a mission chief in Washington, former President Climaco Calderon having been dismissed as envoy to Washington after the *coup d'état* in 1900. Philippe had been cabling his friends in Panama and Colombia and pressing the government for action on the waterway, and Carlos Martinez Silva entered the history of the canal, arriving at his post in February 1901. During his tenure, he kept in touch with Philippe.

Although Silva did not have the power to negotiate a treaty, he was convinced that the best interests of the waterway lay in transferring the canal property to the United States. The Commission drafted an *aide-memoire* which Walker submitted to Silva for consideration. At this time, Silva objected to a perpetual lease and the inclusion of the cities of Colon and Panama within the proposed canal zone, but he forwarded the draft to Bogota.[137]

The envoy took an active interest in the fate of the canal, and his own views were modified after his conversations with

Bunau-Varilla. Silva showed Philippe the voluminous correspondence he had sent home favoring a canal convention,
and added: "You preach to a man who is already converted. I
should be happy if the authority of your name were added to
corroborate my opinion."[138] But as soon as Colombia learned
of the approaching signing of the Hay-Pauncefote Treaty, it
began to act as coy as the French company. With the approval
of the minister, Philippe began a strange, one-sided correspondence with Bogota, mostly by the way of expensive
cables. On February 23, 1902, on learning through Silva that
he was about to be superseded by Jose Vicente Concha,
Bunau-Varilla spent over $300 on a cablegram to Marroquin,
excerpts of which stated:

> Request pressing President of Republic to hear cry of danger
> uttered by uncompromising defender enterprise Panama and
> faithful friend Colombia. . . . If blind . . . advice induces
> Colombian Government to ensure the victory of Nicaragua by
> delaying protocol or formulating exaggerated demands, I
> assert that the Panama conception will be killed
> . . . no European Government, from fear of American hostility,
> and no private company, from fear of Nicaragua competition,
> will ever resume works if abandoned, and this enterprise will
> remain an historical disaster for moral and material interests
> both Colombian and French. . . . The danger is extreme. There
> is not one minute to lose, nor one mistake to commit to fix
> Destiny and arrest Fortune.[139]

Jose Vicente Concha was only thirty-five, with no diplomatic experience to his credit. He was a newsman who had
founded the daily El Dia in Bogota, and more recently had
held the portfolio of war.[140] The American proposals and
Silva's views were known in Panama and Bogota, and Silva
had become the target of misguided patriots such as the
interim governor of Panama, Aristides Arjona, who sent the
envoy the following cable:

> Our patriotism takes offense at the stipulation. . . . In
> renouncing sovereignty, and in allowing the establishment of
> a Foreign Power [The United States], on our own territory,
> Colombia is ignominiously humiliating her most precious

jewel, Panama. It would be preferable that the negotiations should fail altogether rather than that we should pay so dearly for them. The inhabitants of the Isthmus protest with indignation against such negotiations.[141]

This salvo was to be the first shot in almost a century of anti-Bunau-Varilla and anti-American jingoism by the Panamanians themselves. Arjona had become acting governor on the death of General Carlos Alban on January 20, 1902. Threatened by the liberal forces which were about to seize Panama and Colon, he had requested United States intervention in accordance with the Bidlack-Mallarino Treaty. American marines disarmed the rebels as well as the civilian population, prevented the routing of the conservatives, and saved the two cities. The liberals blamed the governor for the landing of the soldiers. Bereft of public support and trying to save himself, Arjona became the most "patriotic" of all citizens blasting the distant Martinez Silva.[142]

Concha arrived in the United States in March 1902, apparently undeterred by the threat from Nicaragua. Philippe's contacts with him were most frustrating. So were those of Cromwell. In sophistication, experience, philosophy and style, Bunau-Varilla and Cromwell were as unlike as two men accustomed to dealing with large numbers can be. Concha was not happy with the ramrod tactics of the lawyer, who annoyed the envoy by writing him treaty proposals which the legation's secretary, Tomas Herran, had to translate to him. Concha did not know a word of English. Moreover, Bigelow's suspicion of Cromwell's maneuvers made him obnoxious to the old statesman, who criticized his methods and detected "his ambitions."[143]

Conscious of the gigantic task of restoring the damages of the civil war in his country, Concha set his sights high. Philippe suggested an indemnity of $9.8 million and an annuity of $250,000 for transferring the concessions to the United States.

Concha demanded immediate delivery of $7 million in cash, plus an annuity of $600,000. If capitalized at 3 percent, that was about $27 million instead of the maximum sum

Philippe had calculated—$14 million. Nicaragua would have been happy to receive one-fourth of that sum.[144]

Political confusion in Colombia complicated the negotiations. In disagreement with Marroquin, Minister for Foreign Affairs Rafael Uribe resigned, and Miguel Abadia Mendez assumed his duties temporarily. Mendez demanded $20 million from the new company for permission to transfer the concession to Washington. American tenure in the canal zone was to be restricted to ninety-nine years, if possible. Mendez, however, seemed willing either to renegotiate the concession every ninety-nine years or to yield a grant in perpetuity over a zone of ten kilometers on both sides of the waterway. But the majority of the Colombian leaders naively believed the United States was willing to sit and wait for the expiration of the French protocol with Colombia.[145]

Concha's basis for a treaty was Silva's project of January 1902, which Philippe had seen. Colombia consented to the new company's transfer of its property to the United States, to the completion of the canal by the federal government, and to the building of new port cities opposite Colon and Panama City, where police and judicial procedures were to be left in the hands of the Americans. Toll rates were to be regulated by the United States. Colombia was to be nominally responsible for the defense of the waterway, but the Bidlack-Mallarino Treaty's proviso, giving the Americans the right to intervene at the request of Bogota in case of disturbance of public or international order was made part of this draft.[146] Philippe had previously convinced Silva that his objections to the inclusion of Panama City and Colon within the canal zone could be taken care of by giving the United States the right to build administrative towns opposite these urban centers. The only question to be agreed upon at this time was tenure, and the canal commission desired perpetuity.

Concha's problems were aggravated by his lack of experience. Ignoring most of Silva's counsel, he sought the advice of Facundo Mutis Duran, a former governor of Panama who was living in New York. In an incredible comedy of errors, Bogota notified Concha that the government had given some instructions for negotiations to Charles B. Hart, the returning American minister. Concha sàt motionless, waiting in vain for Hart to deliver these guidelines.[147] Instead, as was procedurally correct, the suggestions were handed over to Hay.

Concha's ineptness and confusion once more bestirred Bunau-Varilla to action. In an open cablegram to Jose Gabriel Duque, the director and owner of the *Panama Star & Herald*, he warned the Panamanians:

> Panama is exposed to terrible danger. Every day's delay in the signature of a very generous protocol is a step towards death. Any financial demand of Colombian government, higher than twelve million and a half dollars for all the rights on the Canal and Railroad or its equivalent in annuity at three per cent for totality of part of it is equivalent to a death warrant and signifies triumph of Nicaragua. I consider sums stated above as extreme and already dangerous limits. Urgently advise to demand less. Immediate action is indispensable to avoid irreparable consequences. Communicate my cablegram to all those who desire that Panama should not be killed.[148]

This message brought about the first face-to-face confrontation between Cromwell and Philippe. Cromwell was alarmed. Not knowing the idiosyncrasies of the Colombians or the real conditions in Panama, he was appalled at the prospect of a rebellion against Bogota.

Philippe suspected that his warning was to be shown to the new military governor, Victor Salazar, who would in turn communicate its contents to Bogota. At the same time, Bunau-Varilla sent a copy of the cable to Concha, appealing once more for a decision:

> The people, quite independently of party politics, will, in fact, hold that they have been materially betrayed in their most legitimate hopes. You have attained, at too young an age, Mr. Minister, to the highest positions in the State not to be endowed by Nature with exceptional faculties. . . . In the hope that a clear statement of the danger involved would lead those most interested to make a salutary appeal to Bogota, I sent yesterday, to the Isthmus, the cablegram of which I consider it my duty to remit to you the enclosed copy.[149]

On the same day, the minister answered Philippe, deploring the sending of the communication, but Bunau-Varilla did not despair. He immediately replied:

> New Willard, Washington (D.C.)
> March 27, 1902

To His Excellency, M. Concha,
  Minister of Colombia, Washington.
Mr. Minister,
  I have the honour to receive your letter in answer to mine of this morning.
  Your elevated conception of the Canal question is absolutely just. The real question, the essential point, is not that of money.
  It is in theory truly monstrous, both on the part of the United States as well as on that of Colombia, that a question of such capital importance should be dependent on some millions of dollars more or less.
  The real interest which each of the Republics ought to attach to the idea of the construction of the Canal at Panama is of such paramount importance that it seems foolish to think that the Panama route may be condemned owing to disagreement bearing on a question of such inferior order.
  It is, nevertheless, I repeat, just because of this inferior point that the conception of Panama is going to perish.
  It is a point of very secondary order, a rock in the ocean; but if the ship strikes against it, a catastrophe is certain.
  It is a point of very secondary order, a tie in a railroad track; but let two or three of them be missing in succession, and a catastrophe is certain.
  It is a point of very secondary order, a loose stone on a road. But if it be placed so that the foot of the traveller slips and the man falls into the abyss, a catastrophe is certain.
  We are today placed, after mortal years of efforts and struggles, in the heartrending situation of beholding everything lost, owing to an element of a merely secondary order.
  It seems impossible to believe such a thing, but you know that such is the case, Mr. Minister. You know that the unanimity of popular sentiment is against Panama, and that only the devotion of a few prominent men, who are risking their popularity for the public welfare, can make it victorious.

They are beaten in advance, and consequently will take no trouble about Panama if Colombia may be accused, with any likelihood, of exercising a pressure, which the passion of our opponents will qualify as blackmail. It is, therefore, on that point of secondary order, that the existence of the entire work depends. All the other conditions, infinitely more important for Colombia, are not exposed, as this one is, to the base appreciation of the masses, and will be settled, I am convinced, in the highest spirit of justice and cordiality by the American government, as well as in accordance with the just aspirations of Colombian patriotism.

In this affair, I am seeking only to avenge the genius of France, odiously misappreciated even by France herself.

The triumph of Nicaragua, owing to a paltry difference of some millions between the demands of the Company and the views of the Isthmian Commission, was prevented through my action in Paris, not more than three months ago. I am conscious of having rendered a service to my country in taking the heavy responsibility of recommending the sale for forty million dollars.

To-day for a paltry question of some millions, Colombia is nigh throwing away the most marvelous privilege that Nature gave to any people.

Everything must be attempted to avoid such a terrible disaster.

> Please, I beg you to accept, etc.,
> P. Bunau-Varilla[150]

At last, on March 31, 1902, when Concha presented Hay a draft of a treaty, Cromwell's fears were allayed. This draft was not too different from that presented by Silva except that it fixed American tenure at one hundred years, renewable at the option of the United States for a similar period. It did not say when, but it was understood that it could be at any time. The canal was to be neutral in perpetuity; it excluded Panama City and Colon from this grant, but permitted the federal government to build any towns needed for the maintenance of the waterway. The administration of justice within the canal zone was left to the decision of future conventions. The provisions of the Bidlack-Mallarino Treaty regarding disturbance of the public or international order were continued, and the initial price for the concession was reduced to $7 million. The question of the annuity was to be decided upon later.[151]

Philippe had acted only instants ahead of disaster by coaxing the lethargic Colombian envoy to present his proposals to Hay. A few days later, Bogota, in complete ignorance of the progress of negotiations, sent Concha entirely new directives in which he was told to negotiate only with the French company. His government would reach a direct agreement with Washington. Obviously, the right hand did not know what the left hand was doing. Bogota chose to ignore the fact that the new company had already been authorized to negotiate directly with Hay and that an agreement had already been reached. Concha was exasperated. He asked to be relieved immediately but, by that time, he could not withdraw the draft proposal.[152] Philippe's pleadings with Silva to waive the objections to transference of the canal property to a foreign power and his pressure on Concha had saved the canal again, because an agreement with Nicaragua had been about to be completed.[153] Hopes for Panama were brighter, thanks to the tireless persistence of Bunau-Varilla, but the battlefield seemed ready for new combat.

8

Colombia Spurns a Canal Treaty
and Philippe Plots a Revolution

Negotiations for a Nicaraguan Canal; Walter Reed Fights Disease in Cuba; The Panama Canal Treaty Is Victorious in Congress; Colombia Spurns It; Three Possible Panamanian Revolutions: Plotting the Bunau-Varilla/Loomis Revolution

The American sentiment for Nicaragua was based on reason, not emotion. In 1893, a handsome caudillo overthrew the conservative government of Roberto Sacasa after heavy fighting, and the land of the two lakes settled into a period of social and economic prosperity unparalleled in Central America. Jose Santos Zelaya, its president, was a typical Latin-American leader, competent with the sword, machete, gun, and pen.[1] Thanks to the United States, he had been able to annex the Mosquito territory which Horatio Nelson, while still an unknown navy commander, had attached to England in 1780.[2] When Washington formally told London that "it would not recognize other government but that of Nicaragua [over the Mosquitos]," it settled the dispute in favor of Managua.[3]

By the Treaty of Managua, the Mosquitos were privileged to surrender their rights as a separate people and be merged into the population of Nicaragua on condition that they submit to the laws and constitution of that state. They availed themselves of this privilege by applying to Zelaya for incorporation as a part of the republic. The resolution passed by the few hundred souls left among the Mosquitos incorporated this land as a part of Nicaragua, a decision which Zelaya himself ratified at once.[4] Thus the new strong man began his rule, indebted to and closely associated with the political and diplomatic tides washing the shores of the Potomac. The former domain of the Mosquitos became the Zelaya Department, and the caudillo ruled like Guzman Blanco, Juan Manuel Rosas, Rafael Nunez, or Porfirio Diaz.[5] During this period, Nicaragua made great strides in agriculture, education, and commerce. Railroad construction was promoted, and the cemeteries were secularized. Zelaya was able to generate the climate of law and order so necessary for the existence of an interoceanic canal. In 1895, El Salvador and Honduras were persuaded by Managua to form a tripartite political union.

Although Zelaya was a dynamic leader, Nicaragua, like Colombia, lacked the most elementary conception of international relations. And like Bogota, Managua played down the threat of Panama, the influence of the French lobby put together by Bunau-Varilla, and the driving persistence of the Frenchman himself. Had Philippe worked for Nicaragua, that country would have emerged the winner in the struggle for the American canal.

As the Anglo-American talks aimed at scuttling the Clayton-Bulwer Treaty appeared to be ending, Secretary Hay was frequently host to Senator Morgan who, at seventy-six, feared that death might prevent him from realizing his dream of a Nicaraguan canal. Morgan's obsession with Nicaragua was surpassed only by Philippe's with Panama. And from the very beginning, conversations with Managua were a carbon copy of those with Colombia. Extravagant demands were slowly reduced and, by 1900, the Department of State was able to sign various protocols with the Central Americans relating to canal construction. These documents were vague and uncertain, but Hay regarded the Central Americans as children who, once shown the strength of Panama, would come to him "like beggars—without being called."[6]

Managua's negotiating power was hampered by its ties with the other states, whose constitutions prohibited territorial concessions under any conditions. But Zelaya and his fellow presidents were still willing to grant exclusive rights for a canal zone "in perpetuity." This suggestion was accepted during the negotiations with Washington in 1900, on condition that the various Central-American states changed their constitution and ceded the land in perpetuity.[7] Once the conventions were ratified, the various governments were to be compensated by Washington with annuities and lump sums of money.

A treaty for a waterway necessitated the use of the San Juan River, bordering Costa Rica, but San Jose was unwilling to negotiate until the constitutional changes were completed.[8] Realizing that the final treaty drafts with these recalcitrant clients were as elusive as negotiations with Colombia, Hay, in February 1902, worked out a convention following the guidelines suggested by Zelaya and interpreting the articles of the protocols of 1900. Even though the initial payment for the concession was to be $6 million,[9] Costa Rica wavered, and the secretary's patience was taxed by the Nicaraguan envoy, Gabriel Corea, who was as mercurial as Colombia's Concha. On May 12, 1902, Hay exploded. He wrote to Morgan:

> It is impossible for you, as it would be impossible for anyone, to appreciate the exasperating difficulties that have been placed in my way in trying to get a definite proposition from our Central American friends.[10]

Hay may not have been entirely sold on the Nicaraguan cause, but his relations with Senator Morgan at this time were criticized by senators Hanna and Lodge. On May 14, 1902, while waiting for the final reply from Colombia, Hay wrote to Morgan:

> If you will use the Colombian proposition now it will subject me, and I think justly, to the severe criticism of your colleagues, who have already, as I told you, complained to the

President of my giving you information which is not communicated to the rest of them. This I hope, is the last appeal I shall
make to your forbearance.[11]

On the surface, Henry Cabot Lodge and John Hay were the
best of friends, but temperamentally they were poles apart.
Senator Lodge entreated Roosevelt, when he became president, to keep Hay in his post, but it was clear to everyone that
the relationship among the three men was strained, especially for Hay, who seemed puzzled by the senator's
growing influence on the president.[12] While Morgan was
approaching Hay on behalf of Nicaragua, Lodge was impor-
tuning the president on behalf of Panama. The secretary of
state, frustrated and resentful of the senator's influence,
retaliated by passing to Morgan confidential data about the
canal talks.

In May 1902, Managua presented a formal treaty to Hay
based on the terms agreed upon earlier, and a month later a
separate convention was signed with San Jose, but the
secretary of state was not pleased with these documents
because the Nicaraguan envoy kept insisting that they were
to be amended later.[13] The multiple negotiations conducted by
Hay during the last four years of his office did much to wreck
his already undermined health.[14] The stage was set for
Francis B. Loomis to handle, behind the scenes, the last great
crisis during Hay's tenure of office—the disposition of the
Panama question.

Walter Reed Fights Disease in Cuba

If order was difficult to maintain in the isthmus, improving
public health was no less a problem. Disease was as rooted in
Panama as subversion throughout Colombia. By 1901, a new
wave of paludal maladies had struck in the canal zone,
sending tremors through the ranks of Philippe's friends in
Washington. Suppose Morgan and his allies began to play up
Panama's Achille's heel—epidemics? The threat of volcanic
eruption in Nicaragua was not comparable to that of epidemics in the isthmus. It appeared to Philippe that if Managua's friends were to exploit Panama's disadvantage, he
ought to be prepared to counterattack.

Bunau-Varilla was familiar with the theories of Dr. Carlos Finlay, whom he greatly admired. But Finlay, like Philippe, had been for decades derided by the scientific world. Certainly, the vindication of the Cuban physician's theories would help Philippe's cause. With these thoughts in mind, Bunau-Varilla decided to see for himself what progress the good doctor had made against the mosquitoes. With his brother, he sailed for Cuba in April 1902. Their host was to be Aniceto Menocal, one of the engineers who participated in the Interoceanic Canal Congress of 1879.[15]

In 1867, Dr. Finlay had decided that an outbreak of cholera in Havana was water-borne, but his views were anathema to beliefs of those days and no one dared to publish his treatise. Since 1872, he had concentrated his efforts on demonstrating that the mosquito was the carrier of both malaria and yellow fever, accurately identifying the species that transmitted yellow fever—*Aedes aegypti*,[16] previously named *Stegomyia fasciata*. There are two variants of yellow fever: one is labeled *urban*, which is transmitted from person to person by "sedentary" or city-wise mosquitoes, particularly the *aedes aegypti*. The other is the *jungle* type, which is transmitted to humans by mosquitoes inhabiting the forests. *Aedes aegypti* multiplies rapidly in valleys and harbors in temperatures above 65°F.[17] Havana, Panama City, and Colon were ideal breeding areas for this species, but the last two towns, being close to both water and jungle, had the unenviable distinction of epidemic outbreaks of a large assortment of diseases. In 1897, an epidemic of yellow fever in Cuba killed more than six thousand people and, during the Spanish-American War, yellow fever decimated both camps.[18]

In his long years of research, Dr. Finlay attracted converts, yet in more than one hundred experiments he had not successfully transmitted the disease, and the medical world still believed the malady was the result of bacterial contamination. Several American sanitary commissions had ruled out Finlay's claims, but the Cubans, like Bunau-Varilla, believed in him.[19] In 1900, an American physician, Walter Reed, arrived in Havana as head of still another sanitary commission, ostensibly to put an end to Finlay's claims. Dr.

Reed and his colleagues, J. Carroll, J. W. Lazear, and Antonio Agramonte, decided to test the theory of bacterial contamination personally, both directly and indirectly. They slept in beds with contaminated patients, ate their food, wore their dress, and closely studied urine and excreta of patients.[20] Although Dr. Lazear died of yellow fever, Finlay's theory had not been disproved.

Obviously, there was something wrong, perhaps not in Finlay's experimental method, but in the nature or duration of his tests. Reed decided to try Finlay's method, but held the mosquitoes longer. He succeeded. The reason for the delay in proving Finlay's theory was that no one had guessed that the agent causing the disease is a virus so small that the microscopes of those days could not detect it. No one considered the possibility that the virus, once in the mosquito, was undetectable during what is called today the "eclipse." Since the mosquito does not digest all of the virus, part of it multiplies in the walls of its stomach. During this gestation interval, the virus cannot be detected. After a period of time, which is influenced by outside temperatures, the virus penetrates the salivary glands of the mosquito. Thus the insect becomes infective. Not even when the virus has multiplied in the insect can it be seen under ordinary microscopes. But once infected, the mosquito remains a deadly carrier for the rest of its life.[21] It is believed that as many as eighteen days are needed to complete the cycle. Dr. Finlay's error was in not keeping his insects longer, and in believing that the *Stegomyia* collected an agent in one human's blood and transmitted it to another. But where does the virus come from? Again, we must go back to the prince of medicine, Hippocrates, who suspected that cesspools, lakes, foul water, bad air, and dirt in general were responsible for the periodic epidemics with which he had to cope in his day.[22]

Once the criminal was found, its elimination followed. That was the job assigned to another American physician, William Crawford Gorgas. The extinction of the mosquito demanded the isolation of the patient, the fumigation of the house, of the neighbor's house, and eventually of the whole town. After the contaminated house was sealed, rolled sulphur, at the rate of a pound to a thousand cubic feet of space, was burned in a Dutch oven placed in a vessel of water or in a box containing sand, to prevent fires. The sulphur fumes, however, damaged fixtures and fabrics; moreover, fumigation with sulphur was expensive. When the landlord was not wealthy, pyrethrum (a variety of chrysanthemum used as an insecticide) was burned, and a "mixture of camphor and carbolic acid" (one part camphor to three parts of carbolic acid) was used. This method took time, because not all the mosquitoes died. Many of them, momentarily paralyzed, later recovered their normal strength, in which case they had to be gathered while they were still intoxicated, and burned.[23]

The difficulty of eliminating yellow fever this way, especially when the armies recruited for the crusade were largely ignorant, can be better imagined than described. When Philippe and his brother arrived in Cuba, Gorgas was engaged in full battle with the mosquitoes. Menocal took Philippe to the marshal's tent, and Commander Gorgas said to him:

> "I hope soon to go and apply the same method in Nicaragua for the construction of the canal."
>
> "Major," replied Philippe, "I am sorry to say such a thing to you, but you will never apply your method in Nicaragua."
>
> "Why?" inquired Gorgas.
>
> "Because Nicaragua will never see the construction of the canal. . . . But reassure yourself, you will rid the isthmus of its plagues, as you have done in Havana."[24]

Later, while undertaking the prophesied job, Gorgas remembered Bunau-Varilla's words.[25]

The Battle in the Senate Committee

Bunau-Varilla returned to Washington from Cuba in early May 1902, and immediately began to act as an unofficial assistant to Senator Hanna. At his suite at the New Willard Hotel or at the senator's apartment in the Arlington Hotel, Philippe prepared charts, data, and estimates to be used by Hanna in the coming Senate debate on the canal. On week-ends he traveled to the Waldorf-Astoria hotel in New York, where he entertained newspapermen and potential witnesses while enjoying the company of his friend John Bigelow, whose house was the center of much pro-Panama activity.[26]

In Havana, Philippe had interviewed many sea captains who knew the Panama route and had made appointments for them to sign affidavits on behalf of Panama at Attorney Cromwell's New York office. These statements were given to Hanna. Philippe also supplied the senator with scientific literature on the subject of vulcanology and canals, and with information about the progress of the war against tropical diseases in Cuba. Hanna was fascinated by science, and he listened attentively. The senator was a gregarious man who seldom ate alone. His house in Cleveland and his apartment in Washington were always full of guests for breakfast or supper,[27] occasions on which he made converts to his new scheme. Hanna's method of work was very much like Philippe's. In order to make his own opinions prevail, he had to be an authority on the issue. Although the senator was dealing with technicalities foreign to him, he was intellectually equipped to grasp them. Not an engineer like Philippe, Hanna was enthusiastic about the opportunity to become an expert in a discipline totally alien to his own.[28]

The battle began in a committee room, the same setting in which the contest had been fought and lost in France. Hanna, coached by Philippe, minutely questioned the witnesses, especially the engineers on the canal commission. He wanted them to make a choice based on engineering grounds. Most of those interrogated favored Panama. Hanna knew that he could not convince the committee, on which Morgan had a majority, but he hoped to swing the Senate to his side on the final vote.[29]

As time for the debate approached, Philippe intensified his behind-the-scenes activity. On May 6, 1902, nature swung decisively to his side. Mount Pelée erupted in Martinique and destroyed the town of Saint-Pierre, leaving thousands dead. Losing no time, Philippe drew a parallel between Nicaragua and Martinique: he sent to every senator, and to President Roosevelt, clippings from the *Evening Post* and the brochure containing the lectures he delivered in 1901. The *Post* had published a comparison between the Lesser Antilles and the Greater Antilles, to the effect that the latter, unlike the former, showed no evidence of subterranean fire. Philippe had made a similar study of Nicaragua and Panama.[30] Senator Hanna asked Philippe for his charts and statistics, and Bunau-Varilla printed *Comparative Characteristics of Panama and Nicaragua* and brought the copies to the Senate for distribution during Hanna's speech.

Philippe's treatise was divided into various categories, illustrated with drawings and with an abundance of data: excavation—Nicaragua, 227,711,605 cubic yards, Panama, 94,863,703 cubic yards; quantity of steel—Nicaragua, 40,500 tons, Panama, 32,624 tons; depth of the cut—Nicaragua, 297 feet, Panama 103 feet (Culebra); cost of maintenance and operation—Nicaragua, 141.88 miles, Panama, 42.09 miles; canal navigation in the shallow area of Lake Nicaragua and Lake Bohio at Panama—Nicaragua, 49.29 miles, Panama, 22.85 miles; curvature and radius—Nicaragua's curvature, 2,339°50′ and average radius, 6,400 feet, Panama's curvature, 771°39′ and average radius, 9,000 feet; sharpest curve outside of lakes and harbors—Nicaragua, 4,045 feet, Panama, 8,202; actual time of sailing, not counting natural delays—Nicaragua, 33 hours, Panama, 12 hours; average crossing of the strait—Nicaragua, 64 hours 30 minutes, Panama, 21 hours; rainfall—Nicaragua, 265 inches annually, Panama (at Colon), 129 inches annually.[31]

Bunau-Varilla estimated that the cost of maintenance would be $130 million less in Panama. Computed at the usual rate of interest for U.S. bonds, it represented a capital saving of $65 million. The cost of construction for Panama being $5 million less, the total saving was $70 million when the capitalized value of operation was taken into account. Philippe also called attention to the importance of the curvature of the canal because, while the ships navigated these areas, their steering faculties were reduced by two-thirds. Consequently, the curves had to be as flat as possible or, in other words, have a very large radius. The abnormal curvatures of the Nicaraguan route were complicated by their sharpness, a fact that Philippe diagrammed in his sketches. The danger of navigation, according to these drawings, increased as the ships traversed the Nicaraguan waterway, but there was no zig-zag navigation in Panama.[32]

Bunau-Varilla, not satisfied to present only his own findings, added statements by other engineers such as George Morison, who testified before the Senate's canal subcommittee that another great obstacle at Nicaragua was night transit. According to Morison, navigation in the dark was not possible in Nicaragua because the large curves and floodless waters would not permit it. Transit had to be stopped between sunset and daylight. Morison asserted that the same objections did not apply to Panama. But even if they did, the waiting period for daylight would be longer in Nicaragua than in Panama because ships traversing the Nicaraguan canal would have to wait outside the route thirty-three hours.[33]

These points were explained by diagrams and charts in a simple but eloquent manner. Although Bunau-Varilla had learned English in college, he had had little opportunity to use the language extensively in writing until he translated his 1892 book. He wrote remarkably well, expounding difficult scientific ideas with elegance. All his writing about the canal at this time was scholarly and to the point, and his erudition was salted with worldliness and wit.

The trade winds, which during most of the year are very strong in Central America and the Caribbean, were shown to blow directly in the direction of Nicaragua. The message was clear: the winds would disturb navigation and throw ships on the rocks. At Panama, the canal was to be at right angles to the direction of the trade winds and shielded from them by mountains.

Last, there was the matter of rain. Since 1888, the isthmus had not experienced the deluges that Krakatoa had generated in 1883, but rain seemed to be eternally antagonistic to

Nicaragua. No mention was made of the typhoon-like inundations that plagued Panama in 1885 and 1886, or in 1888, when Philippe almost lost his life.[34] Nor was disease mentioned. Each page of the prospectus was a dart at Nicaragua. Since much of the brochure quoted figures from the Isthmian Canal Commission, Bunau-Varilla could not be accused of inventing. Hanna read the pamphlet on June 1, 1902, and toasted Philippe in his apartment with a glass of punch.[35] The next day, Hanna distributed the treatise to every senator.

Debate on the Senate Floor

The Senate's debate on the canal began on June 4, 1902, and lasted seventeen days. After permitting Panama's enemies to indulge in oratory, and following a pre-arranged signal from Hanna, Senator John C. Spooner offered an amendment to the Hepburn Bill which left nothing of the House measure except its enacting clause. It directed the president to purchase the franchise and the French installations for no more than $40 million; to secure by treaty with Colombia a canal zone; and then to build the canal. The executive branch was authorized to re-examine the Nicaraguan route if it was unable to reach a satisfactory bargain with Colombia or acquire the French property.[36] The amendment threw the Nicaraguan supporters into disarray, placing them on the defensive.

Philippe had anticipated the possible charges against his canal. A few days before the senatorial debate began, he met, at Bigelow's, the owner and the editor-in-chief of the *New York Sun*, Francis Dana and Edward P. Mitchell. After four hours of conversation, the two publicists fell under Bunau-Varilla's spell, and their newspaper embraced Panama's cause.[37]

Following this meeting, the *Sun* said editorially that Nicaragua's most pronounced liability was her beautiful volcanoes, especially Conseguina which, in the eruption of 1844, had wrought great damage as far as one hundred fifty miles from its epicenter. Nicaraguan volcanoes had always been in the forefront of seismology and had been surpassed only once, in 1883, by the mighty Krakatoa. Nothing similar could be feared in Panama, where there was no volcano, active or inactive, within one hundred eighty miles of the projected canal zone.[38]

Nature smiled again on Philippe on May 13, when Momotombo erupted in Nicaragua, and the witty Mitchell chided Morgan in the pages of the *Sun*:

> His great voice has uttered a warning of incalculable value to the United States. "Here is," wrote the eminent journalist, "what it said": "My compliments to Senator Morgan. I beg leave to inform that gentleman, and others whom it may concern, that I am not only alive but am capable of sending down, without notice, through Lake Managua and the Tipitapa River into the adjacent Lake Nicaragua, a tidal wave of sufficient volume and malignity to overwhelm any canal that engineering skill can construct through this country, and to wipe out every dollar of the two or three hundred millions which the United States Government may be foolish enough to invest within the reach of the waters subject to my power. Precisely the same thing can be done with equal facility, and on equally short notice, by my neighbors and allies, Pilas, Nindiri, Zelica, Santa Clara, Oros, Isla Venada, Fernando, Macaron, Zapatera, Mancaroncita, Madera, Omotepe, and the Hell of Masayany, one of them or all combined."[39]

Undismayed by the Spooner Amendment or the recent evidence of seismic activity in Nicaragua, the energetic Morgan opened up his attack on Panama, following precisely the strategy anticipated by Bunau-Varilla. Morgan's speech was not to be dismissed as a mere exercise in rhetoric. He concentrated on Colombia's chief liabilities—political unrest and pandemia. He also pointed out the weakness of the Colombian protocol prepared by Concha, and he questioned the legality of the Bogota regime led by Manuel Marroquin. He even accused the isthmus of having seismic tremblors.[40]

On June 5 and 6, Hanna made an important speech in favor of the Spooner Amendment. Oratorically he was well prepared, but he had written not a word except a short outline consisting of page numbers of reports and data furnished by Philippe. His secretary sat behind him with all the literature the speaker intended to use. The senator spoke calmly, as if he were talking individually to each of his colleagues. But after he had been on the floor over an hour, Bunau-Varilla began to fear Hanna's collapse. The senator had not been well and his health seemed to have taken a turn for the worse in recent weeks. Afflicted by typhus in early life, Hanna had traveled to Europe for a cure of the swelling of the knee joints, but his disregard of medical treatment hampered his recovery.[41] After two hours, his knees gave out. Again, Bunau-Varilla's victory seemed so near and then, once more, the threat of death hung over his most powerful sponsor.

But the next day, experiencing acute pain, Hanna rose again and concluded his speech with a short argument. It was followed by a bitter attack on Panama by Senator John H. Mitchell of Oregon, who gave eleven eloquent reasons why the Nicaraguan route should be chosen:

> [Panama] is a sewer. It is the certainty of moral defilement. It cannot be touched without the certainty of deadly moral infection. All the waters of the multitudinous seas cannot wash Panama clean. It is simply too rotten to be looked at without nausea. Panama cannot be touched with safety by the American people. It must be shunned as a place incurably affected with the most deadly plagues. It is a dung-heap of crime. It is a perpetual monument to human credulity and human villainy. It is a sink of iniquity wherein no nation can delve without certainty of irremediable pollution.[42]

This tirade indicated that the rational arguments in support of Nicaragua had evaporated. Imaginatively, Senator Mitchell had personified the Panama route, an inanimate strip of land devoid of moral qualities, as a hateful and vile creature. But passions were so intense that most of the Nicaraguan lobby applauded him. The *Washington Star* lampooned Hanna with cartoons portraying the senator as a madman drawing volcanoes.[43] It was, however, under such highly emotional conditions that Philippe was most rational.

The Testimony of the Nicaraguan Stamps

For some time, Philippe had thought that he might have to present visual evidence of Nicaraguan volcano activity to the Senate. There was no possibility of taking the senators to Nicaragua, but if they could not go to the mountain, Philippe was ready to bring the mountain to them. Not wishing to arouse suspicion, and accompanied by his child Giselle, he visited every stamp dealer in Washington and bought ninety stamps depicting Momotombo in majestic eruption. Bunau-Varilla placed each stamp on a sheet of paper and wrote: "Postage Stamps of the Republic of Nicaragua." Below the stamp was written: "An official witness of the volcanic activity on Nicaragua." On June 16, Hanna had one of these sheets on every senator's desk.[44]

The reaction was instantaneous. Several uncommitted senators, such as Jacob H. Gallinger, asked the Senate if it was reasonable to undertake the colossal task of building an interoceanic canal in a country which had taken a volcano in eruption as its emblem on its postage stamps. But Morgan and his majority were not to be moved. Morgan appealed to the Managuan envoy, who requested an official denial of volcanic activity from Santos Zelaya, and the president complied: "News published about recent eruptions of volcanoes in Nicaragua is entirely false."[45] Encouraged, Morgan, repeating charges of intrusion on the duties of the canal committee, attacked Cromwell. The attorney's presence had become conspicuously annoying to the partisans of Nicaragua and even to the Colombian legation.[46] Actually, Cromwell was confusing both sides.

Senator Hanna Turns the Tide

Sensing that the battle had not yet been won, Hanna took the floor on June 18 and made a last appeal on behalf of Panama. His words were remarkably effective. He repeated the advice of the engineers and the ship masters. His words, in contrast to the tirades of the enemies of Panama, were cool and candid. Because of the expert advice he had received, Hanna approached the problem without passion.

When Hanna finished, many of his colleagues rushed to his side to congratulate him. Hundreds of copies of the speech were requested. Senator Orville Platt stated that it was the most effective oration which had been delivered in the Senate during his incumbency. The Spooner Amendment was approved on June 19 by eight votes—forty-two to thirty-six with twelve abstentions. It was clear that Hanna's speech, so admirably delivered and so well documented, made converts of nonbelievers and doubters. Herbert Croly, in his biography of Hanna, states that "The incident constituted the most conspicuous single illustration of Senator Hanna's personal prestige."[47] It was the culmination of a long and successful career in politics and industry which marked the Ohioan as a statesman and a patriot. The final vote stood at sixty-seven to six, which meant that, after being defeated, the legislators in favor of Nicaragua did not want to go on record against an interoceanic canal.

After the passage of the Spooner Amendment, Philippe sent to his newspaper, Le Matin, the following message:

> Washington, June 19. After fifteen days of desperate struggle the majority of the Senate, answering the call of Truth and Science rather than that of popular prejudices half a century old, has adopted the Panama route, the French project, in preference to the Nicaraguan route, the American project.
>
> This memorable victory of French genius, unappreciated and proscribed by France, is the everlasting condemnation of the calumniators who have poisoned public opinion and thus excited a blind and criminal ostracism against the glorious conception of Panama. P. Bunau-Varilla.[48]

The American press gave wide coverage to this cable, and the Times of London, as it had Ferdinand de Lesseps many years earlier,[49] praised Philippe as the "ablest of French civil engineers" but warned him of still more battles to be fought before the war was over.[50] The amendment had to go through the House of Representatives first and then fulfill the two conditions attached to the preference for Panama—acquisition of the French company's property and negotiation of a treaty with Colombia.

The caution conveyed to Philippe by the London *Times* was shared by Bigelow and Asher Baker, who still feared Senator Morgan. Despite the victory in the Senate, the rumor persisted that Roosevelt and Hay were not totally committed to the idea of Panama. The *Tribune*'s silence was interpreted as ominous. Reid's newspaper had not attacked Panama, but it had not defended it lately. Was this neutrality due to deference to John Hay or to the approaching presidential election of 1904? It was speculated that Marcus Hanna might challenge Roosevelt for the nomination.[51]

Victory in the House of Representatives

Experience had trained Philippe to overcome all obstacles for the cause of Panama. Knowing that there was much Morgan-inspired opposition in the House of Representatives, Bunau-Varilla went to New York with his child Giselle to purchase five hundred of the Nicaraguan stamps depicting smoky volcanoes. A few days later, every Congressman found on his desk a sheet of paper with the stamp in the middle, and the necessary explanations printed above and below it. On June 25, 1902, the House committee abandoned the Hepburn Bill and made way for the Spooner Amendment. Two days later, the full House Chamber accepted the Spooner Amendment by a vote of 260 to 8. On June 29, Roosevelt signed the document into law.[52]

Philippe was the recipient of many congratulatory messages. One from Myron T. Herrick:

> Cleveland, Ohio, July 12, 1902
> Your success in Washington gave us great delight. We spent the 4th of July at the Hannas' and you were mentioned many times. Senator Hanna is, of course, greatly pleased with your success, and spoke in the highest terms of you.[53]

And Jose Vicente Concha's congratulation said:

> Washington, June 19, 1902
> I remain very grateful to you for the important work that you have accomplished. It is beyond doubt that in the result of today much is due to your effort. I congratulate you on it.[54]

Title to the new company's property was acquired by the federal government shortly after a lawyer from the Department of Justice, Charles W. Russell, researched its archives in Paris. On October 25, 1902, Philander C. Knox, the attorney general, endorsed the Russell findings.[55] Another obstacle had been overcome.

The "man [with] a plan for a canal in Panama" had accomplished a miracle, and it was because of his well-planned strategy. First, Philippe had transmitted his ideas and expertise about the waterway to the engineers on the canal commission, and they had inserted these conceptions and data in their official report of January 1902 as if they were their own. Second, Bunau-Varilla presented these opinions to Hanna for delivery to the Senate as the doctrine and beliefs of a variety of experts, including those on the commission. Not one of Morgan's supporters detected the stratagem. The Alabama senator was much too busy attacking Panama to perceive Philippe's well-contrived maneuver.

Nevertheless, sentiment continued to be positively and aggressively against Panama. The consensus was that the president would have to fall back on Nicaragua in the end. In a flippant mood, the *New York Press,* one of the mouthpieces of the Nicaraguan lobby, assured its readers that the canal at Panama was never going to be completed.[56] The *Press* was very nearly correct.

Negotiations with a Colombia Wracked by Civil War

Negotiations between the Colombian legation and Hay had not progressed markedly since Concha's memorandum to the Department of State in April 1902, but on July 1 Roosevelt ordered Hay "to take personal direction" of the negotiations, and four days later Cromwell submitted a redraft of the early proposal in Concha's name.[57] It appeared at this time that the envoy was rapidly losing all desire to continue negotiations. The minister was connected to the "generation of '98," those who wept for the defeat of Spain in the Spanish-American War. Concha felt too much of the heat generated by the American power structure and press, now enjoying the halo of Manifest Destiny, and his residence in Washington was a traumatic experience.[58]

Hay still thought that a good treaty could be negotiated and, on July 13, 1902, the secretary sent Concha a new draft incorporating the amendments desired by various senators.[59] The envoy was now convinced that his country could not resist the American demands for control of the canal zone in perpetuity, and he began a series of cable exchanges with the foreign office and with President Marroquin, ending in late August, when Bogota instructed Concha to accept the amendments but to state that the final word on the treaty belonged to the Colombian Senate. The minister's frustrations surfaced on September 18, 1902, when American marines landed at Colon to keep traffic open on the railroad.

The arrival of the soldiers was not unusual. They had landed many times before under similar circumstances, but now Bogota silently acquiesced to their presence. Concha exploded in rage. He protested the landings and addressed himself to Hay and to the home office:

> The chief of the American forces has assumed executive power in the isthmus, which is not in the hands of the rebels [Liberals]. Colombian troops are disarmed by the United States and are guarded by them. The governor is in custody and the American commander has informed the government and the rebels that he will not permit [fighting]. Last, the minister in Washington [Concha], when he asks for the necessary information to formulate an official protest according to the canons of international law, is silenced by the chief executive of Colombia and his foreign minister.[60]

At that moment, Concha developed an intense aversion to the covenant proposals and to Hay, whom he considered a hard bargainer. Concha soon departed for home in ill health, leaving the legation's secretary, Tomas Herran, in charge. Meanwhile, Admiral Silas Casey arrived in Colon on the warship *Wisconsin* to talk with government officials. The civil war ended two days later with a treaty which spared the lives of the rebels and declared a general amnesty throughout Colombia.[61]

Although Concha's departure may have been dictated by his own somber mood, it is reported that Secretary Hay asked Bogota to recall him.[62] However, Philippe wrote to Marroquin:

Marroquin, President of Republic, Bogota:
. . . Either the final selection of Nicaragua as the Spooner Law orders; or the loss of all the results obtained and indefinite postponement if everything is not voted and settled; or the development of international events of the gravest order, from which might result that the Canal be made at Panama against Colombia instead of being made with her amicably. The only hope is in a decisive radical action of the Supreme Government of the Republic. P. Bunau-Varilla.[63]

By his own choice, Minister Concha's incumbency came to an end. The establishment in Colombia, like a committee in the American university system, made decisions without explaining to anyone. Deeply hurt by his government and by Hay's prodding, the envoy understood his own position very well but overlooked the problems of the secretary of state.[64] Concha's political survival required that he should have some breathing room on his return to Bogota, and that he be able to criticize President Marroquin. On the other hand, John Hay needed to subdue the anxieties of both friends and foes of Panama in the Senate.

Following his own timetable, Bunau-Varilla entreated the newly appointed chargé d'affaires, Herran, to seek a quick solution to the impasse. In the beginning, Herran proved more conciliatory than his predecessor, but the thorny question of money eventually reached crisis proportions. Hay, ably seconded by Francis Loomis, decided not to offer Colombia more than $10 million. It must be remembered that Nicaragua had asked for only $7 million as the total indemnity and $10,000 more as the annual payment. Philippe persuaded the Americans to raise the amount of the annuity to $100,000, but Colombia demanded $500,000. It seemed that the more given, the more was requested. Finally, Bunau-Varilla "shrewdly guessed that the American government would agree to $250,000 to make sure of the other articles."[65] This was the maximum that Philippe had recommended to Concha in April. Under mounting pressure from Bunau-Varilla, Herran agreed to these terms but, in order to insure approval, Philippe cabled Marroquin:

> Marroquin, President of Republic, Bogota:
> Situation improved by removal of diplomatic representative. Colombia is exposed to new and grave perils, on the question of annual rental.
> Though the Government here thinks to have reached the maximum with $10 million cash and annual rental of $100,000, I believe that a firm decision of the Colombian Government to accept $10 million plus annual rental of $250,000 would have much chance of saving the situation if the offer of signing immediately the Panama Canal Treaty accompanies the said proposition. P. Bunau-Varilla.[66]

After reporting to Hanna, Philippe sailed for home, spending Christmas at sea. On January 21, 1903, a day before the Herran-Hay Treaty was signed, he became anxious about the convention's fate and took a ship back to America. On this trip he again met Pedro Nel Ospina, who was about to become vice-president of the Colombian Senate.[67] Ospina's ideas about the canal were typical of Bogota's attitude, in that he detested dealing with problems and loved to avoid them. Philippe pleaded with him to exert his influence at Bogota in favor of the treaty, but the Frenchman's words were as popular in Colombia as a Baptist preacher's in a Las Vegas casino.

Senatorial debate in Washington lasted until March 17, 1903, and Morgan filibustered against the treaty during most of the session. The senator attacked the document, the Colombians, and the isthmians with gusto. He called attention to Bogota's close ties with the Vatican, to the filthiness of the canal zone, and to the degradation of the people, whom he called "stupid" and "slothful." Again, Cromwell became the whipping boy, portrayed now as an agent of the railroads. Morgan suggested numerous amendments to the convention, including reducing the indemnity to $7 million and eliminating the rent.[68] But there were no amendments, and the protocol was approved seventy-three to five, with twelve abstentions. Philippe returned to France to await ratification.

Prior to the debate, Nicaragua, urged by Morgan, had accelerated negotiations and was reported ready to grant any terms including perpetuity, within a large canal zone.[69] Colombia's reaction to the treaty demonstrated ignorance of these moves as well as contempt for Panama. The newly elected Colombian Senate was called into session in late June 1903, and most of the enemies of the canal were now entrenched in the chamber. On June 13, Bunau-Varilla cabled Marroquin once more:

Marroquin, President Republic, Bogota.

Beg to submit respectfully following: (1) One must admit as a fundamental principle that the only party that can now build the Panama Canal is the United States and that neither European Governments nor private financiers would dare to fight either against the Monroe Doctrine or the American Treasury for building Panama Canal, in case Americans return to Nicaragua, if Colombian Congress does not ratify Treaty. (2) It results from this evident principle that failure of ratification opens two ways: Either construction of Nicaragua Canal and absolute loss to Colombia of the incalculable advantages resulting from construction on her territory the great artery of universal commerce, or construction of the Panama Canal after secession and declaration of independence of the Isthmus of Panama under protection of the United States as has happened with Cuba.[70]

Colombia Spurns the Canal Treaty

Marroquin never believed these words. Philippe compared the president's position to Pontius Pilate's. In his address to Congress, Marroquin pointed out that the net result of the treaty was of tremendous importance for Colombia. Industry and commerce were to gain much from ratification. But, the chief executive expressed relief that the final decision was not his. "It is not my intention to allow my opinion to weigh in this matter."[71] The human termites were now free to undermine the structure Bunau-Varilla had built so laboriously. Old war-horse Jose Joaquin Velez thundered from the pages of *Nuevo Tiempo*, proclaiming that the construction of the canal was a violation of the fatherland's sovereignty. If it was not to be a native canal, it should not be built.[72] The affairs of men had to wait until Colombia rid herself of subversion—which, in geological parlance, meant until the Andes melted away. Like sharks scenting blood, the Colombian Senate sprang to life. A well-organized campaign in the press began to hint at ludicrous accommodations which were later formalized by the politicians. The twenty-four senators[73] referred the treaty to a committee of their own while proposals multiplied.

La Revista Blanca, El Sumapaz, and *Autonomista (White Review, Peace,* and *Autonomous)* competed in the search for new schemes. Without the slightest sign of embarrassment, these journals suggested that if the isthmus were to secede and join the United States, Colombia should sell it to the federal government at a good profit:

> [We] suggest the granting of sovereign power to the United States over the canal at both entrances in the Atlantic and Pacific oceans. . . . They will be our allies and they shall give us $100 million which we will invest as follows: $20 million to pay the foreign debt, $30 million to redeem the fiat money in circulation and $50 million for the construction by France or the United States of a railroad from Puerto Colombia to Bogota.[74]

The *Autonomista* of May 12, 1903, echoing the rumors of juntas and "annexation calls," reported the existence of a widespread feeling for uniting Panama to the "Northern Republic."[75] Evidence of the collective greed was Nicolas Esguerra's suggestion for renewal of the French company's grant. Colombia was to receive $10 million for this privilege, $2 million in 1904, 1905, 1906, 1907, and 1908, plus the cost of sanitation in Panama City and Colon.[76] So great was the ignorance that Esguerra found widespread public support for an *aide-memoire* to the government in which the following premises were advanced:

1. Nicaragua is inferior to Panama, territorially and econom-
   ically.
2. Americans are good businessmen and they will not enter
   into a bad deal [Nicaragua] if a better one is in view.
3. The Central-Americans will never accept conditions which
   we refuse.
4. Our isthmus has a permanent value which cannot be
   diminished by the failure of the new company or the
   refusal of the United States.[77]

In such an atmosphere, not only money, but reason itself
was devalued and debased. Large expenditures of public
funds, both for counter-revolutionary activities and graft,
increased the national debt monthly, and for a time the
regime looked to Washington for a loan which never came.
There was a brief moment of hope when the Colombian
senators expected the United States Senate to reject the
Herran-Hay convention just as it had refused to grant cash
advances to Bogota. President Marroquin publicly thanked
God for that denial, reasoning that had his government
received the requested loan, Bogota would not be able to
oppose the Americans' demands.[78] Nationalistic sentiment
cried out for an all-native canal: "The canal should not be
opened through our land no matter how empty the treasury
and how large the sum offered for our sovereignty." Colombia herself would someday finish the canal:

The nationalists studied the Constitution of 1886 and the
laws subsequently passed. Notwithstanding the authority
granted the president to deal with disruption of public order,
"Sanclemente had no right to authorize the extension of the
French concession beyond 1904." They found that even the
law of May 25, 1888, which gave the executive sweeping
powers to control subversion and execute rebels, conduct
radical administrative reforms, and re-orient the economy,
did not entrust the president with treaty-making powers. If
the treaty were approved, Colombia would nullify the French
grant.[79]

Shortly after this public debate, the Senate committee,
backed by such influential citizens as Pedro Nel Ospina and

Rafael Reyes, unveiled its plan to confiscate the French company's property after October 31, 1904:

> By the 31st of October of next year, that is to say when the next Congress shall have met in ordinary session, the concession will have expired and every privilege with it.[80]

The prospect of Colombia's acquiring, by forfeiture, the assets of the French company appalled the Americans. Hay, who held very rigid convictions about property rights, was disgusted. Roosevelt, Lodge, Hanna, and Hay searched the dictionary for suitable epithets to apply to the Colombian politicians. The president called them "homicidal corruptionists" and "contemptible creatures," and Hay labeled them "greedy little anthropoids."[81]

Philippe was kept informed of the separatist hopes of the Panamanians, whom he secretly encouraged from Paris.[82] Since 1899, isthmian citizens had become outspoken in their demands for a quick solution to the canal problem. Men such as Jose Agustin Arango, Jeronimo de la Ossa, Gerardo Ortega, Emilio Briceno, and Francisco Ardila wrote columns in *El Cronista* (*The Chronicler*), *El Lapis* (*The Pencil*), the *Isthmian*, *El Duende* (*The Gnome*), *El Aspirante* (*The Suitor*), and *La Verdad de Colon* (*The Colon Truth*).

Nicolas Esguerra, a member of a commission which had gone to Panama to study the canal works, wrote home:

> Our Isthmus is not like the other Departments of the Republic. Those who set foot on this part of the nation from the interior of the country feel immediately like foreigners.[83]

The commission felt that the Panamanians were frustrated by Colombia.

Many liberals, who had lost the recent civil war, also had access to these media, but expressed their feelings differently. By politicizing the treaty, they sought to subvert the central government. The liberal list included Dr. Carlos A. Mendoza, Rodolfo Aguilera, Simon Rivas, Jose C. Argote, Edmundo Botello, Federico Escobar, and Dr. Joaquin P. Franco, who satirized Tomas Herran with the following "sonnet."

If I could catch
the troublemakers and
Herran [I]
will punish their designs
Cutting them into a
Canal.[84]

The verse is indicative of the ignorance in which isthmian youth was kept. The gravity and importance of the negotiations escaped these men. Unwittingly, they almost caused, if not the abortion of the revolution, perhaps much bloodshed. In May 1903, in violation of the Treaty of Wisconsin, the government executed Victoriano Lorenzo, an Indian caudillo who had fought with the liberals. Criticism of this crime in the press was countered by temporary military rule in the isthmus. The commanding general of the province, General Jose Vasquez Cobo, dismissed the civilian governor and assumed his duties. Several newspapers were invaded and the writers mauled. Prominent citizens were incarcerated but, thanks to the intervention of the Bishop of Panama on July 26, 1903, Cobo relented and allowed the return of civilian rule. One of the men beaten by the soldiers later died, and the governor telegraphed Bogota: "The garrison is demoralized. Military scandals hurt our canal postures. Please punish the culprits."[85]

Had the general not rescinded his orders or had he remained in power longer, the revolutionaries might not have been so lucky and heavy casualties might have occurred. Despite the return of the legal regime, surveillance of those suspected of treasonable designs was tightened and, in October when Amador traveled to Washington, his movements were an open book.

On August 12, 1903, Senator Miguel Antonio Caro morbidly explained, before the final vote in the Senate, that the delay in its decision was due to a misunderstanding concerning how to "embalm" the "dead" treaty.[86] What the legislators did not comprehend was that they were killing Colombia, not Panama. The Colombian senators, in order to allay the canal company's fears, reported to the French press that the validity of the concession's extension had never been doubted by Bogota.[87]

The duplicity of the Colombian lawmakers energized Philippe. Instead of the victory he hoped for, he saw Panama advancing toward the abyss. The possibility of revolution had never left Bunau-Varilla's mind, and throughout the summer he had discussed this idea with his house guest, John Bigelow, who had considered that very subject before leaving for France with Francis B. Loomis. Like Caesar at the Rubicon, Philippe had no choice but to plot to circumvent the inefficient bureaucracy entrenched at Bogota.

Meanwhile Hay, to cushion the blow of rejection, brought the Nicaraguan alternative to the president's attention:

> You will, before Congress meets, make up your mind which of the two courses you will take . . . the simple and easy Nicaraguan solution, or the far more difficult and multifurcate scheme, of building the Panama Canal *malgré* Bogota.[88]

Plotting Three Possible Revolutions for Panama

Loomis' reports concerning the possibility of rebellion were much too pressing to ignore, and Secretary of State Hay also ventured to broach that subject in writing to President Roosevelt:

> There is a question whether we ought:
> 1. To save time and . . . say to the Colombians that we will not for a moment consider the propositions they are now discussing; or
> 2. Say nothing and let them go on making fools of themselves until you are ready to act on some other basis. . . . It is altogether likely that there will be an insurrection on the Isthmus against the regime of folly and graft that now rules at Bogota. It is for you to decide whether you will (1) await the result of that movement, or (2) take hand in rescuing the Isthmus from anarchy, or (3) treat with Nicaragua. Something we shall be forced to do in the case of a serious insurrectionary movement in Panama, to keep the transit clear. Our intervention should not be at haphazard, nor this time should it be to the profit, as heretofore, of Bogota.[89]

Hay ended his memorandum by suggesting that the president wait two or three weeks to see what happened.

And from Paris, after a night at the opera with friends of Philippe, Henry Cabot Lodge wrote to Roosevelt:

> At this distance it is hard to form an opinion on the canal business, but I do hope that we shall not go to Nicaragua. While the thing is pending, you are not bound to take any action, and when Congress comes together, we will introduce a bill, if thought best, to modify the mandatory clause, and whether it passes or not, that will enable you to take your time. I am in strong hopes that either under the Treaty of '46, or by the secession of the Province of Panama, we can get control of what is undoubtedly the best route.[90]

Earlier suggestions by Senator Shelby Cullom of Illinois also gained momentum: that the federal government pay no attention to Colombia, finalize the purchase of the French works, and open the waterway under the justification of "universal public utility."[91]

Colombia's rejection of the treaty had left the Panamanians without means of survival, and Jose Agustin Arango looked destiny in the eye. The revolutionary movement took shape in the home of this citizen who had modeled his life according to the precepts of Plutarch. For security reasons, Arango told no one of the plans but closely allied males: only his sons, Jose Agustin, Jr., Ricardo, and Belisario; his sons-in-law Samuel Lewis, Raul Orillac, and Ernesto T. Lefevre; and Carlos Constantino Arosemena.[92]

From the columns of *Le Matin*, Philippe warned Colombia once more of her folly, made an open call to the Panamanians to revolt, and invited Roosevelt to employ force and obtain what was guaranteed to his country by the Bidlack-Mallarino convention of 1846. Bunau-Varilla discussed the rights granted to the United States under that treaty and prodded the isthmians to rise in arms as they had in 1840 and 1856. Once secession was proclaimed, the rights of the treaty of 1846 would be vested in Panama alone, whose leaders would call on the United States to protect interoceanic communication.[93] Bogota did not heed the warning, but the Panamanians heard the call to rebellion. Philippe sent copies of the article to influential friends in the United States, including President Roosevelt and Herran. Recipients in Panama were Amador Guerrero, Federico Boyd, Manuel Espinosa Batista, Ricardo Arias, and Nicanor A. De Obarrio, all of whom knew Philippe. They joined the secret movement initiated by Arango, now in progress.[94]

Bunau-Varilla's call to revolt, the encouraging news from Panama, and the illness of his son sped Philippe's departure for New York, where he arrived on September 22, 1903. Meanwhile Loomis and Hay were scheming secession in Washington. The assistant secretary of state did not know the potential revolutionaries in Panama, but he knew that Bunau-Varilla was acquainted with most of them. By September 23, 1903, at least three revolutions were on paper: the high-level plans of the federal government, which could not be initiated without Roosevelt's assent; the often-planned coup outlined so many times to Loomis by Philippe; and the all-Panamanian movement, which Arango had begun months before the scuttling of the Hay-Herran treaty. In the end, all three plots found a guiding spirit and most enthusiastic supporter in Bunau-Varilla.

The Failure of the All-Panamanian
Revolution Sponsored by Cromwell

Bunau-Varilla's secret Panamanian contact in New York was J. J. Lindo, a wealthy merchant with connections in the isthmus. In September, after Philippe's call to arms, Arango, on the advice of J. R. Beers, an officer of the railroad, decided to send Amador to New York to appraise the situation. Through Lindo, Amador advised Bunau-Varilla in Paris of his projected trip to the United States. By that time, the movements of the suspected conspirators were being closely watched by Bogota, a vigilance suspected by Amador. Beers, entirely unaware and much less informed of Philippe's conspiratorial moves, suggested that Amador see the lawyer W. Cromwell.[95]

The Panamanians' struggles had been unknown to Cromwell until they were revealed by Philippe in his first message to Marroquin in 1902. Complications developed when Jose Gabriel Duque, owner of the *Star & Herald* and *LaEstrella de Panama*, who was in Washington, gained an interview with Hay to report on conditions in the isthmus.[96] Pressed by Duque and Amador, and not seriously concerned with spying activities or aware of the precariousness of his position as lawyer for the French company, Cromwell promised the presidency of the new republic to Duque, and guaranteed Amador an interview with Hay.[97]

Although Secretary of State Hay promised Duque nothing, the publisher made a serious error. Fearing detection and attempting to reinforce Philippe's warnings, he called on Herran and served him with an ultimatum: approval of the treaty or revolution.[98] The foolhardy conduct of both Cromwell and Duque revealed the all-native plot to Bogota. Herran cabled home:

> Revolutionary agents of Panama [are] here. Yesterday the editor of *La Estrella de Panama* had a long conference with the Secretary of State. If treaty not approved, there is the probability of revolution with American help.[99]

After warning Cromwell that his activities had endangered negotiations, Minister Herran wrote home the details of the conspiracy, implicating the administration of the railroad in the plot. Meanwhile, Duque, duplicating Philippe's technique, gave interviews to the press in which he made veiled threats of secession.[100] Intimidated by Herran, Cromwell refused to see Amador and sailed for France. The all-native revolution had failed.

All-American Revolution

From his summer home at Oyster Bay, New York, President Roosevelt began to work on a plan similar to that proposed by Bunau-Varilla in the article printed in *Le Matin*, September 2, 1902, and identical to that suggested by Senator Cullom of Illinois: namely, to acquire the French canal property and then build the waterway, ignoring Colombia. The scheme involved Loomis, who at that time was politically very close to the president. Before Loomis' appointment to the Department of State, the president had received him and his wife at dinner at the White House, rare deference to a mere diplomat,[101] but the correct procedure when dealing with a prominent member of the Ohio gang and an intimate of Whitelaw Reid. Roosevelt was already thinking of the presidential election three years off.

In 1903, because of Hay's illness, Roosevelt was giving instructions directly to Loomis in regard to appointments, resignations, or transfers in the foreign service.[102] As the state conventions approached, Roosevelt relied heavily on Loomis' political wisdom. While traveling in the state of Washington, the president urged Loomis to keep the Midwestern delegates to the convention in line and on his side:

> The president has the utmost confidence in the loyalty and discretion of you and Senator Foraker. . . . He leaves the matter entirely in your hands and will be absolutely satisfied with whatever action you take. Wire me at Walla-Walla date of the Pennsylvania and Ohio conventions.[103]

Hours after this wire was sent, Roosevelt telegraphed again, addressing Loomis as secretary of state:

> Pasco, Washington, May 25, 1903. Those who favor my administration and my nomination will endorse them, and those who do not would oppose. The president was deeply touched by the action of President McKinley's home county, in which Canton is situated, in instructing so heartily in his favor. Nothing could have pleased him more.[104]

Loomis had engineered this maneuver, which was aimed at diffusing any opposition to the president's nomination.[105] By July, Roosevelt was not only seeking Loomis' political advice but his diplomatic counsel concerning the mounting Panama crisis:

Oyster Bay, July 21, 1903
To the Secretary of State
My dear Mr. Secretary: The President requests me to write

you to ask if you can not come here and take lunch with him on Saturday, the twenty-fifth, at half after one o'clock. You can take the train leaving Long Island City at eleven A.M. arriving here at twelve twenty.[106]

A week later, the president wrote confidentially to Loomis, asking him not to name, as secretary to the embassy in Paris, a protégé of Senator Thomas Platt and ordering that the new German ambassador, Baron von Sternberg, be brought to Oyster Bay to present credentials. Loomis was instructed to tell the diplomat to prepare for a round of practice shooting after the ceremony—"I will play with him at the butts in the afternoon," Roosevelt wrote.[107]

During these meetings in July between Loomis and Roosevelt, the *espinosa* (thorny) Panama situation was raised.[108] At this time, the acting secretary of state brought the president a personal letter sent to Loomis by one of his Venezuelan diplomatic acquaintances, Carlos Zumeta, who had just arrived from Germany. The epistle enclosed a résumé of several articles published in Berlin by the Pan-germanic League, in which the canal problem was cleverly tied to German designs on Venezuela. Zumeta's translation included the statement that the "sphere of influence of the United States is indisputably up to the Nicaraguan canal." The implication, as stated by Zumeta, was that the canal at Panama was to be part of a German sphere of influence, since the Kaiser, as "leader of the European entente," had to "protect the German residents of Venezuela against ever-recurring revolts."[109] Even the German historian Theodore Mommsen asserted that the "United States has become a robber power, a piratical power," and that by pouring her incomparable resources into expansionist designs she might menace the world's quiet and might, like Rome, "carry forays into every continent."[110] Mommsen's statements were shown to Andrew D. White, the ambassador to England, who commented that they might hurt Professor Mommsen with the people who were his greatest admirers outside Germany.[111] These publications and comments, especially coming from one of the greatest historians of modern times, disturbed Hay and Roosevelt.

A second item treated during these meetings between Roosevelt and Loomis was a decoded cable from H. M. Beaupré, the minister to Bogota. Beaupré anticipated the defeat of the treaty. He had learned that Herran should not have signed the document and that, pretending that instructions had arrived much too late, he had signed it, anyway.

Discussion of this cable is important because Herran had been telling Hay, Loomis and Cromwell that the treaty would be approved, one way or another, either by the Colombian Senate or by executive fiat,[112] an unlikely occurrence because of the opposition of Miguel Antonio Caro and his followers. Antagonism against the convention had manifested itself in Panama among the ranks of those who had lost the civil war and wished to embarrass the Marroquin regime, particularly Belisario Porras, who thought it a certainty that he would be left out of any role in the new Panamanian deal, secession or not.[113]

On August 15, 1903, Loomis transmitted to Roosevelt the opinion of John Bassett Moore, the international lawyer and former secretary of the peace commission in Paris, whose views Loomis had solicited earlier, in preparation for a possible coup at Panama:

Dear Mr. President:

When I was at Oyster Bay some days ago, I had the honor of speaking to you for a moment with reference to the views of Professor John Bassett Moore concerning the diplomatic and international aspects of our relations to the Panama Canal treaty and problem. It will be admitted, I think, that Professor Moore is one of the most profound and accurate students of international law in the United States, and that he has had a great deal of extremely valuable experience in the practical application of the principles of both public and private international law. I asked Professor Moore to put his views into writing in order that you might look over them if you so desire, and I herewith enclose a copy for your perusal. I think you will find some strong and well supported suggestions in this memorandum, which, in the event of the failure of the

treaty at Bogota, which now seems probable, may be of the
very greatest importance.
Very respectfully,
Francis B. Loomis.[114]

Because of the coming elections, Loomis' counsel did not
inspire any overt presidential moves. Roosevelt's fears were
no secret. Loomis, as well as Philippe, knew that a badly
organized coup at Panama, even with the open intervention
of the United States, had its risks. Heavy civilian casualties in
the isthmus might jeopardize the administration despite
Loomis' careful political dealings. A fiasco like the later Bay of
Pigs[115] was not altogether impossible, particularly if the
discontented liberals managed to fan the embers of nationalism against the Americans.

Under these uncertain conditions, Roosevelt decided, in
early September 1903, to play the role of a corporation
executive. Why not leave the coup in the hands of Loomis
and Bunau-Varilla? If the scheme succeeded, he would
support Hay, who would, in turn, back Loomis. If it failed,
Hay needed only to dismiss Loomis. In the corporate world,
the president always supports the executives in whatever
they do. The president also ratifies and confirms all measures
taken, if successful, and opposes them if they are not. The
high-level "managed" revolution was thus shelved.

The Bunau-Varilla-Loomis Revolution

While Roosevelt remained preoccupied with political affairs
and Hay well-protected by illness, the two chefs, Bunau-
Varilla and Loomis, were left in charge of the revolutionary
stew. They had the not-too-reliable and distant human support promised by Amador, and the seasoning of Philippe's
money. On September 23, Bunau-Varilla and Amador held
their seminar on revolution. It was not the first time the two
men had talked of a coup. Many years before, Philippe had
heard talk of revolution and had chided the Panamanians for
not taking the direct route to independence.[116]

The Panamanian told his story well. General Esteban

Huertas, who commanded the garrison at Panama City, was ready to cooperate, and the élite of the isthmus would make any sacrifice in order to provoke the intervention of the United States. Moreover, if the Colombians should attempt to send reinforcements from Colon, the most probable origin of any counter-revolutionary army, the administration of the railroad was willing to perform as Philippe had in 1885 during the double rebellion at Colon and Panama City.

"Are you certain that we have everyone that counts on our side?" questioned Bunau-Varilla.

"Positively," answered Amador, "but our position is precarious, I don't know where we stand. We were led to believe that the United States would give us all the money needed to buy arms and ships. Also pay the troops."[117]

Without revealing to Amador that he had already discussed these possibilities with Loomis, Philippe assured the physician that if what he said was true, there was no problem whatsoever. Then he startled Amador by asking, "How big a sum do you consider necessary to begin the revolution?"

"Six million dollars," Amador replied.

Without raising his voice or losing composure, Philippe answered, "Six million, my dear friend, that's quite a lot of money. I don't think the government is ready to hand that large a sum to total strangers without assurances of success. Let me see what I can do. Remain here in New York until I find a way to proceed. See nobody, talk to no one, and write not a note. When calling me, your name is Smith and mine Jones. It may be days or weeks before we can work out this matter."[118]

Bunau-Varilla suspected that the United States wanted nothing to do publicly with a revolution, but one managed by remote control was another matter. Philippe had read the press, especially the *New York American* and the *New York Herald*, which were still rousing public opinion against Panama and in favor of Nicaragua. He concluded that it was dangerous to deal in revolutions before the election. A dinner in Washington with Loomis at the New Willard Hotel gave him at least a glimpse into the president's mind. The acting secretary of state assured Philippe that Roosevelt had read his articles in *Le Matin* and that he was familiar with the theory proposing to deal directly with the new company and ignore Colombia. Loomis did not say a word about having sent Bassett Moore's views on the canal to the president, but Bunau-Varilla surmised that the professor was Loomis' friend.[119]

Through Moore's colleague on the faculty of Columbia University, Canal Commissioner William Burr, Philippe managed an introduction to the international lawyer, and again there was friendship and identity of ideas at first sight. Bassett Moore assured Bunau-Varilla that the treaty of 1846 gave the United States the right to carry out the work necessary for the canal. The professor wondered who had propounded the same theory in *Le Matin*. Philippe had a copy of that edition in his pocket and, when the paper was unfolded, the secret was no more. Bunau-Varilla urged Bassett Moore to publicize his views and offered to send a reporter from the *Sun* to interview him, but the professor insisted that their conversation had to be secret. Again prodded by Philippe about the mystery, Bassett Moore retorted that "The conditions under which I was led to formulate this idea are such that I can no longer consider it my own."[120]

The "man with a canal" reasoned that it was to Roosevelt himself that the professor had expressed his opinion. He knew that Bassett Moore, as assistant secretary of state in 1898, had been Roosevelt's colleague when the president was under-secretary of the navy. Moreover, he had recently read in the press of Moore's visit to Oyster Bay. Not even the chief executive of the United States could keep canal schemes from Philippe. If Bunau-Varilla's reasoning was correct, Roosevelt still wished that someone, somehow, would extricate the administration from the quagmire of the Herran-Hay fiasco without directly compromising the government.

Suddenly, Philippe understood the theme of the plot and the role assigned to him: (1) Roosevelt was ready to employ coercion, but only at the right time; (2) if he unchained the revolution at Panama by giving Amador money, he had to tell his plans to an American official but the information would be given on a personal basis—Loomis had to be that man; (3) once the action had begun and had become a *fait accompli*, Washington would be "forced" to declare a protectorate over the isthmus or to annex it; (4) Philippe was not to arouse suspicion that the American government knew about his plans; (5) at no time were the insurgents to communicate directly with the United States government.

Philippe had wondered whether he was taking the right step. The answer was yes. He had warned Silva, Concha, Herran, Marroquin, Ospina Perez, and all Colombian officials of the threat of revolt if the treaty was not ratified. He also felt that his ties were with Panama, not with Bogota. Anything that seemed to dim the future of the isthmus distressed him. It was there that French "genius" had located the interoceanic canal, and it was time to fulfill that purpose even if it meant revolution.[121]

Philippe and Loomis visited the White House at noon on October 9, 1903. They found the president in an expansive mood. Roosevelt asked Bunau-Varilla what the outcome of the Panama impasse was to be, and Philippe replied, "Revolution." The president turned toward Loomis, winked, and murmured hopefully, "Revolution." Roosevelt ventured to ask how it could be done, and Philippe spent the last thirty minutes of the interview explaining potentialities and stating what arrangements were in progress.[122] No commitments were made, but there was no sign of vexation or apprehension about Philippe's prophesy.

From October 10 to 15, Philippe wondered how he could raise $6 million. Although a wealthy man, he did not have that in cash, and liquidating some of his assets would surely betray the secret of the revolution. Having guessed that the Panamanians, thanks to the probable intervention of the United States, needed no ships or mercenaries, he offered Amador $100,000 from his own pocket for pay owed to the troops—at $20 each, that amounted to only $10,000—and for rifles and munitions. Once the treaty with the new republic was signed, Panama would take care of the rest of the expenses.[123] He met Amador on October 15.

The septuagenarian doctor had fallen into a melancholy mood. He had received a letter from Carlos C. Arosemena stating that Senator José de Obaldia had returned to the isthmus as governor with the secret purpose of advancing the fortune of General Rafael Reyes in the presidential elections of 1904. Obaldia confided to the revolutionaries that Reyes, once elected, would engineer the approval of the treaty in Congress or by executive sanction.[124] The suggestion was not without risk to Philippe. If the enemies of the new company succeeded in declaring the Sanclemente extension void in 1904, the French company stood to lose everything.

Amador proved uncompromising. Without realizing the secret nature of the plot, he insisted upon talking directly to Roosevelt or, at least, to Hay. The $10 million promised to Colombia in the Herran-Hay document seemed too little to Amador. The $40 million promised to the new company were almost as intoxicating to him as to Bogota. Amador left the Waldorf-Astoria Hotel[125] dejected, only to return on the morrow to accept Philippe's modest offer. He still had to wait for last-minute instructions, and possibly for the money.

Philippe Drafts a Panamanian Constitution, Designs a Flag, and Finances a Revolution

After leaving Amador, Bunau-Varilla went to the office of his lawyer, Frank Pavey, where he worked out a draft of a proclamation and a constitution which was to be handed over to Amador before his departure. Philippe's constitution was modeled after Cuba's, and it gave the United States the right of intervention when order was disturbed. Returning to the hotel, Bunau-Varilla received a call from Loomis, who asked him to stop at the Department of State the next day, when Philippe was scheduled to attend the ceremonies for the unveiling of the statue of General William Tecumseh Sherman. While he was in Loomis' office, Hay came in "by accident." The secretary had interrupted his sick leave to receive a group of ambassadors at noon. Philippe had met Hay years earlier at Bigelow's home, and, without difficulty, a private meeting was arranged for mid-afternoon at the secretary's home.[126]

At his house, Hay asked Philippe to talk freely about Panama and the plans for the revolution about which he had heard from Loomis and Roosevelt. Bunau-Varilla laid his cards on the table, eliciting from Hay compliments and admiration but no direct orders or indirect backing. Just before leaving, the secretary turned the conversation to a book he had just finished reading, the story of Captain Macklin, a West Point officer who enlisted in the forces of a French general engaged in a Tarzan-like adventure in the jungles of Central America. Would Philippe read the book? "It is yours," said Hay. "I am certain you will enjoy it as much as I did." And just before departing with a firm handshake, the secretary turned back to the subject of the revolt. "If there is to be trouble in Panama, we might as well order units of the Pacific fleet to the Gulf of Panama." On October 22, the press announced the departure from San Francisco, in a southerly direction, of the cruisers *Mohican* and *Marblehead*.[127]

This veiled command to continue his job did not escape Bunau-Varilla, who recognized that Hay had already cast him as the "French general," and Francis B. Loomis as the "West Point captain." Bunau-Varilla had knocked at the doors of a fortress, and the doors had opened. He took the next train to New York to meet Amador, assured him of American support, and described to him the role each one was to play in the coup. He presented Amador with the projected proclamation and constitution and sketched a flag to be ready on the 20th of October. Delivery of the $100,000 from his bank account was promised when their goal was achieved. The old doctor was ecstatic. In exchange, Philippe asked to be named minister to the United States. Amador argued that isthmian citizenship was necessary and that the other members of the junta would certainly object. Philippe reminded Amador that

Colombia's first diplomatic representative was the Spaniard Don Manuel Torres (1764–1822). "Don't you recall, my dear doctor, that in 1822 Senor Torres placed in the hands of President Monroe the credentials of the Colombian government, by virtue of which he became the first diplomatic agent in Washington representing a Latin-American republic?" Amador asked time out to think it over.[128]

The septuagenarian Amador was a good man, but he had already visualized himself signing treaty commitments as the envoy of Panama.[129] Like all physician-politicians—and there have been many in Latin America[130]—Dr. Amador had no political perspective. His outlook was rather myopic and his background barren of skills for dealing with such extremely complex and urgent problems as the creation and recognition of a new state. In a final burst of energy, he had assumed the leadership of the movement and was reserving for himself the later pleasure of saying to the Frenchman, "Thank you for your efforts. We shall remember you."

Amador's role in the revolution was not a difficult one. For the first time in the history of the province, Arango had succeeded in unifying the élite against Bogota. Long and lasting ties with the lower classes assured their support for the movement. The opportunity was not to be wasted. Reluctantly, the physician promised Philippe the post of envoy extraordinary and minister plenipotentiary to Washington. But more discussion was needed to set the time to launch the revolt.

Amador requested two more weeks after his landing in Panama but Philippe insisted that the revolution begin not later than November 4, if possible, November 3. By that time, he estimated, most of the votes would have been cast in the American elections. But the country doctor argued that he had to meet with various committees. It was necessary for Bunau-Varilla to reveal to Amador what he had learned from Loomis, that Colombian troops were being mobilized for shipment to Panama. "If you don't act soon enough, the opportunity will be lost," said Philippe. The Panamanian relented, promised to begin the insurrection as early as November 1, and boarded a steamer for Colon on October 20.[131]

After Amador's departure Bunau-Varilla requested the money from his brokers in Belgium and Paris:

> Balse, 7, rue d'Aremberg, Brussels. Can you lend me two hundred and fifty thousand francs on securities you hold in safeguard for me and, if so, remit immediately funds to agence B Credit Lyonnais. Answer me Waldorf Astoria New York. Philippe Varilla, Thursday, October 22, 1 A.M.[132]

Five and a half hours later the answer arrived:

> Philippe Varilla, Waldorf Astoria, N. Y. We agree to lend two hundred fifty thousand francs on your securities held in safeguard for three months or later if new agreement prorogrates loan we are remitting Credit Lyonnais agence B. Balser, October 22, 1903, 6:36 A.M.[133]

> Credit Lyonnais, 55, Champs-Elysees, Paris. Can you lend me two hundred and fifty thousand francs on securities you hold in safeguard for me and remit immediately funds to my account agence B. Answer me Waldorf Astoria, New York. Varilla, Thursday, October 22, 1:00 A.M.

> Bunau-Varilla, Waldorf Astoria
> Agree for two hundred and fifty thousand francs which we transfer to your account agence B letter follows. Credionnais.[134]

> Agency B. Credit Lyonnais, Place Bourse, Paris. First: You certainly have received five hundred thousand francs from Balser and Agence A. S. Second: Instruct Heidelback Ickelheimer to deliver me any sums I require against drafts I shall issue up to a total of five hundred thousand francs as is done for letters of credence. Third: Answer me Waldorf Astoria. Philippe Bunau-Varilla, Sunday, October 25, 1903, from Highland Falls, 6:30 P.M.[135]

The transaction was not very different from that in which his ancestor Antoine Varilla had been involved with the

Austrian emperor's agents and the Dutch bankers a few years before the outbreak of the French Revolution.[136] In this case, however, Philippe stood to lose a fortune, besides the dream of his canal, if he made a false step. He was about to cross his Rubicon.

9

Revolution in Panama and the

Canal Treaty of 1904

The United States Backs the Bunau-Varilla-Loomis Revolution by Showing the Flag;
Colombia Tries to Negotiate with Washington but Fails; The Panama Canal Treaty Is
Signed; France and Panama Thank Bunau-Varilla

The task of mobilizing the American fleet fell to an assistant secretary of the navy, James Darling. The head of the department, William Henry Moody,[1] like Hay, was not at his post. While Philippe was securing the money for the revolution, Loomis was insuring the wireless communications:

October 23, 1903.
J. A. Beard, Esq.,
Secretary, Central and South American Telegraph Co.,
66 Broadway, New York City.
    Dear Sir: Will you kindly tell me whether your company has a station at Punta Arenas, Costa Rica, and whether the line is likely to be working as well at that point irrespective of disturbances south of Panama?

Very truly yours,
F. B. Loomis[2]

Some isthmian liberals suspected that important events were in the making. Not yet sure if they wished to abandon

Bogota,[3] they almost aborted the revolution. Another peril presented itself in the lack of discipline of those who had been encouraged by Bunau-Varilla's separatist propaganda. This group was eager for direct action without a script. After a short visit to Nicaragua, the gunboat *Nashville* appeared at Colon on October 11.[4] Secret information had reached the navy that an arsenal had been shipped to Panama early that month by mysterious agents in the United States.[5]

Four thousand Winchester rifles and 1.5 million rounds of ammunition were loaded at Morgan City, Louisiana. The ship sailed for Progresso but the cargo was met off the coast of Yucatan and then transferred to a second vessel that had cleared Kingston, Jamaica. The latter craft's destination was Rio Indio, a few miles north of Colon. Information provided by revolutionaries to Colombia made possible the success of this operation. While six hundred misinformed soldiers were combing the jungles in search of weapons at Rio Indio, the arms were safely unloaded at Porto Bello.[6] The arrival of the *Nashville* on October 11 was dictated by these rumors. Historian Gonzales Valencia states that the revolt was plotted by "a small group of politicians and business interests" and that "the great mass of the people were entirely alien" to the coup.[7] Yet even the foreign element was secretly seeking secession, among them the Millers, the Pizas, and Jose Gabriel Duque, owner of the *Star & Herald*.

Extortion in Panama

To most of the governors of Panama, it did not matter whether a citizen was a conservative, a liberal, or neutral. General Carlos Alban asked members of his own party for $60,000. He withdrew from the room and surrounded the building with troops. Later he reappeared and insisted on having the money; otherwise no one would leave. The money was given. Extracting "voluntary" subscriptions under duress was the most common means of raising money. When Harmodio Arosemena, a banker, was told that $25,000 was needed, he had it reported that he had gone to Ecuador. Troops were billeted in his house and the governor told the family, "Cable him for the money." Actually Arosemena was hiding in his own house, where he remained a prisoner for nine months. The soldiers on guard had to be fed all that time. On different occasions within five years, not reckoning the quartering of the troops, the Arosemenas paid more than $150,000 in "voluntary subscriptions to the government."[8]

Oscar Miller, a jeweler, showed receipts for "war loans" of $80 to $100 a month. Although of German parents, he was born in the isthmus, and he had no protection. One day when he was asked for a voluntary subscription of $1,250, he removed everything from his safe and refused to pay. A commission came to force the safe. Miller gave the combination rather than see the safe blown up. Only old papers were found in it, so his house was locked and no one could come out. For twenty-four hours the family was besieged. Finally, Miller compromised for $300, but he had to pay $5 more for the man who had come to blow up the safe and who had "lost his time." Miller also had to pay $6 for the advertisement of the intended sale of his store.[9]

Carlos Miller, Oscar's brother, was similarly treated. His haberdashery was locked up for four days until he subscribed $1,250. When the public sale of his goods was advertised, he yielded. At the house of Domingo Diaz, the soldiers occupied Senora Diaz' bedroom, and for two nights the women folk had no place to sleep.[10] Federico Boyd was held up for $10,000 but settled for $5,000. To avoid a "voluntary subscription" which he heard was to be requested of him, De la Espriella, the future foreign minister, left for Costa Rica. He returned just as Bunau-Varilla was arranging the revolution.[11]

Carlos Icaza, before he could escape, was taxed $5,000. Jose Gabriel Duque's manager at Colon, R. Cortez, who was a native Colombian but took no interest in politics, was assessed $600 for being "indifferent."[12] Importers were a favorite target. The alcaldes were never paid, and pardons were sold in open court. Petty blackmail was exacted from the poor and grand blackmail from the rich.

The isthmians looked forward to the completion of the canal because it meant the United States would control it, and with that control would come peace and order. Annexation was not rejected, but welcomed. Separation and independence was a stage which could not be achieved without the constant vigilance of Washington. But this protection would not be easily granted, nor was it forthcoming until solid guarantees of the canal agreements were given. Under these conditions, the opportunity offered by Philippe's ingenious scheme was not to be wasted.

Philippe Delivers His Promise

In addition to a proposed proclamation, constitution, and flag, Amador carried with him a code composed by Bunau-Varilla with which the two were to communicate and the draft of a telegram to be sent immediately after the coup began.[13] From October 28, when Amador was to arrive at Panama, to November 5, Philippe was as nervous as a man waiting for the birth of his first child. His wife was in New York sharing his anxiety.

The *Nashville's* wanderings raised his hopes. The ship had returned to Caimanera, Cuba, but then sailed again for Jamaica, on October 28, whence it was commanded to return to Colon on the morning of October 31. The rebels were pragmatic souls; they wanted visual evidence of American aid. Amador was forced to cable Philippe: "Fate news bad powerful tiger. Urge vapor Colon, Smith." Decoded, the message was certainly alarming: *Fate:* This cable is for Philippe; *News:* Colombian troops arriving; *Bad:* Atlantic; *Powerful:* Five days; *Tiger:* More than two hundred. In the excitement the nervous Amador improvised new words. The last half, "Urge vapor Colon" (demand steamship at Colon), was not in the proper code.

Bunau-Varilla thought that this might be a trick of the revolutionaries to see if he was with them,[14] but the original group had expanded to include such prominent citizens as Tomas Arias, owner of the electric company, and Manuel Espinosa Batista. Room had also been made for the liberals, and Eusebio A. Morales, Carlos A. Mendoza, and Juan Antonio Henriquez were brought into the plot. Some of these late-comers did not know Philippe as well as Arango, Boyd, Espriella, and Amador, and wanted more concrete evidence of his backing. Still trying not to offend Bogota, the insurgents were waiting for October 31, the date the Colombian Congress was to adjourn. Until the arrival of Bunau-Varilla's money, expenditures to take care of the troops were to be secured from the $145,000 held by Isaac Brandon and Brothers and Henry Ehrman, in charge of the departmental treasury, who were in on the secret of the revolution. General Esteban Huertas needed $10,000 to send some of the less reliable troops away from Panama City to investigate an "invasion." General Ruben Varon, who commanded the man-o'-war *Twenty-First of November*, also needed $25,000. His chief engineer and artillery boss would settle for $10,000 each.[15] Until these matters were taken care of, the revolt could not begin.

Philippe managed to interpret Amador's message and, that evening, he called on Loomis and acquainted him with developments. He recounted again what had happened in 1885, when both ends of the isthmus were involved in subversion, and impressed upon Loomis the need to protect transit, lives, and property.[16] The two friends arranged to meet again in the late morning of October 30.[17]

After consulting with the president, Loomis met Philippe and remarked that it would be deplorable if the rebellions of 1885 were repeated in Panama. Loomis thought that adequate measures would be taken to prevent casualties and protect isthmian transit, when—and if—the revolution started on November 3, as Bunau-Varilla had informed him it would.[18] That's all Philippe needed to hear. He cabled Amador from Baltimore: "Pizaldo, All right will reach ton and half obscure. Jones." "Pizaldo" was a contraction of the shipping and merchant firm of the Piza Nephews, with which Lindo was associated. The decoded telegram read: "All right will reach two days and a half. This is for Amador. Philippe."[19] On November 2, Bunau-Varilla cabled Amador a last message before the outbreak of the coup: "Boy." In the prearranged code, this meant: "Nothing has happened which requires modification. Proceed." Nevertheless, the ships that were sailing toward the isthmus, as Hay had promised Philippe on October 16, were not in sight of Panama, and the insurgents were uneasy.

Since the revolution should have started by November 2 and things seemed quiet, the American consul at Panama City sent the following coded message: "The White House, Washington, Hay: No uprising yet reported. Will be in the night. Situation critical. Ehrman."[20] Meanwhile, the under secretary of the navy had instructed the captain of the *Nashville*:

> Washington, November 2, 1903.
> Nashville, Care of American Consul Colon
> Secret and Confidential
> Maintain free and uninterrupted transit. If interruption threatened by armed forces, occupy the line of the railroad. Prevent landing with hostile intent of any armed force, either Government or insurgent either at Colon, Porto Bello or other point. Send copy of instructions to the senior officer present at Panama upon arrival of Boston. Have sent copy of instructions and have telegraphed [the] *Dixie* to proceed with all possible dispatch from Kingston to Colon. Government force reported approaching the isthmus in vessels. Prevent their landing if in your judgment the landing would precipitate conflict. Acknowledgement is required.
>
> > Darling, Acting[21]

The Triumph of the Revolution

The last dispatch that left the isthmus while it was still part of Colombia reached the Department of State at 10:53 A.M. on November 3:

> Colon, Colombia, November 3. It is rumored that startling developments pointing to the independence of the isthmus are on foot. Everything is quiet here. The United States gunboat *Nashville* arrived here yesterday. The Colombian Gunboat Cartagena arrived at Colon today from Sabanilla with several hundred troops on board.[22]

At 5:00 P.M. the same day, the municipality of Panama City

proclaimed its secession from Colombia. Amador cabled directly to Hay: "Panama, November 3, 1903. His Excellency, Secretary Hay. Isthmus independence proclaimed without bloodshed. Canal treaty saved. Amador."[23] Ehrman also cabled Hay:

Panama, November 3, 1903. Hay, Washington.

Uprising occurred tonight six; no bloodshed. Army and Navy officials taken prisoners. Will organize government tonight, consisting of three consuls, also organize cabinet. Soldiers changed. Suppose same movement will be effected in Colon. Order prevails so far. Situation serious. Four hundred soldiers landed Colon today Barranquilla. . . . Ehrman.[24]

The condition of the Colombian army was indicated by eyewitness accounts of the landing of 400 soldiers at Colon in the company of an equal number of camp followers. Suffering from *mal de mer*, the women lay down in the streets seeking relief.[25]

Under secretary Darling instructed the *Dixie* and the *Atlanta* to detour from Jamaica to Colon, and the *Boston* to go from San Juan del Sur, Nicaragua, to Panama City. The president left early on November 3 for Oyster Bay to cast his ballot in the election. Loomis and Darling stayed at their desks. On receipt of the last cable from Ehrman, which both under secretaries read, the cruisers *Wyoming*, *Marblehead* and *Concord* were alerted for proceeding to Panama from Acapulco.[26] That evening, Roosevelt returned to Washington and conferred with Loomis and Darling. Minutes later, Hay was also asked to come to the White House. By 10:00 P.M., another message reached Loomis from the navy's decoding room:

Colon, November 3, 1903. Secretary of State.

Troops from vessel Cartagena have disembarked; are en- camping on Pacific dock awaiting orders to proceed to Panama from commander-in-chief who went there this morning. No message from Nashville received. Malmros.[27]

While the world press busied itself printing news of the events, Philippe at last heard from Amador, who repeated the cable he had already sent to Hay.[28] Every news item out of Panama gave the impression that the object of the coup was annexation to the United States.[29] The details of events at Panama that day are well known, and we do not restate them here. However, this cable from Consul Malmros to Hay gives a clear picture of those happenings:

> Colon, Nov. 4, 1903. Secstate, Washington.
> Met Captain of Nashville at 6 P.M. yesterday. Heard that message had been delivered to Captain boat alongside of wharf instead of to me. No rebels or invading force near Panama or Colon or line of transit and the latter is in no danger. Panama intended revolutionary movement known here to four persons only up to eight A.M. today. Revolutionary Committee of six in Panama at six P.M. took charge Revolutionary movement. General Juan Tobar and five officers taken prisoner. Panama in possession of Committee with consent of entire population. This fact not known as yet to conservatives in Colon. Panama committee expect to have fifteen hundred men armed by this time. State of affairs at Panama not known by Colombian force at Colon as yet. Committee ordered in name of Tobar the force disembark to proceed to Panama in order to capture them on arrival. Official in command of disembarked force applied for transportation this morning. Captain meanwhile communicated to Committee about ten P.M. last night his refusal to allow train with force to be sent to Panama and the Committee assented this leaves Colon in the possession of the [Colombian] Government.[30]

Almost simultaneously, the captain of the *Nashville* received the following telegram from Panama City:

> Gunboat Colombia shelling Panama. Send immediately battery three-inch gun and six pounder with a force of men to Panama to compel cessation of bombardment.[31]

And Bunau-Varilla, through Lindo accepted this message from Amador:

> This dispatch is for Bunau-Varilla
> Ask pressingly Bunau-Varilla 100,000 pesos—
> town bombarded to-night by Bogota—
> urge ships Pacific.[32]

Philippe had just returned from Washington, where he had conferred with Loomis and received confirmation that a confrontation at Colon, with possible loss of lives, was not unexpected. The revolutionaries themselves caused this crisis by not following Philippe's instructions. Colon should have been captured by the insurgents before or at the same time as the coup at Panama City. Almost no one at Colon knew of the plot. With the landing of the *Cartagena*, armed confrontation developed. It should not have been forgotten that the United States intervention could not begin "until communication had been disturbed."

Philippe and the merchant J. J. Lindo correctly guessed that Amador had no control over the isthmus as yet, therefore, Bunau-Varilla's part of the bargain was not yet due. Nevertheless, the Frenchman arranged through his bankers for the delivery to Amador of $25,000 (50,000 pesos),[33] a sum which helped avert armed confrontation at Colon. When the two generals, Juan B. Tobar and R. G. Amaya, were seized in Panama City on November 3, the regiment at Colon was left under the command of Colonel Eliseo Torres. On November 4, Torres placed his men in battle formation and faced the marines protecting the railroad terminal and telegraph office. The following day, a high-ranking general, Pompilio Gutierrez, arrived, and command of the troops passed to him. After two hours of continuous talks in which several Colombian civilians participated, Torres was persuaded to leave, but not before he was given $8,000 in "expense money" from the funds Bunau-Varilla had transferred to the junta. Torres' officers received $500 each.[34] It was reported that General Gutierrez reluctantly accepted $14,445, a year's salary in the Colombian army.[35]

Urged by a distinguished citizen, Porfirio Melendez, the civilian authority at Colon, represented by P. A. Cuadros, Eleazar Guerrero, and O. L. Martinez, exonerated Colonel Torres of any cowardly act:

> We are witness to the heroic conduct of Colonel Eliseo Torres and his soldiers. However, in the presence of the American position, and to avoid conflict in the city of Colon,

[Colonel Torres] decided to take his troops to Cartagena with weapons and munitions.[36]

Natural catastrophe and disease in Panama, and political chicanery, and bribery in France had almost terminated the canal project. In the end, another natural catastrophe, the timely eruption of the Nicaraguan volcanoes, the control of disease by the serendipitous testing of Finlay's theory, Bogota's attempts to blackmail the French company, the cooperation of the United States navy, and bribery in Panama with the money supplied by Bunau-Varilla fulfilled the revolutionary aims of the isthmians in a bloodless coup expertly managed by Philippe.

By 11:55 A.M. November 6, conditions appeared normal, and Felix Ehrman cabled Hay:

> The situation is good. Isthmus had obtained so far success. Colon and interior provinces have enthusiastically joined independence. Not any Colombian soldiers known on Isthmian soil at present. Padilla equipped to pursue Bogota. Bunau-Varilla has been appointed officially Confidential Agent of the Republic of Panama at Washington.[37]

Simultaneously, J. J. Lindo handed Philippe the following telegram in Spanish: "Tower, N.Y., hostile troops re-embarking. Demand from Jones for more money."[38] Not a word was sent to Bunau-Varilla about his ministry to Washington. Clearly the ruling triumvirate of Arango, Boyd, and Arias was not informed of this argument. Ignoring Amador's message, Philippe cabled back:

> November 5, 1903, Amador, Panama. Wish to beg Government to send me in plain language the message agreed between us on October 20, when you came to see me the last time before embarking. It will allow me through my official authority to solve political and financial questions, the latter being on a wider base than projected. These two public missions are inseparable, as was explicitly understood between us. I decline any responsibility in the future, if Government Republic prefers any other solution. My hands will be tied; my heart will remain the same.[39]

On November 6, the junta, unaware of Philippe's cable, wired Bunau-Varilla:

> Philippe Bunau-Varilla, Waldorf Astoria, New York: We are declaring today, November 6, to the Secretary of State that Colon and all the towns of the Isthmus have adhered to the Declaration of Independence proclaimed in our capital. The authority of the Republic of Panama is obeyed on all its territory. Press recognition of the Republic by the Government. Arango, Arias, Boyd.[40]

It seems clear that Amador was maneuvering to thwart Philippe's appointment. Again, Philippe came to a crucial decision and instructed the triumvirate to convey to the American Consul at Panama their decision about him, one way or another. Already in sore need of money to satisfy its creditors, the junta yielded and Bunau-Varilla became envoy extraordinary and plenipotentiary of Panama to Washington.[41] The revolution had ended according to the program worked out by Philippe, but not before Amador had injected into it the first hint of internal rivalry.

Fearing rebellion in the states of Cauca, Magdalena, and Bolivar, Bogota made no public mention of the coup for some time. Had these lands seceded, Colombia would have become another Bolivia, deprived of coasts.[42] Rumors of attack by Bogota plagued the isthmians for months, therefore, the junta created an army and made Domingo Diaz its first general. And the gunboat *Padilla* was placed under the command of a West Point graduate, H. C. Jeffries.[43]

The World's Press Reacts

Newspaper reaction to the coup was divided. The *New York Times* played the role of Cassandra, and the *New York World* had reservations. Said the *New York Times*:

> Theodore Roosevelt is as little likely as any president we have ever had to fall victim to the wishes of other men, or to become the dupe . . . of schemes. If he has ever been betrayed into folly it was his own notion. . . . If [he] pursues a course which will result in the dismemberment of . . . Colombia and

thereafter proceeds with the Panama Canal undertaking . . .
all the world will conclude that the instigation of the revolt . . .
were one and all measures of our own national policy.[44]

Overseas, the *Frankfurter Zeitung* in Germany believed the
United States had abetted the revolution.[45] The London *Times*
of London editorialized that Colombia was guilty of wanton
procrastination in regard to her canal obligations, which she
had fully abdicated: "There seems every justification for
saying that she has been trying to blackmail the United States
on one hand, the French Panama Company on the other."[46]
Naturally, most of the Parisian press was overjoyed.[47] And,
finally, the *New York Herald* surrendered.[48]

However, throughout the crisis, the administration and
Bunau-Varilla's shield against all comers was the *New York
Tribune*. Day after day, editorially, by the publication of every
newsworthy item about Panama and the printing of large
photographs of daily life scenes in the isthmus, it kept public
opinion well-informed about the events dealing with the
secession.[49] "The United States in sending a force to the scene
. . . is doing only what it has done before on several occasions in accordance with the Treaty of 1846."[50] On November
6, it wrote: "The strategic position of the United States is so
strong and the assurances that 'things will come our way' is
so ample, that there is no need or excuse for anything that
would even look like interested interference."[51] On November 8, the *Tribune* editorialized, applauding the decision to
prevent the landing of Colombian troops at Porto Bello,[52] and
on November 15 it chastised those "who are appalled" at the
prospect of "successfully conducted negotiations with the
new Republic of Panama."[53] Whitelaw Reid wrote to Roosevelt:

> It looks as if your Panama coup would be overwhelmingly
> successful. . . . It is obviously the right thing for the country,
> which according to my notion has the right to assert its
> paramount authority in the region of the Caribbean Sea or the
> Gulf of Mexico.[54]

The United States and France Recognize Panama; Morgan Fights Back

On November 5, the Department of State recognized the de facto regime, but Bunau-Varilla's role was still imperiled, this time by his own exultation and by Amador. On learning that the *Herald* changed sides, Philippe cabled its owner, James Gordon Bennett, in Paris, "the gratitude of Panama" for this sensible step. Then he wrote to Senator Morgan suggesting that he correct his previous mistakes by rallying to the side of Panama. Meanwhile, he granted interviews with delight.[55] These moves, while Philippe was still waiting to be received as the official representative of Panama, irritated Senator Morgan, abetted the self-serving Amador, and disturbed Philippe's backer, John Bigelow.

Caught by surprise, Morgan declared that the revolution would make the canal at Panama "an impossibility."[56] The senator called the recognition of Panama a "shameless absurdity" because he felt that the isthmian government was unable to guarantee order around the canal. He demanded that Panama City and Colon be conquered and forecast continuous harassment of the new state by Colombia if the entire country was not annexed. He reminded Roosevelt that Colombia had offered to sell the isthmus at least twice, and that the people there "would prefer to be annexed, and we better take the responsibilities directly than in any empty bargains with a little straw republic."[57]

Morgan exploded upon learning that the Frenchman had much to do with the revolution. He demanded a congressional inquiry into the affair and accused Bunau-Varilla of attempted intimidation because of his newly acquired rank. Philippe, who expected to be formally received at the state department on November 9, was instead invited to lunch by Loomis at Hay's house. He returned to New York that night, but not before being prodded by Loomis to get treaty-making powers from the junta immediately. Philippe told the press that Colombia had wasted time in the past, and "for the general good, delay in this matter cannot be permitted. Panama and the United States want the canal. Why should we wait?" The minister ended the interview by adding that "the two tricolor flags will be once more associated with the great enterprise which France began and which the United States will finish."[58]

His newspaper, *Le Matin,* praised the Americans for saving the honor of France:

> . . . generous Americans, who gladly recall the indispens-
> able services rendered to them by France in the War of
> Independence and afterward in offering them for a nominal
> price the empire of Louisiana. If only a part of the capital
> invested by France is recovered, the canal would be saved.
> There would be compensation for the balance in the closer
> friendship between the United States and France.[59]

Bunau-Varilla's sudden outburst of rhetoric again alarmed his friends, who threw a protective cordon around him and urged the utmost caution. Frank Pavey, who had become counsel of Panama, the young Pablo Arosemena whom Philippe had named consular agent in New York, John Bassett Moore, and faithful Bigelow entreated Bunau-Varilla to be quiet.[60] Even a Parisian daily raised a question about Philippe's not asking the foreign office's permission to represent Panama.[61] Bigelow, who loved Philippe like a father, admonished him. "Lend your ears only and not your tongue to newsmongers. Give the public now some eloquent flashes of silence. You have done a deed that surpasses Bolivar, Cortez, and Iturbide."[62]

Morgan's fireworks needed to be defused quickly, because an enraged Senate could force any envoy's departure. Philippe quieted things down by telling the press that his letter was written as a private citizen.[63] This was not unusual, for he had previously addressed himself to senators Hanna and Lodge. Nevertheless, the epistle was written on stationary bearing the imprimateur of the "Legation of Panama."[64] The fact remained that he had not been officially received as the plenipotentiary of that country.

In open conflict, the best defense is to attack. On November 10, the Republicans acted on a suggestion by Loomis to remove Morgan from his chairmanship of the Committee on Interoceanic Canals, a post which fell to Hanna.[65] The Alabama senator quieted down but the Democratic Party's leadership took up the fight, declaring that they could not approve a treaty except with Nicaragua.[66] Philippe realized the urgency of presenting his credentials and negotiating a treaty. It had to be done before Panama's enemies awoke from the political cyclone he had unleashed. He began drafting a protocol with the aid of his advisor, Frank Pavey.

Colombia Tries to Negotiate

News of the isthmian secession reached Bogota by way of Ecuador on November 5. The Colombian minister to Quito, Emiliano Izaza, sent his government two telegrams with details of the events.[67] The consul at New York, Arturo Brigard, Marroquin's nephew, was either unwilling to notify his superiors or unable to send messages.[68] Later, he helped spread the rumor that his country was about to become a German protectorate.[69] Afterward, in response to sympathetic telegrams from the Peruvian and Ecuadorian presidents, Marroquin named a commission presided over by General Reyes for the purpose of bringing Panama back into the fold. Bogota was at last ready to cooperate with Washington and, by the use of his constitutional authority, Marroquin was willing to declare martial law, approve the treaty by executive fiat, and call extra sessions of the Congress for its ratification.[70]

The last-minute recantations by Bogota revealed the charade in which the Colombian politicians had been engaged for months. If the government now found itself powerful enough to sanction the protocol, it certainly had the power to do so before. The new Congress would probably have been docile, thanks to the bayonets. The news of General Reyes' mission brought both hope and fear to Panama—hope of endangering Bunau-Varilla's ministerial appointment and fear of Reyes. Meanwhile Bunau-Varilla, in fulfillment of his pact with Amador, authorized J. J. Lindo to place at the junta's disposal the rest of the money he had promised for the revolt. But this sum was not enough. At the insistence of the isthmians, Bunau-Varilla named the firm of J. Pierpont Morgan and Company financial agents of the new nation, and a credit of $350,000 was immediately extended to the junta.[71]

Reyes' trip brought about, for the first time, a spirit of *retrovogue*, a vision of the past which romanticized the Colombian occupation. This feeling later pervaded the intellectual community of Panama.[72] These people thought: After all, what Panama desired was the canal, not independence. Why break away from Simon Bolivar's mother country, the home of the Liberator's image and traditions?

The Amador Mission

Amador, who already had upstaged Arango, the soul of the separatist movement, began to plot to supplant Philippe in Washington. After communicating with Cromwell, who was about to sail from Le Havre for New York, the Panamanian had himself appointed head of a commission to travel to Washington to write the treaty.[73] The duties and movements of the group were kept secret, and the press was the first to inform Philippe of its existence.

Amador was ready to play the role of the Colombian Senate; and procrastination might be the first order of business. If he prolonged the negotiations, Washington would eventually have to deal directly with the junta. He could gently push Bunau-Varilla to the sidelines, while moving to the center of the stage himself. Hay's reaction to the appointment of the commission, news that both the secretary and Philippe had read in the newspapers, was enigmatic. It appeared strange to both that, after being named to minister, Panama was about either to supersede or to ignore Philippe. Again, Bunau-Varilla seized the initative. He cabled the junta asking for clarification of the newspaper's reports and reported that he had denied to Washington that the commission's role was to discuss or sign treaties.

The reply is indicative of the confusion generated by Amador's gyrations:

> We approve that you have denied that Commissaries go to discuss and sign Canal Treaty, all things that exclusively concern Your Excellency. Amador and Boyd have no mission to the American Government, but only the mission communicated to Your Excellency in yesterday's cablegram to avoid loss of time.[74]

And what was the substance of "yesterday's cablegram," which Philippe received a few hours after he sent his message?

> As it is thought convenient to avoid your request for advice on objects of urgent resolution, tomorrow [Tuesday Nov. 10], Amador and Boyd will leave, carrying your letters of credence.[75]

On the same day, consul Ehrman confirmed Philippe's and Hay's suspicions. The delegates were to cable "arrange in satisfactory manner to the United States the Canal Treaty and other matters. Pablo Arosemena, attorney, follows by next steamer."[76] After receiving Philippe's cable of November 9, however, the junta confirmed that Bunau-Varilla was the sole representative empowered to negotiate and sign treaties: "I am officially informed that Bunau-Varilla is the authorized party to make treaties. Boyd and Amador have other missions and to assist their Minister.—Ehrman."[77] It appears that the triumvirs at Panama remained constant despite Amador's trip to Washington. On November 6, they cabled Philippe:

> The Junta of the provisional government names you Envoy Extraordinary and Minister Plenipotentiary to the government of the United States, with full powers to conduct political and financial negotiations.—Arango, Boyd, Arias, and F. V. de la Espriella.[78]

On November 13, it was again revealed that Philippe had full power to negotiate treaties and that the constitution of Panama was not to be like Colombia's: "It will permit the alienation of territory." The tract of land was to be double that designated by the Herran-Hay Treaty in the "interest of the maintenance of order along the canal."[79] Bunau-Varilla immediately presented his credentials to Roosevelt in a history-making ceremony which the envoy wished his son to witness. Twelve-year-old Etienne Bunau-Varilla followed the offical carriage in a landau in which he was the only passenger.[80]

General Reyes' Mission—and Others

Reports of indignation in Colombia and preparations for invasion were not taken lightly in Panama.[81] The American minister to Bogota, who had been left in a most uncomfortable position, was told that he was "at liberty to leave," and in a gesture of national unity the liberals offered their support to the government to retake Panama and execute the leaders of the revolt.[82] Philippe had advised the junta not to receive Reyes unless he came as an envoy of Colombia, but the general offered to make Panama City the capital of his country.

The Reyes mission was not the only group seeking to talk with Panama and the United States. A group composed of Drs. Francisco Pavon, E. Partega, Nicanor Isignares, General Demetrio Dairia, and Francisco Valez arrived in Galveston, Texas, on the steamer *Scotia* of the Hamburg-American Line, with hopes of attaching the Department of Bolivar to Panama, with United States help.[83] Several other prominent Colombians who liked the Herran-Hay Treaty supported this move, which they visualized as the beginning of a federation of discontented states, with Panama as its capital.[84]

Bunau-Varilla discouraged such activity and cabled the junta not to fall for these pledges. As the voice of his adopted country, he told reporters:

> Panama would absolutely refuse to listen to any overtures on their part [the Colombian suitors] toward a federation—we are wedded to the United States, contented and happy under her protection, and we have no desire to take another husband.[85]

While Amador was at sea, these groups were converging toward Washington. Meanwhile, the Nicaraguan minister, Gabriel Corea, convinced that there was to be a battle royal among the revolutionaries about treaty terms, slipped out of

Washington for Managua to promote constitutional changes in Central America and expedite a canal treaty.[86] Still another ominous threat appeared with the French press organized a campaign asking the stockholders of the French Company to force the corporation to cancel its sale to the United States.[87] Morgan continued to thunder against an accord with Panama short of annexation. His friend, Senator Edward Carnack of Tennessee, offered a resolution to build the canal through the Nicaraguan–Costa Rica border. He argued that "reasonable time" for acquiring the Panama route had elapsed with the death of the Hay-Herran Treaty, leaving the president no alternative but to build the canal "on the most northerly Isthmian route." At a caucus of Democratic senators, it was tentatively agreed that the party might vote for a treaty "if the right articles appear because it might be in the national interest." Only the two senators from Texas dissented. They, like Morgan, wished annexation.[88] What were "the right articles"? Perpetuity.

It was clear that unless perpetuity were granted in what the *New York Tribune* stated was a treaty of which "a good deal . . . is already done," the Senate would introduce myriad amendments.[89] The newspaper continued its editorial drive in support of the coup: "Is there a civilized government in the world that under similar circumstances would not say and do the same things?"[90] "Bogota had her chance. She frittered it away."[91] Two days later, the *Tribune* editorialized:

> There will be a cause on November 26, among our other grounds for national thanksgiving, for profound and devout gratitude that the government has not been foolish enough or weak enough to put the United States into a situation so imbecile. . . . We wanted the canal at Panama. Some of the critics particularly wanted it there in preference to anywhere else. . . . It is not business of ours that Panama has seceded from Colombia.[92]

On November 6, the United States took over the Guantanamo naval station in Cuba,[93] and the consul in Panama City transmitted to Washington the desires of the Panamanians who "want annexation or anything that will ensure the construction of the Panama Canal and the subsequent prosperity of the isthmus."[94] Despite its threats of invasion, Colombia backed up the Reyes mission with a direct appeal to the U.S. Senate, to the world at large, to the pope, and to the stockholders of the French company.[95] Simultaneously, another commission representing Bogota traveled to Washington to offer all the facilities needed for the building of the canal. This group was formed by Don Doncio Jimenez, Dr. Antonio R. Blanco, and Julio C. Zuniega.[96] Whitelaw Reid and Bunau-Varilla chided Marroquin for his belated attempts to subvert the isthmian republic. Said Reid:

> One of the most extraordinary incidents of the whole Panama business is the audacity of the President's demand or appeal [to the U.S. Senate]. It is strange that so accomplished a scholar should be so ignorant of the United States Constitution which makes the conduct of negotiations with foreign powers an executive function.[97]

And Philippe: "Before appealing to the sense of justice of the American people, President Marroquin would do well to appeal to his own sense of veracity."[98]

It was still possible that, through threats and persuasion, Bogota might be able to extract an accommodation from the United States. It was not only in the American Congress or in pro-Nicaraguan newspapers that pleas were heard and read—demands for abandoning Panama to Colombia, annexing the isthmus outright, or giving Bogota another chance. General H. O. Jeffries, who commanded an almost disabled three-ship flotilla for Panama, declared publicly that he was still "hopeful that Washington negotiate with Colombia directly."[99] One question had not been answered by Bogota: amnesty for the rebels. Under such confusing signs and ominous indications of a long debate if treaty terms were not quickly drawn and approved, Bunau-Varilla signed the document presented to him by Hay on the evening of November 18, 1903.

At a time when President Woz y Gil of Santo Domingo was

begging the United States to annex that state,[100] the canal treaty was a compromise between those who advocated union with Washington and those who wished to negotiate with Colombia. The protocol guaranteed what the Panamanians desired most at that moment: the canal, and the end of status as a protectorate of Bogota. In exchange for United States protection against Colombia or any other nation, the Republic of Panama granted territory for the waterway to the extent of five miles on each side and other lands necessary for the maintenance of the same.

By article 3, Panama ceded to the United States, within such lands, authority "as if it were the sovereign." Article 5 granted perpetual monopoly of any system of communication across her territory by canal or railroad to the federal government.[101] In article 2, which Bunau-Varilla had written, "leases in perpetuity" was changed by Hay to "grants to the United States in perpetuity."[102]

Two hours after the signing of the document, Amador, Boyd, and Carlos C. Arosemena reached Washington. They might have arrived earlier, but Amador decided to await Cromwell's return from France, a few hours after his own arrival. It was at this meeting that the two men began a partnership aimed at denigrating Philippe and compromising the treaty. Speaking to reporters in New York, Amador expressed hope that "annexation comes later." Debarking in Washington, he almost died of shock when Bunau-Varilla announced that he had signed the convention.[103]

After reading the treaty, the commissioners cabled Panama and justified its terms. The junta in turn cabled Philippe: "Explanation received from Amador-Boyd on the powerful reason which made you sign treaty."[104] Amador's craving for personal recognition was temporarily satisfied when he was received by Hay and Roosevelt. On November 20, at a formal presentation to the secretary of state by Bunau-Varilla, Amador expressed deep gratification at the terms of the covenant, provisions which he labeled "generous." He was convinced that "no time will be lost in its ratification, which I believe could be accomplished in the first ten days of December."[105] The group, led by Hay, went into the oval office. Roosevelt thanked Amador and Boyd for their unqualified support of the treaty, and the physician took the opportunity to pay tribute to Philippe's efforts on behalf of Panama. The president also praised the minister and allowed Amador to pin to his coat a miniature flag of the new nation, which Roosevelt wore the rest of the day.[106] The reception was both dignified and hearty.

While the commissioners spent the rest of the day sightseeing, the minister expressed shock at the efforts of English bondholders to persuade the Netherlands not to recognize Panama until it assumed an equitable share of the Colombian debt. Bunau-Varilla rejected the suggestion in the same manner in which he had objected to Hay's proposal to give Colombia half of the $10 million indemnity which had been allocated to Panama. "Panama," said Philippe, "had no part to the original loan nor had she received benefits from it, because the debt was contracted while Panama was still part of Spain from 1810–1821. Yet the isthmians had paid a high interest on the debt from 1821 to 1903.[107]

After the failure of his diplomatic mission at Colon, Reyes threatened war on Panama.[108] Meanwhile, another Colombian mission, led by Dr. Antonio Blanco, arrived in Washington and offered a six-mile or more canal zone in perpetuity, in exchange for a lump sum of $10 million. Of course, Panama's protection had to be withdrawn.[109] Realizing that Panama's recognition by the international community was imperative (only France, China, and the United States recognized the coup), Philippe enlisted the aid of the doyen of the diplomatic corps, Count Alexiev O'Cassini of Russia, to distribute to his colleagues a request for recognition signed by Bunau-Varilla.[110] In the expectation of diplomatic changes and waiting to hear from the Colombian missions traveling to Washington, the British declined to recognize Panama at that time.[111]

Panama Ratifies The Treaty; Old Allies Fall Out; Roosevelt Denies All

Amador's meeting with Cromwell in New York harbor on

November 17 only complicated the story of the canal. All signs pointed to the beginning of an ensconced and jealous opposition to Bunau-Varilla. And Reyes' arrival was imminent. The only solution to the crisis was to present Amador, Cromwell, and Reyes with a *fait accompli*, ratification by Panama. Philippe cabled the junta a summary of the protocol, urging approval. The document was wrapped in the flag of Panama, sealed with the family crest of John Bigelow, and placed on board the steamer *City of Washington* en route to Colon.[112]

General Reyes was a charismatic man. Philippe and the junta knew him well. His reputation had preceded him to the United States. He was considered capable of canceling the secession, and such a move did not appear impossible to the junta. Even the *New York Tribune* advised discretion when dealing with the envoy:

> For years he has been looked upon as one of the very foremost statesmen and soldiers of his much troubled country, as a man possessing at once integrity of character, amplitude of scholarship, and force of will.[113]

The *Tribune* regretted only the general's statements at Colon, where he had threatened the United States with a "second Boer War" if recognition of Panama was not withdrawn.[114]

In youth and in old age men do reckless things. In the twilight of his life, Amador, who had upstaged Arango, could not reconcile himself to seeing Philippe surrounded by the press, granting interviews, and signing documents on behalf of Panama. Amador wished to re-open discussions on the treaty, a dangerous move in view of the unsettled business with Colombia. But the physician's hopes of becoming Panama's first chief executive were enhanced when his friends in the isthmus began a campaign to reward him with the honor.[115] If he could not both sign the treaty and become president, he would settle for the latter. And immediately upon landing in New York, he made his son Panama's consul general.[116]

While Philippe waited to hear from the junta, Senator Morgan lined up his ducks and began to fire. He did not openly resent being replaced as chairman of the Committee on Interoceanic Canals, but he accused Roosevelt of bad faith. He attacked Loomis, whose statements about American rights to keep peace in the isthmus were, he thought, "the grimmest piece of irony that ever graced diplomatic annals."[117] The senator promised continued opposition to the treaty.

Influenced by Amador, the junta hesitated to approve the treaty. On November 24, Senator Hanna told Philippe about the conditions Reyes was bringing to Washington. The envoy had been authorized to grant the United States all the terms agreed upon in the Hay–Bunau-Varilla convention except the $10 million proviso, which Bogota now declined to accept. The canal was to be free to its builder. Colombia's capital was to be Panama City. Loomis confirmed these terms to Philippe, [118] and Amador was diverted from his unrealistic schemes on hearing these terms. He cabled the Junta, suggesting approval which could later be ratified by the municipalities.[119] On the twenty-fifth, Philippe demanded that the triumvirs ratify, or accept his resignation.[120]

At 10:00 A.M. the next morning, the junta and the Cabinet unanimously approved the treaty:

> In view of the approbation given by the delegates, Amador and Boyd, to the Hay–Bunau-Varilla treaty, you are authorized to notify officially the government of the United States that as soon as the document is received by the Junta of the Republic of Panama it will be ratified and signed. Arango, Arias, Espinoza, Espriella.[121]

Unaware of Amador's cable to the junta, Philippe was surprised at the speed with which he received his answer. But public attention had turned to the Reyes mission. While the news of the junta's ratification appeared on page 3 of the *New York Tribune*, page 1 headlined Reyes' statements and his new threats of invasion. General Victor Salazar, bitter because in 1902 the American navy had prevented his army from marching on Panama City, was now ready to march on Colon and settle old and new scores with the Panamanians[122]

Philippe did not feel that Panama was secure until Reyes' threat had ended. He continued his drive to get more recognition from the international community. He received assurances from Austria-Hungary on November 26, but England was still silent, a delay caused by the complaints of the holders of Colombian bonds. They had discounted the payment of $10 million, a good share of which they hoped would be applied to partial reimbursement of these bonds, which rarely if ever had paid any interest. Colombia's financial predicament meant ruin for its bondholders. Panama was their only prospect. Bogota hoped that the British would remain firm in their stand.

Without consulting Amador, who was in New York in conferences with Cromwell, Bunau-Varilla persuaded the junta to reach an understanding with London. On November 26, Philippe announced to the British ambassador that Panama would assume her share of the Colombian debt, in proportion to the population of the respective countries. The offer dissipated all objections, and England's recognition was transmitted to the minister the same evening. Shortly thereafter, Denmark, Sweden, Belgium, Switzerland, Norway, Peru, Costa Rica, Nicaragua, and Cuba did the same. Germany, Italy, and Japan sent word that they would soon follow suit.[123] Reyes' dreadnought was left without moorage space, thanks to Bunau-Varilla.

Still, commissioners Reyes and Ospina Perez represented the last hope of the Nicaraguan lobby. In their first interview, to the *New York Herald* on November 28, they stated that Colombia was ready and willing to build the canal at any cost.[124] On the eve of the mission's arrival, another daily, the *World*, perhaps with knowing Reyes' terms, asked in an editorial "Why $10 million?"[125] The general answered this question by saying: "We want the canal, and I have come to Washington to see what the people of the United States are prepared to accept. I come with direct instructions from the President [Marroquin]."[126] A few hours later, Reyes confirmed to the *New York Tribune* what Philippe had known for a week. He had offered the canal concession free and urged the

United States to destroy the Republic of Panama and deal with Colombia:

> My energies are devoted to the granting of the canal concession to the United States without payment of a cent. Even at this, Colombia will be the gainer. Colombia is afire with zeal for the building of the Canal by the United States.

The envoy ended the interview by saying that the treaty had not yet been ratified and promised that he would personally "put rebellion down."[127] The Colombian emissary also spoke of war:

> So tense is the feeling and so national the spirit of determination to bring the Isthmus back into the Republic, that President Marroquin will have no trouble in raising an army twice the size necessary to put down the disturbance. Such an army can march overland to the Isthmus, the opinion of ill-advised persons to the contrary notwithstanding.[128]

Neither open conflict nor guerrilla warfare, which several senators including Morgan predicted, was welcomed by Roosevelt. He was unwilling to risk political disaster at home by engaging Colombia in an undeclared jungle war which might attract worldwide sympathy for Bogota. Reyes' statement that the treaty was not yet ratified increased Philippe's concern for its final approval. His attempt to get the document back from Colon failed. Mystified but suspicious, Bunau-Varilla ordered the junta to deliver the treaty to the American consul immediately after ratification "because the Panama Railroad no longer offers the necessary guarantees for the transporting of the treaty."[129] The railroad owned the shipping line whose board chairman, G. Edward Simmons, was an intimate of Cromwell.

Amador's and Cromwell's antagonism toward Philippe was expressed in a wire which threw the junta into confusion on November 30:

> Several cables urging immediate appointment of Pablo Arosemena [replacing Philippe] have been sent to the Junta since Friday. Minister of Panama is trying to disturb the Junta by cabling that Washington will make a trade with Reyes. . . .

Mr. Cromwell had direct assurances from President Roosevelt, Secretary Hay, Senator Hanna, and other Senators that there is not the slightest danger of this. . . . We have the fullest support of Mr. Cromwell and his friends who have carried victory for us for the past six years. . . . Objection exists in Washington to the Minister of Panama, because he is not a Panamanian, but a foreigner; and initially has displeased influential Senators regarding character of the former Treaty. . . . He is recklessly involving Republic of Panama in financial and other complications that will use up important part of the indemnity. . . . Delegates here are powerless to prevent all this.[130]

Cromwell has reason to be concerned about Philippe's diplomatic agreement with the British. He was already discussing with Amador the investment of the $10 million indemnity while preparing his bill to the French canal company for services rendered in the past. The lawyer had not spoken with the president, Hay, Hanna, or Lodge since his return from France on November 17.[131] Certainly, Cromwell was not suggesting that one of the "influential senators" was Morgan, because Morgan disdained the lawyer. Cromwell was not naïve enough to approach Loomis and propose dispensing with Bunau-Varilla, and any suggestion of this kind to Hay would have been known to Loomis.[132]

It appears that Amador, the revered country doctor and patriot, had become a political animal. It was at this moment that "Varillitis" was invented by frustrated men who owed their place in the canal battles to Philippe. It was no conspiracy of the weak or oppressed against a tyrant or manipulator. It was a conspiracy of the worry-free and securely placed whom Bunau-Varilla had discovered, and who were now greedy for glory and fame and ready to sacrifice their savior. A silent, well-organized, and vicious campaign against Philippe spread.

Bunau-Varilla's work for the cause of Panama stirred up envy and rancor. Little did his detractors understand that it was his pragmatism that had brought Panama so close to success. Fortunately for the Panamanians, the junta was of a different mind. It ignored the Cromwell-inspired message and ratified the covenant: "at this moment, at eleven-thirty, the junta of the Provisional Government had just approved and signed the Treaty. Espriella."[133] At 6:00 P.M., another message arrived:

> Panama, December 2, 1903: It is most agreeable to inform Your Excellency that unanimously and without modification, we have ratified the Canal Treaty. This action of the Government had attracted unanimous approval. J. A. Arango, Tomas Arias, M. Espinoza.[134]

The junta sent the treaty in a sealed folio to Bunau-Varilla by Dr. Guy L. Edie, of the sanitary commission, who traveled to the United States on the steamer *City of Washington*. The twenty-four hours between December 14 and 15 were momentous in the history of the canal. Roosevelt submitted a message to Congress about his Panama policy and the treaty talks, Philippe was informed by the junta that all the municipalities had ratified the convention, and William Buchanan sailed on the *Yucatan* to take up his post as the first envoy to the new nation.[135]

Almost simultaneously with Reyes' arrival, Amador departed on the steamer *Sequrança*. Ratification by the junta was a severe blow to Reyes, but not the end of the war, for he was as persistent as Bunau-Varilla. On December 3, General Reyes and Herran were asked to lunch at Hay's, where Reyes informed the secretary of state that he had no idea what he was going to ask of Washington. The next day he presented his credentials to Roosevelt, who received him cordially and informally. They reminisced about old times and toasted each other. Roosevelt ended the private meeting by telling Reyes that he should address himself to Hay from then on.[136]

Meanwhile, newspaper reports and confidential information confused the picture of the Reyes mission. William H. Taft relayed to Loomis the words of James A. Scrymser, of the South American and Telegraph Company of New York, dealing with contemplated uprisings in the provinces of Cauca and Antioquia. The acting secretary wrote: "We shall be exceedingly obliged for any information bearing upon the possible purpose of Colombia to dispatch troops to the Isthmus." Loomis requested that all cables from Buenaventura to him be enclosed in an envelope marked "Personal."[137]

Before his arrival, Reyes had written to the president and to Loomis asking that all negotiations with Panama be suspended until he was received by Roosevelt; otherwise, he would support an invasion of Panama. The president ordered Loomis to warn Colombia, for "they will be repelled and their ports blockaded." The acting secretary left the matter to Hay,[138] who conveyed no such statement to Reyes.

Meanwhile, the Colombian found a strange ally in Morgan, who, acknowledging his defeat in the matter of the treaty, opened a campaign against Roosevelt and all those who had been at the center of the revolt. Armed with the article written by Philippe in Le Matin, September 2, 1903— the article in which Bunau-Varilla outlined the revolution— Morgan took the floor at the first meeting of the Senate, on January 4, 1904. Morgan charged collusion between Philippe and Roosevelt: "If the President did understand the situation at that time and did not state it to him, Bunau-Varilla is a great mind reader. Here is the plan worked out exactly, which he projected and prognosticated in September 1903."[139] Other senators took the cue and charged the two men with collusion.

As expected, that same day the president sent the treaty to the Senate with a message on his Panama policy. He rebuked Morgan for all "the injurious insinuations which have been made of complicity by this government in the revolutionary movement in Panama," which were "as destitute of foundation as of propriety." Roosevelt denied any participation in the coup or any expectation of an explosion of this character. He urged Congress to ratify the protocol.[140] The Senate leadership promised that debate would not be delayed beyond February, but prospects of quicker ratification were poor because of Hanna's and Hay's maladies. The recent political exertions of the former and the diplomatic anguish of the latter had much to do with their deteriorating physical conditions.[141]

Loomis and Bunau-Varilla Campaign for Senate Approval of the Treaty

On December 15, Loomis and Philippe had appeared as guests of the prestigious literary Quill Club of New York City,[142] and their talks made a profound impression upon the listeners. Loomis declared that had Colombia been allowed to renege on the concession, Paris might have violated the Monroe Doctrine and allocated her canal investments by force. On this occasion Roosevelt wrote: "My dear Loomis: On all sides I hear voices of praise for your admirable speech. I think it was most timely, and you brought out the points in excellent shape. Sincerely yours, Theodore Roosevelt."[143] Two days later, Philippe spoke before another influential group whose chief officer wrote to him afterwards: "Permit me to present to you the formal thanks of the American Academy of Political and Social Science for the admirable address delivered at the session last Friday evening. . . . Leo S. Rowe, President."[144]

On December 19, after a Cabinet meeting, the president publicly praised Loomis' speech, while several anti-Panama senators, led by Arthur Gorman of Maryland, criticized it in Congress. Lodge and Foraker defended Loomis, and Reyes refused to treat with the acting secretary.[145] Hay's illness necessitated the postponement of a formal presentation of Reyes' memorandum and the impasse continued. Loomis, thanks to Philippe, already knew what was on the envoy's mind. The two had conferred in the New Willard Hotel's lounge, where the general had reminisced about old times in Panama and urged the Frenchman to back him up. Reyes made frequent calls at the State Department in the hope of seeing Hay. After one of these visits, Loomis wrote to Buchanan:

> Reyes was in again to-day; he is evidently going to try to get the Panama people or some of them to agree, after the canal

question has been settled according to the treaty, to become re-incorporated in Colombia and have the capital at Panama. No arrangement could be more objectionable than this. The President asked me to say that he hopes you would take pains to discourage heartily any such notion if it creeps up. . . . It will not be necessary to keep copies for the record or to confirm in your letters any confidential telegrams which come to you with the signature group of figures meaning Legantic. Anything of a confidential nature for the Department or the President you will please address to "Legantic, Washington." F. J. Loomis.[146]

As 1904 approached, and in view of Hay's condition and Reyes' refusal to deal with Loomis, Secretary of War, Elihu Root, received the envoy, who by this time was no longer optimistic. The general told Root that his mission was diluted because his people were angry and divided. Since Root's reply was not to his liking, Reyes excused himself from the New Year's reception at the White House and began to prepare for his journey home.[147]

The general's proposals were translated and sent to Bassett Moore and to Bunau-Varilla for comments.[148] Reyes was secretly giving his government the impression that Washington had changed its position and would allow Colombian troops to land at Panama; but Loomis put a stop to this delusory information in a strong note to Herran.[149] Reyes' offer to submit the matter of Panama's share of Colombia's debt to the Court of International Justice at the Hague evaporated when Philippe stated that "Panama would not object to assuming her proportion of the Colombian debt." Allegations by Reyes that the United States had usurped Colombia's rights in the treaty of 1846 were dealt with by Bassett Moore, whose opinion was that the protocol did not bind the federal government to protect Colombia against revolution, but obliged her to "guarantee to us a free and open transit. We have had to secure it for ourselves."[150]

Later, Loomis wrote Bassett Moore' that "what Bunau-Varilla had to say is authentic. The Panama people have officially notified us [through Philippe], that they are willing to assume a share of the Colombian foreign debt based upon a per capita proportion."[151] The international lawyer then prepared to advise on a formal reply to Reyes, and Bunau-Varilla and Loomis submitted considerable material to him. By this time, attention was again focusing on the Senate, which had moved to start an inquiry into the conduct of the government during the critical days of the revolution.[152]

Colombia Tries to Move against Panama, but the U.S. Fleet Is There

Bunau-Varilla dismissed the rumors of invasion of Panama by Colombia as a purely "Quixotian enterprise,"[153] but Roosevelt took no chances. On December 8, American marines from the armada near Colon bivouacked at Capira, west of the canal, and troops at Fort Sheridan, Illinois, Fort Thomas, Kentucky, and Fort Riley, Kansas, were alerted for action in Panama.[154] Colombia had precipitated this reaction by landing eleven hundred men at the mouth of the Atrato, and General Daniel Ortiz exhorted the troops near Cartagena: "It is preferable to see the Colombian race exterminated than to submit to the United States."[155] The war vessels *Pinzon* and *Cartagena* took positions in the Gulf of Darien.[156]

In mid-December, contingents from the cruiser *Prairie* encamped at Yaviza, east of the canal, and the force on the *Dixie*, 330 strong, was sent ashore.[157] These maneuvers, and the government's delay in answering Reyes' *aide memoires*, gave hope to Morgan and his friends, who prayed for an incident which would help forestall the treaty with Panama. Newspaper reports seemed alarming to Lodge, who visited the president in the company of five other influential senators. Roosevelt was told to expect bitter opposition to the protocol in Congress. He was also advised to let Bogota take the initiative in any armed conflict.[158] After a consultation with Moody, it was decided to intensify the American military and naval demonstrations and thereby discourage Colombia from any armed move. In spite of her miserable army, Bogota, by sheer numbers, could have put down the rebellion, as Reyes boasted, for Panama's forces were even more ludicrous. The commandant of the marines, General

George F. Elliott, was dispatched to the isthmus with more men and an order to await developments.[159]

Panama claimed that it could put more than fifty thousand men under arms to resist an invasion or put down any insurrection, but the fact is that it would have taxed all the resources of the new republic to arm and equip even fifteen hundred men for active service: At that, they would have had to go into the field without uniforms and with a varied assortment of arms. The army of the new nation was little more than a name. The Colombian battalion that arrested the officers sent by Bogota were mostly recruited from Cauca. It numbered only two hundred, but it was able to impress the public when turned out on parade in gaudy yellow, blue, and gold uniforms. It had a multiplicity of generals, colonels, captains, lieutenants, and sergeants, each dazzling in gold lace and resplendent accoutrements. Fearful of invasion, the new government was eager to recruit in a hurry. Little judgment was exercised in enlisting men for service, however, and in February 1904 the Panamanian army looked like a high-school cadet corps. A large number of boys under fifteen were part of this force, but it had been so in Colombia for a century, and the Colombian army was not much better off. Surely with armies such as these only Don Quixote, as Philippe said, would dare challenge the United States.[160]

By the middle of January 1904, while Hanna's and Hay's physical condition continued to deteriorate,[161] Senator Morgan was warming up for the second of a total of thirteen speeches he delivered against the treaty. Once more, Bigelow was enlisted, this time to influence some of the politicians in the Democratic camp. The sage diplomat, like Philippe, was convinced that the canal was necessary to promote world trade. Both men foresaw the rise of a new world power in Japan and, thereby, a threat to the United States. With arguments like these, Bigelow had little trouble appealing to the Democratic presidential candidate of 1904, Alton Parker, who promised not to make an issue of the canal during the political campaign.[162]

Roosevelt himself tried to allay the suspicions of collusion between himself and Bunau-Varilla in a grand manner. On the night of January 14, 1904, at the reception before a state dinner for the diplomatic corps, the president seemed to be awaiting a special guest. When Philippe arrived, Roosevelt, followed by the Cabinet, the doyen of the corps, and other high-ranking diplomats, greeted the Panamanian envoy effusively. The chief executive marveled in a loud voice at Bunau-Varilla's cunning in guessing what he had discussed with Bassett Moore in early September 1903. Philippe replied that it was a matter of logic, "for logical minds meet." Roosevelt responded, "If that is so, you are the greatest logician I have ever known, sir. They say that I have inspired you. It would be much more true to say that you inspired me.[163]

The Departure of General Reyes' Mission

The barrage of memoranda from Reyes to Hay which began on December 23 and ended on January 5, 1904, shows the general's increasing frustration with events, as well as the influence of persons unfriendly to Bunau-Varilla. At first Reyes appeared confident of achieving a rapprochement between Panama and Colombia. Advised by the veteran lawyer, Wayne McVeagh, former attorney general under Cleveland, the Colombian continued to ask for a settlement of the debt question, to insist that the United States guarantee Colombian sovereignty over the isthmus, and to declare that the French company had no right to sell its concession to anyone. Later, he assured Hay that the "mother country commands sufficient forces to subdue the rebellion" and, finally, he condemned the way in which the new state was created, "by a *coup de main* effected by the winning over of troops who have fought against no one, assaulted no entrenchment, captured no fort, contenting themselves with putting in prison the constituted authorities." Reyes charged that the revolutionists were "counseled by speculators of several countries who had assumed the direction of affairs. . . . Thousands of the inhabitants of Panama condemned the separatist movement.[164]

Wishing to draft a final reply to these charges before senatorial debate reached a climax, the secretary of state summoned Philippe. Would Colombia invade the isthmus? Would the United States pay Bogota a large indemnity, as Reyes suggested? The answer was no. Considering the rugged terrain south of Panama City, there could be no invasion without a bona fide army and navy. Paying indemnity would be construed as an admission of guilt. Do the Panamanians abhor secession from Colombia, as Reyes affirmed? Philippe did not think so, but the reply was to offer a plebiscite to the citizens of Panama. As for Bogota sharing in the $10 million windfall and the French company's sale of its property, submit this claim to the Court at the Hague and submit the company's rights to the French tribunals. These and other suggestions were taken into consideration in the final reply to Reyes, which ended:

> Any charge that this Government, or any responsible member of it, held intercourse, whether official or unofficial, with agents of the revolution in [Panama], is utterly without foundation. Equally so is the insinuation that any action of this Government, prior to the revolution in Panama, was the result of complicity with the plans of the revolutionists. The department sees fit to make these denials and it makes them final.[165]

With these words, Reyes' mission came to an end and the envoy departed for home.

The secretary's note met the highest diplomatic requirements, for it was true that no one in the government had had direct contact with any Panamanian, revolutionary or not. Its talks were with a foreigner, Bunau-Varilla, who was not overtly engaged in actual revolution but was covertly pulling strings behind the scenes. He had presented to Loomis only the possibility of a disturbance which might have interrupted isthmian communication, as had happened so many times before. Reyes' accusations were partly based on Amador's indiscretion in rushing to cable Hay first, rather than Bunau-Varilla, about the successful coup. Amador's eagerness to place himself at the center of the stage proved to be counterproductive, for he knew nothing of the contortions of high diplomacy.

American Reaction

Twice in January, Morgan-inspired resolutions to investigate Bunau-Varilla's role in the revolution were introduced into the Senate. These salvos were cleverly answered by Edward P. Mitchell of the *New York Sun*, who wrote:

> The Committee on Foreign Affairs is hereby instructed to investigate and ascertain whether [Tomas] Estrada Palma and other persons residing in the United States, and subject to our laws, did aid or promote an insurrection in Cuba against the Kingdom of Spain.[166]

But if one can cope successfully with frontal attacks, one is always vulnerable to the enemy within. On January 17, 1904, the *New York World* splashed on its front page the words of Reyes' memorandum to Hay making direct and careless accusations against Pablo Arosemena, Federico Boyd, Carlos Constantino Arosemena, Amador, and Philippe, all of whom appeared beside the caption "Panama Revolution a stock gambler's plan to make millions." "The Real Story" told of a "syndicate" with branches in Paris and New York, whose "clever agent" had carried out his promises "that the United States would furnish aid and would recognize the new republic."[167] By the very absence of his name, one person became universally suspected of planting the story—William Nelson Cromwell.

Years later, the federal government sued the newspaper, and in a post-mortem investigation in the House of Representatives instigated by Congressman Henry T. Rainey of Illinois, this and other articles in the *World* became boomerangs, causing Cromwell irreparable damage. The editors of the *World* disclosed the source of information to Bunau-Varilla:

> New York, July 2, 1909, to Philippe Bunau-Varilla
> 53 Avenue D'Iena, Paris, France:
> . . . I have informed Mr. Lindsay, with the consent of Mr. Piza, of the nature of your standing in the matter, and add for

your own information that you can accept my word that the article about which you desired information came directly from the office of William Nelson Cromwell to our editors through the medium of Jonas Whitley, his press agent, who is closely associated with Roger L. Farnham, Mr. Cromwell's general representative in such matters. Both Mr. Farnham and Mr. Whitley were employees of the *World* before going into the pay of Mr. Cromwell, whom up to the time of his canal performance, had not participated in public affairs, but was regarded as an extraordinarily keen lawyer. . . . I give you my word in this matter. . . . Mr. Lindsay bears with him much information of interest and value to you personally which he will gladly place at your service. . . . Greatly regretting that I am unable at the moment to greet you in person, I am, Sincerely yours, Don C. Seitz, Assistant Vice-President.[168]

John D. Lindsay, legal counsel for the *World*, traveled to Paris to see Philippe at the insistence of the journal's owners. At the congressional proceedings, Rainey charged that Cromwell had become another Aaron Burr. Other witnesses characterised Cromwell as the rapist of the isthmus.[169] Cromwell was not that kind of a Machiavelli, but he had acquired enemies as ships acquired barnacles. His testimony implicating Hanna, eight years dead, did not befit a distinguished lawyer.

Seeking sole credit for Hanna's conversion to the cause of the Panama Canal, Cromwell charged that the senator's change was not a question of the mind or the heart, but of the hand. Hanna, said Cromwell, accepted $60,000 for his campaign fund in 1902.[170] Although Philippe stated that the lawyer had charged the French company this sum for expenses, there were no records to prove that Hanna received it.[171] From 1900 to 1902, the senator received nearly $3 million for electoral expenses but, in two specific cases, considerable sums were returned to the surprised donors after the election. Hanna's honesty in dealing with financial supporters increased their confidence in him and in his party: when contributions implied the promise of particular services, the money was returned.[172] Finally, a staff correspondent for the *World*, Earl Harding, corroborated Seitz' letter of 1909 to Bunau-Varilla, in which he stated that "the facts were brought to the *World* by Jonas Whitley of Mr. Cromwell's staff of press agents, and the *World* holds a receipt for $100 for the tip."[173]

One of the witnesses, however, Henry N. Hall, either intentionally or in total ignorance of facts, gave Cromwell the credit for the $100,000 loan Bunau-Varilla had advanced to the revolution, and named Cromwell as the real hero of the plot. Fortunately, Philippe's former lawyer, Frank D. Pavey, was still living, and in 1913 the investigation was reopened to hear his testimony and to insert into the record Bunau-Varilla's "Statement on Behalf of Historical Truth." Pavey's testimony helped dispel some of the lies and half-truths elicited at the hearing in 1912. The new edition of *The Story of Panama*, in 1913, was more in line with the facts.[174]

At the time of the accusations, Philippe's first impulse was to sue the newspaper, but Pavey and Bigelow dissuaded him from this course. Shortly thereafter, however, the *New York Tribune* and the *Sun* gave wide coverage to Bunau-Varilla's reply:

> All the slanders published in Paris, and which have been echoed by some American newspapers, are themselves echoes of some of the calumnies which have been during the many years the missive with which Frenchmen unworthy of that name have attacked all those who served Panama. It is necessary to recall that even President Loubet has been attacked by these vile methods for having tried to protect the canal interests. . . . I have been so much exposed to calumny in my long fight against ignorance and falsehood that I feel myself immune against their attacks. . . . I have served the Republic of Panama in a diplomatic capacity . . . . Her interests are coincident with those of the canal. Once the treaty is ratified I will have fulfilled the pledge I made to myself twenty-three years ago in the Ecole Polytechnique at the conclusion of a lecture delivered by de Lesseps himself.[175]

Ironically, in the last stages of the epic of Panama, Bunau-Varilla's greatest opponent was not Colombia, volcanoes, pandemia, Morgan, or the junta, but Cromwell, who by his lack of foresight missed a true place in the history of the Panama Canal. A newspaper report in 1908 described the lawyer as "five feet, eight inches high" and of medium build, like Philippe. His brilliant light-blue eyes were as innocent looking as a boy's, but they hid a steely mind that could deal ruthlessly with the mightiest of foes.[176] Like Bunau-Varilla, he talked fast and was capable of conveying his ideas and wishes clearly and persuasively.

Both men were about the same age, Cromwell being two years older than Philippe. John Bigelow who, unlike Cromwell, sensed that he was near the vortex of history-making events, kept records of the movements of his protégé and never for a moment doubted Bunau-Varilla's ultimate triumph. Because of his style, the Frenchman attracted more supporters to the Panama cause than Cromwell. Both warriors were good speakers and there was great dignity in their bearing and grace in their gestures, but because Philippe had more experience with the canal and Panama, his arguments were strong and clear. He spoke precisely and to the point, without the slightest hesitation. The difference between the two men was one of character. Philippe's ultimate victory was due to persistence, for the problem he was tackling needed a confident realist more than a dedicated public-relations gladiator like Cromwell.

The Senate Debates and
Ratifies the Treaty with the Republic of Panama

Senator Hanna's condition kept him from participating in the canal debate, but in the end his illness was to decide its favorable outcome. His influence was missed, particularly in curtailing the natural desire of legislators to introduce amendments. Hay had to press the senators for a quick ratification—but just then, when he needed support, he remarked that the "treaty is not so advantageous to Panama."[177]

All over the world, this statement, betraying an unexpected elasticity of conscience, had a deleterious effect on the treaty. In signing the document, Bunau-Varilla had not only interpreted the desires of the junta, which was ready to accept annexation, but also guaranteed the security of the waterway. He believed that perpetual freedom of transit could not be guaranteed without a stable Panamanian commonwealth. But soon he was to feel the darts of ingratitude from the very isthmians whom he had helped to revolt and had firmly established under the protection of the United States.

Despite orchestrated attacks against Philippe, the *Washington Post* and the *New York Evening News* had joined the *New York World* singing Cromwell's opera, the opposition to the treaty in the Senate[178] and in academia.[179] The departure of Reyes ended the impasse and relaxed the tension. Although Colombia continued to talk of war,[180] the envoy privately expected that his country would be recompensed for the loss of Panama, an accommodation which he could expedite by his return home. Reyes was the choice of Marroquin and his cronies in the 1904 elections. His failure in Washington threatened that arrangement, because Jose Joaquin Velez and Jose Vasquez Cobo were maneuvering to put up a ticket headed by themselves; and Reyes' friends in the State of Bolivar urged his return. The general's last suggestion was to have either Buchanan or H. Bowen (the American minister in Caracas), sent to Bogota as special ambassador to renegotiate the issue of Panama. He thanked the government for the courtesies he had received and separately visited senators Lodge, Spooner, and Elkins. And Bunau-Varilla.[181]

As February approached, senatorial opinion began to change, but most of the Democratic newspapers, such as the *Brooklyn Eagle*, the *Hartford Times*, and the *Atlanta Constitution*, continued their attacks. Southern legislators like the two senators from Georgia and from Texas remained adamantly opposed to the canal at Panama.[182] They were ready to die for Nicaragua. A favorite slogan of the Democratic solons was that the canal through Nicaragua "is a Democratic route. No matter how badly conceived it is, we must support it for the sake of the party."[183]

Roosevelt discussed the treaty with as many as thirty senators at a large dinner given for him by the attorney general. Hanna was well enough to attend and, with Lodge and Platt of Connecticut, persuaded the rest that all amendments to the treaty should be dropped. The junta, said

Hanna and Roosevelt, had given assurances through Bunau-Varilla that arrangements about harbors, sanitation, and the limits of Panama and Colon—cities that Morgan and others wanted included in the canal zone—would be worked out. Slowly, Democratic opposition began to crack, and the first one to concede the final victory of Bunau-Varilla was John Tillman of Mississippi, who stated: "I shall make no set speech on the Panama Treaty, but I shall sit in the Senate and throw rocks at it as it passes by." The solid opposition of the Democrats seemed shattered. Morgan introduced a bill providing for the annexation of Panama.[183] Another Democrat, Senator Warren Simmons of North Carolina, advocated ratification because it was not realistic to leave Panama at the mercy of Colombia, although he still yearned for a Nicaraguan canal.[184]

The Latin-American press was also responding to the Hay-Bunau-Varilla accord by that time. In the *Noticiero* of San Jose, Costa Rica, Dr. Modesto Garcia, a Colombian who had favored the Herran-Hay protocol, stated that his country had mistreated the isthmians and that the treaty was a good thing for Panama.[186] Don Francisco Serrano, another exiled Colombian, declared in *El Comercio* of Quezaltenango, Guatemala, that "we expected the revolt of Panama after the treaty was rejected."[186] San Salvador's *El Latinoamericano* envied the position of Panama which now "owes its existence to the United States."[187] *El Telegrafo* of Guayaquil expressed the same feelings.[188] The Chilean journals which had at first opposed the secession, such as *El Ferrocarril (railroad)*, *La Tarde (Afternoon)*, *El Mercurio (Mercury)*, and *El Chileno*, swung over to Panama by the end of December. Characteristic of their policy is an editorial from *El Chileno*:

> It is impossible to deny the impressive tendency of the United States. North American advances with gigantic steps on the road to progress, while South America represents, in the majority of her people, the past, in a few ways only the present. . . . Lucky Panama who will soon prosper.[189]

The junta, for its part, contributed to the ratification by

formalizing the establishment of a permanent government with the selection of a constituent convention which, by February, was about to finish its job. The charter provided for no death penalty, no army, no business monopolies, an efficient police force, a free press, a four-year presidential term, and three vice-presidents elected for a two-year period and chosen from both parties. More important for the canal, the convention approved the draft of the treaty referring to territorial boundaries, and delimiting the canal zone as specified in the Hay-Bunau-Varilla convention. A supplementary bill approved all the acts of the provisional government—including, Philippe's appointment as envoy extraordinary and his signing of the treaty.

Amador personally proposed to the delegates the insertion of the following proviso:

> Should public peace or constitutional order be disturbed in any part of the Republic of Panama, the government of the United States may intervene to restore peace and order, in the event that the United States, by treaty or convention, shall have assumed, or expressed the intention of assuming, the obligation of guaranteeing the independence and sovereignty of this republic.[190]

Agitation against the treaty within and without Congress, plus the well-publicized attacks against Philippe inspired by Cromwell, suddenly died in February, when three unexpected events monopolized the headlines and preoccupied the legislators. The last tirades against Bunau-Varilla and Roosevelt in the House and Senate were delivered on February 1.[191] Senator Hanna took to bed on the same day, after attending the Ohio gridiron dinner on January 30, and he never walked again. His condition became serious when it was announced that he had contracted "irregular typhoid" and, after the tenth, his death appeared inevitable. He died on the fifteenth "of a very virulent typhoid fever."[192]

A second unexpected event occurred in Baltimore. At 2:00 A.M. on February 8, a conflagration of gigantic dimensions spread through Baltimore's business and middle-class residential districts. The fire, which lasted more than sixteen hours, dislocated transit between New York and Washington and, when it was over, Baltimore was two-thirds smaller. The loss was estimated at $150 million,[193] as much as the projected cost of the canal. An important enemy of the treaty, Maryland's Senator Arthur Gorman, had much more to worry him now.

Almost simultaneously, in faraway Port Arthur, the Russo-Japanese conflict, which Bunau-Varilla had predicted in 1900, exploded. In an attack similar to the one on December 7, 1941, against Pearl Harbor, the Mikado sank or disabled the entire and highly rated Russian fleet in the Far East.[194]

Each of these events directly influenced the fortunes of the treaty. The "most sorrowful scene" said Senator John Spooner, "which I ever saw was in the Senate when we sat and waited for the news" of Hanna's death. Debate on the treaty remained in abeyance and, upon Hanna's death, the Senate adjourned and began preparations for his two funerals, one in Washington and the other in Cleveland.[195]

The New York Times tried to keep the issue alive by printing a long interview with Reyes, who was on his way to Paris in a belated attempt to derail the transfer of the new French company's assets to the United States. The journal praised Reyes, as the representative of "intelligent Colombians who have gained control of the country" and compared him with Porfirio Diaz, nevertheless rejoicing that "his face has no trace of Indian blood," for he is "a Biscayan by descent who belongs to the large element in Colombia which has never admitted the blood of the aborigines in their blood." The newspaper regretted that a handful of traitors in one of the smallest provinces had taken advantage of Bogota which, confronted by the irresistible power of the United States, found itself without a friend among the nations.[196]

Editorially, the New York Times charged that most of the French company's stock had been bought by Americans. Without paying attention to Cromwell's denials of the story, it chastised Loomis for his speech at the Quill Club on December 16. "Now," said the New York Times, "his canvas is simply blown from its frame by the disclosure."[197] The editor had still more lances to throw, and these were hurled at Roosevelt a few days later, when the Republican Party announced that the success at Panama would be campaign propaganda. The *New York Times* sarcastically editorialized: "Admirable! Perfect! President Roosevelt rode down all law and smashed a treaty in the accommodation of the Panama Canal Policy."[198]

While Hanna's funeral was taking place in the marble hall of the Capitol, Amador was being elected president by Panama's constitutional convention; and the European nations, alarmed at the unexpected course of the Far-Eastern war, were preparing for mobilization. The kaiser openly supported the czar, and although France declared neutrality, the French were on Russia's side. England's sympathy was with Japan, and American public opinion was divided.[199] Under such ominous signs, it was advisable to reach a quick decision on the treaty. Morgan, who did not eulogize Hanna, sat behind Bunau-Varilla who, with the rest of the diplomatic corps, outranked the Senate. Among the many floral tributes was a large wreath, in the shape of the isthmus, bearing the colors of the flag of Panama. Morgan did not need to be told who had ordered this display.[200] Out of respect for Hanna, and because many senators accompanied the cortege to Cleveland, the Senate adjourned until December 22. Vote on the treaty was set for the twenty-third.

A last-minute attempt to appease Bogota failed when an amendment by Senator Augustus Octavius Bacon of Georgia, giving Colombia a huge indemnity for the loss of Panama, was voted down forty-nine to twenty-four. Just before the final balloting, Senator Edward Carnack of Tennessee repeated the ludicrous charges of the *World*, and other misinformation appearing in *La Libre Parole*. He claimed to have received "compromising documents on the Panama Canal."[201] However, the saddened Senate, preoccupied with the furious succession of recent events, ignored him and ratified the treaty by a vote of sixty-six to fourteen. Philippe cabled Amador:

> While defending the great enterprise, almost killed by falsehood and calumny, I acted in the capacity of a French citizen defending the great moral interest of France. This

excludes all idea of material remuneration, therefore I request the Government of the Republic of Panama to withhold the salary of my office. It will form the nucleus of a fund for the erection of a monument by the grateful Panamanians to Ferdinand de Lesseps, the great Frenchman, whose genius has consecrated the Isthmus to the progress of the world.[203]

On February 25, Roosevelt and Philippe signed the treaty at the White House. Senator Kittredge of South Dakota received the pen used by the president; Bunau-Varilla gave his to Lodge.[204] The final examination of the treaty's semantics and the issuance of the formal proclamation came the next day at the State Department. Hay, Philippe, Sidney Smith (chief of the Diplomatic Bureau), and Eddie Savoy were present. Savoy was a career messenger, and an expert in sealing original treaties, which had to be framed with the traditional red ribbons in a rhomboid shape. Again Bunau-Varilla and Hay had to affix their names to the treaty, and this time the pens used went to Loomis and Savoy.[205]

Panama Thanks Bunau-Varilla

Panama's first president was in the twilight of his life. Self-conscious about his age, he wished to depart in a flash of glory. After the ratification, Amador atoned for his tardiness in giving due credit to Philippe:

Panama, February 24, 1904, Bunau-Varilla, Washington (DC)
I publicly declare to the American government and its generous and great people the most sincere expression of gratitude from our nation for the services rendered by you to our country from October 11, 1903 to this date. These services will always live in the hearts of our countrymen and will last longer than the bronze of the statue of the great Frenchman to which erection you so generously are contributing now. Amodor.[206]

And the Constituent Convention expressed its collective gratification to Philippe for the same services. The presiding officer of this body, Pablo Arosemena, wrote:

Panama, February 27, 1904
Senor Don Philippe Bunau-Varilla, Washington.
I have the great distinction of communicating to you that the

National Convention, which I preside, adopted yesterday the enclosed proposition which I presented myself: The National Convention holds in great esteem the services which Mr. Philippe Bunau-Varilla has rendered to the Panamanian people contributing with his perseverance and intelligence to the adoption by the United States, of the Panama route to build the interoceanic canal.

I rejoice with you in the adoption of this resolution which is nothing but an act of strict justice. I avail myself of the opportunity to reiterate to you the expression of my highest personal esteem. Pablo Arosemena.[207]

The junta wanted Philippe to return to his native France as Panamanian envoy in order to expedite the settlement of the Colombian shares in the canal company, but he thought it unnecessary because the matter was in the hands of the courts. According to Bunau-Varilla, international precedent made the new republic, as the sovereign of the isthmus, heir to those certificates. Therefore, Philippe had advised the junta to acquiesce in paying for a fraction of the Colombian debt, a sum proportionate to the population of Panama. This sum was approximately $1 million, provided Bogota recognized the secession. Philippe figured that by obtaining these shares, valued at one hundred francs each, the republic would make a profit of $222,222 at the then-current rate of exchange. Colombia had received the securities in partial payment for the extensions of the canal contract signed earlier by Napoleon Bonaparte Wyse.[208]

In April, after Pablo Arosemena, the new minister to Washington arrived, Philippe left for France, where he plunged himself into activities in connection with his journal and his mining and railroad interests in Africa and Europe. There was still the possibility that he might accept a place in the new canal commission, as Roosevelt wanted, but the appointment of his friend, Professor William Burr of Columbia University, guaranteed that his views on the waterway would be heard by the commission.[209]

On April 22, 1904, the deed transferring the property of the French canal company to the United States was signed in

Paris in Philippe's presence. The payment of $40 million was made by the United States through J. Pierpont Morgan and Company, New York bankers, acting as an agent of the federal government. The money was first paid to "J. Pierpont Morgan & Company of New York City, Special Disbursing Agent" on May 9, 1904, by a treasury warrant on the assistant treasurer of the United States at New York and then transmitted to Paris by J. P. Morgan and Company, partly in bullion and partly by the purchase of exchange between March 9 and June 2, 1904, payment of the total amount being made to the Bank of France. The French company bore the expense of the transmission of these funds, for which the Morgan bank charged $35,000.[210]

The fund of $40 million paid into the Bank of France produced a net sum of 206 million francs. Of this, 128 million francs were placed, pursuant to the decision of the arbitrators, to the credit of the old French interoceanic company, and 77.4 million francs were placed to the credit of the new French company. The liquidator of the old company, acting under the direction of the Civil Tribunal of the Seine, distributed the amount that came into his hands to the claimants of that company, that is, to the bondholders of the old company. None of the stockholders of the old company received any dividend whatsoever. The number of claimants and bondholders was 226,296, and the average amount paid was $156, or 650 francs.

The amount paid to the French new company in liquidation was distributed among its shareholders through four leading banks—the Credit Lyonnaise, Societé Genérale, Comptoir Nationale d'Escompte de Paris, and Credit Industriel et Commerciel—in three separate installments: July 15, 1904; February 3, 1908; and June 15, 1908. The amount so paid to the shareholders of the new Panama canal company was approximately 129.78 francs per share, the par value of each share being 100 francs: that is, they received only the capital originally invested, with interest of less than 3 percent per annum. The number of shareholders existing at the time of the distribution was 6,796, and at least 70 percent of shareholders were stockholders when the company was organized[211]

Philippe made no financial profit from these transactions, but Cromwell did.[212] Since not one of the stockholders of the old company received any dividend, Bunau-Varilla received only the $50,000 he had invested in the corporation in the 1880s. His salary of $1,000 a month as minister of Panama, totaling by the end of March no more than $5,000, had been donated to the Amador regime to memorialize the history of the canal and build a statue to de Lesseps.

No expense money was allocated to Philippe during his tenure as diplomatic agent of the republic, nor has Panama ever suggested he or his heirs be repaid the enormous sums he spent to promote the cause of Panama in Europe and America. His residences in the United States—the Waldorf Astoria, the New Willard Hotel and, for five critical months, for Panama in 1903 and 1904, the Hotel Amsterdam in New York, where he housed his family—cost more than $20,000. Cables; secretarial and entertainment expenses to influence legislators, and prominent people in industry, banking, and shipping; tips to newsmen; printing the numerous data to advance the cause of Panama; his transatlantic voyages; his trips on this continent, to Cuba, Venezuela, and within the United States, cost more than $100,000. Not one penny of those expenses has ever been returned to him, his heirs, or his memory. His missionary work in Europe and Africa, plus his pro-Panama expenses in Paris and at the long sessions at his home in Paris, also reach the six digit mark.[213]

France Honors Bunau-Varilla

At the initiative of President Loubet and Foreign Secretary Theophile Delcassé, Philippe was made grand officer of the Legion of Honor.[214] But Bunau-Varilla was not a man to forget his friends. During the summer and early autumn of 1904, Philippe's brother almost died of an attack of appendicitis, and "my poor little Giselle nearly lost her life. She fell vertically 15 feet on a brick staircase through a glass roof. She remained unconscious for 12 hours, but after two months she is nearly completely well again."[215] Nevertheless, during those same months, Philippe kept asking the French government to decorate Loomis and Hay. Finally, on October 21, he wrote his friend: "Delcassé proposes to confer the Legion of Honor on you and will speak to Porter about it at the next diplomatic reception," and he hoped that Loomis was already recovered from "the terrible trial of this year."[216] Loomis, like Bunau-Varilla, was being victimized by slander and jealousy, this time from H. Bowen, his successor in Caracas. This crisis was not resolved until 1905.[217]

A year after leaving the post of Panamanian envoy to Washington, Philippe was back in New York, invited by the president and the canal commission to express his views on how to tackle the problem of the ditch.

On March 29, 1905, Philippe sold the president on his plan for a semi-rigid lock canal, which was later to be converted to sea-level. For the next few days, Bunau-Varilla, Roosevelt, William H. Taft, and several engineers discussed this plan. Philippe's suggestion to create an international consulting board was followed, and the group met in September. Engineers Burr, Parsons, Canal Commissioner Davis, and the experienced canal builder G. Quellennec were on the board. Quellennec was named at the request of Philippe, whose busy schedule prevented him from attending all the sessions. For a time it appeared as if the provisionary lock canal would win. The elated Bunau-Varilla wrote Loomis:

> We just learned that the greatest danger of the Panama Canal, the perpetual locks, have been condemned to death. This ensures tomorrow or day after the "strait" because the execution of the narrow sea level and locked canal will soon appear entirely impracticable.[218]

After much discussion, however, the consulting board decided on a lock-type seaway. For reasons of economy and time, and because of the difficulty of diverting the Chagres, two of Philippe's early backers, Alfred Noble and John Frank Stevens, changed their minds. The decision was also inspired by the suddenly heated international situation, the result of the Asian war. Reluctantly, Roosevelt and Taft threw their support behind the immediate solution, and Philippe's better-planned but more complicated canal was shelved. "When Stevens saw how time-consuming and expensive it would be to divert the river, he was converted from sea-level to lock canal and managed to convince others that he was right."[219]

Steven's switch to a rigid-lock canal brought about the resurrection of Adolphe de Lepinay's plans, which Philippe had suggested. If the waterway was to have locks, it would be necessary to build a water reservoir to feed the canal by damming the Chagres at Bohio.[220]

Stevens was the second chief engineer appointed by the United States. The first, John F. Wallace, left the job "in a devil of a mess" because he received little cooperation from the civilian crews. Yellow fever and malaria were still rampant, and morale was poor. "Decent food was hard to come by and expensive when available. Eggs sold for $1.50 a dozen."[221] It was get-rich-quick time in the isthmus again.

During Stevens' tenure as chief engineer, Dr. Gorgas arrived in Panama to repeat his Cuban success against the mosquitoes. Like Bunau-Varilla, Stevens was cheerful and optimistic. Unlike Philippe, his optimism caused him to underrate difficulties and ignore detractors. Yet the speed, extent, and permanance of Stevens' sanitation work are unquestionable proof of his engineering ability. Like Bunau-Varilla, he had to bend to opposition, especially from some of the commissioners who called him a crank and from ignorant natives who called him "loco Stevens." At great cost, every dwelling in Panama and Colon was fumigated, and thousands of contaminated household items were sprayed or burned, as had been done in Havana. These precautions spawned protest demonstrations.[222]

Window screening costing $90,000 was installed on all the buildings left by the French. "Owing to the good material and thorough workmanship employed by the French companies, the greater part of the buildings were in such condition as to warrant [only] repairs even after standing unused for ten years or more." The French plans and buildings, mostly constructed during Philippe's tenure as chief engineer, "furnished valuable features of tropical architecture. These were fully appreciated by the Architectural Department and were later incorporated in the design of the buildings erected by the Commission."[223] The hospitals left by the French, equipped and staffed by Bunau-Varilla, were "facilities [which] were well provided for, and excellent care was taken of the patients."[224] For five months there was not one case of yellow fever.

Bunau-Varilla kept in touch with the commissioners, and with Loomis, Lodge, and Roosevelt, about canal construction. Bunau-Varilla's proposals seemed too costly for the board—actually, this opinion was due to the erroneous unit prices the board adopted. Every engineer suggested a bottom width no greater than one-hundred-fifty-feet. Philippe toyed with the idea of a one-thousand-foot-deep channel, but he feared being called a lunatic and compromised on a five-hundred-foot channel. When the consulting board adopted this depth for the sea-level sections of the lock passage, Philippe began to campaign for one-thousand feet, the width of the Havre-Rouen canal in France.[225]

In 1906 the board reported:

> Mr. Bunau-Varilla has outlined to the Board a very ingenious procedure to be followed in effecting such a transformation [lock canal to straits], with special reference to the difficulties of eliminating the locks successively and of disposing of the excavated material.[226]

The Board was concerned with the underwater excavation, which it found costly but not impossible to realize, and finally recommended against Philippe's plan because the construction of the large locks "required under present law . . . makes it quite impossible to complete the preliminary lock canal . . . within the period stated." It was also argued that "the excessive cost of transformation" [of the lock canal to a sea-level passage] was prohibitive, and since "the lock canal is likely to be retained for many years, it should be made for the most efficient service and not to be encumbered with modifications."[227]

The two essential arguments were the cost and that the lock canal was to be retained for eons (without consideration of increases in tonnage or of the size of future vessels). The most optimistic expectations of the commission anticipated tonnage at 11.375 million ten years after the opening of the canal,[228] but Philippe insisted that the figure would be over 24 million.[229] The board, while expressing its adherence to a rigid-lock canal, concluded that Bunau-Varilla's ideas were not unrealistic:

> The Committee is of the opinion:
> 1. That it is possible to turn any lock canal, which it has considered, into a sea-level canal without interrupting the traffic on it.
> 2. That it is practicable from an engineering standpoint to transform any lock canal, which it has considered, into a sea-level canal, but that the cost of such transformation is so great as to render such a change impracticable from a financial standpoint, until traffic should have so increased as to tax the capacity of the lock canal, or until other good and sufficient reasons existed for such a change[230]

Philippe's campaign in favor of the strait was appreciated in America, where his words were instantly reprinted:

> My dear Mr. Loomis,
> I am glad you have read with interest my lecture to the Society of Arts. It has brought out two important points. The first is the qualified backing of Sir John Wolfe Barry, the greatest structural engineer in England (he who made the Tower Bridge in London) to my plans and to my principle of carrying out the work of the Straits of Panama. The second is what I have explained: that a provisional canal entirely suffi-cient for a fleet to pass from one ocean to the other in twenty-four hours can be constructed in three years.[231]

Bunau-Varilla recommended that the Gatun Dam be aban-doned because of the "unsatisfactory borings" and that this decision would certainly lead to "the strait." In the same letter, commenting on Japan's status, he wrote: "The United States must acknowledge that Japan is unstable to the highest degree, owing to the absence of a Balance of Power in the Pacific. This balance will be immediately established by the opening of the Panama Canal to men-of-war."[232]

Three years after the adoption of the rigid-locks canal, Alfred Noble evaluated Philippe's proposal:

> Such a broad channel [five-hundred-feet] at sea level as the one advocated by the eloquent and ingenious Bunau-Varilla, and by him appropriately designated the "Strait of Panama," would afford quicker and safer navigation than any other lock or summit-level canal. But on account of its enormous cost and the prolonged period required for completion, the "Strait of Panama" must long remain a work of the imagination, rather than of practical realization.[233]

Had Noble lived twenty years longer, he would have been the first to recognize that the "enormous cost" of which he spoke was being met by enormous fleets, enormous tonnage and tremendous increase in canal traffic—not to mention the increasing responsibilities of the United States in a world with a huge population with enormous needs and the astronomical cost of such a strait in the twenty-first century.

10

Bunau–Varilla's Last Campaigns

For economic reasons, long before the Bowen affair, Francis Loomis had announced to Hay his intention to retire from diplomatic work. The controversy actually delayed his leaving until full exoneration was achieved. By 1906, he had moved to Burlingame, California, and a few years later he began his long association with the Standard Oil Company of California. Roosevelt, and later Taft, further distinguished Loomis by naming him envoy extraordinary to Japan in 1908, and in 1912, commissioner general to the Turin Exposition and Delegate to the Berlin International Congress. Wherever Bunau-Varilla and Loomis were, they corresponded frequently.[1]

Mining enterprises and a trip to Panama in 1907 did not appeal to Philippe. He declined Loomis' offer to engage in mining:

> I have received with great pleasure your letter of March twenty-third referring to a mining enterprise which you

intend to start in the neighborhood of the mines you actually possess in your California ranch. I am now too much tied to the French soil to go and investigate the matter myself and I have adopted as a principle never to go into an industrial business without looking into it with my own eyes.[2]

But Bunau-Varilla did not remain idle after his Panama years. He kept himself busy with many projects and social engagements, and he still found time to secure a mining expert, Jules Hunebelle, for his friend Loomis: "a very nice man and a good friend of mine who is very much interested in American mines and has some capital invested in them." As for the trip to Panama, "Of course I would desire to go but not at the present time." At that moment, engineering problems, the result of human errors, threatened the canal. He advised Loomis "to keep in constant watch the monthly excavation and the monthly expenses. They will tell more than anything on the Isthmus about the veracity of the prophecies made."[3]

Regardless of his schedule, Philippe found time to attend to Panama's troubles. Mesmerized by Cromwell, Amador had agreed to an investment of $6 million in real estate by Sullivan and Cromwell, a deed which Panamanians have extolled, but which proved a financial mistake. In 1906, Bunau-Varilla counseled the Panamanian to terminate the contract and invest the funds in stock or in United States securities[4], but Amador spurned the advice.

Philippe remained optimistic about the future of the Isthmians and regarded Amador's indiscretion lightly. Little did he suspect that the country physician was preparing an all-out assault on him. On his death, Amador left behind a legacy of rancor and jealousy magnified by those who had contributed nothing to the canal or the republic and who later exaggerated the roles of Amador and Cromwell to the point of being historically incorrect. In spite of their not-too-happy relationship, at the news of Amador's death, Bunau-Varilla cabled the government, his condolences:

His name will remain forever associated with the work of the Union of two oceans, a thing which would have remained a chimera without the formation of the Republic of Panama. My mind goes back with emotion towards those tragic moments of September, 1903, when Amador, betrayed and abandoned, confided in me his despair, and when we took together the liberation of the Isthmus. . . . The slaying of oppression has unchained Progress.[5]

The new chief of state, Jose de Obaldía, responded:

I am grateful to you for the share you take in the sorrow caused by the death of President Amador. The remembrances you recall have deeply moved the public sentiment. It is a page of our history. Our people will keep eternally engraved in their memory your fruitful services, and will put in a pre-eminent place the names of Amador and your own. The national gratitude gives them the title of "Benefactors of Panama." Obaldía.[6]

This was to be the finest and last tribute ever paid by the isthmians to their "benefactor."

Having refurbished his magnificent home on the Avenue d'Ienna, Philippe spent much time there, at the Bois de Boulogne, or at his brother's country estate at Orsay, in the company of his family.[7] Trips to Portugal, Spain, Mexico, and the United States interrupted this well-earned peace. In 1910, he traveled to Mexico for the centennial of the revolution to discuss railroad construction to Tampico and from Oaxaca to the Pacific with President Diaz and the positivist Jose Limatour.[8] Visual evidence of progress was everywhere in the towns, but Bunau-Varilla sensed the underground discontent with the regime and concluded that "it is absolutely impossible to think of seeing the great French capitalists invest in an enterprise of this nature now."[9] Months later, the government collapsed, and Mexico became another Colombia, seething with violence.

Bunau-Varilla and the Tolls Question

As the waterway took shape, the question of tolls arose and Philippe was repeatedly asked, in America and in Europe, for his views on the issue. In a series of letters to Loomis (who was returning from an Asian tour on behalf of the Standard Oil Company of California), Bunau-Varilla confronted "the whole body of the theory which solves entirely the tolls puzzle." He viewed the American and British theories as identical:

> Once the mandate of civilization is accomplished and the distribution of the cost of operation and interest made on *all ships using the canal,* the Hay-Pauncefote Treaty is respected and the United States is free from any further obligation. She then fully enjoys the capacity of paying back the tolls to all her ships whether coastways or not, if she likes. You will see by the commentary of the *Shipping World* of September 4 that the shipping people in England openly welcome my theory.[10]

Philippe urged Roosevelt to speak up, cut the Gordian knot and

> . . . declare himself for *the free passage of all ships flying American flags* and at the same time for the absolute respect of the letter and of the spirit of the Hay-Pauncefote and Hay-Bunau-Varilla treaties. This can be done by reimbursing on the national resources the tolls paid according to the law of equal reparation on terms of absolute equality, as the treaties require, of the canal expenses.

He concluded by saying that "there will be a rush for all ships to fly the American flag and this would enhance the prestige of the United States."[11] Most of his ideas were eventually incorporated in the tolls agreement with the English.

Bunau-Varilla spent the last days of the summer of 1913 at Loomis' country estate near San Francisco, where the two friends surveyed the future of the world. They reminisced about their friend Bigelow, who had just died, then turned their thoughts to the clouds of war. Philippe was certain of a European conflict involving France and Germany in the next three years, and he wondered if the United States would act as decisively as in 1905.[12]

Philippe's Last Journey to Panama

The year 1913 was the quadricentennial of Balboa's arrival at the Pacific, and the canal engineers rushed their work to meet the historic deadline. Philippe gladly accepted an invitation to the ceremonies because he feared that war might prevent him from traveling in 1914, when the canal was scheduled to be opened to world traffic. In the fall of 1913, he spent less than a week in Panama, where he "enjoyed a most interesting visit and a very kind reception from every side and everyone."[13] His daughter Giselle crossed the canal with him, a thrilling experience in which she recalls "the hurrying sail boats and canoes trying to be the first to get over the line, into the Pacific's waters. I was alone with my father in one of the boats and my heart burst into happiness that he should see this experience the result of his gigantic effort."[14] Philippe left almost immediately after the ceremony because of the sudden death of "one of the best men on the staff of *Le Matin*, Monsieur Charles Lauerwein, which makes my return indispensable by the way of New York."[15] He had intended to go back to Loomis' ranch in California.

Philippe said that the trip from the East Coast to California in the company of Loomis, and thence to Panama "will remain as one of the most agreeable and pleasant journeys I have ever undertaken." He promised to return soon if the international situation improved.[16] He kept his pledge, for he was back in New York in the summer of 1914. But as he prepared to sail for Panama to participate in the official opening of the waterway, the tragedy of Sarajevo struck. He left for France at the end of July.

The *New York World* seized upon the forthcoming inauguration of the waterway as an occasion for glorifying William Nelson Cromwell's role in the Panama revolution and attacking Roosevelt, Loomis, and Bunau-Varilla. On this occasion, the former president wrote to Loomis from Oyster Bay, New York:

> My dear Mr. Loomis:
>   Keep a watch on the *New York World*, which is beginning a series of articles on the matter. Of course, I am not going to bother with the *New York World*, because to do so would give it the advertisement that it is looking for. But you very properly

can handle it, and I wish you would take it up, go over it minutely and crush it. The *World* has always thought that Nelson Cromwell had something to do with the revolution, but, as you know, Nelson Cromwell was very much irritated because the revolution took place without his knowing anything about it. There were dozens of revolutionary movements on at that time, but I have always supposed that *the real leader of this one was Bunau-Varilla.*

Faithfully yours, Theodore Roosevelt.[17]

Loomis responded gallantly through the pages of the *New York Tribune*, the *Sun*, and the *San Francisco Chronicle*, meriting Roosevelt's accolade: "Mr. Loomis, that's fine! I have seen Mr. Bunau-Varilla and had a very satisfactory conversation with him!"[18]

The dream of centuries became reality on August 14, 1914, when the first commercial vessel, the *Ancon*, safely navigated the passage. The Peruvian destroyer, *Teniente Rodriques*, was the first war vessel to traverse the water route,[19] but the clouds of war which had prevented the real hero of the canal, Bunau-Varilla, from attending, robbed the ceremony of gaiety.

The Bunau-Varillas and World War I

World War I was a reality, and while Philippe and his son were about to don martial dress, Philippe took time to answer the many congratulatory messages he received on the occasion of the opening of the canal. He wrote Loomis:

> I received in time the welcome and charming letter you were kind and thoughtful to write to me on the 15th of August on the occasion of the opening of the canal. I appreciate very much indeed the cordial expression of your friendship on that memorable day, as much as I appreciate the fact which you omit to mention that it was very largely owing to your help and support that the greatest final crisis of the struggle for the Panama canal was victoriously tided over.[20]

Philippe excused himself for not answering earlier "because I have decided to consecrate all my thoughts, time and endeavour to the service of my country. I have gone back into service with the rank of Major of Military Engineers." Bunau-Varilla had directed the building of various bridges over the Marne, Oise, and Aisne rivers, and he praised his son, who had become, like his father, a hero:

> My son, Etienne, has made the great war on horseback as sergeant of dragoons. He was in all the great battles of Charleroi, of the Marne, and of the Aisne. In that capacity he made five German prisoners, I must say three of them wounded, in a castle near the Marne. The interesting thing is that he did it with a single comrade.[21]

The visionary Bunau-Varilla had anticipated the role of the airplane in war, and he had made his son a pioneer aviator. As Mrs. Rocco reported:

> My father, as always, was glad to be in the forefront of anything worth while. Thus he gave my brother a plane in 1910 when he successfully finished his class examinations. It was a biplane [Voisin]. Etienne was very gifted as a pilot and proved it by rapidly mastering the know-how of flying with no one to guide him.[22]

Giselle Bunau-Varilla also flew in an airplane in 1910, but not with her brother, for her mother would not allow the two to ride together:

> In those days there was no "body" of the plane. Just a small stool on which the pilot sat with his legs on a board. This board was where I sat, while the pilot let me rest between his knees. As we took off all went well, but shortly after he bent over to my ear and said, "You must catch the loose wire because if it gets in the propeller we have had it," which, of course, I did after several unsuccessful efforts. The pilot's license of my brother was No. 16, between Bleriot's after his record flight over the Channel and Wilbur Wright's (No. 16 in the world).[23]

Philippe's children inherited his daring and adventure-seeking spirit.

No wonder, then, that once Etienne's talents as a pilot were recognized by the high command, he traded a horse for an airplane:

Since the beginning of October, my son Etienne has been mounting the aerial guard in Paris and so fight the attacks of the German planes. He is about to leave for the battlefront again but this time flying a plane.

Not all news was good. Bunau-Varilla's son-in-law, Viscount de Rancoiegne, was made a prisoner of war at Lille after a desperate battle in which his colonel and almost all his regiment "of Chasseurs found a heroic death. When the ammunitions were spent nothing remained for the rest but to surrender. He is now at Darmstadt Hesse."[24]

For two weeks in late January and early February of 1915, Philippe came to the United States to lobby for his country, but on his return he was entrenched in the camp guarding Paris. Life was very dull in the trenches and he asked transfer to the fighting lines:

I am now *Commandant Adjoint du guerre du 14th Corps d'Armée*. Regulations prohibit me to say where I am and where the 14th Army Corps is. . . . We have here all kind of warfare, the subterranean war, the war of mines and unexpected explosions, and the trench war on the surface with an adequate distribution of shell bombs. At certain points the trenches are so near as not more than twenty feet separate the enemies. It is needless to say how passionately interesting is my life.[25]

Philippe extolled the morale of the troops under fire and their stoicism in battle, but his pride was his children, all in uniform. Giselle had joined the Red Cross, and he did not forget his son's early association with the birth of independent Panama:

Etienne, the little boy who was a witness on the thirteenth of November 1903 of the reception by the President of the United States of the Minister of Panama, and therefore of the first recognition of the new republic is now in the flying corps as *Commandant d'Aeroplane*. His service has been very distinguished. He was proposed for the military medal and mentioned in the order of the day which gives him the Cross of War for having succeeded in accomplishing missions under atmospherical conditions which prevented all the other aeroplanes to accomplish it.[26]

Two weeks later, he expressed concern for Mrs. Loomis, who had been ill, and confirmed that Etienne had been decorated with the Croix de Guerre, highest class, for his exploits in shooting down two German planes:

> The text of the meritorious service award is very flattering and you will see that the little boy who was a witness of the recognition of the Republic of Panama by President Roosevelt on the 13th of November 1903 has not degenerated in 1915.[27]

The commendation praised Etienne for his "bravery, his tenacity and skillfulness in difficult circumstances. Also for fulfilling his missions with the greatest courage when his apparatus had been pierced several times by enemy projectiles." Loomis sent Philippe *Panama and Castilla del Oro,* by J. Bishop, along with other publications about the canal. Bunau-Varilla considered Bishop's information "false and offensive to the French," the result of fabrications and innuendos.[28]

The Chlorination of Water for the French Troops

Because of his years at Panama and his meetings with Finlay, Goethals, and other medical experts, Philippe became keenly interested in the purification of water, which he considered the clue to the elimination of typhoid fever. He never forgot the agony of Marcus Hanna, who worked so hard for Panama's victory. Typhoid fever, an infectious septicemic disease propagated by the bacillus *Salmonella typhi,* causes symptoms similar to yellow or blackwater fever. Typhoid bacilli, however, persist after recovery. They may be found in the intestinal and urinary tracts as well as the gallbladder long after health has been restored to the patient. The cured become carriers.[29]

Infection is oral, through ingestion of food or water polluted by fecal matter, flies, unclean dishes, or hands. Water contaminated by fecal matter, directly or by leakage from a sewer system, is a major source of epidemics. In the first two decades of the twentieth century, thousands died of typhoid all over the world because of unsafe water systems. While

Senator Hanna was dying, Pittsburgh had the highest typhoid death rate in the United States.[30]

Hope of controlling the noxious bacteria in water was enhanced in Germany in 1894, where the first known experiments with chlorine were conducted, and chlorine was first used in municipal water supplies in the United States by John L. Leal and George A. Johnson in 1908.[31] After 1894, every major industrial nation was experimenting with chlorine, trying to reduce deaths from typhus. But there was confusion and doubt as to how to use chlorine, as the amount of chlorine to be added to the water depended on many factors—type and concentration of the chlorine, contact time, water characteristics and temperature, and the type and number of organisms to be destroyed.

In France, particularly, no standard method of guaranteeing safe water existed, and epidemics persisted. Preliminary research into this problem was done by the Pasteur Institute in 1911, under the direction of Dr. R. de Roux, as well as by a chemist, L. Dienert. De Roux was convinced that one milligram of chlorine was enough to eliminate bacteria in one-half gallon of water in three hours; other researchers insisted on 0.5 milligrams, or 3.00 milligrams.[32]

After his trip to Mexico in 1910, Bunau-Varilla devoted time to the study of contaminated waters. Because of his academic background, world travels, and bouts with diseases, Philippe was eminently qualified to research this subject. In 1915 he was appointed *Directeur du Service des Eaux*, and during the critical weeks of the battle of Verdun, his immediate task was to provide safe water for the troops. He took over command of the water corps when confusion reigned. Without considering the quality or quantity of the water or such elementary precautions as regard for sedimentation, coagulation, and filtration, technicians were mixing 1.0, 2.0, 3.0, and even 4.0 milligrams of chlorine per liter of water, all of which were much too strong. Soon after Philippe's arrival, general headquarters ordered that 0.5 milligrams of chlorine be considered the standard mix.[33]

Before the battle of Verdun, reinforcements arrived from

Africa and Indochina, and the water problem became critical—especially after it was discovered that some of the Asian
troops were suffering from colitis, an inflamation of the large
bowel or colon caused by bacteria, viruses,fungi, allergies,
and nutritional deficiencies. The disease has no universal
etiologic agent. Symptoms such as abdominal pain, bleeding,
and diarrhea are common, but these are also characteristic of
dysentery, tuberculosis, and the dread typhoid fever. The first
step in diagnosing colitis is to isolate the causative agent, and
the panic-stricken paramedics in the army, who feared a
typhus epidemic, isolated the sick men and hoped for the
best.

By this time, Bunau-Varilla had mastered the complexities
of chlorine disinfection and was capable of designing better
chlorination facilities. One of the baffling problems was
whether to add chlorine at or ahead of the filters and
sedimentation units which Philippe had already constructed
("prechlorination") or to add it after the water had been
treated. At the moment, it was urgent to make safe water
available to as many troops as possible. Philippe wrote to
headquarters:

> If the typhoid bacillus is more resistant than the *Bacterium
> coli*, it is absurd to argue that the complete destruction of the
> latter is necessary. It is only necessary under these circum-
> stances to achieve antiseptic success by dissolving a propor-
> tion of chlorine enough to destroy *Bacterium coli*. In this way I
> am sure that every colibacillus will be destroyed.[34]

Here was the practical mind of the genius again. He had
proposed a semi-rigid lock canal to solve the immediate
problem of transoceanic navigation which later, at a more
leisurely pace, could be transformed into a strait. At Verdun,
he suggested immediately attacking the threat of a colitis
epidemic. Controlled sanitation would avoid the arrival of
typhus, which was only feared at the moment.

After weeks of research, Bunau-Varilla discovered that only
one-fiftieth of a decimilligram of chlorine was enough to
insure post-chlorination but, to be on the safer side, he used

one-tenth of a decimilligram per gallon. In this way, superchlorination was avoided, colitis was defeated, and typhus was held at bay. But the experiments almost cost Philippe's life. One afternoon in the late summer of 1916, his treated water tanks were bombed. Headquarters gave immediate orders to restore the containers during the night, and Bunau-Varilla insisted on supervising the installation. While he was at the site, the officer in charge of the anti-aircraft platoon told Philippe that he was going to die soon, killed by a bomb. Bunau-Varilla was attempting to dispel the officer's fears when a solitary warplane appeared and dropped a bomb. Philippe's escort died, and his own severely wounded leg had to be amputated above the knee. He telegraphed his children in Switzerland: "Leg cut above the knee, temperature 38°C, pulse 72. Sadness is futility." Etienne, after bombing the Alinin factories in Germany, had experienced engine trouble and had landed in Switzerland, where he was interned, and his sister Giselle was with him at the time.[35]

"The loss of his leg never diminished his activity. He chose the stump kind and not the articulate one, as he said it slowed down his movement. He suffered from sores at first but he courageously overcame this by strict discipline of walking a mile a day." Wherever he went, especially at the Riviera, he looked at the town's map to calculate "which streets to walk and cover the specified number of kilometers. Thus, in this way he kept himself always fresh and alive."[36]

His contact with Loomis never ceased, and on learning of Myron T. Herrick's defeat in his race for the Senate in Ohio, Philippe was "bitterly disappointed. He is such a splendid and noble type of man. He would have been of such service to your great country and to Humanity in the American Senate." As in his fight for the canal, he renewed his determination to go "on the good road to the final victory of liberty over slavery."[37]

After the armistice, Philippe enthusiastically greeted the creation of a permanent apparatus to keep the peace and "the Atlantic entente" between the United States and France, a foundation which "we established in 1905 in Monsieur Rouvier's office at the Quai d'Orsay, with Senator Lodge." As he

Philippe Bunau-Varilla, Washington, January 23, 1904.

Senator Henry Cabot Lodge (circa 1922) sitting on the porch of his home in Massachusetts. Lodge was a staunch supporter of the Panama route and a loyal friend of Bunau-Varilla.

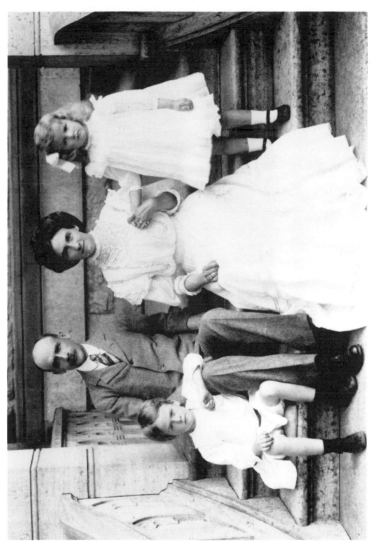

Francis Butler Loomis, U.S. minister to Venezuela, 1897–1901, Mrs. Loomis, and their two children, Florence and Francis Jr.

William Nelson Cromwell

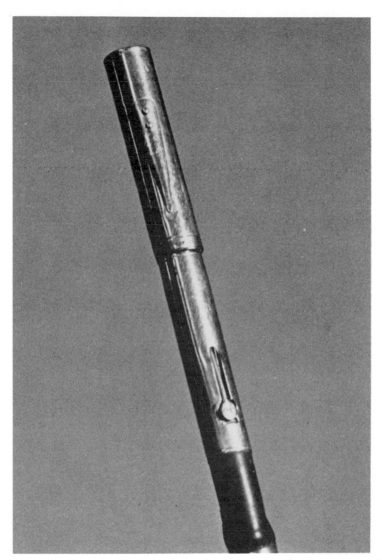

One of the pens used to sign the Bunau-Varilla/Hay Treaty of
November 18, 1903, now owned by Madame Giselle Bunau-Varilla
Rocco.

Left to right: Etienne Bunau-Varilla, Philippe Bunau-Varilla, and Giselle de Rancorigne (?).

Philippe Bunau-Varilla in the uniform of Lt. Colonel of the French Army, November 1936, during the commemoration of the Armistice, ending World War I on November 11, 1918.

Philippe Bunau-Varilla (third from right) with World War I comrades and other army officers at the Franco-American monument, Verdun, November 1937.

Residence of the Bunau-Varillas in Paris, 53 Avenue d'Iena. Philippe and his brother, Etienne, also owned a country estate at Orsay, today a part of the University of Paris.

Commander Etienne Bunau-Varilla, only son of Philippe, in the
uniform of the French Air Force. He learned to fly in 1910, piloting a
Voisin airplane purchased by his father, and was issued license
number 16 (world) after Bleriot and Wilbur Wright. An officer in
World War I, Etienne was a resistance fighter during World War II.
He died in 1968.

Philippe Bunau-Varilla II, son of Etienne Bunau-Varilla and grandson of Philippe, as a member of the French Air Force (circa 1970). He is now a banker in France, Egypt, and the United States.

Madame Giselle Bunau-Varilla Rocco, only daughter of Bunau-Varilla, has lived in Naiwasha, Kenya, since 1929, where she works as an artist. Her sculptures have been exhibited in France as well as in Kenya.

Dorian Rocco, only son of Colonel Mario Rocco and Madame Giselle Bunau-Varilla Rocco, is an industrialist in Naiwasha, Kenya.

Colonel Mario Rocco, Italian Army retired, and Madame Giselle Bunau-Varilla Rocco at their estate in Naiwasha, Kenya (circa 1976).

Oria Douglas Hamilton, daughter of Giselle Bunau-Varilla Rocco and wife of Iaian Douglas Hamilton, is an ecologist. She and her husband are considered to be authorities on elephants and have recently published a book, *Among the Elephants*, on the subject.

Grandchildren of Madame Giselle Bunau-Varilla Rocco and daughters of Dorian, Mirella, and Oria.

Madame Giselle Bunau-Varilla Rocco feeding a favorite pet in the garden of her estate in Naiwasha, Kenya (circa 1975).

Prisca Bunau-Varilla, daughter of Etienne Bunau-Varilla and grand-child of Philippe, lives in Paris, where she is a fashion designer and model.

prepared for another transatlantic voyage he thought "more than ever before that this is the great and unique guarantee of future peace . . .," and urged Lodge and Loomis to work for it and so prevent another world conflagration.[38]

The Bunau-Varilla family left the battlefield decorated and promoted. Philippe was now a full colonel and it was time to visit America again, and possibly Asia, a trip recommended by Loomis. After spending two weeks at Loomis' home in California, he sailed home by the way of Japan, via Suez. While at sea, Philippe thought about writing another book on the canal and his experiences at Verdun. He chose to name his chlorination progress *"verdunization."* He also outlined an essay "The German Menace."[39]

Philippe's mind grew as he grew older, for his was a remarkable old age. At a time when most people were harboring lifelong prejudices, the war and the ingratitude of Panama changed his philosophical outlook from the paro-chial to the cosmic. Despite his battle wounds, he enjoyed an unusually healthy life after his sixties. His home, and his brother's country estate at Orsay, attracted the élite of four continents who discussed and even formulated the latest international and financial trends. His American friends found a warm welcome. Henry Cabot Lodge II and Florence Loomis remember him as a "veritable dynamo of energy. When we were leaving France in 1923, after a memorable sojourn with the Bunau-Varillas, he and his wife came aboard to bid us farewell and he brought me a bag of oranges. . . . He was such a warm person." And Henry Cabot Lodge II reminisces: "I have a warm and vivid memory of Philippe Bunau-Varilla." On the occasion of the young Henry Cabot Lodge's visit to France, his grandfather wrote to Philippe, "Let me thank you for your kindness to my grandson. He returned most enthusiastic with your goodness to him and all you did for him. ... I desire to thank you most cordially for all you did for the boy, and you may rest assured that he fully appreciated it."[40]

Rewriting the History of Panama

In the 1920s, while plotting the diffusion of his chlorination process, Philippe became interested in a new scheme to make steel "from the ore without coke" which had proved to be both practical and economical in France. Loomis and others had shown interest in this novelty, and Bunau-Varilla was ready to satisfy their curiosity.[41] News from Panama, however, turned his attention to America again. In 1904, William H. Taft, as secretary of war, had signed a temporary protocol with Panama—suspending, for the period of canal construction, some of the clauses of the Hay–Bunau-Varilla Treaty. In 1910, while visiting the isthmus, President Taft had implied that the document was to be renegotiated once the canal was completed. The Panamanians insisted on this promise, but the United States, because of the crisis provoked by the war, delayed negotiating.[42] In their frustration, the isthmians, led by the wily Belisario Porras, turned their ill feelings against the distant Philippe.[43]

By 1920, after the untimely death of President Ramon Valdes, Porras again contrived his own election, with the aid of the United States minister to Panama, William Jennings Price. Porras feared to press the renegotiation of the Taft Convention, intensified the anti-Bunau-Varilla campaign, and mesmerized the public with showy public works, which he paid for by contracting huge loans abroad and by reviving an old frontier dispute with Costa Rica which led to armed conflict.[44]

Porras also decided to rewrite history. In a lapidary account on the walls of the old fortress at Panama City, Bunau-Varilla was ignored. "In fact," says historian Enrique Arce, Philippe "shines by his very absence because everyone knows what he did for Panama." To which this author replied, "But Uncle Henry, generations die and fifty years from now lies will become history." The sage professor answered, "Then do something about it."[45]

The Porras-inspired "history" of the canal speaks of the "heroic perseverance" of the engineers and contractors, of the "formidable obstacles" they confronted, of the "great breach open through the formidable reef at Culebra," of "the powerful machinery," of the "gigantic plant," of the "thousand structures," and so forth, but there is not a word about the man most responsible for these titantic works. Thus, the history engraved on the monument erected to the glory of France at the entrance of the canal gives a false version of the origin and the building of the passage.

It omits the name of the real conqueror, "that of its greatest engineer, Philippe Bunau-Varilla, yet his name is everywhere engraved on the soil of the isthmus and particularly on its principal work, the great breach opened through the formidable reef of Culebra." The Parisian newspapers chided Panama for its "hypocritical method of writing history . . . the classical method of German propaganda, which consists of distortion of history by omission of true facts and by the commission of forged statements."[46]

Two men came to the defense of Bunau-Varilla. At the glittering banquet given by the American ambassador to France, Myron T. Herrick, himself part of the story of the canal, rose and proclaimed, to the applause of more than five hundred persons, "Without Philippe Bunau-Varilla the Panama Canal would never have been constructed." Later, Charles de Lesseps came out of retirement to praise "our friend, Bunau-Varilla, this man of genius, without whom Panama would have remained the figment of a dream."[47]

Philippe's Interest in Postwar International Problems

Although he was born in the state of New York, Charles Gates Dawes was a member of the Ohio Gang, like Reid and Loomis—and consequently, a friend of Bunau-Varilla's. He had introduced Philippe to Hanna,[48] and they remained close friends through the stormy days of canal confrontations. Dawes' parents moved to Ohio, and after he graduated from Marietta College and the Cincinnati Law School in 1886, he moved to Nebraska, where he became a member of the bar. By 1895, Dawes was deeply engrossed in the utility industry. He bought Northwestern Gas, Light and Coke Company, and other concerns, making his home in Evanston, Illinois. Soon afterwards he entered politics under the guidance of Hanna, and with Reid and Loomis, he plotted the election of McKinley.

Dawes's connections, plus his book, *The Banking System of*

the United States and Its Relations to the Money and Business of the Country (Chicago, 1892), won him the office of comptroller of the currency. Long before World War I, he sold his utility empire to Samuel Insull.[49] With the entrance of the United States into the conflict, he became, with the help of his Nebraska friend John J. Pershing, Brigadier General in charge of procurement and supplies, with orders to coordinate supply operations with General Ferdinand Foch. Dawes performed splendidly. He renewed his friendship with Philippe on the battlefront and at Pershing's headquarters at Ogden Mills' mansion in Paris. In return, Bunau-Varilla received his host at Orsay or at 53 Avenue d'Ienna.

Both Dawes and Philippe had reservations about the reparation figures. By the terms of the Versailles protocol of June 19, 1919, Germany was to be given a bill for war damages done to the people and countries of the allied nations, including pensions for veterans and bereaved families. And during the difficult years when a settlement was being worked out, Philippe was a sought-after man on the continent, by Americans as well as Europeans. His correspondence with Loomis, Dawes, Lodge, and others reveals his versatililty.[50]

The Mellon Plan

The war left the economy of the United States in bad shape, and the task of solving this problem fell on the shoulders of financier Andrew William Mellon, another friend of Philippe's who had been indirectly associated with the canal. The Mellons had their home in Pittsburgh, Pennsylvania, headquarters of their banking empire. Advised by Bunau-Varilla, Andrew Mellon had formed a construction company which helped build the canal.[51] On his becoming secretary of the treasury in 1921, Mellon reduced the national debt,[52] but later he had to face the problem of inter-allied debts, which by 1923 had reached the critical stage. Mellon made a series of bilateral agreements with the European nations at the same time that Dawes was trying to solve the reparation problem. Mellon's covenants postponed the payments due the United

States for several decades, until the economy of the debtor nations recovered. The agreement with France, signed in 1925, was called the Berenger-Mellon Treaty.

Victor Henry Berenger, author and editor of *l'Action*, was a veteran politician and a friend of Philippe's. Before he left for Washington to discuss the pact, he had several talks with Bunau-Varilla. Philippe favored the agreement, but he cautioned Berenger: if the treaty were not tied to a sound system of repayments to the lender states by Germany, it would become a useless document. He suggested that Berenger secure from Mellon a reduction in tariffs to enable these countries to earn money in trade and meet their payments. Without these clauses, Philippe prophesied, "The result will be general default in payments followed by a world economic crisis."[53]

The Dawes Plan

To resolve the reparation impasse, Henry Barthou, another friend of Bunau-Varilla and president of the Reparations Commission, adopted Philippe's suggestion to turn the matter over to an international group of financiers. He hoped for Charles Dawes' participation. As Bunau-Varilla predicted, the United States readily agreed to this move. Dawes and Owen D. Young of New York became the American representatives.[54]

During the financial meetings in Paris, Dawes was a frequent guest of the Bunau-Varilla brothers, and Philippe enthusiastically approved the plan that bears the name of his friend:

> Our common friend, Charles Dawes, is making a magnificent campaign against demagoguery which will have important bearings not only on the political destiny of the United States but of the world. If as everyone expects, the people of the United States ratify his principles, he will have the extraordinary characteristic in history not only to have formulated the plan which brought peace to Europe but also to have injected in the American mind a new antiseptic at demagogic infection.[55]

As the economic clouds darkened, Philippe began to publicize his views about the problems of war debt and reparations, which he considered the key obstacle to economic stability and world peace. In an open letter which appeared in several dailies and which was intended for the American public, he revealed that France had no money. Fortunes which, in the prewar years, had been worth $40,000 now amounted to "only $4,032, because tax is 90 percent for singles and 75 percent for married with an income of $14,-000." France was to pay in gold if the debt were reduced by half, in accordance with the Berenger-Mellon Treaty, but because the scheduled payments for reparations were not being made, France could not do so. In the name of the French government, Bunau-Varilla proposed:

> That the United States relinquish in toto her credit with all peoples with whom she was associated during the war, under the double condition: (1) That in turn each of those people will relinquish their total credit with the allies; (2) that they shall abandon to Germany two thirds of the proceeds derived from the execution of the Dawes Plan, the last third remaining with them as partial compensation for the damages of the war.[56]

This appeal, backed by the government, caused much reaction on both sides of the Atlantic. Philippe was besieged with requests for interviews, especially from American newspapers. Edward Price Bell of the *Chicago Daily News* traveled to Paris to see him. Out of these meetings came a series of newspaper reports supporting the engineer's views.[57] In his correspondence with Price Bell, Bunau-Varilla again showed his keen mind at work:

> I am sending your copy of the *Figaro's* article of August 15 of which I gave you one this morning. I add to it a *Paris Herald* of the same day with reference to my proposal. I also enclose five other papers beginning with an article in the *Figaro* in which I show the weakness of the Berenger-Mellon Treaty, and the only remedy to its ratification.[58]

To relax international friction because of the war debts, Philippe suggested that his government lighten Germany's reparations burden. His recommendation had been adopted by the ministry in power.[59] Sensing the historic importance of his interview with Philippe and the value of the handwritten correspondence from him, Price Bell wrote his home desk in Chicago: "This man is the engineer whom Roosevelt described as bringing the Panama Canal to him 'on a gold platter.' Colonel Bunau-Varilla lost a leg at Verdun. Will you kindly preserve this letter for me?"[60]

Philippe Works for Peace

Aristide Briand, another publisher-politician, had succeeded in negotiating a series of multilateral pacts with most of the European nations, known as the Locarno Treaties. These agreements were designed to preserve the peace and the postwar status quo. But Philippe insisted that none of these arrangements were guarantees to peace as long as the United States was not a party to them.[61] Price Bell and Bunau-Varilla's campaign for world peace took the form of a forceful newspaper crusade in the pages of the *Figaro*, the *Lanctern* (Briand's daily), *Temps*, and *Le Matin*. In America and elsewhere, Price Bell disseminated Philippe's ideas, and Bunau-Varilla congratulated the newsman on his articles.

> . . . which apparently have reached every chancellory, including Japan's. Your appeal to the world chancellories is a forceful and substantial pledge for the authority of the articles and of the book you are preparing for solving problems of inter-allied debts. I have given to you my solution. If the United States adopts this plan (disarmament and cancellation of the reparation bill paralleling the end of the war debt), Washington will be in a position to rely on Germany's cooperation because she will be forced to accept strict disarmament not in intention but in fact. The United States is the only power on earth capable of imposing the peace. Had she taken that attitude in 1914 there would have been no war. . . . Germany will not repeat the disaster of 1914 if the United States insists that her own generosity with the Germans be repaid in good will.[62]

By mid-1927, the general mood was one of frustration and pessimism. There were few Bunau-Varillas to spread optimism and try to persuade an isolationist Congress in Washington to keep peace in the world. The high expectations generated by the Locarno Treaties were waning rapidly, although there were many who hoped that the spirit, if not the form of the treaties, would keep that peace.[63] Disarmament was, as always, a baffling problem. So preoccupied was the world with disarmament that Briand decided to try his luck in convincing the United States that it should help preserve the status quo.

Three times during late March of 1927, Philippe played host to dinners attended by Poincaré, Briand, and Herrick. "I knew not what they talked about," says Madame Bunau-Varilla Rocco, "but the conversations were always pleasant and flavored with the unparalleled wines from my uncle's cellar. Uncle Maurice was a connoisseur of good wines."[64] As arranged at 53 Avenue d'Ienna, on April 6, 1927, the tenth anniversary of the United States' entry into the World War, Briand issued a statement calling on American idealism to protect the very structure of civilization "now in danger of destruction."[65] He then proposed exactly what Philippe, Lodge, and Loomis had discussed on the eve of the memorial service for John Paul Jones in 1905,[66] namely, that France and the United States give up war as an instrument of national policy and give public and concrete evidence of their attachment to the everlasting principle of democracy.[67]

Conversations on the subject continued at a high level in Paris until abruptly interrupted by a happy event which was to dramatize the geographical proximity of France and the United States, the epic flight of Charles Lindbergh on May 20, 1927.[68] At a huge reception for the new hero, Myron T. Herrick again recalled the deeds of Philippe, who had recently been declared persona non grata by Panama's Assembly. Attempts at renegotiating the Taft Convention in accordance with Panamanian wishes had failed, and the Isthmians once more vented their frustration on Bunau-Varilla.[69] At this reception, Ambassador Herrick toasted the man who had united the continents—Lindbergh—and the one who had united the oceans—Philippe.[70]

On June 3, 1927, Herrick was officially approached with a suggestion "for the negotiation of a treaty between France and the United States for the elimination of war and the promotion of lasting peace between the two nations."[71] Considerable effort was made by Bunau-Varilla's friends to promote his candidacy as ambassador to Washington and in this way expedite his peace schemes, but his numerous jobs—director-in-chief of the Madrid-Caceres and Portugese railroads, of the Congo Railways, of various corporations, including L'Union Miniere du Katanga (the Belgian Congo), plus his crusade for chlorination—prevented him from encouraging this idea:

> . . . not the slightest chance of seeing the politicians abandon a part of the cake they exploit in common for what they think to be of benefit to a person not belonging to the sacred phalanx. . . . The parliamentarians monopolized for themselves and their families not only the cabinet posts but the high diplomatic missions. They were too ignorant and jealous to appreciate the value of a given man in a given place, and their minds had become pregnant with the notion that an individual if elected today is fit to be tomorrow chief engineer of all public works (Minister of Public Works); Chief banker of all financial establishments (Finance Minister); Chief of Education of the French Youth (Minister of Public Instruction); or any other position which commands the welfare of France. To tell these fools that a given man may be useful as ambassador would attract the reply: "Is he a deputy or a Senator?" If he is neither, he knows nothing and cannot do anything in a great public office.[72]

The Declaration of Paris

Because of Price Bell's and Bunau-Varilla's efforts, the French proposals were well-received in the United States, especially by Frank Billings Kellogg, the secretary of state. Through Dawes, Kellogg suggested that the pact include all the great powers. The final document was signed by sixteen nations on August 27, 1928. Sixty-two countries ultimately subscribed to the pact, which was ratified by the United States on January 15, 1929.[73] Like the Hay–Bunau-Varilla

Treaty, the Kellogg-Briand protocol was opposed in the United States Senate, and the secretary of state, exactly as Hay had done in 1903, made private statements which eventually reached the press and weakened the treaty. Kellogg said that the pact did not outlaw wars of self-defense, and the French found it necessary to add that it did outlaw wars of aggression.[74]

The signing of the World Peace Treaty, another name by which the document is known, was one of humanity's finest hours, but its spirit, like the spirit of Locarno, did not last long. The key to world peace, as it has ever since, rested in Washington. In 1931, President Herbert Hoover proposed a moratorium on German payments for one year. There was much debate in Congress, and the French did not like the idea, but Philippe's opinion was that:

> Roosevelt would have cut the Gordian knot quicker if he had been there with you as advisor. But the Hoover remedy, although good, could not be enough to reestablish confidence. We are on the eve of great economic and military convulsions. . . . We are going all over the earth to pay for the pachydermic ignorance of our Wilsons "yours and ours."[75]

President Woodrow Wilson's postwar arrangements were not well received in Europe, but his 1914 statement deprecating and minimizing the acquisition of canal rights by the United States has no parallel in naiveté.[76] His incredible utterances, possibly politically inspired, lined Wilson up against all the heroes of the saga of Panama—Bunau-Varilla, Loomis, Roosevelt, Lodge, Dawes, and others—and they never forgot them. On the occasion of the eighty-third anniversary of the founding of Wells Fargo, Wilson's words were revived, this time to be universally ridiculed.[77]

Chlorination and Ozonation

After the war, Philippe was also occupied with promoting the discovery he had made at Verdun. As he wrote Loomis:

> I have intended several times to write to you but the intense pressure of business did not allow me to make that intention a

reality. Giselle has moved to Africa with her husband and correspondence does not reach in less than a month and a half. My son is very well and successful in various enterprises among which are two companies of automobile business. My wife, as always, is leading a very retired life and sends to you and Mrs. Loomis her kindest regards. As for myself I am very much engaged with a struggle for the propagation of a very simple and efficient system of water sanitation which prevents typhoid, dysentery and yellow fever from spreading. It is not a financial business and consequently I could not think of deriving profit from it. As soon as verdunization shall have won the final battle I will go to the States and hope to see you.[78]

Although not as intense as the canal battles and the confrontations with Cromwell and Amador, Philippe's campaign to have his method of water purification adopted was not easy. The crux of his discovery was finding the proper proportion of chlorine to mix with drinking water. The absence or excess of chlorine had been the main factor hindering progress in this field. His work for the army, which resulted in mixing regular proportions of chlorine and water in one hundred twenty-five pumping stations built under his supervision, considerably alleviated the misery of the troops. This initial success elicited favorable comment from the allied command and the personal congratulations of General Foch.[79]

When he became a civilian again, Philippe dared the scientific community to disprove his findings about water sanitation. By then, he was also moving toward another method of sanitizing drinking water: ozonation, which is the addition of ozone, instead of chlorine or any of its collateral products and compounds, to water. Ozone can be produced by three techniques: (1) electrical discharge; (2) electrolysis of perchloric acid; and (3) ultraviolet exposure to oxygen. At room temperature, ozone is a colorless gas which has an unpleasant odor. It frequently appears in the atmosphere after an intense electrical storm, or near electrical discharges.[80]

Ozone, being one of the most powerful oxidizing agents, is

very unstable and must be produced on the site of application, a necessity which makes the process more expensive
than chlorination. What Philippe proposed was to test in the
laboratory the method of ultraviolet exposure of oxygen. This
method, according to Bunau-Varilla, not only killed the bacilli
in water but very probably transformed them into vitamins in
the same way in which ultraviolet sunlight energized
plankton.[81] Philippe also enlisted the aid of several professors
at the Val-de-Grace Institute in testing chlorine. The director
of epidemic services of the army and Dr. Jean de Rien
reported to the medical academy that "the Bunau-Varilla
method of treating waters is now generalized in the 2nd and
4th armies. Although the quantity of chlorine in the water is
minimal, the system has proved completely satisfactory."[82]

The campaign for chlorination made decisive progress
when Dr. L. Techoueyres, disciple of Pasteur and director of
the Bureau of Hygiene, decided to chlorinate the water at
Reims, a city which was being reconstructed after the war.
When these experiments succeeded, Bunau-Varilla asked the
scientist to embark upon one final series of tests to verify his
theory, which explains the production of ultraviolet rays that
eventually destroy most microbial life. With weak doses of
chlorine, it was not possible to attribute this destruction to
chemical action.

This was Bunau-Varilla's first explanation of the phenomenon revealed in another series of experiments conducted at the Bar-le-Duc laboratories by technicians in his
pay. The elated Dr. Techoueyres invited Bunau-Varilla to
report his findings at the Eleventh Congress of Hygiene,
which met at Reims in October 1924. Here, before a large
audience of experts and health officials from the continent
and the colonial empire of France, Dr. Techoueyres introduced Philippe:

> The system of water purification through the use of hypo-
> chlorite in minimal doses, product of the brilliant imagination
> of Philippe Bunau-Varilla and tried in the Army at Verdun,
> combined with the necessary apparatus for auto-chlorination,
> has solved forever the baffling problem of water purification in
> small and large cities.[83]

Reims, the medieval city where the French kings were crowned, was the first jewel in Bunau-Varilla's new crown. Since water sources in those days were not as polluted as they became later, most towns, for reasons of economy, adopted chlorination instead of ozonation, which according to Philippe required expensive electrical equipment if ozone were to be produced by electrical discharges.[84]

At the learned assembly in Reims, Philippe proposed to fill quartz tubes with colon bacillus solution into which hypochlorite had been poured. If ultraviolet rays occurred in the exterior fluid, they would penetrate the tubes and kill a certain quantity of colon bacilli. By comparing their number with those in identical tubes immersed in the same water but without the added chlorine, one would be able to determine if it were the irradiation which destroyed the microbes.[85]

Dr. Techoueyres used and improved this apparatus, experimenting for three months. It resulted in a 30 percent reduction in the number of microbes exposed to the irradiation. Sixty experiments were performed, and all gave the same result. Dr. Techoueyres asked the director of the Pasteur Institute, Dr. R. de Roux, to present the results to the Academy of Sciences but he refused, saying that there had not been enough tests. Dr. Techoueyres and his staff continued the experiments, refining the shape of the tubes, and eventually showed that almost 25 percent of the colon bacilli in the second set of tubes were killed. Finally, on May 25, 1925, a chemist, Dr. Jean Perrin, presented these findings to the Academy of Sciences in the names of Philippe and Dr. Techoueyres.[86] At last, Bunau-Varilla's 1916 theory had been demonstrated.

Chlorination and Infant Mortality

In 1926, Philippe proposed a novel consequence of the effects of ultraviolet rays in chlorination. He had deduced that ultraviolet rays must not only kill colon bacilli but also transform them into carriers of vitamins. He reasoned that ultraviolet rays from the sun affect life in the sea, and the end result is the "magic" cod-liver oil. He also knew that egosterol, nonsaponifiable animal grease, is transformed into vitamins A (growth) and D (antirickets) when struck by ultraviolet rays. He concluded that the deadly germs were not only destroyed by chlorination, but were also changed into carriers of vitamins A and D. Consequently, chlorination, he believed, must favorably influence the vitality of youth.

These assertions could only be demonstrated by statistical evaluation of a large number of cases of infant mortality. Control of infectious diseases cannot lower the death rate from zero to one year of age and from one to twenty years a great deal. But after the application of chlorination, statistics showed the result which Philippe presented to the Eleventh Industrial Congress on Chemistry, where he demonstrated the reduction in infant mortality of ages zero to five years after the adoption of chlorination: in Lyons 26.4 percent; Reims, 29.5 percent; Bar-le-Duc (Haute Ville), 27.2 percent. Yet, Bunau-Varilla was not satisfied with these figures. He waited too see the statistics on Paris, where the chlorination of 700,000 cubic meters of water from the rivers Seine, Marne, and Oureq was introduced in 1930. Distribution, however, did not begin until 1932. Because of the opposition of Dr. Roux, Paris was not in a hurry to become "verdunized." But the support of the prefect of the city, the president of the Municipal Council, Robert Bos, and the backing of several scientific luminaries such as Nobel prizewinner Alexis Carrel won the day in 1929.[88] By 1937, infant mortality in the zero to one-year age bracket compared favorably, on the average, with that of the years 1925 to 1929 and showed a reduction of 56 percent. The reduction of mortality in ages one to twenty, inclusive, was 57 percent. Naturally, if mortality in youth is reduced, it affects all ages. In the five years preceding the adoption of chlorination, the average mortality rate was 14.4 per 1,000 inhabitants. After the introduction of chlorination in 1932, mortality during a period of six years continued to decline. In 1933 it was 13.0; in 1934, 12.8; in 1935, 12.2; in 1936, 11.98; and in 1937, 11.92. The annual average number of deaths in the five years preceding the chlorination was 41,581, but by 1937 this number was reduced to 33,739.[89]

The city of Lyon learned the hard way. After a devastating

typhus epidemic in 1928, the town's mayor, Edouard Herriot, forced chlorination upon the people. Months of experimentation established a recommended application of one decimilligram of chlorine per litre of water. In the end, the statistics confirmed Bunau-Varilla's theory again.[90] Henceforth, the French municipal system had faith in Philippe. The municipalities of Auxerre, Bar-le-Duc, Calvi, Carcassonne, and Dieppe followed Reims' example, and the statistics spoke for themselves. The reduction of pandemia, especially typhoid fever, caused a stampede in which every town and city competed for the right to be next. Larger cities—Monte Carlo, Vichy, and Nancy—followed. Soon they all began to name their main avenues "Bunau-Varilla."[91]

The success of "verdunization" transcended frontiers, seas, and oceans: Lisbon, Port Said, Ismailia, Port Thewfik, Suez, Caracas, Saigon, Hanoi, Madrid, Barcelona, Geneva, Lausanne, Coimbra, Manressa, Seville, Saint Croix and Bellaigues (Switzerland), Trinidad, Douala (Cameroon), Lobito (Angola), Rabat, Aleppo, Aley (Algeria), Beirut, Brussels, Trieste, Dakar, and so on, were all "verdunized."[92] While Bunau-Varilla was negotiating with Addis-Ababa for the installation of water purification machinery in Abyssinia, the Italo-Ethiopian War erupted, but Mussolini's legions carried "verdunization pills" with them.[93] Before the adoption of Philippe's purification method, mortality (especially among infants) in most of these cities, stood above 15.4 per 1000. By 1937, it had been reduced to 11.02, and more than ninety cities in and out of France had adopted chlorination.[94]

More importantly for the satisfaction of Bunau-Varilla and unlike his pro-Panama campaigns, he received for these triumphs the world's gratitude. City after city struck commemorative medals honoring him. It started with Carcassone, Reims, and Lyons in 1929. Soon, Lisbon, Lausanne, and Dakar, followed suit, and he eventually received the Grand Gold Medal of Paris in 1936, an honor that municipality had bestowed on only two others before, one of them Charles Lindbergh.

Of his campaign for chlorination, Philippe wrote to

Loomis: "My dear friend, what obstacles I found in my way, almost as much as for making the Panama Canal and freeing the Isthmus from Colombia. Human ferocity against any new scheme producing unlimited benefits to the world is always the same." Regardless of his occupations, Bunau-Varilla would drop all schedules to entertain friends: "Let me know in advance when you expect to arrive so that I may keep my time free from any incumbrances when you are here."[95] He did the same for Charles Dawes:

> My dear friend;
> I hasten to reply to your cordial note of December 31st written before you left for the States, hoping that it will reach you in Washington where you expect to stay a week. You spent your Christmas with Dawes. I spent New Year's Day with him. I was greatly pleased with his good health. He, as well as Mrs. Dawes, seem to be in the most perfect physical condition. . . . He was here with his adopted daughter and his nephew, who is his secretary, both charming and bright young people.[96]

When the battle for chlorination appeared to be ending, Philippe took time off to visit his daughter and her family in Africa. They had acquired "a property near Lake Naiwasha in Kenya, three hundred miles east of Lake Victoria in a region settled by Sir William Mac Kinnon," Philippe's colleague as a director of the Congo railway.[97] "He walked all around," writes Madame Giselle Rocco, "and was enthusiastic about the prospect of a gold mine which did not amount to anything. But he seemed relaxed and very happy." On his way back, however, Philippe became depressed by the world crisis, which had worsened because of the conquest of Abyssinia by Italy, the invasion of Manchuria by Japan, and the beginning of the Spanish Civil War. French governments rose and fell amid daily charges and countercharges of corruption and sell-outs in the Chamber of Deputies.[98] The optimistic Philippe, remembering the heroic generation of 1914, used to say that "France cannot fall except by the deeds of her own children."[99]

On September 10, 1936, before an assembly of scientists,

health officials, city employees and citizens, municipal coun-
cillor Raymond Laurent decorated Philippe with the Grand
Gold Medal of Paris. The Loomis family was present. Said
Laurent: "It is now possible not only for us in Paris but for all
those within the French Empire to revere the name of the
man who dedicated his life to this process which has saved so
many lives: Philippe Bunau-Varilla." The prefect of the Seine,
Achille Villey, congratulated Philippe for his scientific contributions and for his heroism at Panama and Verdun.[100] Bunau-
Varilla responded to the honor by sharing his glory with
those who had helped in the laboratory and in the field—
Robert Langeron, prefect of police, and Robert Bos, the
municipal official, both of whom had embraced
"verdunization" early—and the scientists at the Pasteur Institute and the Academy of Sciences who had encouraged his
research.[101] Alexis Carrel wrote: "I regret not being able to
attend the ceremony in which you are being so justly honored with the Grand Medal of the city of Paris. I not only join
but applaud the public recognition of your great work."[102]

Having been honored for his engineering, diplomatic,
military, and scientific skills, Philippe was still to become a
laureate in literature. Two months later, the French Academy
granted him the grand prize Marcelin-Guerin for his book *De
Panama à Verdun* (Paris, 1936). In this book he summarized his
previous work, especially his Panama success and his battlefield experiences. The book had first appeared in London
in 1920, under the title *The Great Adventure of Panama*. *De
Panama à Verdun* was dedicated to those who helped him in
the struggle for Panama, especially Loomis, Lodge, Hanna,
and Roosevelt. In both editions, he explained what Roosevelt
meant when he said "I took Panama." "It meant," said
Roosevelt to William Morton Fullerton in an interview at
Oyster Bay in 1914, "because Bunau-Varilla brought it to me
on a gold platter." Philippe explained that Roosevelt's words
meant that Bunau-Varilla took Panama away from Colombia
"not because the interests of the United States demanded it,
but because he wished to protect her." "At her pressing
request," he delivered her from "the tyrannical greed of

Colombia, because her own preservation and the world's interests wanted it."[103]

Nicaragua a Threat Again?

Philippe's continuing interest in Panama is evidenced by his reaction to new overtures to build a Nicaraguan waterway. Informed of these proposals by Loomis, he replied:

> It would have been better to formulate a resolution prohibiting nature to shake down the dams and locks needed for this illusory endeavor to make a stiff canal where a flexible structure is necessary. Every time the United States takes seriously-in-hand the Nicaraguan Canal, a momentous seismic accident prevents her from carrying out the project. The same thing happened a few years ago. Colonel Lultau, in his report, inflamed by a feverish enthusiasm, declared that Nicaragua was less exposed than Panama to seismic disturbance. A few days later, the town of Managua was wiped out of existence by an earthquake. I hope the United States will receive the same seismic manifestations before spending any money on that foolish enterprise.[104]

The Hearst newspapers, especially the *San Francisco Chronicle*, embraced these chimeras, and Philippe commented about articles which Loomis sent him:

> As the Hearst publications have much power, these articles will push the project and inflate the illusion on which it floats. But their power will not be enough to pacify the earth tremors of the great society of Nicaraguan and Costa Rican volcanoes, dangerous neighbors of the proposed canal.[105]

Declining Health

Bunau-Varilla, as the sage professor Antony E. Raubitschek of Stanford University used to say, did not resent growing old because he well knew how many of his generation had been denied this privilege by the Great War. As the eternal game of international politics intensified, it was not difficult to deduce that air power would be a decisive factor in the approaching holocaust. The romantic Philippe had anticipated this change in military technology early in the century, having prepared his son to do battle in this element and having campaigned through the 1920s and 1930s for air supremacy. It was clear by now that Bunau-Varilla's most persistent adversaries were the politicians—whether in France, the United States, Colombia, or Panama. The high command in his own country, led by General Maurice Gamelin, exhibited little desire to present the parade of unstable regimes that competed to succeed each other in Paris[106] with an aggressive defense program. Philippe was not alone in his idea; young officers in the armed forces, such as Charles de Gaulle, were of the same mind but were also powerless to change a climate of inertia so well represented by citizens like Pierre Laval.[107]

Influential veteran's groups conceived the idea of paying national homage to Bunau-Varilla on the golden jubilee of his canal crusade. Although he was considered a national hero by the populace, official recognition was long overdue. No date could have been more appropriate than Bastille Day. On this day in 1938, he was awarded the Grand Cross of the Legion of Honor, and the officers corps presented him with a gold plaque bearing this inscription: TO COLONEL PHILIPPE BUNAU-VARILLA, 1888-1938, FROM HIS COMRADES EXPRESSING THE GRATITUDE OF FRANCE FOR HIS CRUSADE FROM PANAMA TO VERDUN. Visibly affected, but still mindful of the imminent peril of war, Philippe responded, "I am very happy to receive this memento from my comrades in war, which demonstrates the solidarity of men, so much needed when the fatherland is in danger."[108] Marshall Philippe Petain, still revered as the epitome of heroism—Foch and Joffre, his greatest competitors for glory, were dead—joined the national homage:

July 13, 1938
My dear friend:
    I rejoice at the news of your nomination for the dignity of the Grand Cross of the Legion of Honor. My happiness is even greater when I recall that this distinction was won at Verdun, which is the glorious name that characterises your genial discovery. . . .
Philippe Petain[109]

The End of a Glorious Life

Philippe's main preoccupation during his last two years of life was the peace of the world. In failing health after 1938 and in the certainty that another great war was about to begin, he mailed many copies of his last book, *From Panama to Verdun*, to his friends in America. He considered the Munich pact, by which Hitler, Mussolini, Edouard Daladier, and Neville Chamberlain agreed to the dismemberment of Czechoslovakia, a stratagem to gain time.

> Everything appears as if Mussolini and Hitler are preparing for a sudden attack in the spring or summer of this or the next year. The whole question seems to me lies in air power. As you can read in my book, detestable influences have prevented us from keeping the first rank we formerly had in the air.

But he had good news to send about chlorination, and abundant statistics, and this was "of course gratifying and I do not think that I have completely lost my time since the end of the war."[110]

Being the greatest living authority on canals, he was asked to give his opinion on the proposed passage through the Isthmus of Kra:

> I had already heard, more than forty years ago, about the canal through the Isthmus of Kra. It is undoubtedly a rather short canal, about seventy kilometers in length shorter than the Panamal Canal. Its military importance is very great because it passes across the back of the Singapore Naval Station. . . . I do not see why it was not undertaken earlier, [unless] on account of England's prohibition to a navigation short circuit leaving Singapore in the air. . . . From the engineering point of view it is a very easy job, but a rather difficult one from a political point of view on account of the obvious and certain opposition of England.[111]

A few months before the outbreak of the war, Philippe commented on the film *Suez*. "Of course it was not true history but it was interesting and entertaining." He agreed with Loomis that a movie on Panama "would offer a field of wide interest with its battles against nature, Nicaragua,

Colombia, etc.," but he left the production to Loomis, who he believed should be one of the main actors in the movie. Watching the clouds of war on the horizon, he feared that the democratic camp might not be able to cope with the double threat of "Bolshevism and Nazism."[112]

Bronchial attacks in the winter of 1940 debilitated Bunau-Varilla. Because of an operation "which cut through my stomach and upper intestine," his condition was aggravated in the spring, yet he felt strong enough to record several speeches for broadcast in the free world promoting the allied cause, because "the gangster operations on weak countries like Denmark and Norway show that the Germans have lost their mental equilibrium."[113] This was Philippe's last letter to Loomis and the second not in his own handwriting since their long association began in the 1890s. The signature lacks the usual vigor, indicating his deteriorating condition. As the Third Republic, a political structure dominated by parliamentary committees, marched toward oblivion, Bunau-Varilla's condition worsened.

In May 1940, the Germans opened their campaign on the western front. Bunau-Varilla was in the American Hospital in critical condition, but war communiqués such as "The general situation is satisfactory," issued while the Netherlands, Belgium and Luxemburg were being crushed,[114] did not deceive him.[115] On May 14, the Nazis pierced the French lines on a sixty-two mile front, and at last General Gamelin admitted that the situation was serious. In emulation of Joffre in 1914, he issued another "conquer or die" proclamation.[116] The next day, Petain was named vice-premier. Later, before Philippe died, General Gamelin was dismissed, and the entire high command was shaken up,[117] but much too late to save the Third Republic. Bunau-Varilla's and de Gaulle's fears had become reality because of the "lack of intelligence" of the military.

On May 17, Philippe was enlivened by a visit from Premier Reynaud and General Petain. On May 18, Edouard Daladier, now foreign minister, and Edouard Herriot, president of the Chamber of Deputies, came. And, when the end seemed imminent, President Albert Lebrun, Minister of Justice Albert Sorel, Georges Mandel of the interior, and the new generalissimo, Maxime Weygand, who had replaced Gamelin as supreme allied commander, also appeared at the hospital. "Finally he grew very weak. He could not sit on his chair; he was not able to rally from the exhaustion produced by the recent operation and he fell into a coma. He died on May 20."[118] On learning of his death, Lebrun, Reynaud, Weygand, and Herriot reappeared at the clinic to extend their condolences to the family.

To prevent the spread of political rumors, the government had ordered the population to remain indoors. Meetings, processions, and funerals were prohibited. In a motorized hearse, Philippe's remains were transferred to the cemetery of Passy, where he was entombed in the family vault. Only government officials and Philippe's close associates attended the private ceremony. The news was not immediately released to the public, perhaps because the Reynaud regime did not want to give the Nazis cause for rejoicing. Philippe had been one of their most uncompromising enemies. Giselle flew to Kenya by way of Italy, thanks to Reynaud. Reynaud also revealed to Maurice Bunau-Varilla the secret of Mussolini's impending declaration of war on France. "My uncle [Maurice] was given the last seat available in the last plane flying to Kenya with some British officers. Since my husband was an Italian commander, I had to return home to take care of my children. We knew Mario would be interned. I was unable to attend the funeral."[119]

Philippe was one of the true geniuses of the late nineteenth and early twentieth centuries. In an age abounding in heroes, Bunau-Varilla ranks with such luminaries as Pasteur, Edison, Madame Curie, Marconi, Walter Kosch, Lindbergh, de Lesseps, the Wright Brothers, Finlay, Ferdinand Zeppelin, Alexis Carrel, Sir Alexander Fleming, and Jonas Salk. People like these are united and driven by principles, and others may be inspired or confounded by them; but history knows that if humanity is to conquer it must have fearless leaders.

Philippe yielded to no obstacle and bowed to no difficulty.

For him, persistence was a creed. In a century of titans, a rather brutal century at that, he achieved the impossible. He was a superb optimist, especially about Panama. Bunau-Varilla had a passion for the democratic process that, according to him, was not to be confused with the committee-plagued Third Republic, which he distrusted. Democracy belonged to ancient Athens and Rome, as well as to the Americans and the French. He saw a political system which contributes to a high standard of living and enhances opportunities. The Panama Canal opened up new avenues through which these goals were to be achieved, for the United States, France, Panama, and all who cherish this legacy. The generations of isthmians who were born after his victories have taken the canal for granted because they knew no better.

Philippe was a true adventurer, like those who founded cities, navigated the oceans, and explored the cosmos. He advanced to the wilderness of the virgin frontier, always seeking new horizons for the well-being of people or attempting to prolong their lives. Bunau-Varilla could not understand why his crusades were so controversial, especially among people for whom he had performed miracles—the Panamanians. He made possible to Panama the double dream of independence and a canal, with an additional gift: protection by the most powerful nation on earth.

It is time for the Panamanians to awaken, recognize, and pay proper homage to their greatest benefactor, without whom, as Charles de Lesseps said, "Panama would have remained but the figment of a dream."[120] He is unfairly portrayed by many aspiring writers as a greedy "betrayer," perpetuating the United States' presence for mere love of money,[121] when money was something he did not need or covet. He spent vast sums in the service of Panama because he had faith in its destiny. While he was engaged in these expenditures, Panama's children were exercising the "right" to eliminate each other.

It might be questioned whether he was a gregarious person, for he was uneasy in crowds, yet he was acclaimed by the world at large outside of Panama for his respect for others, regardless of color, religion, social station, or economic condition. Let it be said that he was at ease in the company of his causes and ideas which were always directed toward progress and peace. Detractors must be reminded that there are those who cause events to occur and that Bunau-Varilla was one of them. Others simply watch events happen, like the Colombians in 1902 and 1903, and many do not know that anything happened at all, like Bunau-Varilla's detractors. Philippe is the prototype of a rebel with a cause.

Let's not forget that the pirate Henry Morgan destroyed Panama once;[122] Bunau-Varilla rescued it from the miserable future to which another Morgan, Senator John Morgan of Alabama, tried to consign it. We take leave of Philippe with Shelley's immortal lines, oft-quoted by Professor Duncan Robinson of the University of Texas at Arlington:

Till the Future dares
Forget the Past, his fate and fame shall be
An echo and light into eternity

Appendix 1

Geneaology of

Philippe Bunau-Varilla

A child with Basque and German relatives on both sides of the family tree—some of them already immortalized by their own deeds in the complicated worlds of diplomacy and history—was born in Paris on July 26, 1859. He was named Jean Philippe Bunau-Varilla.

Among his illustrious ancestors was Count Henry Bunau, 1697–1792, statesman and historian who became an intimate of and a court advisor to King Augustus III of Saxony, later ruler of Poland. Count Bunau also served with distinction as counselor to Holy Roman Emperor Charles VII. Count Bunau's library, which contained forty-two thousand volumes, was one of the best of its kind in private hands. Among its treasures was the first translation into the Tuscan language of the works of Tertulian and an original copy, with its translation, of the rare history of the late Roman Empire by Ammianus Marcellinus. These translations had been made by the celebrated Renaissance humanist, Niccolo Niccoli. Count Bunau himself wrote the *History of Germany and of the Holy Roman Emperors to 918 A.D.*, published in Leipzig in 1718, and *History of the War between France, England and Germany*, printed at Regensberg in 1763.

Another of Philippe's ancestors was the brilliant Antonio Varilla, whose parents migrated from the Basque country to Geret, France, before 1626, the year of Varilla's birth. Early in life the young Varilla found himself at court, where his talents were acknowledged. He became the tutor and official chronicler of the Duc d'Orleans, royal librarian, and advisor to several leading figures of the realm, including Pedro Depuy and Jean Baptiste Colbert. His influence and charm must have been vast, because, by 1668, his friends at court secured for him a life pension of 1,200 pounds a year, very probably to enable him to devote his full time to writing. Varilla did not disappoint his patrons, for he became one of France's most prolific historical essayists, although he also became the target of lesser minds, envious of his success. He died in 1696 at a time when his diplomatic counsel was once more being eagerly sought because of the international crises that exploded in the Great Northern War, 1697–1710, between Poland, Russia, and Denmark vs. Sweden, and in the War of the Spanish Succession, 1700–1713.[1] Antonio Varilla is not a source to be overlooked if one wishes to research the history of the West during the post-Renaissance decades.

Felipe Varilla, son of Antonio and a Parisian lady, traveled to Madrid shortly after the end of the War of the Spanish Succession, when the Bourbons had been universally recognized by the Treaty of Utrecht of 1713 as the new ruling family of Spain. On the accession of Philippe Anjou to the throne of Ferdinand and Isabella in 1700, the French began to take advantage of the many opportunities offered to the devotées of trade and commerce within the imperial domains of the crown. Thus, Felipe Varilla might have been sent to America on a business mission by one of the Franco-Spanish guilds or may have wandered on his own to the River Plata province. He later settled in Chile. The hamlet that bears his name is located in the Department of Putaendo, Province of Aconcagua.

Felipe Varilla must have devoted much of his energy while in America to the boundless opportunities that had opened up in the continent, thanks to the new economic policies of the Spanish government originating in the mind of the very able Minister of State, Jose Campillo.[2] Felipe returned to France a wealthy man and, by the end of the *ancien régime*, his granddaughter, Gabrielle Varilla, married Alexander Bunau, grandson of Henry Bunau.[3]

Gabrielle's father was the dashing Etienne Varilla, who also enjoyed great financial talents. Through a highly complicated monetary transaction, Etienne became a millionaire. In order to please his Brabant subjects, Holy Roman Emperor Joseph II seriously contemplated opening the navigation of the Scheldt River, an act which might have curtailed Dutch trade considerably. Desiring to thwart this move, the Dutch bankers (in utmost secrecy) contrived to offer the monarch several million gold francs. Emperor Joseph could not accept this money in Antwerp or Vienna. It was decided that the sum was to be placed in the hands of several Parisian financiers who assumed the responsibility—for a high fee—of depositing the funds safely in Austria.

Etienne Varilla was one of the manipulators of this scheme, which was carried out during the emperor's state visit to Versailles. An innocent victim of this clever transaction was the unfortunate Marie Antoinette. The transmission of the assets from France to Vienna was enough to quicken the already insidious malevolence toward the queen, who was accused of giving immense sums in cash to her favorite brother, Joseph II. Hostility toward her increased when several gold trading firms throughout Europe declined to confirm that the Dutch-inspired transaction had taken place, and it was even rumored that the financial maneuver was only a canard fabricated to protect Marie Antoinette.[4]

The children of Alexander Bunau and Gabrielle Varilla used the name Bunau-Varilla. There were four—three boys and a girl. The girl either married and changed her name or died young. The two older sons were casualties of the Napoleonic wars, but the youngest, Antoine Bunau-Varilla, became the father of Philippe Bunau-Varilla. Antoine died a few months after Philippe's sixth birthday, leaving his family well provided for, as he had invested wisely in Parisian real estate and in the mines of Asturias. There was another child, Maurice Bunau-Varilla, for whom Philippe showed great affection throughout his life.[5]

Commemorative Medal Struck by the city of Reims in 1929 Honoring Bunau-Varilla.

The words read:	Homage to the discoverer [inventor]
The city of Reims to her benefactor Philippe Bunau-Varilla	of the verdunization process after five uninterrupted years preventing epidemics of Typhus and Disentery God bless him

Commemorative Medal Struck by the city of Carcassonne in 1929
Honoring Bunau-Varilla.

The city of Carcassonne in
homage 2nd recognition to
her benefactor.

By a decree of the municipal
council of November 20, 1926,
Mr. Philippe Bunau-Varilla is
made [honorary] citizen of
Carcassonne.

Commemorative Medal Struck by the City of Lyon in 1929 Honoring
Bunau-Varilla.

The city of Lyon in recognition
of Philippe Bunau-Varilla services.

Verdunization protects Lyon
against water epidemics.
Forward, forward for a better
Lyon, June 1929.

DOCUMENT H'

Form No. 1516.   **CABLE MESSAGE.**
THE WESTERN UNION TELEGRAPH COMPANY.
—— INCORPORATED ——
ROBERT C. CLOWRY, President and General Manager.

TWO AMERICAN CABLES FROM NEW YORK TO GREAT BRITAIN.
CONNECTS ALSO WITH FIVE ANGLO-AMERICAN AND ONE DIRECT U. S. ATLANTIC CABLES.
DIRECT CABLE COMMUNICATION WITH GERMANY AND FRANCE.
CABLE CONNECTION WITH CUBA, WEST INDIES, MEXICO AND CENTRAL AND SOUTH AMERICA.
MESSAGES SENT TO, AND RECEIVED FROM, ALL PARTS OF THE WORLD.

OFFICES IN AMERICA:
All Offices (23,000) of the Western Union Telegraph Company and its Connections.

OFFICES IN GREAT BRITAIN:

547 Pm.

RECEIVED at   Wyatt Building, Washington, D. C.

February 24, 1904.

480/HY BI Panama 71

Bunau-varilla, Washington (DC)

Suplicoos manifestar al ilustrado gobierno americano y a su grande
y generoso pueblo expresion sincero reconocimiento nombre gobierno
pueblo nuestra naciente republica los valiosos servicios prestado-
,s por ud a esta nacion del 11 de octubre de 1903 a esta fecha
viviran siempre en el corazon de sus habitantes y perduraran
aun mas que el bronce de la estatua del gran frances a cuya erecc-
ion contribuye ud tan generosamente
Amador

TEXTE EN ESPAGNOL	TRADUCTION EN FRANÇAIS	TRADUCTION EN ANGLAIS
February, 24 1904 Bunau-Varilla Washington, D. C.	24 février 1904 Bunau-Varilla Washington, D. C.	February 24, 1904 Bunau-Varilla Washington, D. C.
Suplicos manifestar al ilustrado gobierno americano y al su grande y generoso pueblo expression sincero reconocimiento nombre gobierno pueblo nuestra naciente republica. Los valiosos servicios prestados por ud a esta nacion del 11 octubre de 1903 a esta fecha viviran siempre en el corazon de sus habitantes y perduraran aun mas que el bronce de la estatua del gran Frances a cuya ereccion contribuye Ud tan generosamente. AMADOR.	Je vous prie de manifester à l'illustre Gouvernement américain et à son peuple grand et généreux l'expression sincère de notre reconnaissance au nom du gouvernement et du peuple de notre république naissante. Les vaillants services que vous avez rendus à ce pays depuis le 11 octobre 1903 jusqu'à ce jour vivront toujours dans le cœur de ses habitants et dureront plus longtemps même que le bronze de la statue du grand Français à l'érection de laquelle vous avez contribué si généreusement. AMADOR.	I beg you to express to the illustrious government of the United States and to her great and generous people, on behalf of the government and of the people of our republic just born, their sincere gratitude. The valiant services rendered by you to this country from the 11th of october 1903 to this day will live for ever in the hearts of its inhabitants and will last aven longer than the bronze of the statue of the great Frenchman to the erection of which you contributed so generously. AMADOR.

República de Panamá.

Convención Nacional Constituyente.

PRESIDENCIA.

Número 60.

Panamá, 27 de Febrero de 1904

Señor Don Felipe Bunau-Varilla
Washington.

Tengo la honra de comunicarle á Ud. que la Convención Nacional, de la República, Cuerpo, del cual soy Presidente, adoptó ayer la proposición que en seguida copio, que fue presentada por mí:

"La Convención Nacional tiene en alto aprecio los servicios que el Señor Felipe Bunau-Varilla le ha prestado al pueblo istmeño, contribuyendo, con labor inteligente y perseverante, á la adopción por los Estados Unidos, de la ruta de Panamá, para la excavación del canal interocéanico"

Me congratulo con Ud. muy sinceramente, por causa de la resolución inserta que es un acto de estricta y merecida justicia, y aprovecho la oportunidad, para ofrecerle á Ud. las seguridades de mi alta estimación personal.

Tito Arosemena

TEXTE EN ESPAGNOL	TRADUCTION EN FRANÇAIS	TRADUCTION EN ANGLAIS
Republica de Panama Convencion Nacional Constituyente Panama, 27 de Febrero 1904 Senor don Felipe Bunau-Varilla Washington	République de Panama Convention Nationale Constituante Panama, 27 février 1904 M. Philippe Bunau-Varilla Washington	Panama Republic National Constituent Convention Panama, February 27, 1904 Philippe Bunau-Varilla, Esquire Washington
Tengo el honor de communicale a Ud que la Convencion Nacional de la Republica cuerpo del cual soy présidente adopto ayer la proposicion que en seguido copio, que fue presentada por mi.	J'ai l'honneur de vous informer que la Convention Nationale de la République, corps dont je suis président, a adopté hier la proposition que je copie ci-après et qui fut présentée par moi :	I have the honor of communicating to you that the National Convention, body of which I am the president, has adopted yesterday the proposition which I copy hereafter and which was presented by myself :
« La Convencion Nacional tiene « en alto aprecio los servicios que « el Senor Felipe Bunau-Varilla le « ha prestado al pueblo istmeno, « contribuyendo, con labor inteli- « gente y perseverante à la adopcion « por los Estados Unidos, de la ruta « de Panama, para la excavacion « del canal interocéanico ».	« La Convention Nationale tient « en haute estime les services que « M. Philippe Bunau-Varilla a rendus « au peuple de l'Isthme en contribuant « par un travail intelligent et persévérant « à l'adoption de la route de Panama « par les Etats-Unis pour l'excavation « du Canal interocéanique ».	« The National Convention hold « in high esteem the services which « Mr. Philippe Bunau-Varilla has « done to the Isthmiam people by his « contribution to the adoption of the « Panama route by the United States « for the Interoceanic canal, thanks « to his intelligent labor and perse- « vering efforts ».
Me congratulo con Ud muy sinceramente por causa de la resolucion inscrita, que es un acte de estricta y merecida justicia, y aprovecho la oportunidad para ofrecerle a Ud las seguridades de mi alta estimacion personal.	Je me réjouis avec vous très sincèrement de l'insertion de cette résolution dans les annales de la Convention, ce qui n'est qu'un acte de justice stricte et méritée, et je saisis cette occasion pour vous offrir les expressions de ma haute estime personnelle.	I feel sincerely very happy with you to see inserted in the archives of the Convention what is nothing but an act of strict and merited justice and I avail myself of the opportunity to offer you the expression of my high personal esteem.
Pablo AROSEMENA.	Pablo AROSEMENA.	Pablo AROSEMENA.

Appendix 2

Ferdinand de Lesseps

and the Suez Canal

For two hundred years before the opening of the modern Suez Canal, the French toyed with the idea of a canal in Egypt. The mathematician Leibnitz proposed one in 1672. The Marquis d'Argenson, in the reign of Louis XV, conceived a canal which was to be for the "common good of all Christians." As the French Revolution approached, royal missions to Egypt multiplied in number. Montigny went in 1776, Choisseul-Gouffier in 1777, and Truguet in 1785.[1]

Once rule by committee was over and moderation returned to Paris, the Marquis de Talleyrand began to dig out the old plans,[2] but many other prominent Frenchmen were also fascinated by the East. Bonaparte was one, and the idea of creating an Army of the Orient to seize Egypt grew in his mind in proportion to his intimate friendship with Monsieur Barras and his love affair with Josephine de Beauharnais.[3] By the end of 1798, the young Corsican was inspecting the area of the canal with his chief engineer, J. Marie Le Père, and other members of his staff.

On orders from the commander-in-chief, and in spite of nearly insuperable difficulties, Le Père presented a report to the government in 1803. He wrote that by means of the canal the route would become as continuous for navigation as that of the Cape of Good Hope. The canal would go from Alexandria to Suez, passing near Cairo. His statement that there was a difference of twenty-nine feet in the levels of the two seas was rejected by the celebrated astronomer, Pierre de Laplace. Perhaps because of Laplace's reservations, or Napoleon's belief that the Turks themselves should build the new canal, the report remained a secret until 1808. Still, for the first time, there was an engineering plan exact enough to provide a basis for technical discussion. This *aide-memoire* of Le Père was the spark that kindled the flame in de Lesseps' mind years later, even though he decided to adopt another route.

Like Panama, modern Egypt needed stability and order, necessary conditions for undertaking and completing a vast project such as the building of the Suez Canal. The reign of the Greek-born Mohammed Ali (1805–1849) brought these assets to the Land of the Nile. He created a state, called in experts from Europe, and inaugurated a vast program of public works. The tranquility of the land was a *fait accompli* when de Lesseps arrived to begin work on the canal. Fearful of being caught in the middle of a power struggle between two aggressive Western powers—England and France—the Egyptian ruler tried to give each something: the English backed a railway and the French were given the canal concession.

Born on November 19, 1805, at the height of Napoleon's military exploits, de Lesseps later followed the advice of his father and, by 1825, had embarked on a diplomatic career. As vice-consul, consul, consul general, and minister to Madrid, the young man not only acquired firsthand knowledge of the very difficult machinations and intrigues of diplomacy but also demonstrated an unselfish attitude and unusual charm. While stationed at Cairo (1833 to 1837), he took direct action, at the risk of his life, to combat the plague. The Egyptian pashas as well as the humble *fellahs* were greatly impressed by this unusual behavior.[4] No doubt good deeds eventually pay dividends, for de Lesseps' courage in the face of death on this occasion was not forgotten. Later, when he sought the canal concession, he had little difficulty enlisting the support of Mohammed Said, the son of Mohammed Ali.

After de Lesseps was forced to retire in 1850, nobody who knew him could imagine him leisurely enjoying the healthy waters of Vichy. He was only forty-four and bursting with physical energy. A good horseman, he was fond of spectacular exploits. As a child he swam the Seine. He also excelled as a marksman with the pistol, and he loved to walk and dance. Despite the epicurean ways of diplomacy, de Lesseps was a sober man of good personal habits. Like the ancient Romans, whose healthy customs he admired, he took hot baths almost daily and fasted one day a week. He was endowed with sound intuition, and once convinced of a course of action, he would proceed fearlessly. He could adapt himself to every geographical and social climate and did not spurn omens and prophecies. Sometimes he played at astrology, reading his destiny in the stars.[5]

In his late childhood, Mohammed Said paid more attention to the fork than to exercise or books. Large in body, he quickly became fat, to the annoyance of his royal sire, who prescribed a spartan diet for him and hired de Lesseps to shape up the uncoordinated and obese prince. The French diplomat instructed well, but he did not starve the boy. On the contrary, he introduced him to the richness of French cuisine and with time, patience, and daily exercise, the shapeless mass of fat transformed itself into a handsome, refined, and athletic young man. He never forgot de Lesseps' kindness, and on his accession to power he asked that his former tutor come to see him "immediately."[6]

Perhaps more by intuition than by coincidence, de Lesseps had been studying every report on the Suez Canal project, especially the memorandum of Le Père to Napoleon, 1804.[7] He sailed from Marseille without delay and disembarked at Alexandria on November 7, 1854. Knowing how much his former teacher liked to ride horses, Mohammed Said invited de Lesseps to ride with him at the head of an army on its way to Cairo. In his pocket the Frenchman had the canal plans, but he decided to wait for an appropriate moment to discuss them. A week later, after he had consulted his horoscope and during the appearance of a brilliant rainbow, de Lesseps revealed his project to his friend, who immediately accepted it. On November 25, at a hastily called consular meeting in Cairo, the monarch made a public announcement of the concession and designated de Lesseps to carry it to its conclusion. The world was caught by surprise, and the unhappy English consul general at Cairo almost collapsed on the spot. He was later reprimanded by his superiors for failing to anticipate this move. But when you deal with the stars and a man of destiny there is little anyone can do.[8]

The official documents were signed on November 30, 1854, but it was clear that this was a personal agreement, for in these papers the ruler refers to de Lesseps as "my devoted friend who is of high birth and noble rank." The profits were to be divided, 75 percent to the shareholders, 10 percent to the founders, and 15 percent to the government. To remove it from the dangers of narrow-minded nationalism, the company was repeatedly described as "universal." No nation was to obtain special advantages of any kind, and the length of the concession was to be for ninety-nine years from the date of the opening of the canal.[9]

Immediately thereafter, England began to apply pressure on the Sublime Porte in Constantinople, urging the rejection of the deal or at least indefinite postponement. Still the nominal overlord of Egypt, the Turkish sultan could do just that. However, like his disciple Philippe Bunau-Varilla in another continent and a later time, de Lesseps was equal to the challenge. He enlisted the support of Emperor Napoleon III,[10] and wrote a series of open letters to the English Parliament, the East India Company, the city merchants, the mining houses, bankers, the chambers of commerce, and the merchants who traded with India and China. He also gave conferences in which maps and graphs were exhibited and visited Queen Victoria, Prince Albert, Gladstone, Palmerston, and many others.

Despite all de Lesseps' veiled diplomacy, Palmerston shot down de Lesseps' plans by direct action. Keeping the real motives for his brutal attacks in the background, the prime minister declared on two successive occasions, July 7 and August 14, 1856, that the canal scheme was a bubble. He claimed that reliable authorities had labeled the project physically impossible, but he explained that his opposition was based on a higher motive—England's altruistic desire to preserve the integrity of the Ottoman domain.[11] The arguments of the English statesman might appear ludicrous at first but, considering what has happened since 1900 in the realm of international relations, we might pause and wonder if it would have been better if the isthmus had never been cut.

As in so many other historical crises, faraway events and de Lesseps' good fortune overcame Palmerston's opposition. By the summer of 1856, the imperial regime in France was at its height. Napoleon III, like his earlier namesake at Tilsit in 1807, was about to dictate humiliating treaty terms to Russia; and the Crimean War, which had drawn France and England together, was coming to an end. Both governments decided to leave matters in the hands of Egypt and Turkey, but the Porte, encouraged by the English minister, would not ratify an agreement.

The situation was almost identical to that which confronted Bunau-Varilla after 1900, when the Colombian Senate refused to ratify the Herran-Hay Treaty and the government remained in the hands of a politically weak octogenarian chief executive with as little real power as the Sublime Porte in Constantinople.

Undaunted by these delays (it had been four years since he won the concession), de Lesseps persisted. Armed with his best assets—charm and persuasion—he set about raising the required capital of two hundred million francs. Each share was worth five hundred francs, and four-hundred thousand shares were issued. He set up a publicity bureau which sought invitations from social and banking circles. He left a favorable impression everywhere, for he was a man of great tact and good manners.

Baron de Rothschild congratulated him on his plan for an international subscription and offered his "uninterested" help at a "modest" price of 5 percent. Without losing his composure, de Lesseps refused this "aid," set up headquarters near the Place Vendôme, and launched a personal tour of Europe.

De Lesseps' selflessness and dauntless courage were already something of a legend. The French middle class, always patriotic, pictured him as an underdog. Within two weeks, in the fall of 1858, twenty-five thousand subscribers applied for the first issue of the shares. By early December, they had bought 207,111 of the 400,000 shares.

Perhaps because of the troubled world situation, which presaged a decade of conflict and readjustment, Austria and the United States refused the block of shares reserved for them. Russia did the same, but for different reasons. England's boycott of the subscription was not unexpected.[12] However, Mohammed Said once again came to the aid of his friend. In addition to the 96,517 shares that he had already taken, he subscribed to the blocks of shares spurned by these countries. Eventually the ruler of Egypt became the largest single shareholder, with 50 percent of the capital. It was this block that Disraeli bought in 1875.

Meanwhile, English public opinion had turned against the canal. It was speculated editorially and privately that if the canal should ever be built, it would not make a pound of profit. It was said that most of the subscribers were waiters, busboys, cooks, grocers, butchers, and in general members of the servant class of France, who had been deceived by de Lesseps' propaganda. The whole business was labeled a gigantic fraud and compared to the Mississippi bubble a century-and-a-half earlier. Nothing was said about Mohammed Said's shares. An enterprise financed in this way today would be labeled a "people's company" or a "third-world economic crusade," but every week from 1854 to 1869, Suez was called the greatest swindle of the century.[13] In spite of all the travail and tribulation at Suez, the agony, near disaster, and the invidious criticism would eventually be drowned in the grandeur of final victory.

England's Obstinacy and Eventual Capitulation

In a ceremony presided over by Mohammed Said, ground was broken on April 26, 1859. Work was begun under climactic conditions similar to those that would be encountered at Panama, except for the massive tropical isthmian jungle. The company was entitled by its charter, thanks to the viceroy, to as many native laborers as it required, up to forty thousand, and at a nominal price. These men were drafted into the company by *corvée*.

Immediately after the arrival of Khedive Ishmail, successor to Mohammed Said, England opened up a new front in her campaign to stop work on the ditch. Coached by the British, Ishmail inaugurated a policy of duplicity which, fifteen years after the completion of the canal, placed the majority of the stock in the hands of Disraeli's government. Proclaiming himself as much a canal enthusiast as de Lesseps, the new Egyptian ruler made his own the protests of England against a "revival of slavery," reduced the number of laborers to only six thousand, and demanded from the company the return of all lands that had been granted to it. While millions of men and women were working in the British Empire under the most miserable conditions, a hypocritical and violent campaign against "forced labor" was loosed throughout England.

Early in 1864, the Khedive was constrained to break the contract with the company and order suspension of the works. Once more the issue escaped the Land of the Nile, and de Lesseps had to request the intervention of Napoleon III in order to face his enemies in Europe. The emperor was named arbiter of the dispute and rendered an impartial but just verdict in the summer of 1864. De Lesseps had the mortification of seeing his little army of *fellahs* disappear as suddenly and irrevocably as an April fog, leaving only their tents behind. Many took their tools with them. The company was compelled to return 148,000 acres of land which it held under the concession.

The company gave Egypt ownership of an already finished fresh-water canal, but kept the right to use it. It received an indemnity of eighty-four million francs[14] and won the most important and essential round: the concession was declared valid by the Sublime Porte.[15]

The logic of the situation suggested to the resourceful de Lesseps the replacement of men with machines, the putting to work of slaves without souls or sensibilities. The inventive genius of France, inspired by the gravity of the crisis, rose to the occasion and in a short time from eighty to one hundred twenty dredges, an equal number of barges, elevators, steam tugs, ferries, and iron mules like the ones later used at Panama took the place of the thousands of men withdrawn at England's instigation. This assemblage of ferrous machinery needed fewer than three thousand five hundred men to handle it, and monthly output was increased from 11,000 cubic meters to over 2 million. More earth was excavated in three years than in the previous seven-and-a-half.[16]

Work continued without further setbacks, especially after the recruiting of more mechanically-minded workers throughout the whole of the Mediterranean. Fifteen thousand "free" workmen—French, Italians, Spaniards, Greeks, Arabs, Illyrians, and Syrians—were obtained. As in the Isthmus of Panama later, the native population contributed few hours of labor to the building of their greatest economic asset.[17]

However, de Lesseps had to face another crisis which, like most of the past troubles, was set in motion by England. Because of the loss of *fellah* labor and the high cost of the machines and their continuous servicing, it became necessary, in 1868, to raise eighty-five million more francs. The resources of the company were small and its credit not great. Thanks to malicious rumors spread in the London stock market, only thirty-three million francs were subscribed for an issue of one hundred million in bonds. Politicians and financiers, sensing victory and profit for themselves and defeat for de Lesseps, closed in on the canal company and nearly snatched his prize from him. The canal builder appealed for the last time to Napoleon III, and his brother, the Duc de Morny, quickly persuaded the legislature to approve a lottery loan. At last completion of the canal was assured.[18]

Although there is no evidence of it in any source, my belief is that one of the strongest reasons for the support of the canal project, first from Mohammed Said and later, in spite of England's obstructive tactics, by the Khedive Ishmail, was national pride. No doubt, de Lesseps' enthusiasm impressed Egyptian ruling circles with the importance of commemorating the nine hundredth anniversary of the founding of Cairo with a spectacle unparalleled in history. (The city of Cairo was founded during the reign of the Fatimi Caliphate, in 969 A.D.)

In 1866, the Khedive began to plan the inauguration celebration. Palaces were built, roads were opened up toward the pyramids, and the opera house was about to be completed. Early in 1869, he went to France to distribute invitations to the event personally. On March 14, the waters of the Bitter

Lakes and the Mediterranean were joined, and on August 15, seven days after the anniversary of the founding of Cairo the two seas were joined at Suez.

The formal dedication took place on November 17, 1869, just two days before de Lesseps' sixty-fourth birthday, but he was to face a last-minute crisis. The ship sent to test the ditch went aground, blocking transit, and Ishmail feared that the celebrations would have to be postponed. De Lesseps calmed the viceroy down by ordering that the ship be blown up, but there was no need. The ship floated free, continuing its testing successfully.

Few times in the history of mankind was a more fantastic event recorded. The imperial yacht *L'Aigle*, as majestic as its passengers, Empress Eugenie de Montijo and a glittering assembly of royalty, led an armada of warships into the Red Sea. At Lake Timsah, thousands of spectators cheered their arrival, while French cannons gave the signal to begin the celebration. The Khedive was host to hundreds of officials, including the Austrian emperor, the prince of Wales, Henry, heir to the Dutch throne, and the crown prince of Prussia. The royal guest list also included a cruiser full of kings and princes. A cross section of Middle East and European high society was also present, including the Algerian leader, Abd-el-Kader, novelists Alexander Dumas, Theophile Gautier, Henrik Ibsen, and Emile Zola, and the painter, Eugene Fromentin, plus hundreds of French political figures, businessmen, engineers, bankers, musicians, and composers. In his speech de Lesseps made no mention of England's opposition. Ironically, the English warship *Royal Oak* collided with a sister vessel while competing for a place in the nautical parade. Both ships were stranded.

De Lesseps gave a formal banquet for a thousand guests and, two days later, an open dinner for twice that number, who ate and drank from tables set on the dunes under the desert stars. The viceroy held several receptions and banquets for an equal number of guests. Several operas were performed, and the Khedive commissioned Giuseppe Verdi, then at the peak of his career, to write an opera in commemoration of the event. The Italian maestro composed *Aida*, which was staged in Cairo in 1871.[19]

A few days later there were more celebrations for those returning from visiting the Valley of the Kings, Elephantine Island, and the Pyramids. To the surprise of everyone, de Lesseps married a young lady who could have been his granddaughter, twenty-one-year-old Mademoiselle de Bragard, a hazel-eyed beauty who was to accompany him to Panama ten years later and give him six sons and six daughters.[20] De Lesseps seems to have been destined to do things in pairs. He had two wives, almost built two canals, worked in two different activities during his life, and enjoyed the friendship and admiration of two loyal friends who made his dreams reality—Said Pasha in Egypt and Philippe Bunau-Varilla in Panama.

Each government represented at the inauguration decorated the canal builder with its highest order. He also received many valuable gifts on the occasion of his second marriage, and at last, his bête noire, England, capitulated to him. De Lesseps was invited to visit a dozen European countries, and everywhere he received the acclamation of the multitudes. Even the British, who had fought him so bitterly, almost killed him with an outburst of tribute. The *Times*, which had been the most brutal instrument of opposition to de Lesseps for twenty years, apologized and made amends in a witty and candid editorial.

> Mr. de Lesseps has arrived in a country which did nothing to help in the construction of the canal, but which since its opening has had more ships passing through it than all the other nations of the world put together. It is this country that will provide him with almost all the dividends which [he] and his shareholders will cash. Let that be the compensation which we offer for all the wrongs which we have managed to inflict upon him in the past.[21]

No tribute could have been more deserved, especially coming from his enemies, for it was de Lesseps alone who made the Suez Canal.

Appendix 3

Treaties between the United States and the Republic of Panama, 1904 and 1977

Convention Between the United States and the Republic of Panama

(1904)

[The attempt on the part of a French company to build a Panama canal was begun in 1879 under a concession from the Republic of Colombia, through whose territory the canal was to pass. When the enterprise was taken over by the United States in 1904, the treaty with Colombia, arranging for United States control of the canal strip, was rejected by the Congress of Colombia. The people of the isthmus, whose prosperity largely depended on the building of the canal, thereupon seceded from Colombia, set up the Republic of Panama, and agreed to the following convention.]

For the Construction of a Ship Canal to Connect the Waters of the Atlantic and Pacific Oceans. Signed at Washington, November 18, 1903. Ratification advised by the Senate, February 23, 1904. Ratified by the President, February 25, 1904. Ratified by Panama, December 2, 1903. Ratifications exchanged at Washington, February 26, 1904. Proclaimed, February 26, 1904.

By the President of the United States of America.

A Proclamation

Whereas, a Convention between the United States of America and the

Republic of Panama to insure the construction of a ship canal across the Isthmus of Panama to connect the Atlantic and Pacific Oceans, was concluded and signed by their respective Plenipotentiaries at Washington, on the eighteenth day of November, one thousand nine hundred and three, the original of which Convention, being in the English language, is word for word as follows:

Isthmian Canal Convention

The United States of America and the Republic of Panama being desirous to insure the construction of a ship canal across the Isthmus of Panama to connect the Atlantic and Pacific Oceans, and the Congress of the United States of America having passed an act approved June 28, 1902, in furtherance of that object, by which the President of the United States is authorized to acquire within a reasonable time the control of the necessary territory of the Republic of Colombia, and the sovereignty of such actually vested in the Republic of Panama, the high contracting parties have resolved for that purpose to conclude a convention and have accordingly appointed as their plenipotentiaries,—

The President of the United States of America, John Hay, Secretary of State, and

The Government of the Republic of Panama, Philippe Bunau-Varilla, Envoy Extraordinary and Minister Plenipotentiary of the Republic of Panama, thereunto specially empowered by said government, who after communicating with each other their respective full powers, found to be in good and due form, have agreed upon and concluded the following articles:

Article I

The United States guarantees and will maintain the independence of the Republic of Panama.

Article II

The Republic of Panama grants to the United States in perpetuity, the use, occupation and control of a zone of land and land under water for the construction, maintenance, operation, sanitation and protection of said Canal of the width of ten miles extending to the distance of five miles on each side of the center line of the route of the Canal to be constructed; the said zone beginning in the Caribbean Sea three marine miles from mean low water mark and extending to and across the Isthmus of Panama into the Pacific Ocean to a distance of three marine miles from mean low water mark with the proviso that the cities of Panama and Colon and the harbors adjacent to said cities, which are included within the boundaries of the zone above described, shall not be included within this grant. The Republic of Panama further grants to the United States in perpetuity, the use, occupation and control of any other lands and waters outside of the zone above described which may be necessary and convenient for the construction, maintenance, operation, sanitation and protection of the said Canal or of any auxiliary canals or other works necessary and convenient for the construction, maintenance, operation, sanitation and protection of the said enterprise.

The Republic of Panama further grants in like manner to the United States in perpetuity, all islands within the limits of the zone above described and in addition thereto, the group of small islands in the Bay of Panama, named Perico, Naos, Culebra and Flamenco.

Article III

The Republic of Panama grants to the United States all the rights, power and authority within the zone mentioned and described in Article II of this agreement, and within the limits of all auxiliary lands and waters mentioned and described in said Article II which the United States would possess and exercise, if it were the sovereign of the territory within which said lands and waters are located to the entire exclusion of the exercise by the Republic of Panama of any such sovereign rights, power or authority.

Article IV

As rights subsidiary to the above grants the Republic of Panama grants in perpetuity, to the United States the right to use the rivers, streams, lakes and other bodies of water within its limits for navigation, the supply of water or waterpower or other purposes, so far as the use of said rivers, streams, lakes and bodies of water and the waters thereof may be necessary and convenient for the construction, maintenance, operation, sanitation and protection of the said Canal.

Article V

The Republic of Panama grants to the United States in perpetuity, a monopoly for the construction, maintenance and operation of any system of communication by means of canal or railroad across its territory between the Caribbean Sea and the Pacific Ocean.

Article VI

The grants herein contained shall in no manner invalidate the titles or rights of private land holders or owners of private property in the said zone or in or to any of the lands or waters granted to the United States by the provisions of any Article of this treaty, nor shall they interfere with the rights of way over the public roads passing through the said zone or over any of the said lands or waters unless said rights of way or private rights shall conflict with rights herein granted to the United States in which case the rights of the United States shall be superior. All damages caused to the owners of private lands or private property of any kind by reason of the grants contained in this treaty or by reason of the operations of the United States, its agents or employees, or by reason of the construction, maintenance, operation, sanitation and protection of the said Canal or of the works of sanitation and protection herein provided for, shall be appraised and settled by a joint Commission appointed by the Governments of the United States and the Republic of Panama, whose decisions as to such damages shall be final and whose awards as to such damages shall be paid solely by the United States. No part of the work on said Canal or the Panama railroad or on any auxiliary works relating thereto and authorized by the terms of this treaty shall be prevented, delayed or impeded by or pending such proceedings to ascertain such damages. The appraisal of said private lands and private property and the assessment of damages to them shall be based upon their value before the date of this convention.

Article VII

The Republic of Panama grants to the United States within the limits of the cities of Panama and Colon and their adjacent harbors and within the territory adjacent thereto the right to acquire by purchase or by the exercise of the right of eminent domain, any lands, buildings, water rights or other properties necessary and convenient for the construction, maintenance, operation and protection of the Canal and of any works of sanitation, such as the collection and disposition of sewage and the distribution of water in the said cities of Panama and Colon, which, in the discretion of the United States may be necessary and convenient for the construction, maintenance, operation, sanitation and protection of the said Canal and railroad. All such works of sanitation, collection and disposition of sewage and distribution of water in the cities of Panama and Colon shall be made at the expense of the United States, and the Government of the United States, its agents or nominees shall be authorized to impose and collect water rates and sewage rates which shall be sufficient to provide for the payment of interest and the amortization of the principal of the cost of said works within a period of fifty years and upon the expiration of said term of fifty years the system of sewers and water works shall revert to and become the properties of the cities of Panama and Colon respectively, and the use of the water shall be free to the inhabitants of Panama and Colon, except to the extent that water rates may be necessary for the operation and maintenance of said system of sewers and water.

The Republic of Panama agrees that the cities of Panama and Colon shall comply in perpetuity, with the sanitary ordinances whether of a preventive or curative character prescribed by the United States and in case the Government of Panama is unable or fails in its duty to enforce this compliance by the cities of Panama and Colon with the sanitary ordinances of the United States the Republic of Panama grants to the United States the right and authority to enforce the same.

The same right and authority are granted to the United States for the maintenance of public order in the cities of Panama and Colon and the territories and harbors adjacent thereto in case the Republic of Panama should not be, in the judgment of the United States, able to maintain such order.

Article VIII

The Republic of Panama grants to the United States all rights which it now has or hereafter may acquire to the property of the New Panama Canal Company and the Panama Railroad Company as a result of the transfer of sovereignty from the Republic of Columbia to the Republic of Panama over the Isthmus of Panama and authorizes the New Panama Canal Company to sell and transfer to the United States its rights, privileges, properties and concessions as well as the Panama Railroad and all the shares or part of the shares of that company; but the public lands situated outside of the zone described in Article II of this treaty now included in the concessions of both said enterprises and not required in the construction or operation of the Canal shall revert to the Republic of Panama except any property now owned by or in the possession of said companies within Panama or Colon or the ports or terminals thereof.

Article IX

The United States agrees that the ports at either entrance of the Canal and the waters thereof, and the Republic of Panama agrees that the towns of Panama and Colon shall be free for all time so that there shall not be imposed or collected custom house tolls, tonnage, anchorage, lighthouse, wharf, pilot, or quarantine dues or any other charges or taxes of any kind upon any vessel using or passing through the Canal or belonging to or employed by the United States, directly or indirectly, in connection with the construction, maintenancce, operation, sanitation and protection of the main Canal, or auxiliary works, or upon the cargo, officers, crew, or passengers of any such vessels, except such tolls and charges as may be imposed by the United States for the use of the Canal and other works, and except tolls and charges imposed by the Republic of Panama upon merchandise destined to be introduced for the consumption of the rest of the Republic of Panama, and upon vessels touching at the ports of Colon and Panama and which do not cross the Canal.

The Government of the Republic of Panama shall have the right to establish in such ports and in the towns of Panama and Colon such houses and guards as it may deem necessary to collect duties on importations destined to other portions of Panama and to prevent contraband trade. The United States shall have the right to make use of the towns and harbors of Panama and Colon as places of anchorage, and for making repairs, for loading, unloading, deposit-ing, or transshipping cargoes either in transit or destined for the service of the Canal and for other works pertaining to the Canal.

Article X

The Republic of Panama agrees that there shall not be imposed any taxes, national, municipal, departmental, or of any other class, upon the Canal, the railways and auxiliary works, tugs and other vessels employed in the service of the Canal, store houses, work shops, offices, quarters for laborers, factories of all kinds, warehouses, wharves, machinery and other works, property, and effects appertaining to the Canal or railroad and auxiliary works, or their officers or employees, situated within the cities of Panama and Colon, and that there shall not be imposed contributions or charges of a personal character of any kind upon officers, employees, laborers, and other individuals in the service of the Canal and railroad and auxiliary works.

Article XI

The United States agrees that the official dispatches of the Government of the Republic of Panama shall be transmitted over any telegraph and telephone lines established for canal purposes and used for public and private business at rates not higher than those required from officials in the service of the United States.

Article XII

The Government of the Republic of Panama shall permit the immigration and free access to the lands and workshops of the Canal and its auxiliary works of all employees and workmen of whatever nationality under contract to work upon or seeking employment upon or in any wise connected with the said Canal and its auxiliary works, with their respective families, and all such persons shall be free and exempt from the military service of the Republic of Panama.

Article XIII

The United States may import at any time into the said zone and auxiliary lands, free of custom duties, imposts, taxes, or other charges, and without any restrictions, any and all vessels, dredges, engines, cars, machinery, tools, explosives, materials, supplies, and other articles necessary and convenient in the construction, maintenance, operation, sanitation and protection of the Canal and auxiliary works, and all provisions, medicines, clothing, supplies and other things necessary and convenient for the officers, employees, workmen and laborers in the service and employ of the United States and for their families. If any such articles are disposed of for use outside of the zone and auxiliary lands granted to the United States and within the territory of the Republic, they shall be subject to the same import or other duties as like articles imported under the laws of the Republic of Panama.

Article XIV

As the price or compensation for the rights, powers and privileges granted in this convention by the Republic of Panama to the United States, the Government of the United States agrees to pay to the Republic of Panama the sum of ten million dollars ($10,000,000) in gold coin of the United States on the exchange of the ratification of this convention and also an annual payment during the life of this convention of two hundred and fifty thousand dollars ($250,000) in like gold coin, beginning nine years after the date aforesaid.

The provisions of this Article shall be in addition to all other benefits assured to the Republic of Panama under this convention.

But no delay or difference of opinion under this Article or any other provisions of this treaty shall affect or interrupt the full operation and effect of this convention in all other respects.

Article XV

The joint commission referred to in Article VI shall be established as follows:

The President of the United States shall nominate two persons and the President of the Republic of Panama shall nominate two persons and they shall proceed to a decision; but in case of disagreement of the Commission (by reason of their being equally divided in conclusion), an umpire shall be appointed by the two Governments who shall render the decision. In the event of the death, absence, or incapacity of a Commissioner or Umpire, or of his omitting, declining or ceasing to act, his place shall be filled by the appointment of another person in the manner above indicated. All decisions by a majority of the Commission or by the umpire shall be final.

Article XVI

The two Governments shall make adequate provision by future agreement for the pursuit, capture, imprisonment, detention and delivery within said zone and auxiliary lands to the authorities of the Republic of Panama of persons charged with the commitment of crimes, felonies, or misdemeanors without said zone and for the pursuit, capture, imprisonment, detention and delivery without said zone to the authorities of the United States of persons charged with the commitment of crimes, felonies and misdemeanors within said zone and auxiliary lands.

Article XVII

The Republic of Panama grants to the United States the use of all the ports of the Republic open to commerce as places of refuge for any vessels employed in the Canal enterprise, and for all vessels passing or bound to pass through the Canal which may be in distress and be driven to seek refuge in said ports. Such vessels shall be exempt from anchorage and tonnage dues on the part of the Republic of Panama.

Article XVIII

The Canal, when constructed, and the entrances thereto shall be neutral in perpetuity, and shall be opened upon the terms provided for by Section I of

Article three of, and in conformity with all the stipulations of, the treaty entered into by the Governments of the United States and Great Britain on November 18, 1901.

Article XIX

The Government of the Republic of Panama shall have the right to transport over the Canal, its vessels and its troops and munitions of war in such vessels at all times without paying charges of any kind. The exemption is to be extended to the auxiliary railway for the transportation of persons in the service of the Republic of Panama, or of the police force charged with the preservation of public order outside of said zone, as well as to their baggage, munitions of war and supplies.

Article XX

If by virtue of any existing treaty in relation to the territory of the Isthmus of Panama, whereof the obligations shall descend or be assumed by the Republic of Panama, there may be any privilege or concession in favor of the Government or the citizens and subjects of a third power relative to an interoceanic means of communication which in any of its terms may be incompatible with the terms of the present convention, the Republic of Panama agrees to cancel or modify such treaty in due form, for which purpose it shall give to the said third power the requisite notification within the term of four months from the date of the present convention, and in case the existing treaty contains no clause permitting its modifications or annulment, the Republic of Panama agrees to procure its modification or annulment in such form that there shall not exist any conflict with the stipulations of the present convention.

Article XXI

The rights and privileges granted by the Republic of Panama to the United States in the preceding Articles are understood to be free of all anterior debts, liens, trusts, or liabilities, or concessions or privileges to other Governments, corporations, syndicates or individuals, and consequently, if there should arise any claims on account of the present concessions and privileges or otherwise, the claimants shall resort to the Government of the Republic of Panama, and not to the United States for any indemnity or compromise which may be required.

Article XXII

The Republic of Panama renounces and grants to the United States, the participation to which it might be entitled in the future earnings of the Canal under Article XV of the concessionary contract with Lucien N. B. Wyse, now owned by the New Panama Canal Company and any and all other rights or claims of a pecuniary nature arising under or relating to said concession, or arising under or relating to the concessions to the Panama Railroad Company or any extension or modification thereof; and it likewise renounces, confirms and grants to the United States, now and hereafter, all the rights and property reserved in the said concessions which otherwise would belong to Panama at or before the expiration of the terms of ninety-nine years of the concessions granted to or held by the above mentioned party and companies, and all right, title and interest which it now has or may hereafter have, in and to the lands, canal, works, property and rights held by the said companies under said concessions or otherwise, and acquired or to be acquired by the United States from or through the New Panama Canal Company, including any property and rights which might or may in the future either by lapse of time, forfeiture or otherwise, revert to the Republic of Panama under any contracts or concessions, with said Wyse, the Universal Panama Canal Company, the Panama Railroad Company and the New Panama Canal Company.

The aforesaid rights and property shall be and are free and released from any present or reversionary interest in or claims of Panama and the title of the United States thereto upon consummation of the contemplated purchase by the United States from the New Panama Canal Company, shall be absolute, so far as concerns the Republic of Panama, excepting always the rights of the Republic specifically secured under this treaty.

Article XXIII

If it should become necessary at any time to employ armed forces for the safety or protection of the Canal, or of the ships that make use of the same, or the railways and auxiliary works, the United States shall have the right, at all times and in its discretion, to use its police and its land and naval forces or to establish fortifications for these purposes.

Article XXIV

No change either in the Government or in the laws and treaties of the Republic of Panama shall, without the consent of the United States, affect any right of the United States under the present convention, or under any treaty stipulation between the two countries that now exists or may hereafter exist touching the subject matter of this convention.

If the Republic of Panama shall hereafter enter as a constituent into any other Government or into any union or confederation of states, so as to merge her sovereignty of independence in such Government, union or confederation, the rights of the United States under this convention shall not be any respect lessened or impaired.

Article XXV

For the better performance of the engagements of this convention and to the end of the efficient protection of the Canal and the preservation of its neutrality, the Government of the Republic of Panama will sell or lease to the United States lands adequate and necessary for the naval or coaling stations on the Pacific coast and on the western Caribbean coast of the Republic at certain points to be agreed upon with the President of the United States.

Article XXVI

This convention when signed by the Plenipotentiaries of the Contracting Parties shall be ratified by the respective Governments and the ratifications shall be exchanged at Washington at the earliest date possible.

In faith whereof the respective Plenipotentiaries have signed the present convention in duplicate and have hereunto affixed their respective seals.

Done at the City of Washington, the 18th day of November in the year of our Lord, nineteen hundred and three.

John Hay.	[SEAL.]
P. Bunau Varilla.	[SEAL.]

And whereas the said Convention has been duly ratified on both parts, and the ratifications of the two governments were exchanged in the City of Washington, on the twenty-sixth day of February, one thousand nine hundred and four;

Now, therefore, be it known that I, Theodore Roosevelt, President of the United States of America, have caused the said Convention to be made public, to the end that the same and every article and clause thereof, may be observed and fulfilled with good faith by the United States and the citizens thereof.

In testimony whereof, I have hereunto set my hand and caused the seal of the United States of America to be affixed.

Done at the City of Washington, this twenty-sixth day of February, in the [SEAL.] year of our Lord one thousand nine hundred and four, and of the Independence of the United States the one hundred and twenty-eighth.

By the President: Theodore Roosesvelt.
John Hay,
Secretary of State.

Panama Canal Treaty

The United States of America and the Republic of Panama,

Acting in the spirit of the Joint Declaration of April 3, 1964, by the Representatives of the Governments of the United States of America and the Republic of Panama, and of the Joint Statement of Principles of February 7, 1974, initialed by the Secretary of State of the United States of America and the Foreign Minister of the Republic of Panama, and

Acknowledging the Republic of Panama's sovereignty over its territory,

Have decided to terminate the prior Treaties pertaining to the Panama Canal and to conclude a new Treaty to serve as the basis for a new relationship between them and, accordingly, have agreed upon the following:

Article I

*Abrogation of Prior Treaties and Establishment of a
New Relationship*

1. Upon its entry into force, this Treaty terminates and supersedes:

(a) The Isthmian Canal Convention between the United States of America and the Republic of Panama, signed at Washington, November 18, 1903;

(b) The Treaty of Friendship and Cooperation signed at Washington, March 2, 1936, and the Treaty of Mutual Understanding and Cooperation and the related Memorandum of Understandings Reached, signed at Panama, January 25, 1955, between the United States of America and the Republic of Panama;

(c) All other treaties, conventions, agreements and exchanges of notes between the United States of America and the Republic of Panama, concerning the Panama Canal which were in force prior to the entry into force of this treaty; and

(d) Provisions concerning the Panama Canal which appear in other treaties, conventions, agreements and exchanges of notes between the United States of America and the Republic of Panama which were in force prior to the entry into force of this Treaty.

2. In accordance with the terms of this Treaty and related agreements, the Republic of Panama, as territorial sovereign, grants to the United States of America, for the duration of this Treaty, the rights necessary to regulate the transit of ships through the Panama Canal, and to manage, operate, maintain, improve, protect and defend the Canal. The Republic of Panama guarantees to the United States of America the peaceful use of the land and water areas which it has been granted the rights to use for such purposes pursuant to this Treaty and related agreements.

3. The Republic of Panama shall participate increasingly in the management and protection and defense of the Canal, as provided in this Treaty.

4. In view of the special relationship established by this treaty, the United States of America and the Republic of Panama shall cooperate to assure the uninterrupted and efficient operation of the Panama Canal.

Article II

Ratification, Entry into Force, and Termination

1. This Treaty shall be subject to ratification in accordance with the constitutional procedures of the two Parties. The instruments of ratification of this Treaty shall be exchanged at Panama at the same time as the instruments of ratification of the Treaty Concerning the Permanent Neutrality and Operation of the Panama Canal, signed this date, are exchanged. This Treaty shall enter into force, simultaneously with the Treaty Concerning the Permanent Neutrality and Operation of the Panama Canal, six calendar months from the date of the exchange of the instruments of ratification.

2. This Treaty shall terminate at noon, Panama time, December 31, 1999.

Article III

Canal Operation and Management

1. The Republic of Panama, as territorial sovereign, grants to the United States of America the rights to manage, operate, and maintain the Panama Canal, its complementary works, installations and equipment and to provide for the orderly transit of vessels through the Panama Canal. The United States of America accepts the grant of such rights and undertakes to exercise them in accordance with this Treaty and related agreements.

2. In carrying out the foregoing responsibilities, the United States of America may:

(a) Use for the aforementioned purposes, without cost except as provided in this Treaty, the various installations and areas (including the Panama Canal) and waters, described in the Agreement in Implementation of this Article, signed this date, as well as such other areas and installations as are made available to the United States of America under this Treaty and related agreements, and take the measures necessary to ensure sanitation of such areas;

(b) Make such improvements and alterations to the aforesaid installations and areas as it deems appropriate, consistent with the terms of this Treaty;

(c) Make and enforce all rules pertaining to the passage of vessels through the Canal and other rules with respect to navigation and maritime matters, in accordance with this Treaty and related agreements. The Republic of Panama will lend its cooperation, when necessary, in the enforcement of such rules;

(d) Establish, modify, collect and retain tolls for the use of the Panama Canal, and other charges, and establish and modify methods of their assessment;

(e) Regulate relations with employees of the United States Government;

(f) Provide supporting services to facilitate the performance of its responsibilities under this Article;

(g) Issue and enforce regulations for the effective exercise of the rights and responsibilities of the United States of America under this Treaty and related agreements. The Republic of Panama will lend its cooperation, when necessary, in the enforcement of such rules; and

(h) Exercise any other right granted under this Treaty, or otherwise agreed upon between the two Parties.

3. Pursuant to the foregoing grant of rights, the United States of America shall, in accordance with the terms of this Treaty and the provisions of United States law, carry out its responsibilities by means of a United States Government agency called the Panama Canal Commission, which shall be constituted by and in conformity with the laws of the United States of America.

(a) The Panama Canal Commission shall be supervised by a Board composed of nine members, five of whom shall be nationals of the United States of America, and four of whom shall be Panamanian nationals proposed by the Republic of Panama for appointment to such positions by the United States of America in a timely manner.

(b) Should the Republic of Panama request the United States of America to remove a Panamanian national from membership on the Board, the United States of America shall agree to such a request. In that event, the Republic of Panama shall propose another Panamanian national for appointment by the United States of America to such position in a timely manner. In case of removal of a Panamanian member of the Board at the initiative of the United States of America, both Parties will consult in advance in order to reach agreement concerning such removal, and the Republic of Panama shall propose another Panamanian national for appointment by the United States of America in his stead.

(c) The United States of America shall employ a national of the United States of America as Administrator of the Panama Canal Commission, and a Panamanian national as Deputy Administrator, through December 31, 1989. Beginning January 1, 1990, a Panamanian national shall be employed as the Administrator and a national of the United States of America shall occupy the position of Deputy Administrator. Such Panamanian nationals shall be proposed to the United States of America by the Republic of Panama for appointment to such positions by the United States of America.

(d) Should the United States of America remove the Panamanian national from his position as Deputy Administrator, or Administrator, the Republic of Panama shall propose another Panamanian national for appointment to such position by the United States of America.

4. An illustrative description of the activities the Panama Canal Commission will perform in carrying out the responsibilities and rights of the United States of America under this Article is set forth at the Annex. Also set forth in the Annex are procedures for the discontinuance or transfer of those activities performed prior to the entry into force of this Treaty by the Panama Canal Company or the Canal Zone Government which are not to be carried out by the Panama Canal Commission.

5. The Panama Canal Commission shall reimburse the Republic of Panama for the costs incurred by the Republic of Panama in providing the following public services in the Canal operating areas and in housing areas set forth in the Agreement in Implementation of Article III of this Treaty and occupied by both United States and Panamanian citizen employees of the Panama Canal Commission: police, fire protection, street maintenance, street lighting, street cleaning, traffic management and garbage collection. The Panama Canal Commission shall pay the Republic of Panama the sum of ten million United States Dollars ($10,000,000) per annum for the foregoing services. It is agreed that every three years from the date that this Treaty enters into force, the costs involved in furnishing said services shall be reexamined to determine whether adjustment of the annual payment should be made because of inflation and other relevant factors affecting the cost of such services.

6. The Republic of Panama shall be responsible for providing, in all areas comprising the former Canal Zone, services of a general jurisdictional nature such as customs and immigration, postal services, courts and licensing, in accordance with this Treaty and related agreements.

7. The United States of America and the Republic of Panama shall establish a Panama Canal Consultative Committee, composed of an equal number of high-level representatives of the United States of America and the Republic of Panama, and which may appoint such subcommittees as it may deem appropriate. This Committee shall advise the United States of America and the Republic of Panama on matters of policy affecting the Canal's operation. In view of both Parties' special interests in the continuity and efficiency of the Canal operation in the future, the Committee shall advise on matters such as general tolls policy, employment and training policies to increase the participation of Panamanian nationals in the operation of the Canal, and international policies on matters concerning the Canal. The Committee's recommendations shall be transmitted to the two Governments, which shall give such recommendations full consideration in the formulation of such policy decisions.

8. In addition to the participation of Panamanian nationals at high management levels of the Panama Canal Commission, as provided for in paragraph 3 of this Article, there shall be growing participation of Panamanian nationals at all other levels and areas of employment in the aforesaid Commission, with the objective of preparing, in an orderly and efficient fashion, for the assumption by the Republic of Panama of full responsibility for the management, operation and maintenance of the Canal upon the termination of this Treaty.

9. The use of the areas, waters and installations with respect to which the United States of America is granted rights pursuant to this Article, and the rights and legal status of United States Government agencies and employees operating in the Republic of Panama pursuant to this Article, shall be governed by the Agreement in Implementation of this Article, signed this date.

10. Upon entry into force of this Treaty, the United States Government agencies known as the Panama Canal Company and the Canal Zone Government shall cease to operate within the territory of the Republic of Panama that formerly constituted the Canal Zone.

Article IV

Protection and Defense

1. The United States of America and the Republic of Panama commit themselves to protect and defend the Panama Canal. Each Party shall act, in accordance with its constitutional processes, to meet the danger resulting from an armed attack or other actions which threaten the security of the Panama Canal or of ships transiting it.

2. For the duration of this Treaty, the United States of America shall have primary responsibility to protect and defend the Canal. The rights of the United States of America to station, train, and move military forces within the Republic of Panama are described in the Agreement in Implementation of this Article, signed this date. The use of areas and installations and the legal status of the armed forces of the United States of America in the Republic of Panama shall be governed by the aforesaid Agreement.

3. In order to facilitate the participation and cooperation of the armed forces of both Parties in the protection and defense of the Canal, the United States of America and the Republic of Panama shall establish a Combined Board comprised of an equal number of senior military representatives of each party. These representatives shall be charged by their respective governments with consulting and cooperating on all matters pertaining to the protection and defense of the Canal, and with planning for actions to be taken in concert for that purpose. Such combined protection and defense arrangements shall not inhibit the identity or lines of authority of the armed forces of the United States of America or the Republic of Panama. The Combined Board shall provide for coordination and cooperation concerning such matters as:

(a) The preparation of contingency plans for the protection and defense of the Canal based upon the cooperative efforts of the armed forces of both Parties;

(b) The planning and conduct of combined military exercises; and

(c) The conduct of United States and Panamanian military operations with respect to the protection and defense of the Canal.

4. The Combined Board shall, at five-year intervals throughout the duration of this Treaty, review the resources being made available by the two Parties for the protection and defense of the Canal. Also, the Combined Board shall make appropriate recommendations to the two Governments respecting projected requirements, the efficient utilization of available resources of the two Parties, and other matters of mutual interest with respect to the protection and defense of the Canal.

5. To the extent possible consistent with its primary responsibility for the protection and defense of the Panama Canal, the United States of America will endeavor to maintain its armed forces in the Republic of Panama in normal times at a level not in excess of that of the armed forces of the United States of America in the territory of the former Canal Zone immediately prior to the entry into force of this treaty.

Article V

Principle of Non-Intervention

Employees of the Panama Canal Commission, their dependents and designated contractors of the Panama Canal Commission, who are nationals of the United States of America, shall respect the laws of the Republic of Panama and shall abstain from any activity incompatible with the spirit of this Treaty. Accordingly, they shall abstain from any political activity in the Republic of Panama as well as from any intervention in the internal affairs of the Republic of Panama. The United States of America shall take all measures within its authority to ensure that the provisions of this Article are fulfilled.

Article VI

Protection of the Environment

1. The United States of America and the Republic of Panama commit themselves to implement this Treaty in a manner consistent with the protection of the natural environment of the Republic of Panama. To this end, they shall consult and cooperate with each other in all appropriate ways to ensure that they shall give due regard to the protection and conservation of the environment.

2. A Joint Commission on the Environment shall be established with equal representation from the United States of America and the Republic of Panama, which shall periodically review the implementation of this Treaty and shall recommend as appropriate to the two Governments ways to avoid or, should this not be possible, to mitigate the adverse environmental impacts which might result from their respective actions pursuant to the Treaty.

3. The United States of America and the Republic of Panama shall furnish the Joint Commission on the Environment complete information on any action taken in accordance with this Treaty which, in the judgment of both, might have a significant effect on the environment. Such information shall be made available to the Commission as far in advance of the contemplated action as possible to facilitate the study by the Commission of any potential environmental problems and to allow for consideration of the recommendation of the Commission before the contemplated action is carried out.

Article VII

Flags

1. The entire territory of the Republic of Panama, including the areas the use of which the Republic of Panama makes available to the United States of America pursuant to this Treaty and related agreements, shall be under the flag of the Republic of Panama, and consequently such flag always shall occupy the position of honor.

2. The flag of the United States of America may be displayed, together with the flag of the Republic of Panama, at the headquarters of the Panama Canal Commission at the site of the Combined Board, and as provided in the Agreement in Implementation of Article IV of this treaty.

3. The flag of the United States of America also may be displayed at other places and on some occasions, as agreed by both parties.

Article VIII

Privileges and Immunities

1. The installations owned or used by the agencies or instrumentalities of the United States of America operating in the Republic of Panama pursuant to this Treaty and related agreements, and their official archives and documents, shall be inviolable. The two Parties shall agree on procedures to be followed in the conduct of any criminal investigation at such locations by the Republic of Panama.

2. Agencies and instrumentalities of the Government of the United States of America operating in the Republic of Panama pursuant to this Treaty and related agreements shall be immune from the jurisdiction of the Republic of Panama.

3. In addition to such privileges and immunities as are afforded to employees of the United States Government and their dependents pursuant to this Treaty, the United States of America may designate up to twenty officials of the Panama Canal Commission who, along with their dependents, shall enjoy the privileges and immunities accorded to diplomatic agents and their dependents under international law and practice. The United States of America shall furnish to the Republic of Panama a list of the names of said officials and their dependents, identifying the positions they occupy in the Government of the United States of America, and shall keep such list current at all times.

Article IX

Applicable Laws and Law Enforcement

1. In accordance with the provisions of this Treaty and related agreements, the law of the Republic of Panama shall apply in the areas made available for the use of the United States of America pursuant to this Treaty. The law of the Republic of Panama shall be applied to matters or events which occurred in the former Canal Zone prior to the entry into force of this Treaty only to the extent specifically provided in prior treaties and agreements.

2. Natural or juridical persons who, on the date of entry into force of this Treaty, are engaged in business or non-profit activities at locations in the former Canal Zone may continue such business or activities at those locations under the same terms and conditions prevailing prior to the entry into force of this Treaty for a thirty-month transition period from its entry into force. The Republic of Panama shall maintain the same operating conditions as those applicable to the aforementioned enterprises prior to the entry into force of this Treaty in order that they may receive licenses to do business in the Republic of Panama subject to their compliance with the requirements of its law. Thereafter, such persons shall receive the same treatment under the law of the Republic of Panama as similar enterprises already established in the rest of the territory of the Republic of Panama without discrimination.

3. The rights of ownership, as recognized by the United States of America,

enjoyed by natural or juridical private persons in buildings and other improvements to real property located in the former Canal Zone shall be recognized by the Republic of Panama in conformity with its laws.

4. With respect to buildings and other improvements to real property located in the Canal operating areas, housing areas or other areas subject to the licensing procedure established in Article IV of the Agreement in Implementation of Article III of this Treaty, the owners shall be authorized to continue using the land upon which their property is located in accordance with the procedures established in that Article.

5. With respect to buildings and other improvements to real property located in areas of the former Canal Zone to which the aforesaid licensing procedure is not applicable, or may cease to be applicable during the lifetime or upon termination of this Treaty, the owners may continue to use the land upon which their property is located, subject to the payment of a reasonable charge to the Republic of Panama. Should the Republic of Panama decide to sell such land, the owners of the buildings or other improvements located thereon shall be offered a first option to purchase such land at a reasonable cost. In the case of non-profit enterprises, such as churches and fraternal organizations, the cost of the purchase will be nominal in accordance with the prevailing practice in the rest of the territory of the Republic of Panama.

6. If any of the aforementioned persons are required by the Republic of Panama to discontinue their activities or vacate their property for public purposes, they shall be compensated at fair market value by the Republic of Panama.

7. The provisions of paragraphs 2-6 above shall apply to natural or juridical persons who have been engaged in business or non-profit activities at locations in the former Canal Zone for at least six months prior to the date of signature of this Treaty.

8. The Republic of Panama shall not issue, adopt or enforce any law, decrees, regulation, or international agreement or take any other action which purports to regulate or would otherwise interfere with the exercise on the part of the United States of America of any right granted under this Treaty or related agreements.

9. Vessels transiting the Canal, and cargo, passengers and crews carried on such vessels shall be exempt from any taxes, fees, or other charges by the Republic of Panama. However, in the event such vessels call at a Panamanian port, they may be assessed charges incident thereto, such charges for services provided to the vessel. The Republic of Panama may also require the passengers and crew disembarking from such vessels to pay such taxes, fees and charges as are established under Panamanian law for persons entering its territory. Such taxes, fees and charges shall be assessed on a nondiscriminatory basis.

10. The United States of America and the Republic of Panama will cooperate in taking such steps as may from time to time be necessary to guarantee the security of the Panama Canal Commission, its property, its

employees and their dependents, and their property, the Forces of the United States of America and the members thereof, the civilian component of the United States Forces, the dependents of members of the Forces and the civilian component, and their property, and the contractors of the Panama Canal Commission and of the United States Forces, their dependents, and their property. The Republic of Panama will seek from its Legislative Branch such legislation as may be needed to carry out the foregoing purposes and to punish any offenders.

11. The Parties shall conclude an agreement whereby nationals of either State, who are sentenced by the courts of the other State, and who are not domiciled therein, may elect to serve their sentences in their State of nationality.

Article X

Employment with the Panama Canal Commission

1. In exercising its rights and fulfilling its responsibilities as the employer, the United States of America shall establish employment and labor regulations which shall contain the terms, conditions and prerequisites for all categories of employees of the Panama Canal Commission. These regulations shall be provided to the Republic of Panama prior to their entry into force.

2. (a) The regulations shall establish a system of preference when hiring employees, for Panamanian applicants possessing the skills and qualifications required for employment by the Panama Canal Commission. The United States of America shall endeavor to ensure that the number of Panamanian nationals employed by the Panama Canal Commission in relation to the total number of its employees will conform to the proportion established for foreign enterprises under the law of the Republic of Panama.

(b) The terms and conditions of employment to be established will in general be no less favorable to persons already employed by the Panama Canal Company or Canal Zone Government prior to the entry into force of this Treaty, than those in effect immediately prior to that date.

3. (a) The United States of America shall establish an employment policy for the Panamanian Canal Commission that shall generally limit the recruitment of personnel outside the Republic of Panama to persons possessing requisite skills and qualifications which are not available in the Republic of Panama.

(b) The United States of America will establish training programs for Panamanian employees and apprentices in order to increase the number of Panamanian nationals qualified to assume positions with the Panama Canal Commission, as positions become available.

(c) Within five years from the entry into force of this Treaty, the number of United States nationals employed by the Panama Canal Commission who were previously employed by the Panama Canal Company shall be at least twenty percent less than the total number of United States nationals working for the Panama Canal Company immediately prior to the entry into force of this Treaty.

(d) The United States of America shall periodically inform the Republic of Panama, through the Coordinating Committee, established pursuant to the Agreement in Implementation of Article III of this Treaty, of available positions within the Panama Canal Commission. The Republic of Panama shall similarly provide the United States of America any information it may have as to the availability of Panamanian nationals claiming to have skills and qualifications that might be required by the Panama Canal Commission in order that the United States of America may take this information into account.

4. The United States of America will establish qualification standards for skills, training and experience required by the Panama Canal Commission. In establishing such standards, to the extent they include a requirement for a professional license, the United States of America, without prejudice to its right to require additional professional skills and qualifications, shall recognize the professional licenses issued by the Republic of Panama.

5. The United States of America shall establish a policy for the periodic rotation, at a maximum of every five years, of United States citizen employees and other non-Panamanian employees, hired after the entry into force of this Treaty. It is recognized that certain exceptions to the said policy of rotation may be made for sound administrative reasons, such as in the case of employees holding positions requiring certain non-transferable or non-recruitable skills.

6. With regard to wages and fringe benefits, there shall be no discrimination on the basis of nationality, sex, or race. Payment by the Panama Canal Commission of additional remuneration, or the provision of other benefits, such as home leave benefits, to United States nationals employed prior to entry into force of this Treaty, or to persons of any nationality, including Panamanian nationals who are thereafter recruited outside of the Republic of Panama and who change their place of residence, shall not be considered to be discrimination for the purpose of this paragraph.

7. Persons employed by the Panama Canal Company or Canal Zone Government prior to the entry into force of this Treaty, who are displaced from their employment as a result of the discontinuance by the United States of America of certain activities pursuant to this Treaty, will be placed by the United States of America, to the maximum extent feasible, in other appropriate jobs with the Government of the United States in accordance with United States Civil Service regulations. For such persons who are not United States nationals, placements efforts will be confined to United States Government activities located within the Republic of Panama. Likewise persons previously employed in activities for which the Republic of Panama assumes responsibility as a result of this Treaty will be continued in their employment to the maximum extent feasible by the Republic of Panama. The Republic of Panama shall, to the maximum extent feasible, ensure that the terms and conditions

of employment applicable to personnel employed in the activities for which it assumes responsibility are no less favorable than those in effect immediately prior to the entry into force of this Treaty. Non-United States nationals employed by the Panama Canal Company or Canal Zone Government prior to the entry into force of this Treaty who are involuntarily separated from their positions because of the discontinuance of an activity by reason of this Treaty, who are not entitled to an immediate annuity under the United States Civil Service Retirement System, and for whom continued employment in the Republic of Panama by the Government of the United States of America is not practicable, will be provided special job placement assistance by the Republic of Panama for employment in positions for which they may be qualified by experience and training.

8. The Parties agree to establish a system whereby the Panama Canal Commission may, if deemed mutually convenient or desirable by the two Parties, assign certain employees of the Panama Canal Commission, for a limited period of time, to assist in the operation of activities transferred to the responsibility of the Republic of Panama as a result of this Treaty or related agreements. The salaries and other cost of employment of any such persons assigned to provide such assistance shall be reimbursed to the United States of America by the Republic of Panama.

9. (a) The right of employees to negotiate collective contracts with the Panama Canal Commission is recognized. Labor relations with employees of the Panama Canal Commission shall be conducted in accordance with forms of collective bargaining established by the United States of America after consultation with employee unions.

(b) Employee unions shall have the right to affiliate with international labor organizations.

10. The United States of America will provide an appropriate early optional retirement program for all persons employed by the Panama Canal Company or Canal Zone Government immediately prior to the entry into force of this Treaty. In this regard, taking into account the unique circumstances created by the provisions of this Treaty, including its duration, and their effect upon such employees, the United States of America shall, with respect to them:

(a) determine that conditions exist which invoke applicable United States law permitting early retirement annuities and apply such law for a substantial period of the duration of the Treaty;

(b) seek special legislation to provide more liberal entitlement to, and calculation of, retirement annuities than is currently provided for by law.

Article XI

Provisions for the Transition Period

The Republic of Panama shall reassume plenary jurisdiction over the former Canal Zone upon entry into force of this Treaty and in accordance with its terms.

1. In order to provide for an orderly transition to the full application of the

jurisdictional arrangements established by this Treaty and related agreements, the provisions of this Article shall become applicable upon the date this Treaty enters into force, and shall remain in effect for thirty calendar months. The authority granted in this Article to the United States of America for this transition period shall supplement, and is not intended to limit, the full application and effect of the rights and authority granted to the United States of America elsewhere in this Treaty and in related agreements.

2. During this transition period, the criminal and civil laws of the United States of America shall apply concurrently with those of the Republic of Panama in certain of the areas and installations made available for the use of the United States of America pursuant to this Treaty, in accordance with the following provisions:

(a) The Republic of Panama permits the authorities of the United States of America to have the primary right to exercise criminal jurisdiction over United States citizen employees of the Panama Canal Commission and their dependents, and members of the United States Forces and civilian component and their dependents, in the following cases:

(i) for any offense committed during the transition period within such areas and installations, and

(ii) for any offense committed prior to that period in the former Canal Zone.

The Republic of Panama shall have the primary right to exercise jurisdiction over all other offenses committed by such persons, except as otherwise provided in this Treaty and related agreements or as may be otherwise agreed.

(b) Either Party may waive its primary right to exercise jurisdiction in a specific case or category of cases.

3. The United States of America shall retain the right to exercise jurisdiction in criminal cases relating to offenses committed prior to the entry into force of this Treaty in violation of the laws applicable in the former Canal Zone.

4. For the transition period, the United States of America shall retain police authority and maintain a police force in the aforementioned areas and installations. In such areas, the police authorities of the United States of America may take into custody any person not subject to their primary jurisdiction if such person is believed to have committed or to be committing an offense against applicable laws or regulations, and shall promptly transfer custody to the police authorities of the Republic of Panama. The United States of America and the Republic of Panama shall establish joint police patrols in agreed areas. Any arrests conducted by a joint patrol shall be the responsibility of the patrol member or members representing the Party having primary jurisdiction over the person or persons arrested.

5. The courts of the United States of America and related personnel, functioning in the former Canal Zone immediately prior to the entry into force of this Treaty, may continue to function during the transition period for the judicial enforcement of the jurisdiction to be exercised by the United States of America in accordance with this Article.

6. In civil cases, the civilian courts of the United States of America in the Republic of Panama shall have no jurisdiction over new cases of a private civil nature, but shall retain full jurisdiction during the transition period to dispose of any civil cases, including admiralty cases, already instituted and pending before the courts prior to the entry into force of this Treaty.

7. The laws, regulations, and administrative authority of the United States of America applicable in the former Canal Zone immediately prior to the entry into force of this Treaty shall, to the extent not inconsistent with this Treaty and related agreements, continue in force for the purpose of the exercise by the United States of America of law enforcement and judicial jurisdiction only during the transition period. The United States of America may amend, repeal or otherwise change such laws, regulations and administrative authority. The two Parties shall consult concerning procedural and substantive matters relative to the implementation of this Article, including the disposition of cases pending at the end of the transition period and, in this respect, may enter into appropriate agreements by an exchange of notes or other instrument.

8. During this transition period, the United States of America may continue to incarcerate individuals in the areas and installations made available for the use of the United States of America by the Republic of Panama pursuant to this Treaty and related agreements, or to transfer them to penal facilities in the United States of America to serve their sentences.

Article XII

A Sea-Level Canal or a Third Lane of Locks

1. The United States of America and the Republic of Panama recognize that a sea-level canal may be important for international navigation in the future. Consequently, during the duration of this Treaty, both parties commit themselves to study jointly the feasibility of a sea-level canal in the Republic of Panama, and in the event they determine that such waterway is necessary, they shall negotiate terms, agreeable to both Parties, for its construction.

2. The United States of America and the Republic of Panama agree on the following:

(a) No new interoceanic canal shall be constructed in the territory of the Republic of Panama during the duration of this Treaty, except in accordance with the provisions of this Treaty, or as the two Parties may otherwise agree; and

(b) During the duration of this Treaty, the United States of America shall not negotiate with third States for the right to construct an interoceanic canal on any other route in the Western Hemisphere, except as the two Parties may otherwise agree.

3. The Republic of Panama grants to the United States of America the right to add a third lane of locks to the existing Panama Canal. This right may be exercised at any time during the duration of this Treaty, provided that the United States of America has delivered to the Republic of Panama copies of the plans for such construction.

4. In the event the United States of America exercises the right granted in paragraph 3 above, it may use for that purpose, in addition to the areas otherwise made available to the United States of America pursuant to this Treaty, such other areas as the two Parties may agree upon. The terms and conditions applicable to Canal operating areas made available by the Republic of Panama for the use of the United States of America pursuant to Article III of this Treaty shall apply in a similar manner to such additional areas.

5. In the construction of the aforesaid works, the United States of America shall not use nuclear excavation techniques without the previous consent of the Republic of Panama.

Article XIII

Property Transfer and Economic Participation by the Republic of Panama

1. Upon termination of this Treaty, the Republic of Panama shall assume total responsibility for the management, operation, and maintenance of the Panama Canal, which shall be turned over in operating condition and free of liens and debts, except as the two Parties may otherwise agree.

2. The United States of America transfers, without charge, to the Republic of Panama all right, title and interest the United States of America may have with respect to all real property, including non-removable improvements thereon, as set forth below:

(a) Upon the entry into force of this Treaty, the Panama Railroad and such property that was located in the former Canal Zone but that is not within the land and water areas the use of which is made available to the United States of America pursuant to this Treaty. However, it is agreed that the transfer on such date shall not include buildings and other facilities, except housing, the use of which is retained by the United States of America pursuant to this Treaty and related agreements, outside such areas;

(b) Such property located in an area or a portion thereof at such time as the use by the United States of America of such area or portion thereof ceases pursuant to agreement between the two Parties.

(c) Housing units made available for occupancy by members of the Armed Forces of the Republic of Panama in accordance with paragraph 5(b) of Annex B to the Agreement in Implementation of Article IV of this Treaty at such time as such units are made available to the Republic of Panama.

(d) Upon termination of this Treaty, all real property, and non-removable improvements that were used by the United States of America for the purposes of this Treaty and related agreements, and equipment related to the management, operation and maintenance of the Canal remaining in the Republic of Panama.

3. The Republic of Panama agrees to hold the United States of America harmless with respect to any claims which may be made by third parties relating to rights, title and interest in such property.

4. The Republic of Panama shall receive, in addition, from the Panama Canal Commission a just and equitable return on the national resources

which it has dedicated to the efficient management, operation, maintenance, protection and defense of the Panama Canal, in accordance with the following:

(a) An annual amount to be paid out of Canal operating revenues computed at a rate of thirty hundredths of a United States dollar ($0.30) per Panama Canal net ton, or its equivalency, for each vessel transiting the Canal, after the entry into force of this Treaty, for which tolls are charged. The rate of thirty hundredths of a United States dollar ($0.30) per Panama Canal net ton, or its equivalency, will be adjusted to reflect changes in the United States wholesale price index for total manufactured goods during biennial periods. The first adjustment shall take place five years after entry into force of this Treaty, taking into account the changes that occurred in such price index during the preceding two years. Thereafter successive adjustments shall take place at the end of each biennial period. If the United States of America should decide that another indexing method is preferable, such method shall be proposed to the Republic of Panama and applied if mutually agreed.

(b) A fixed annuity of ten million United States dollars ($10,000,000) to be paid out of Canal operating revenues. This amount shall constitute a fixed expense of the Panama Canal Commission.

(c) An annual amount of up to ten million United States dollars ($10,000,-000) per year, to be paid out of Canal operating revenues to the extent that such revenues exceed expenditures of the Panama Canal Commission including amounts paid pursuant to this Treaty. In the event Canal operating revenues in any year do not produce a surplus sufficient to cover this payment, the unpaid balance shall be paid from operating surpluses in future years in a manner to be mutually agreed.

Article XIV

Settlement of Disputes

In the event that any question should arise between the Parties concerning the interpretation of this Treaty or related agreements, they shall make every effort to resolve the matter through consultation in the appropriate committees established pursuant to this Treaty and related agreements, or, if appropriate, through diplomatic channels. In the event the Parties are unable to resolve a particular matter through such means, they may, in appropriate cases, agree to submit the matter to conciliation, mediation, arbitration, or such other procedure for the peaceful settlement of the dispute as they may mutually deem appropriate.

Done at Washington, this 7th day of September, 1977, in duplicate, in the English and Spanish languages, both texts being equally authentic.

For the Republic of Panama: Omar Torrijos Herrera,	For the United States of America: Jimmy Carter,
Head of Government of the *Republic of Panama.*	*President of the* *United States of America.*

Treaty Concerning the Permanent Neutrality and Operation of the Panama Canal

The United States of America and the Republic of Panama have agreed upon the following:

Article I

The Republic of Panama declares that the Canal, as an international transit waterway, shall be permanently neutral in accordance with the regime established in this Treaty. The same regime of neutrality shall apply to any other international waterway that may be built either partially or wholly in the territory of the Republic of Panama.

The Republic of Panama declares the neutrality of the Canal in order that both in time of peace and in time of war it shall remain secure and open to peaceful transit by the vessels of all nations on terms of entire equality, so that there will be no discrimination against any nation, or its citizens or subjects, concerning the conditions or charges of transit, or for any other reason, and so that the Canal, and therefore the Isthmus of Panama, shall not be the target of reprisals in any armed conflict between other nations of the world. The foregoing shall be subject to the following requirements:

(a) Payment of tolls and other charges for transit and ancillary services, provided they have been fixed in conformity with the provisions of Article III (c);

(b) Compliance with applicable rules and regulations, provided such rules and regulations are applied in conformity with the provisions of Article III;

(c) The requirement that transiting vessels commit no acts of hostility while in the Canal; and

(d) Such other conditions and restrictions as are established by this Treaty.

Article II

The Republic of Panama declares the neutrality of the Canal in order that both in time of peace and in time of war it shall remain secure and open to peaceful transit by the vessels of all nations on terms of entire equality, so that there will be no discrimination against any nation, or its citizens or subjects, concerning the conditions or charges of transit, or for any other reason, and so that the Canal, and therefore the Isthmus of Panama, shall not be the target of reprisals in any armed conflict between other nations of the world. The foregoing shall be subject to the following requirements:

(a) Payment of tolls and other charges for transit and ancillary services, provided they have been fixed in conformity with the provisions of Article III(c);

(b) Compliance with applicable rules and regulations, provided such rules and regulations are applied in conformity with the provisions of Article III;

(c) The requirement that transmiting vessels commit no acts of hostility while in the Canal; and

(d) Such other conditions and restrictions as are established by this Treaty.

Article III

1. For purposes of the security, efficiency and proper maintenance of the Canal the following rules shall apply:

(a) The Canal shall be operated efficiently in accordance with conditions of transit through the Canal, and rules and regulations that shall be just, equitable and reasonable, and limited to those necessary for safe navigation and efficient, sanitary operation of the Canal;

(b) Ancillary services necessary for transit through the Canal shall be provided;

(c) Tolls and other charges for transit and ancillary services shall be just, reasonable, equitable and consistent with the principles of international law;

(d) As a pre-condition of transit, vessels may be required to establish clearly the financial responsibility and guarantees for payment of reasonable and adequate indemnification, consistent with international practice and standards, for damages resulting from acts or omissions of such vessels when passing through the Canal. In the case of vessel owned or operated by a State or for which it has acknowledged responsibility, a certification by that State that it shall observe its obligations under international law to pay for damages resulting from the act or omission of such vessels when passing through the Canal shall be deemed sufficient to establish such financial responsibility;

(e) Vessels of war and auxiliary vessels of all nations shall at all times be entitled to transit the Canal, irrespective of their internal operation, means of propulsion, origin, destination or armament, without being subjected, as a condition of transit, to inspection, search or surveillance. However, such vessels may be required to certify that they have complied with all applicable health, sanitation and quarantine regulations. In addition, such vessels shall be entitled to refuse to disclose their internal operation, origin, armament, cargo or destination. However, auxiliary vessels may be required to present written assurances, certified by an official at a high level of the government of the State requesting the exemption, that they are owned or operated by that government and in this case are being used only on government non-commercial service.

2. For the purposes of this Treaty, the terms "Canal," "vessel of war," "auxiliary vessel," "internal operation," "armament" and "inspection" shall have the meanings assigned them in Annex A to this Treaty.

Article IV

The United States of America and the Republic of Panama agree to maintain the regime of neutrality established in this Treaty, which shall be maintained in order that the Canal shall remain permanently neutral, notwithstanding the termination of any other treaties entered into by the two Contracting Parties.

Article V

After the termination of the Panama Canal Treaty, only the Republic of Panama shall operate the Canal and maintain military forces, defense sites and military installations within its national territory.

Article VI

1. In recognition of the important contributions of the United States of America and of the Republic of Panama to the construction, operation, maintenance, and protection and defense of the Canal, vessels of war and auxiliary vessels of those nations shall, notwithstanding any other provisions of this Treaty, be entitled to transit the Canal irrespective of their internal operation, means of propulsion, origin, destination, armament or cargo carried. Such vessels of war and auxiliary vessels will be entitled to transit the Canal expeditiously.

2. The United States of America, so long as it has responsibility for the operation of the Canal, may continue to provide the Republic of Colombia toll-free transit through the Canal for its troops, vessels and materials of war. Thereafter, the Republic of Panama may provide the Republic of Colombia and the Republic of Costa Rica with the right of toll-free transit.

Article VII

1. The United States of America and the Republic of Panama shall jointly sponsor a resolution in the Organization of American States opening to accession by all States of the world the Protocol to this Treaty whereby all the signatories will adhere to the objectives of this Treaty, agreeing to respect the regime of neutrality set forth herein.

2. The Organization of American States shall act as the depositary for this Treaty and related instruments.

Article VIII

This Treaty shall be subject to ratification in accordance with the constitutional procedures of the two Parties. The instruments of ratification of this Treaty shall be exchanged at Panama at the same time as the instruments of ratification of the Panama Canal Treaty, signed this date, are exchanged. This Treaty shall enter into force, simultaneously with the Panama Canal Treaty, six calendar months from the date of the exchange of the instruments of ratification.

Done at Washington, this 7th day of September, 1977, in duplicate, in the English and Spanish languages, both texts being equally authentic.

For the Republic of Panama:

Omar Torrijos Herrera,

*Head of Government of the
Republic of Panama.*

For the United States of America:

Jimmy Carter,

*President of the
United States of America.*

Notes 1

1. Emilio Castelar y Ripoll, *Historia del Descubrimiento de América* (Madrid, n.p., 1892), p. 524. Castelar is certain that Columbus was in the Isthmus of Panama in 1497 (see pp. 525–26). Also see Modesto Perez y Pablo Nougues, *Los Precursores Españoles del Canal Interocéanico* (Madrid: Parlando Paez y Cia., n.d., but probably 1920), p. 14. These two authors state that the Admiral of the Ocean Sea entered the mouth of the Chagres on November 2, 1497. Also see Columbus' letter to the queen, in Alexander von Humbolt, *Examen Critique* (Paris, n.p., 1836), p. 11.

2. Pietro Martire d'Anghiera, *De Rebus Oceanicus il Orbe Novo: Deuxieme Decades*, ed. by Paul Gaffarel (Dijon, France: Derantiere Press, 1895), pp. 11–19. Martire calls Balboa *egreguis digladiator* and states that Alonso Martin was the first European to navigate the Pacific Ocean, on the day of its discovery, September 29, 1513. Also see Gonzalo Fernandez de Oviedo, *Historia Natural y General de las Indias* (Madrid, 1554), book 29, chap. 3, and Pietro Martire d'Angehiera, *Decadas del Nuevo Mundo*, ed. by Edmundo O'Gorman and Agustin Millares Carlo (Mexico City: Jose Porrua e Hijos, sucesores, 1964), vol. 4, book 3, pp. 314–15.

3. Manuel Cano y Leon and Guillermo Brockman y Arbazuza, *El Canal Interocéanico* (Madrid, n.p., 1879), pp. 19–22.

4. Francisco Lopez de Gomara, *Crónica general de las Indias* (Zaragosa, 1552), vol. 2, p. 91, and Bernal Diaz del Castillo, *Verdadera Historia de los Sucesos de la Conquista de Nueva España* (Madrid: Imprenta del reyno, 1632), as quoted by Nougues, p. 33. Cortez (says Diaz), was "of good height and long hair . . . a dice player and liked women . . . spent freely in women, friends and wardrobe. He was clean . . . ate well and drank well . . . was jealous in his house and bold in those of others . . . a characteristic of a whore man." Translation by the author.

5. Ibid., p. 48.

6. Joaquin Garcia Icarbalceta, *Colección de Documentos para la Historia de Méjico* (Mexico City, 1558), vol. 1, pp. 490–98. *Especeria* is interpreted either as "land of the species" or "land of the fish." Translation by the author.

7. Hernan Cortez to Charles V, Oct. 30, 1520, in Michael Chevalier, *L'isthme de Panama* (Paris: n.p., 1844), p. 22. The Aztec court painters also seem to have been good geographers.

8. Felix Belly, *L'Isthme de Panama* (Paris: n.p., 1858), pp. 28–29.

9. Pascual Guayonges, Introduction to *Cartas y Relaciones de Hernán Cortéz al Emperador Carlos V* (Paris: n.p., 1866), p. 23, and F. de Arragoiz, "Hernán Cortéz comprendio desde luego lo importante de la situacion del istmo de Tehuantepec," *Boletin de la Sociedad Geografica de Madrid* (Madrid, 1881), vol. 11, p. 55.

10. Antonio de Herrera, *Historia de las Indias,* as quoted by Nougues, pp. 114–15.

11. Gonzalo Fernandez de Oviedo, vol. 3, book 29, chap. 32, pp. 168–69.

12. D. Juan Bautista Munoz, *Historia de la Conquista de América* (Madrid, 1793), vol. 79, folios 305–7, and Nougues, p. 135.

13. Ibid., p. 136. They were Antonio de la Gama, Pascual de Andagoya, Juan de Velasco, Alvaro de Guijo, Toribio de Montañez, Juan de Castaneda, and the royal treasurer, Jeronimo Martel.

14. Munoz, vol. 79, folio 307, and Nougues, p. 139.

15. Ibid.

16. Ibid., pp. 166–67.

17. Munoz, vol. 80, folio 256.

18. Ernesto de J. Castillero, *Communicación Interocéanica* (Panama City: n.p., 1935), p. 15.

19. Ibid., folio 257, and Nougues, p. 173.

20. Ibid., p. 180, and Munoz, vol. 79, folio 256.

21. Ibid. Says Andagoya: *"Lo util es limpiar el Chagres, por do se puede ir a la sirga, tanto que faltan hasta Panama sobre cinco leguas, las cuales se podrían hacer de calzada . . . La cédula para ver como se puede juntar esta mar con la otra procede de aviso dado sin conocimiento."*

22. Gomara, chap. 104, pp. 1–19, 211–12: *". . . dádme quien lo quiera hacer, que hacer se puede; no falte ánimo, que no faltara dinero, y las Indias, donde se ha de hacer, lo dan . . . para un rey de Castilla, es poco lo imposible."*

23. The king did not issue a decree, as is reported by many writers, threatening with capital punishment anyone who should dare to make any further investigation in regard to the building of a canal in America. No such document has been found in the Spanish archives. But the monarch was worried because a canal would have opened the way to Peru and increased the danger of aggression against his empire. Castillero, p. 15, and Enrique Arce, *Historia de Panama* (Panama: n.p., 1911), p. 128–9.

24. Ibid. Other adventurers who sought a passage were Juan de Fuca in 1592, Pedro de Ledesma in 1616, Francisco de Vergara in 1636, Pedro Porter y Casante in 1640, and Diego Mercado early in the 1700s.

25. Clarence Henry Harding, *The Buccaneers* (New York: n.p., 1910), pp. 52–112.

26. Ibid., pp. 356–72. Also see H. Morse Stephens and Herbert E. Bolton, *The Pacific Ocean in History* (New York: Macmillan, 1917), p. 124; Charles Loftus Grant Anderson, *Castilla del Oro* (Boston: n.p., 1914), p. 471; and Robert Tomes, *Panama in 1855: An account of the Panama Rail-Road* (New York: Harper and Brothers, Publishers, 1855), p. 127.

27. Mario Hernandez de Sanchez-Barba, *La Ultima Expansion Espanola en America* (Madrid: n.p., 1957), pp. 238-50; Salvador de Madariaga, *The Fall of the Spanish American Empire* (New York: n.p., 1947), pp. 339–62; and Samuel F. Bemis, *John Quincy Adams and the Foundations of the American Foreign Policy* (New York: Knopf, 1949), p. 12 ff.

28. Alexander Von Humboldt, *Viajes a las Regiones Equinoxiales de America* (Santiago: n.p., 1898), pp. 73–77.

29. Ibid. Also see Stephens and Bolton, pp. 125–26.

30. Ibid., p. 126.

31. Ibid., pp. 126–27.

32. Ibid., p. 126.

33. New Orleans, *States-Item*, Dec. 23, 1972, p. 1.

34. William Spence Robertson, *General Don Francisco de Miranda and the American Independence* (New York: n.p., 1929), pp. 166, 325–42.

35. Ibid.

36. Castillero, p. 25.

37. Ibid., p. 27.

38. Miles Percy Duval, Jr., *Cadiz to Cathay* (Stanford, Calif.: Stanford Univ. Press, 1939), p. 26. Henry Clay, secretary of state in 1826, sponsored a search for a canal in Nicaragua and Panama. Aaron H. Palmer of New York City formed a corporation for this purpose. Not enough capital materialized and Palmer dissolved the company.

39. *Italian Encyclopedia* (Rome, 1949), vol. 35, pp. 188–89. Da Verrazzano captured two ships sent to Spain from Mexico by Cortéz in 1522. He may have died on the coast of Darien after 1528, not far from the site of the present Panama Canal.

40. L. M. A. D. Milet Moreau, *Voyage de la Perouse autor du monde* (Paris, 1797), vol. I, pp. 71–85. La Perouse's voyage was a serious attempt by the *ancien régime* to find an east-west passage. He explored the western coast of North America, the western Pacific, and the coast of China from 1778 to 1783.

41. Raul de Cardenas, *China en la Apertura del Canal de Panama* (Havana, Imprenta Soler, 1929), pp. 2–5.

42. Emory Adams Allen, *Our Canal in Panama* (Cincinnati: Cincinnati Publishing Co., 1913), p. 89.

43. Cardenas, pp. 3–4.

44. Nancy Baker, "The French Intervention in Mexico: Nexus of Interventionists," Southwest Social Science Association annual meeting, Dallas, March 23, 1973.

45. In order to sustain the administrations of General Zuloaga and of Marshall Miramon, a Mexican citizen of Swiss extraction, Juan Bautista Jecker, redeemed the national debt for 75 million francs. The government of Benito Juarez refused to recognize his claims after 1859. Jecker, who had strong ties with leading European bankers and who was the friend of the duc de Morny, is partly blamed for bringing the French to Mexico. Many years later, while Paris was being governed by the radical commune of 1871, he applied for a passport to return to the Mexico of Porfirio Diaz, who might

have welcomed him. He was recognized within a few days and ordered shot on May 26, 1871.

46. Robertson, pp. 219–31.

47. William M. Malloy, *Treaties and Conventions of the United States* (Washington, D.C., 1910), pp. 128 ff. E. G. Bourne, "United States and Mexico, 1847–48," *American Historical Review*, vol. 5, (1899–1900), pp. 492 ff.; and Albert K. Weinberg, *Manifest Destiny, a Study of National Expansion in American History* (Baltimore: John Hopkins University Press, 1935), p. 65.

48. The British presence was evidenced in Honduras, at Belize. See the statement of Sir Henry Bulwer to President Fillmore on the occasion of the signing of the Clayton-Bulwer Treaty. Gerald M. Capers, *Encyclopedia Americana* (New York, 1970), vol. 7, p. 39.

49. John Bassett Moore, *A Digest of International Law* (Washington, D.C., 1906), vol. 3, pp. 8–10, and Bourne, pp. 49 ff.

50. M. M. Alba C., *Cronologia de los Gobernantes de Panama* (Panama: n.p., 1935), p. 92. The unhappy governor who had to offer reparations to the English was Manuel Jose Hurtado.

51. See J. Bosquet, *Communicacion entre el Senor Carlos Biddle, Coronel de los Estados Unidos del Norte y la Sociedad Amigos del Pais* (Panama City, 1836), and "Decree of the executive authority adjudicating the privilege for opening an intermarine communication through the isthmus of Panama," Bogota, June 22, 1836; *Congressional Record*, 25th Cong., 2nd. Sess., House Document no. 228, vol. 8. The decree was signed by Francisco de Paula Santander, as chief of state, and Lino de Pombo, the foreign minister.

52. J. Franklin Jameson, H. Barrett Learned, James Brown Scott, and Samuel Bemis, *The American Secretaries of State and Their Diplomacy* (New York: Pageant Book Co., 1958), vol. 5, p. 41. Senator Clayton, the future secretary of state who later signed the Clayton-Bulwer Treaty of 1850, introduced his resolution on March 15, 1835. It was approved by the Senate but remained in abeyance.

53. From the correspondence of the French legation at Bogota, December 1848, and Bourne, p. 42. Also, Luis Hoyos to the author, March 30, 1971.

54. Carlos Portocarrero M., *Tratados y Convenios Comerciales de Colombia* (Bogota: Imprenta Nacional, 1946), pp. 79–93. The treaty was signed on December 12, 1846 and ratified on June 10, 1848. Pedro Alcantara Herran signed for Colombia and James Buchanan for the United States. Also see Malloy, p. 1282; and Benjamin Biddlack to James K. Polk, August 9, 1846, *Despatches, Bogota*, vol. 17.

55. Moore, vol. 3, pp. 8–10.

56. Ibid., vol. 2, p. 39; Arias, pp. 16–17; and Forsyth to Biddle in Document 21, Special Message of the President, March 13, 1838, p. 97.

57. Philippe Bunau-Varilla, *The Creation, Destruction and Resurrection* (New York: McBride, Nast and Co., 1914), p. 295.

58. Jameson et al., p. 42.

59. W. H. Welk, *The Monroe Doctrine and the Control of the Isthmus* (New York: Nassau Street Printers, 1881), pp. 5–11.

60. Jameson et al., pp. 43–44.

61. Ibid., p. 46. Polk's statement favoring the annexation of Texas, on the eve of the national convention in 1844, gave him the nomination and the election in detriment to old stalwart Martin Van Buren. Four years later, Van Buren paid him back. He used his influence and prestige to engineer the defeat of the Democratic party and to help the Whigs win the election.

62. Ibid., p. 60.

63. Capers.

64. See "British Diplomacy and the Clayton Bulwer Treaty, 1850–1860," *Journal of Modern History*, vol. 11 (June 1939), p. 168.

65. Jameson et al., p. 69.

66. Henry Cabot Lodge, *Selections from the Correspondence of Theodore Roosevelt and Henry Cabot Lodge* (New York: Scribner's, 1925), pp. 484–88.

67. In the 1960s, Egypt, the Republic of Yemen, and Syria established the United Arab Republic, which disintegrated a few years later and was reshaped into the Lybian-Egyptian Union. The same is true of the Central African Republic and the Senegalese Union.

68. Henry Cabot Lodge, *Historical and Political Essays* (Boston: Houghton, Mifflin, 1892), p. 171.

69. In the State of Panama alone, there were four attempts at secession from Bogota between 1821 and 1830, and five coup d' etats within the isthmus, most of them successful. Strangely enough, only one of the rebel leaders was executed—Colonel Eligio Alzuru, in 1831. Alba C., p. 89.

70. Robertson, p. 302; Orlando Fals Borda, *La Subversion en Colombia: Vision del Cambio Social en la Historia* (Bogota: n.p., 1968), pp. 19–31; and G. Anguizola, *Hispanic American Historical Review*, vol. 48, no. 4 (November 1968), pp. 724–25.

71. Bolivar's former adversary, Don Francisco de Paula Santander, helped promulgate a new constitution in 1832 which changed the name of the country to Nueva Granada. Scalabrini Ortiz, *Politica Britanica en el Rio de la Plata* (Montevideo: n.p., 1901), p. 4, and G. Anguizola, *Hispanic American Historical Review*, vol. 47, no. 3 (August 1967), p. 442.

72. The first operating locomotive was built by Richard Trevithick and pulled a load of twenty-five tons nine and one-half miles in four hours, five minutes from an iron plant near Abercydon, Wales, February 21, 1804. *Daily News* (Arlington, Texas), April 19, 1973, p. 7.

73. During the administration of President Barriga, the first steamboat from New York, the *Falcon*, arrived at the mouth of the Chagres, and this was the occasion for a great celebration. Dr. Enrique Arce to the author, January 15, 1940.

74. The exchange of ratifications of the Bidlack-Mallarino treaty took place in Washington on June 10, 1848. Alba C., p. 100.

75. Jameson et al., p. 219. Secretary Calhoun discussed Mosquera's request with President Tyler.

76. *Panama Star*, April 25, 1850. The contract was signed in Bogota on April 15, 1850, but news in those days was slow in reaching the isthmus. See

Republica de Colombia, *Anales Diplomaticos y Consulares* (Bogota, 1900), vol. 1, pp. 33–49. Victoriano de D. Paredes signed the contract as foreign minister, and John Lloyd Stephens signed for the corporation.

77. Conversation with Arce. The guests toasted each other with coconut milk spiced with rum.

78. Rodrigo de Bastidas is credited with being the first European to land in the isthmus, in the spring of 1502.

79. Claude Levi-Strauss, *Tristes Tropiques* (Paris: n.p., 1955), pp. 56–91. Levi-Strauss theorizes that in the underdeveloped world change can evolve only from inside the primitive forest.

80. Etruscan sculpture found in Arezzo, Italy. Its early origin (circa 700–650 B.C.) evidences a strong Hellenistic influence. In Greek mythology, a chimera is usually depicted as a she-monster with a lion's head vomiting flames, a goat's body, and a serpent's tail.

81. Tomes, pp. 76–77.

82. Gil Gonzalez Davila navigated the Pacific Ocean in 1521 by following the course of the Chagres River. When water ran out, he used mules to take his vessels to the west coast. See Antonio de Herrera y Tordesillas, *Historia General de los hechos de los castellanos en las islas y Tierra Firme del mar Oceano índico* (Madrid, 1615), vol. 3, pp. 19–88.

83. Duvon Clough Corbitt, *A Study of the Chinese in Cuba, 1847–1947* (Wilmore, Ky.: Asbury College Press, 1971), p. 4.

84. Ibid.

85. Conversations with Abel de la Lastra, December 1941, and between Kito Chen and Antonio Anguizola, Sr., March 15, 1940. Mr. Chen was a prominent Panamanian merchant who on many occasions after concluding business transactions with my father, enjoyed reminiscing about the early Asians in the isthmus. Twice I had the privilege of hearing these conversations, but I had no opportunity for questions. I was always kept well supplied with Chinese pastry and tea.

86. Conversation with Lastra, December 1946.

87. In 1940, Panama's chief executive, Arnulfo Arias, decreed that all foreigners owning a retail or wholesale business must take a native-born citizen as a partner. Most Chinese sold their stores.

88. Ruben D. Carles, *Historia del Canal de Panamá* (Panama City: n.p., 1973), pp. 8–9.

89. Panama, Archivo Nacional, *Presidentes de Panama*, vol. 1, pp. 19–20. In Panama: Jose de Obaldia, Tomas Herrera, Carlos Icaza Arosemena, Manuel Maria Diaz, Juan A. Bermudez, Antonio Planas, Bernardo Arce, Salvador Camacho R., Bernardo Arce, Jose Maria Urrutia, Bernardo Arce, Juan Echeverria, Isidro de Diego, Manuel M. Diaz, Juan Pacheco, Justo Arosemena, and Francisco Fabrega. At Bogota: Jose Hilario Lopez, Jose de Obaldia, Jose M. Obando, Jose Maria Melo, Tomas Herrera, Jose de Obaldia, and Manuel M. Mallarino. See Ernesto Camacho-Leyva, *Quick Colombian Facts* (Bogota, 1946), p. 72, and República de Colombia, Academia de la Historia, *Boletin* (Bogota, 1900), pp. 547–51.

90. Carles, p. 8.
91. Allen, p. 103.
92. *New York Tribune,* March 13, 1855, p. 1.
93. Ibid.
94. M. Emile Chevalier, "L'isthme de Panama," *Revue des Deux Mondes,* Paris, June 1, 1850.
95. The *Panama Star,* Jan. 28, 1855, p. 1.
96. Carles, p. 9.
97. Tomes, pp. 130–31.
98. Ibid., pp. 122–23.

Notes 2

1. After the rise of General Charles de Gaulle in 1958, France remained internationally aloof and did not participate in the drafting of the agreement pertaining to the nonproliferation of atomic weapons. Instead, de Gaulle successfully nuclearized the strike force of the French arsenal. See Jacques de Launay, *De Gaulle and His France* (New York: Julian Press, 1968), pp. 91–179, and Wladyslaw Wszebn Kulski, *De Gaulle and the World: The Foreign Policy of the Fifth French Republic* (New York: Syracuse Univ. Press, 1966).

2. J. Franklin Jameson, H. Barrett Learned, James Brown Scott, and Samuel Bemis, *The American Secretaries of State and Their Diplomacy* (New York: Pageant Book Co., 1958), pp. 305–6.

3. Patricia Denault, *American History Illustrated*, vol. 5, no. 6 (October 1970), p. 26.

4. Ibid. The Illinois politician gallantly threw his support behind Buchanan, a move that increased his prestige.

5. W. H. Welk, *The Monroe Doctrine and the Control of the Isthmus* (New York: Nassau Street Printers, 1881), pp. 5–11.

6. Maron J. Simon, *The Panama Affair* (New York: Scribner's, 1971), pp. 6–7.

7. Lawrence Greene, *The Filibuster: The Career of William Walker* (New York and Indianapolis: Bobbs Merrill Co., 1937), pp. 19–91.

8. Ibid.

9. Ibid.

10. Ibid.

11. Ibid., pp. 119–33.

12. Ibid.

13. Welk, p. 6.

14. Conversation with Dr. Enrique Arce. Arce stated that the Russians left by the Pacific route, ostensibly for Alaska.

15. M. M. Alba C., *Cronologia de los Gobernantes de Panama* (Panama: n.p., 1953), p. 112.

16. Octavio Mendez Pereira to the author, December 15, 1943. Also see idem, *Justo Arosemena* (Panama City: n.p., 1949).

17. Alba C. p. 95. The document was signed by the Granadan secretary for foreign affairs, Mariano Ospina Perez, and the English charge d' affaires, Robert Pitt Adams. In 1902, Minister Tomas Herran, following closely the

intransigent line of his predecessor, Pedro Alcantara Herran, refused American terms in another treaty and opened the door for the eventual success of Bunau-Varilla.

18. Ibid., p. 12. With pomp and circumstance, the British rendered public homage to the hirsute monarch, who, according to witnesses, appeared more like an ersatz human product rather than a bona fide Indian. Conversation with Arce. The vigorous protests of Panama's secretary for foreign affairs, Don Mariano Arosemena, were not dignified with a reply by the British.

19. "This contract made with an English naval officer at a time when our country was powerless to support the declaration of the Monroe Doctrine . . . in defiance of the Clayton-Bulwer treaty, is proof of the intention of England to obtain control of the Isthmus." Welk, p. 6.

20. At Appomattox Court House, Virginia, General Robert E. Lee surrendered to the Union forces led by General Ulysses S. Grant, April 9, 1865, officially ending the American Civil War.

21. Conversations with Arce. As in Panama, where the Solomon contract became the model for the Aspinwall concession, the Vanderbilt document was the guideline in Mexico.

22. Sullivan and Cromwell, *Documents Relative to a Trans-Isthmian Canal*, (New York: Evening Post Job Printing House, 1902), vol. 2, pp. 668–69.

23. Welk, p. 7.

24. Metz, 316 kilometers from Paris, is where Marshall Bazaine surrendered his army to the Germans after the battles of Borny, Gravelotte, and Saint Puvat, Aug. 14–18, 1870. Sedan, on the Meuse River, is where the army of Marshall MacMahon capitulated, Sept. 1, 1870. See *Larousse du XXe Siecle* (Paris: Librairie Larousse, 1931), vol. 4, p. 846, and vol. 6, p. 271.

25. Welk, p. 7.

26. *London Globe*, Nov. 30, 1858, p. 2. Disraeli bought the canal shares from Khedive Ishmail with Rothschild money. Parliament later gave its approval.

27. Literally, strong civilian government as distinguished from naked military rule. Some presidents of the State of Panama held office only a few days, so great was the personal and political rivalry. One of these coups prevented Manuel Amador Guerrero from becoming head of the State of Panama, for he had been selected in advance in true *personalismo* style. Later, he held office for a very short time. See Alba, C., pp. 122–29.

28. Dr. Nunez, as consul in Liverpool, enjoyed a long stay in England (1860–1874). He began his political career as a Liberal but turned Conservative. President from 1880 to 1882, 1884 to 1886, and 1892 to 1894, he died in office. Nunez' *ensayos* are some of the best writings in nineteenth century Latin America. His *Reforma Política en Colombia* (Bogota: n.p., 1885) is a treatise dealing with the serpentine politics of his country. Mosquera also traveled abroad widely and was twice minister to Britain as well as to other countries. Immensely rich, he gave his fortune to the nation. He began his political career as a Conservative but turned Liberal. He was president from 1845 to

1849, 1861 to 1864 and 1866 to 1867. Among his literary works are *Exámen Crítico* (Valparaiso, Chile: n.p., 1843) and *Ojeada Sobre la Situación Politica y Militar de Colombia* (Bogota: n.p., 1877). Under the leadership of these two men, Colombia enjoyed its only years of peace in the nineteenth century. Both these pragmatic statesmen were proponents of a canal, especially if the waterway were to be built by the United States or France. See Francisco Garcia Calderon, *Latin America, Its Rise and Progress* (London: n.p., 1911), introduction by Raymond Poincaré.

29. Alba C., p. 12.

30. Related to the philosophy of August Comte and the Count de Saint Simon, who advocated, through their American admirers, economic expansion through supervised government controls.

31. Cisneros fled Cuba after the failure of the *grito de Yara* in 1868, led by Carlos Manuel de Cespedes against Spain. He later became an American citizen.

32. Hernan Horna, "Railroad Construction in 19th Century Colombia," Symposium on Economic Development in 19th Century Latin America, American Historical Association, Annual Meeting, New Orleans, Dec. 30, 1972.

33. In 1869, President Ulysses S. Grant had proclaimed "an American canal for the Americas under American control." Ruben Carles, *Historia del Canal de Panama* (Panama: n.p., 1973), p. 10.

34. Arce to the author, December 10, 1949. Article 10 of the contract. Also see Sullivan and Cromwell, pp. 1255–67, and S. A. Hurlbut to H. Fish, February 1, 1870, Executive E, Confidential, 41st Cong., 3d. Sess.

35. "This treaty could have saved Colombia [economically] and would have assured for her the perpetual sovereignty of the Isthmus." Octavio Mendez Pereira to the author, June 19, 1944.

36. Carles, p. 10, and Sullivan and Cromwell, pp. 1268–69.

37. Bunau-Varilla made a chronological table of the riots and disorders which had taken place near his proposed canal during the last fifty years. Perhaps the most serious of these bloody incidents was the well-known Watermelon Massacre of April 15–16, 1856. Seventeen Americans and one Jamaican were killed by bullets and daggers. The teasing of a watermelon salesman by Jack Oliver sparked the riot, which was fanned by a language barrier. Threatened with the occupation of Panama by the United States, the government of treaty-maker Manuel Maria Mallarino paid an indemnity of 400,000 gold pesos to the families of the deceased. Arce to the author, Jan. 15, 1939. Similar events forced the United States to land its armed forces to protect lives and property in the Isthmus in 1860, 1873, 1901, and 1902. And in 1861, 1862, 1885, and 1900, Bogota officially requested armed intervention in Panama. See Alba C., p. 121.

38. Elisée Reclus also wrote a book about Nueva Granada's struggle for independence.

39. Onesime Reclus traveled widely. He wrote *La Terre a Vol d'Oisseau;*

l'France et ses Colonies; and *le Plus Beau Royaune sous le Ciel.* See *Larouse de XXe Siècle,* vol. 5, p. 959.

40. Philippe Bunau-Varilla, *The Creation, Destruction, and Resurrection* (New York: McBride, Nast and Co., 1914), p. 20. Also, conversation with Arce. Turr was born in Hungary and, through his wife, was related to Bonaparte Wyse, who in turn was the grand-nephew of the great Corsican. Turr received Italian citizenship early in his youth. Arce told the author that the concession was secured in the last days in office of interim President Santiago Perez.

41. Andre Siegfried, *Suez and Panama* (Oxford, Eng.: Alden Press, 1940), p. 231. For a vivid account of the fantastic dealings and "serpentine maneuvers" of these two men, between themselves and against each other, see Simon, pp. 183–229.

42. Emory A. Allen, *Our Canal in Panama* (Cincinnati: Cincinnati Publishing Co., 1913), p. 110.

43. The president of the Department of Panama entertained the survey party royally, gave them food, supplies, horses, and guides, and even accompanied the expedition to Darien. See Carles, pp. 10–11.

44. Ley 28 de 1878. See Lucien Napoleon Bonaparte Wyse, *le Canal de Panama: l'Isthme Americain, Explorations: Comparaison des traces etudies negociations etat des travaux* (Paris: Hachette et Co., 1886), p. 371.

45. Ibid., p. 372.

46. Ibid., p. 373. Article 10 of the concession.

47. William Fletcher Johnson, *Four Centuries of the Panama Canal* (New York: Henry Holt and Co., 1906), p. 154. Johnson counts fifty-five major disturbances in Panama from 1821 to 1903.

48. Mariano Arosemena, *Apuntamientos Historicos* (Panama City: n.p., 1949), p. 282. This author adds ten serious attempts at secession from Greater Colombia, Nueva Granada, and Colombia in eighty years. In each of these riots, *levantamientos*—risings of any kind against constituted authority, *cuartelazos*—a barrack-inspired or revolutionary movement, or *golpes*—a coup d'état or attempt at it militarily or civilian inspired, considerable number of lives were lost and property damage rose to millions of gold pesos.

49. *Le Matin,* May 16, 1789, p. 1.

50. Henry Adams, *The Education of Henry Adams* (Boston: n.p., 1918), p. 114.

51. Pedro J. Sosa to Ricardo Casorla, governor of the State of Panama, May 31, 1879. Before Sosa's letter arrived in Panama City, the governor had been overthrown by a coup d'état and replaced by Gerardo Ortega. Conversation with Arce.

52. Siegfried, p. 232, and conversation with Arce.

53. Siegfried, p. 244. Conversion into dollars has been made in accordance with the rate of exchange for the last months of the decade of 1870, which was from 3.00 to 3.65 francs for the dollar in the transactions at the Paris bourse.

54. *Le Matin* (Paris), May 30, 1879, p. 1.

55. Aeschylus tries to demonstrate that one of the most pervasive negative

traits in man is hybris, excessive pride, self-confidence, or arrogance. Throughout his works, Aeschylus advises his audience to practice humility.

56. Horace, *Odes*, trans. by Helen Rowe Henze (Norman: University of Oklahoma Press, 1961), pp. 129–31, and Horace, *Odes*, trans. by Kenneth J. Reckford (New York: Twayne Publishers, 1969), vol. 3, no 5, pp. 80–81. Regulus is the most famous hero of the first Punic War, 264–242 B.C., and one of America's first missiles was named after him.

57. *New York Times*, May 15, 1973, p. 1.

58. Ibid., May 4, 1973, p. 9.

59. The Brooklyn Bridge, built by John A. Roebling and his son Washington after fourteen years of vicissitudes not unlike those suffered by de Lesseps in building the Suez Canal, was dedicated by Grover Cleveland and President Chester Arthur in May 1883. See Allan Keller, "The Great Brooklyn Bridge," *American History Illustrated*, vol. 8, no. 1 (April 1973), pp. 1–11, 44–48, and the *New York Times*, May 21, 1973, p. 33. Because of the energy crisis, population explosion, and pollution, a century after the opening of the bridge Manhattan and Brooklyn are once more regularly serviced by ferry boats (*New York Times*, May 18, 1973, pp. 1 and 56). We must not overlook another nationalistic extravaganza of those years, the 1876 American Centennial Exposition, which opened in Philadelphia on May 19, 1876, and cost millions of dollars. *Dallas Morning News*, May 19, 1973, p. 3.

60. Conversation with Dr. Harmodio Arias, Feb. 19, 1955. Arias was quoting E. Langlais, who at one time was France's minister to Panama.

61. The canal group stopped in Guadaloupe and Martinique before reaching Colon. Ibid. Also, conversation between Eusebio A. Morales and Antonio Anguizola, Jr.

62. With the dry season, the streams stagnate, forming numerous ponds of water where mosquitoes thrive, for there is no rain or hard current to wash away the larvae. Dr. Carlos Finlay, a Cuban-born physician, is the Copernicus of the malaria and yellow fever theory. Dr. Walter Reed became its Galileo by proving that the theory was sound, exactly as Leonardo da Vinci advised centuries ago: "Practice must be preceded by sound theory."

63. William Crawford Gorgas, *Sanitation in Panama* (New York and London: D. Appleton, 1918), pp. 13–17; Carlos E. Finlay, *Carlos Finlay and Yellow Fever* (New York: Oxford Univ. Press, 1940); and W. B. Bean, "Carlos Finlay," *Current Medical Digest*, no. 37 (1970), pp. 336–67.

64. Ernesto de J. Castillero, *Communicacion Interoceanica* (Panama: n.p., 1935), pp. 12–14, and Siegfried, p. 246. Also, conversation with Arce.

65. De Lesseps visited New York, Chicago, San Francisco, Boston, and Washington. He was received by President Rutherford B. Hayes, who cooled his ardor by sending a message to Congress declaring that "the policy of this country is to advocate a canal under American control." Siegfried, p. 247.

66. Ibid., p. 247.

67. Ibid.

68. Ibid., p. 248.

69. Unfortunately Paris has changed, and skyscrapers are beginning to blight the once-matchless vistas (*New York Times*, May 21, 1973, p. 8).

70. *Le Matin*, March 4, 1881, p. 1.

71. Ibid.

72. Jose Ives Limantour, born of French parents, became the archpriest of *positivismo* in the Mexico of Porfirio Diaz. He was the first Mexican named to the French Academy of Political and Moral Sciences. His numerous writings testify to his unusual financial talent. He believed in the abolition of trade restrictions as a means of increasing economic development. See *Encyclopedia Universal Ilustrada Europeo-Americana* (Barcelona, 1924), vol. 30.

Notes 3

1. A share of the Suez Canal, which had been worth $58 in 1869 and had sunk to $37 in 1872, suddenly rose to $250 in 1880. It continued to rise very rapidly. By 1912 it was worth over $1,200; after World War I, over $5,000. See Philippe Bunau-Varilla, *The Construction, Destruction and Resurrection* (New York: McBride, Nast and Co., 1914), p. 24. Now that we have reached the American phase of the canal, we shall state money in dollars instead of francs.

2. Ibid., p. 28.

3. Ibid., p. 29.

4. Ibid., pp. 29–31. Address by Abel Couvreux, June 9, 1880, on the occasion of a public homage to de Lesseps designed to raise enthusiasm and money for the canal project.

5. Paludism derives from the Latin *palus* and *paludis*, meaning "marsh" or "swamp." Similarly, malaria is literally *mal aire*, or "bad air" in Italian, and very probably originated in the ancient suspicion that swamps, such as the Pontine marshes near Rome, had something to do with the large numbers of cases of malaria and of fever epidemics (probably yellow fever) that afflicted the Imperial City from time to time. This belief was officially expressed when Gaius Julius Caesar designed the drying of the marshes as a means of exorcising the *mal aire*. His assassination might have postponed the work for two millenia. It was not until the arrival of Benito Mussolini that the swamps were permanently dried, in 1926. There is widespread evidence of abundant health in Rome, and throughout Italy and the Empire, during the principate, a strong indication that perhaps the Pontine marshes were drained early in the Augustan age, although no proof of this hypothesis has been found. Certainly the Eternal City was not a healthy place to live during the High Middle Ages, a fact that provided the cardinals with another excuse to move the papacy to Avignon at the invitation of the French monarchs.

6. Bunau-Varilla, p. 30. The effect of pandemia—paludism, tick paralysis, equine encephalitis, beri-beri, dysentery, snake and scorpion bites, blackwater fever and yellow fever—on the canal works will be described later.

7. *Panama Star and Herald*, March 13, 1881, p. 1. Also, conversation with Dr. Enrique Arce.

8. Conversation with Arce.

9. Every five weeks the aborigines, especially the Cunas from the archipelago of San Blass, arrived in the towns to exchange goods with the merchants or buy luxury items such as mirrors or silk. As a child, I met many of these friendly Indians at my maternal grandmother's store.

10. At the end of the War of the Spanish Succession, which lasted from 1701 to 1713, the super powers made peace, reshaped the map of the world, and regulated the slave trade. England claimed the monopoly in this horrible business. *Asiento* is interpreted by some as a "royal grant," or something close to tenure authorized by a royal person. These agreements were common after Father Bartolome de las Casas persuaded the Spanish Crown to substitute Indian labor for African slaves. See Helen Miller Bailey and Abraham P. Nasatir, *Latin America* (Englewood Cliffs, N.J.: Prentice-Hall, 1960), p. 204. However, the word *asiento* literally means "to be seated" or "to have a seat"; it was probably applied to the slave trade because the slave-transporting vessels used to drop anchor near the coast of West Africa and wait weeks, sometimes months, for a good cargo to be brought to the shore by the slave hunters or the African traders. As a general rule, because of papal bulls and royal concern, the Spaniards and Portuguese waited for their slaves in America.

11. The French also brought from Guinea and Dahomey slaves who generally went directly to Haiti. Fernando Ortiz is quoted by Hubert Herring as saying that the Dahomeans were "bad slaves, prone to suicide and nostalgia." See Hubert Herring, *History of Latin America* (New York: Alfred Knopf, 1961), p. 108; and Donald Marquant Dozer, *Latin America: An Interpretive History* (New York: McGraw-Hill, 1962), p. 138.

12. "The Negroes of the Cameroons and Gaboon were regarded as the least useful . . . they are purchased so cheaply on the coast as to tempt many captains to freight with them." Herring, p. 109. Also see Andre Siegfried, *Suez and Panama* (Oxford: Alden Press, 1940), p. 252. For a good account of the slave trade, see James L. Stokesbury, "The Triangle Trade," *American History Illustrated*, vol. 8, no. 2 (May 1973), pp. 4–9, 44–50.

13. Emory Adams Allen, *Our Canal in Panama* (Cincinnati: Cincinnati Publishing Co., 1913), p. 119.

14. Siegfried, p. 250. Also, conversation with Arce. In the very last days of the third administration of President Tomas Cipriano de Mosquera in 1867, and no doubt because of his pro-American sympathy, a bill was introduced into the Colombian legislature prohibiting the building of a canal in greater Colombia without the consent of the Panama Railroad. It became law during the interim presidency of Santos Acosta. General Turr and Bonaparte Wyse were aware of this law when they negotiated their canal concession in 1878. It might have been better for de Lesseps if he had abandoned the canal venture at this stage.

15. Siegfried, p. 25.

16. Siegfried, p. 252, and Ruben D. Carles, *Historia del Canal de Panama* (Panama: n.p., 1935), p. 18. Also, conversation with Arce, Octavio Mendez Pereira, and Abel de la Lastra.

17. In Panama, the company accepted fifty thousand snow shovels when what they needed was one hundred thousand raincoats or umbrellas. It paid for fifteen thousand steel lanterns to mark the canal route on the day of its inauguration and sixty luxurious yachts to be launched as soon as water filled every mile of the ditch. By 1885, over $200,000 had been spent for "paper, pens, ink, and paper clips." When Bunau-Varilla succeeded in transferring the works of the company to the United States, after securing the secession of Panama, the new canal authorities found two tons of new pens and fifty barrels of red, black, blue, and green ink. Also much furniture. Fito Aguilera, *Cincuenta Millas de Heroicidad* (Panama City, n.d.), pp. 80–82. Also, conversation with Arce.

18. Siegfried, p. 252. In control of the *asiento*, the British chose the best slaves for themselves. "The Negroes most in demand at Barbados, are the Gold Coast, or, as they call them, Cormantines, which would yield three or four pounds a head more than the Whydahs [Dahomeans]." "To Windward they approach in Goodness as is the distance from the Gold Coast; so, as at Gambia, or Sierraleon, to be much better, than at any of the interjacent places." John Atkins, Surgeon in the Royal Navy, *A Voyage to Guinea, Brazil, and the West Indies* (London, 1735), as quoted by Herring, p. 108.

19. Conversation with Arce. "To Leeward from thence, they alter gradually for the worse; an Angolan Negro is a *Proverb* for worthlessness; and they mend (if we call it so) in that way, till you come Hottentots, that is, to the Southernmost extremity of Africa." Atkins, quoted by Herring, p. 108.

20. John Bigelow, *Report to the Chamber of Commerce of New York* (New York: Chamber of Commerce Press, 1886), p. 6. Also, conversation with Arce.

21. Bunau-Varilla, p. 49.

22. In my first year at Indiana University I was appointed by the newspaper *La Razon* of David Chiriqui, in Panama, to cover the celebrations of the bicentennial of Goethe in Aspen, Colorado. Dr. Schweitzer was one of the celebrities who took part in this event in the summer of 1949. I had the privilege of talking to him and of hearing on at least three occasions his philosophical and scientific disquisitions to small groups of young people like me who came to Aspen to be rewarded with a word from him.

23. Allen, p. 124.

24. Ibid., pp. 24 ff. Also conversation with Arce.

25. Conversation with Arce. *Altiplano* is the plateau of Bogota.

26. Aguilera, pp. 80–81. The employees of the company were entitled to a five-month vacation after two continuous years of work. Many of these workers did not return. Aguilera says that the minor contractors had to "kick back" to the company's directors in France; most likely they also had to pay high fees to the Colombian government and the departmental authorities for the privilege of bidding for the contracts. This was particularly true for the Chinese and other foreigners.

27. See Byron Stinson, "The Frank Leslies," *American History Illustrated*, vol. 5, no. 4 (July 1970), pp. 19–20.

28. Madame Giselle Bunau-Varilla Rocco to the author, January 15, 1973.

29. Bunau-Varilla, pp. 36–37.

30. For a study of the influence of the loess in civilization, and of its distribution pattern, see V. K. Ting, "Professor Granet's *La Civilisation chinoise,*" *Chinese Social and Political Science Review,* vol. 15 (1931), pp. 267–69. Loess is a deposit formed by winds, usually yellowish and calcareous. In the United States it is found in the Mississippi Valley.

31. *New York Times,* May 29, 1972, p. 1. The isthmus of Panama and the Mediterranean Sea were formed in a few days, seven million years ago.

32. Bunau-Varilla gives credit for this idea to Godin de Lepinay, a French engineer who made a study of the canal route in 1879. Bunau-Varilla, p. 27.

33. Ibid., p. 42

34. Ibid., p. 46.

35. Ibid., p. 48.

36. The Viet-Nam war cost $102 billion. *Dallas Morning News,* March 30, 1973, p. 1.

37. *Sancocho* is a chicken stew to which shrimp, lobster, oysters, or pork are sometimes added, plus a dozen native roots. This dish is a delicacy of the élite, popularized by a former mayor of Panama City named Alfredo Aleman. In his old age, Aleman claimed that he owed his good health and longevity to this protein-rich *caldo* (soup). However, the dish known as *sancocho popular* (native soup) is mostly chicken and pork plus the ever-present native roots. It is prepared in the following manner: 5 lbs. chicken, 1 lb. corned pork, 1 lb. otoes (tropical root), 1 lb. sweet potatoes, 3 corn cobs, 1 lb. ñame (another tropical root), 1 lb. brisket, 1 lb. yucca, 3 plantains, 1 lb. ñampi (another tropical creation), onions, tomatoes, peppers, salt, and pepper. Boil the chicken, pork, 1 lb. brisket, and the tomatoes, onions, peppers, salt, and pepper in 4 quarts of water for 1½ hours. Add the otoes, sweet potatoes, corn, and plantains. Take them out when done. Add the rest of vegetables and cook until everything is done. Serve in soup plates with a side dish of vegetables and, if available, a cup of fried rice, several *tostones* (green plantains fried in hot lard), and a tall glass of cold *marañon, nance,* guanabana, pineapple, or papaya drink. Recipe of Elvira P. Anguizola and Abigail Anguizola de Arias, the author's paternal grandmother and a paternal aunt.

38. Bacalao is salted cod fish. Yucca, otoe and ñame are tropical carbohydrates. Otoes and ñame appear in multicolored forms—yellow, light purple, deep purple, reddish, and white.

39. Conversation with Arce.

40. Bunau-Varilla, p. 48.

41. Ibid. Also, conversation with Gallegos. Professor Gallegos' grandmother was one of the grande dames of Panama's high society at the end of the nineteenth century. In our conversations in Spain, he referred to the frequent trips his grandmother took on the railroad with some of Bunau-Varilla's Colombian guests. On these outings, Madame Gallegos learned much about the origins of the canal entrepreneurs.

42. M. M. Alba C., *Cronologia de los Gobernantes de Panama* (Panama: n.p.,

1935), pp. 126–27. Eager to stymie his opponents, Dr. Nunez ran for the office of departmental governor of Panama in 1882. Once elected, he named Dr. Damasco Cervera his legate in Panama. Dalva C. Figueroa, "El Istmo Durante el Periodo del Estado Federal," *Patrimonio Historico* (Panama, February 1971), vol. 1, no. 1, p. 98.

43. Conversation with Gallegos. Also, Bunau-Varilla, pp. 39–40.

44. *Personalismo* implies choosing a successor by manipulating the ballot box.

45. Alba C., p. 128.

46. B. Sanin Cano, *Administracion Reyes, 1904–1909* (Lausane: Imprenta Jorge Bridel and Co., 1909), p. 21. Also, conversation with Gallegos. Ogé and L'Overture were heroes of the Haitian independence movement. Leclerc was the French commander sent by Napoleon I to quell the revolt.

47. Cano, p. 209.

48. Bunau-Varilla, p. 40.

49. Alba C., pp. 128–29.

50. Carles, p. 25. Also, conversations with Gallegos and Arce. Two of these citizens, Belisario Porras and Pablo Arosemena, owed their lives to their disguise.

51. Cano, p. 209; Bunau-Varilla, p. 40. Commander Kane apparently expected an invitation to land from General Vila, but the governor, for political reasons, hesitated to ask for American help.

52. Cano, pp. 208–18. Also, conversation with Gallegos.

53. Conversation with Gallegos.

54. Cano, pp. 208–9.

55. Ibid., and Carles, p. 25. Also, conversation with Gallegos. On April 26, 1885, after much bravado, Aizpuru called the doyen of the consular corps, Federico Boyd, and announced that he was ready to resign.

56. Conversation between Mario Menocal and Antonio Anguizola, Jr., June 1940, and conversation with Gallegos and Arce.

57. Conversations with Gallegos, Lastra, and Anguizola, Jr. The followers of Aizpuru were Cholos Indians who had been exposed to the culture of the West. They are called Ladinos in other American countries. Those who enlisted in Prestan's crusade were blacks, originally from Caribbean islands other than Jamaica.

Notes 4

1. These tourists were visitors who claimed they had relatives living in Panama. Many came to look for work or to visit the excavation sites. *El gran Francés*, "The Great Frenchman," was a title accorded de Lesseps in France, and Philippe preferred not to be addressed this way and seemed embarrassed by it. Conversation with Carlos M. Gallegos.

2. An *abanderado* is "a flag man," the host of the festivities that day, who carries a huge flag on horseback; a *corrida de toros* is a "bullfight", colloquially a festivity of any kind.

3. From Henri Cermoise, *Deux Ans à Panama* (Paris: E. Flamarion, Imprimerie Balback et Thomes, 1886), pp. 144–45. The author, one of the first young engineers to go to Panama with the company in 1883, refers to Rabelais' *Gargantua et Pantagruel. Viva* is "long live" to the person whose name is added.

4. Cermoise, p. 145.

5. The anniversary of the Battle of Boyaca, July 19, is Colombia's national holiday; the *grita* is the "cry" that sparked the movement for independence from Spain in 1821, celebrated throughout Panama on November 28; and the Feast of the Immaculata, December 8, is "Mother's Day" throughout Latin America.

6. Under these social conditions, agriculture and business languished, Latin-American economies were stifled, and many fortunes were squandered. There grew up a parasitical class that thrived on the ephemeral enterprises related to these festivities, such as pyrotechnics, bullfighting, couture, and gambling. My grandfather closely escaped economic disaster because of this foolish tradition. My father, made more wise by his father's experience, escaped the lasso of the professional fiesta committees and often left the festivities on convenient "business calls." He was caught twice, and on each occasion the expenditures for just one day as flag man reached over two thousand gold pesos.

7. Jose Agustin Arango, who became head of the separatist junta in 1903.

8. Huacas are Indian burial grounds containing much gold in the form of small figurines or animals such as frogs. See the *Dallas Morning News*, July 2, 1973, p. 3. My grandfather found several of these items made of solid gold. He presented a gold frog to William Howard Taft in 1904. In 1940, there were

still huacas to be found. My uncle presented another item, a gold knife, to Henry Wallace on the occasion of his visit to Panama. Bunau-Varilla did not travel to Chiriqui, but he later invited Sr. Anguizola, Sr., to come to Panama City to attend a banquet for Ferdinand de Lesseps. (Conversation with Antonio Anguizola, Jr.)

9. Conversation with Anguizola, Jr.

10. J. W. Judd, "The Eruption of Krakatoa and Subsequent Phenomena," Part 1, *Report of the Krakatoa Committee of the Royal Society,* ed. G. J. Symons (London: n.p., 1888).

11. "[They were] gentle of character, easily taught, skillfull, indefatigable traders, generous, frank [and] hospitable." Hubert Herring, *History of Latin America: An Interpretative History* (New York: McGraw-Hill Book Co., 1962), p. 101. Also, conversation with Anguizola, Jr.

12. An earlier report on the worth of the Jamaicans stated: *"Ces Jamaicans faisaient des travailleurs excellents, bien plus actifs et plus energiques que les naturels de l'isthme, et surtout beaucoup plus faciles a conduire."* Cermoise, p. 247.

13. Robert Blake, *Disraeli* (New York: St. Martin's Press, 1967), and Donald R. Morris, *The Washing of the Spears* (New York: Simon & Schuster, 1965).

14. Cermoise, p. 81.

15. This punishment is called *planazo.*

16. A *trocha* worker is an expert in making a trail in the thick jungle. Cermoise, p. 83.

17. Alfred Edward Taylor, *Thomas Hobbes* (London: Archibald Constable and Co., 1907), pp. 81, 83.

18. Giselle Bunau-Varilla Rocco to the author, July 15, 1973.

19. See *The Confessions of Jean-Jacques Rousseau,* with a Preface by Edmund Wilson. Smith College Editions in Modern Languages. (New York: Knopf, 1923), vol. 1, pp. 114–15.

20. Rocco to the author, July 15, 1973.

21. Conversations with Dr. Enrique Arce and Gumersinda Paez.

22. Conversation between Bunau-Varilla and Rocco as related to the author by Rocco, April 1, 1972.

23. Philippe Bunau-Varilla, *The Creation, Destruction and Resurrection* (New York: McBride, Nast and Co., 1914), pp. 51 ff.

24. Ibid.

25. Ibid., p. 54.

26. Ibid.

27. M. la Vielle, consul of France, in the name of his colleagues, to the Quai d'Orsay. Ibid.

28. Conversations with Anguizola, Jr., and Gallegos. Also, Bunau-Varilla, p. 56.

29. Ibid.

30. Conversation with Arce.

31. Bunau-Varilla, p. 58.

32. *Bulletin du Canal Interoceanique* (Paris, August 1, 1886), p. 1.

33. Open letter of Ferdinand de Lesseps to the canal shareholders, September 15, 1883, distributed as a handbill in Paris: *"Nous avons la certitude d'achever et d'inaugurer le Canal maritime de Panama en 1888. . . . Nous ne negligerons rien de ce qui pourrait devancer—ne fut-ce que d'un mois—l'achevement d'une oeuvre dont la realisation est attendue avec impatience par les marins et les commercants du monde entier."* Letter in the author's possession.

34. Ibid. Other banks were the Banque de Paris et des Pays-Bas, the Societé Genérale pur favoriser le developpement du Commerce et de l'Industrie en France, the Societé Genérale de Credit Insustriel et Commercial, and the Banque d'Escampte de Paris.

35. Maron J. Simon, *The Panama Affair* (New York: Scribner's, 1971), p. 193.

36. Ibid., p. 194.

37. Bunau-Varilla, p. 57. Also, conversation with Arce.

38. Conversation with Arce.

39. André Siegried, *Suez and Panama* (Oxford: Alden Press, 1940). p. 263.

40. Gustave Anguizola, "The Committee System throughout the Ages and in the American University System," Arlington, Texas, 1972.

41. E. C. Barksdale, chairman, Department of History, University of Texas at Arlington, to the author, December 11, 1972.

42. John Bigelow, *Report to the Chamber of Commerce of New York on His Trip of Inspection of the Panama Canal in February, 1886* (New York: Press of the Chamber of Commerce, 1886), pp. 3–5.

43. Ibid., and Bunau-Varilla, p. 59.

44. Rocco to the author, August 10, 1973.

45. Ibid.

46. Conversations with Anguizola, Jr., and Jose E. Lefevre, December 1941.

47. Use 5 lbs. *corbina*, 3 chopped onions, 2 cups of lime or lemon juice, salt to taste, 1 tablespoon of olive oil, and 2 hot yellow peppers. Recipe by Rita de Duran as told to the author by Angelita Munoz Boyd de Lew in conversation, January 1974.

48. Conversations with Garay, Anguizola, Jr., and Lefevre.

49. 2 lbs. of *masa*, 2 lbs. pork chops, 2 small onions, 1 chicken, ½ cup tomato sauce, 16 olives, 2 tablespoons of salt, hot pepper or tabasco to taste, 1 lb. tomatoes. See *Club Interamericano de Mujeres* (Panama: Department of Bellas Artes, 1957), p. 84.

50. 12 ears of young sweet corn, 2 eggs, ¼ tsp. salt, ½ tsp. vanilla, 1 tsp. sugar, and ¼ tsp. cinnamon. Recipe by Alicia Marine de Talbott as told to the author by de Lew in conversation, January 1974.

51. 3 lbs. yucca, salt to taste, 1 lb. ground meat, ½ onion, 1 clove garlic, scallion and parsley, 1 tsp. tomato paste, 1 tsp. Worcestershire sauce, 1 tsp. salt, ⅛ tsp. sugar, 1 tsp. vinegar, capers. Recipe by Laura Lindo, as quoted to the author by de Lew in conversation, January 1974.

52. Conversation with Gallegos.

53. De Lew to the author, September 14, 1973.

54. Conversation with Juan Antonio, Carbone, March 1955, and with

Florencio Harmodio Arosemena, March 1940. Senor Arosemena, a railroad engineer by profession, was president of Panama in the 1920s.

55. Conversations with Octave Mendez Pereira and Arce.

56. Conversation with de Lew.

57. Conversations with Gallegos, Arce, Anguizola, Jr., and Carbone.

58. Rocco to the author, August 20, 1973.

59. Ibid.

60. Conversations with Carbone and D. P. Schouwe.

61. Today, Marcus Junius Schouwe's grandson, Diogenes Paul Schouwe, an engineer by profession, owns a refrigeration business in Chicago.

62. Bunau-Varilla, p. 59.

63. Conversation with Carbone. Also, Siegfried, pp. 264–65.

64. *Panama Star and Herald*, March 3, 1886, p. 1.

65. The insane war cry of the fascist Spanish General Queipo del Llano during the Spanish Civil War. Dr. Juan Maria Aguilar to the author, December 30, 1944. But the cry was heard earlier in Panama, at the height of the mortality caused by disease when many canal workers, considering themselves doomed, resorted to heavy drinking.

66. Bunau-Varilla, p. 60. Also, Rocco to the author, August 20, 1973.

67. Ibid.

68. Bunau-Varilla, p. 81.

69. Conversations with Arce, Carbone, and Anguizola, Jr.

Notes 5

1. J. W. Judd, "The Eruption of Krakatoa and Subsequent Phenomena," Part I, *Report of the Krakatoa Committee of the Royal Society,* ed. by G. J. Simons (London: Simons, 1888)

2. "Krakatoa," *Encyclopedia Britanica* (1973), vol. 13, pp. 485–86.

3. Judd, pp. 321 ff.

4. Ibid.

5. Sir Robert Sharwell Ball, *Consequences of the Krakatoa Explosion* (Philadelphia: J. B. Lippincott Co., 1882), pp. 318–19.

6. Conversation with Chi-Kao-Wang. Dr. Wang resided in Indonesia for more than eight years, visiting many of the islands of this archipelago. He lived in Batavia at different times.

7. Ball, p. 322.

8. Ibid., pp. 324, 333–40.

9. Reverend Philip Neale, "An Effect Near Merak on Western Java, of the Krakatoa Eruption," *American Journal of Science,* vol. 30 (July–December, 1885), pp. 175–80.

10. Ibid.

11. Ball, p. 340. Also, conversations with Antonio Anguizola, Jr., and Pilar Gomez Guerra, the author's grandmother.

12. Ball, p. 339. Also, conversation with Luis Ramon Salvat, December 1940. Dr. Salvat was the author's tutor in physics and later became professor of physics at the National Institute and the University of Panama.

13. Henri Cermoise, *Deux Ans à Panama* (Paris: E. Flamarion, Imprimerie Balback et Thomas, 1886), pp. 144 ff.

14. As we mention later in this chapter, one was the family of the Patrenotres. Madame Giselle Bunau-Varilla Rocco to the author, July 15, 1973.

15. Cermoise, p. 196.

16. Conversation with Oscar G. Carrera, M.D., September 1968.

17. Ibid. Many years later, I witnessed the recuperation of several people in this manner. The *corozo* is a diminutive nut the size and shape of a golf ball. When ripe, it is brown. Boiled for several hours and later peeled, it reveals a pink-brown edible flesh tasting somewhere between bread-fruit and apple. Its core has more secrets. When cracked open, it unveils a nucleus of sweet and hard coconut the size of a marble. The palm's trunk and leaves are a nuisance to man and beast seeking the fruit, for they are covered with

needlelike thorns. While in the palm tree, the nuts resemble a giant bunch of grapes. Because of the abundance of this plant in the canal zone, one of the workers' camps was named Corozal, "land of the corozo." Today it is the site of a healthful and pleasant town.

18. *"Sont insectes imperceptibles qui s'entrouduisent souls la peau des doigts de pied principalement et determinent par leur presense une inflammation qui-peut amener la gangrene. . . . Les nigues constituent un des grands disagaments du pays, et les indigenes sont nambreus qui ont perdu de cette facon quelque phalange de doigts de pieds."* Cermoise, pp. 75–78. This is one of the several species of siphonaptera fleas and a close relative of the African and Indian varieties named Pulex or Tunga *penetrans*. Some authorities believe that these varieties originated in America and then spread to Africa and India. See Folke Henschen, *The History and Geography of Diseases* (New York: Delacorte Press, 1962), pp. 159–60.

19. Conversations with Manuel Samper, M.D., and Anguizola, Jr.

20. C. D. Griswold, *The Isthmus of Panama: And What I Saw There* (New York: Dewitt and Davenport, 1852), p. 65.

21. Conversation with Anguizola, Jr.

22. Conversation with Dr. Enrique Arce. Also, Rocco to the author, July 15, 1973.

23. *New York Times,* May 25, 1973, p. 13. I remember being bitten by a tick at the age of eight, while visiting my grandfather. The wound was treated and bandaged, but the toxicity of the bite caused a high fever which lasted for two days. A few years later, an uncle was bitten by a gnat or a tick near his sawmill and died while he was being taken by hammock to the nearest town. My mother told me that he "had turned purple immediately," signifying that his blood had coagulated at once.

As world population increases, so do the millions of insects carrying lethal germs. Rare, almost unknown in the United States until recent years, ticks are now growing in numbers and causing outbreaks of many diseases in various areas of the country. In July 1974, a widespread outbreak of Rocky Mountain Fever (another name for this illness) was reported in Colorado, New York, and part of New Jersey. *Dallas Morning News,* July 7, 1974, p. 7.

24. Ibid., May 24, 1973, p. 39.

25. Rocco to the author, March 15, 1973.

26. Conversation with Carrera. Also, *Encyclopedia of Science and Technology* (New York: McGraw-Hill Book Co., 1966), vol. 5, p. 242.

27. Ibid.

28. Conversation with Carrera. Dr. Carrera was quoting from *Malariology: A Comprehensive Survey of All Aspects of This Group of Diseases from a Global Standpoint,* a two-volume work edited in 1949 by Mark Frederick Boyd. Also see *Encyclopedia Britannica* (1971), vol. 14, p. 672.

29. Sydenham Society, *The Genuine Works of Hippocrates,* trans. by Francis Adams (London: n.p., 1894), vol. 1, pp. 1–74.

30. *Encyclopedia Britannica* (1971), vol. 14, p. 672. Also, conversation with Carrera.

31. Conversations with Manuel Samper, M.D., and Antonio Anguizola, Sr. Also, conversation between Bunau-Varilla and Santos Zelaya as related to the author by Delores Sunley in conversation, December 1973.

32. Bunau-Varilla believed that several young Frenchmen on his staff—who had no previous history of paludal disease—died shortly after contracting blackwater fever. Rocco to the author, August 10, 1973.

33. Ibid.

34. D. W. Devins, "Non-Fossil Energy Alternatives" *The Review* (Indiana University Alumni Association of the College of Arts and Sciences Graduate School, Indiana University, Bloomington) vol. 16, no. 1,(Fall 1973): p. 4.

35. Rocco to the author, March 15, 1972.

36. Bunau-Varilla, p. 60.

37. As already noted, malaria had been diagnosed by Hippocrates. In his treatise "On Airs, Waters, and Places," the father of medicine blamed the malady on stagnant waters, the stench of cesspools and *retretes,* and decomposed food. He also made a distinction between a more serious illness with almost similar symptoms (yellow fever?) and malaria. "There are two kinds of fever, the common to all is called the plague, and the other being connected with vitiated food in those who use it. The air, then is the cause of both of these." The Greek savant explained how the sickness behaves, appearing daily (quotidian), on alternate days (tertian), or three days apart (quartan). Hippocrates also recommended treatment for the ailment, advising everyone to be careful where "you establish residence, for places with bad airs and stagnant waters are a sure source of the disease."

Despite the wealth of knowledge bequeathed by Hippocrates, the etiology of these diseases was not properly studied for 2,300 years. After Hippocrates, most students of medicine sought the consequences of malaria rather than its cause. Paludal sources were blamed for inflammation of the lungs and the liver as well as for brain tumors, sterility of women, mental depression, early childbirth, and possible insanity. Any kind of estivo-autumnal fever was suspected to be malaria; therefore, it was very difficult to isolate and trace the disease.

See "Analysis," by E. Coray, *Traité de Hippocrates, Discours preliminaire,* Sydenham Society, vol. 7, pp. 22–23; Francis Clifton, *Hippocrates upon Air, Water, and Sanitation* (London, 1734), pp. 71–74; and Sydenham Society, *Hippocrates "De Morbis,"* vol. 4, p. 28.

38. L. Markham, *A Memoir of the Lady Ana de Osorio* (London: n.p., 1869), and *Espasa-Calpe S.A.* (Barcelona: n.p., 1924), vol. 68, p. 1,301. Also, conversation with Ambassador Oscar Benavides of Peru.

39. Espasa-Calpa, S.A., vol. 68, pp. 1,301 ff.

40. Ibid., and *Larousse du XXe Siècle* (Paris, 1929), *Supplement au tome 2,* p. 215. Leopold of Austria and his wife the Archduchess Isabelle were appointed to this post by the Spanish King Phillip IV in 1646.

41. Conversations with Samper, Benavides, Arce, and C. D. Richards. Professor Richards taught the history of England at the University of Texas at Arlington.

42. A. F. Villemain, *Histoire de O. Cromwell* (Paris, 1819); idem, *Historia de Oliverio Cromwell* (Seville, 1842); and Anonymous, *Paralelo entre Cesar, Cromwell, Carlomagno y Bonaparte* (Madrid, 1804). Also, *National Enquirer,* July 15, 1973, p. 9. Cromwell is quoted as saying that he would not permit himself "to be Jesuited to death."

43. See Diego Mendoza, *Expedición Botánica de José Celestino Mutis por el Nuevo Reino de Granada* (Madrid: n.p., 1909), and A. F. Gredilla, *Biografía de Don José Celestino Mutis* (Madrid: n.p., 1911).

44. Hipolito Ruiz Lopez, *Quinologia: o tratado del arbol de la quina o Cascarilla—con su descripcion y la de otras especies de quinos—del modo de beneficiarla* (Madrid, 1792), en la oficina de la viuda de hijo de Marin, and idem., *Suplemento a la Quinologia* (Madrid 1801) pp. 191–224. Profusely illustrated with drawings and diagrams (Ruiz took two artists with him on his trips through the jungle), these publications are a clear challenge to Mutis' glory. See *Lopez Ruiz,* nos. 1–26, in the National Library of Colombia, Bogota, and "Lopez Ruiz," a rare manuscript in the library of the heirs of Enrique J. Arce of Panama City.

45. Jose Celestino Mutis, *El Arcano de la Quina* (Bogota, 1793) pp. 11-19, and J. Mendez y Pelayo, *Historia de la Poesia Hispano-Americana* (Bogota and Madrid: n.p., 1913), vol. 2, chap. 7. Most of Mutis' works are now at the Botanical Museum in Madrid. They were taken to Spain by his nephew, the Colombian naturalist Sinforoso Mutis. For an account of the confrontation between Mutis and Lopez Ruiz, see Enrique Perez Arbelaez, *Jose Celestino Mutis y la Real Expedicion Botanica del Nuevo Reino de Granada* (Bogota: Antares, Tercer Mundo S. A., 1967), pp. 62, 111-13, 118.

46. *Encyclopedia Britannica* (1971), vol. 15, p. 109.

47. Ibid., Acosta de Samper, *Compendio de Historia de Colombia* (Bogota: n.p., 1909); and Francisco Jose de Caldas, *Escritos Varios* (Bogota, 1803).

48. Gordon Cevell, "Relationship between malarial parasitemia and symptoms of the disease: A Review of the Literature," *World Health Organization Bulletin* no. 22 (1960), pp. 604-6, and Tuan Tze Chen, *Research in Protozoology,* 4 vols. (New York and Oxford: Porgen Press, 1967).

49. Cevell, pp. 604 ff.

50. See *Directory of Scientific Biography,* ed. Charles Coulston Gillispie (New York: Scribner's, 1971) vol. 4, pp. 619–20; Carlos Finlay, "The Mosquito hypothetically considered as the agent of transmission of Yellow Fever," (Havana, 1881); "Yellow Fever: A symposium in commemoration of Carlos J. Finlay," *American Journal of Tropical Medicine* vol. 4, no. 4 (July 1955); and J. D. Gillett, *The Mosquito: Its Life, Activities, and Impact on Human Affairs,* (Garden City, N.Y.: Doubleday, 1972), pp. 209–11, 251–52.

51. A Nobel Prize winner, chemist Dr. Linus Pauling, firmly believes that vitamin C prevents the common cold. *New York Times,* October 26, 1973, p. 87. His *Vitamin C and the Common Cold* was a best seller.

52. Conversations with Samper and Carrera.

53. *Fort Worth Press,* February 10, 1974, p. 17A.

54. Conversations with Samper, Carrera, Anguizola, Sr., and Guerra.

55. *Fort Worth Press*, February 10, 1974, p. 17A.

56. Conversation with Arce.

57. Conversation with Anguizola, Jr. The memoirs were probably Markham's *A memoir* . . . Philippe probably also owned a best seller of those days, H. A. Wedell's *Histoire naturelle des Quinquinas* (Paris: n.p., 1849.) Triana's book was published in Paris in 1870.

58. Rocco to the author, July 14, 1973.

59. Converstion with Arce.

60. Rocco to the author, July 14, 1973.

61. Bunau-Varilla, pp. 52–53.

62. J. M. Keating, *The Yellow Fever Epidemic of 1878 in Memphis, Tennessee* (Memphis: Howard Association, 1879), p. 13.

63. *Chapman's Homer: The Iliad, the Odyssey and the Lesser Homerics*, ed. by Allardyce Nicoll (New York: Pantheon Books, 1956), and Thucydides, *The Pelopennesian War*, trans. by Crowley (New York: Modern Library, Random House, 1951), pp. 110–15.

64. Sextus Julius Frontinus, *The Stragems, and the Aqueducts of Rome*, trans. by Charles E. Benett (Cambridge: Harvard University Press, 1961; London: W. Heinemann, 1961).

65. Howard A. Kelly, *Walter Reed and Yellow Fever* (Baltimore: Medical Standard Book Co., 1906), and William Crawford Gorgas, *Sanitation in Panama* (New York: D. Appleton, 1915), pp. 1–10. The Greek savant was handsomely rewarded by the grateful state with a gold crown and many other honors, and perhaps for some time Athens was a much healthier place to live. Yet, forty years later, Aristophanes, in *Athenian Women*, portrayed women who threw every conceivable kind of debris, including excreta, into the thoroughfare. The stage was set for another epidemic of the fever or related disease. See Aristophanes, *Ecclesiaszusae: The Congresswomen*, trans. by Douglas Parker (Ann Arbor, Mich.: University of Michigan Press, 1967), pp. 18–19.

66. Plinius Secundus, *Natural History*, trans. H. Rochman (Cambridge: Harvard University Press, 1958; London: W. Heinemann, 1958), vol. 2, pp. 621–22.

67. My alert grandmother, who had heard about Carlos Finlay's theories, always fumigated her house with the smoke of burned wood or leaves. At dusk, before seating herself with family and friends in the patio or portal of her home to hear or recount stories, she supervised her Indian boys in the stacking of two piles of wood. These were always placed against the breeze, and much of the wood was green logs chosen to generate and prolong the spiral of white fumes.

68. Conversation with George Octave, November and December 1973. Octave was 105 years old in 1974, and lived outside New Orleans. Also, conversation with Guerra.

69. Bunau-Varilla, p. 61.

70. Conversation with Octave. Also, Rocco to the author, March 15, 1973.

71. Bunau-Varilla, p. 62.

72. Rocco to the author, July 4, 1973.

73. Ibid. Also, Bunau-Varilla, p. 64.

74. Boyer died on May 1, 1886. Ruben D. Carles, *Historia del Canal de Panama* (Panama City: n.p., 1973), p. 16, and Bunau-Varilla, p. 66.

75. Catalino Arrocha Graell, *Historia de la Independencia de Panamá: Sus Antecedentes y Sus Causas—1821–1903* (Panama: Star & Herald Co., 1933), pp. 244–45. Professor Graell (a good friend of my father's) describes Bunau-Varilla in this book: "A man of great intelligence, and of a most active and daring temperament." Privately, Graell was even more generous in his appraisal of the canal wizard, whom he called "the most brilliant of all men who at any time, past and present, had anything to do with the planning and building of the canal." Conversation, December 1941.

76. A badge, as the device on a shield or coat of arms; emblem of a city or ship.

77. John Bigelow, *Report to the Chamber of Commerce of New York on His Trip of Inspection of the Panama Canal in February 1886* (New York: Chamber of Commerce Press, 1886), pp. 16 ff.

Notes 6

1. There are years when, in late June and early July, the temperature in the North Atlantic reaches a low of 30 degrees F. While I was crossing the ocean in 1965 and 1966 (June 29–July 8), the thermometer fell below 35°F. every afternoon after 4:30.

2. Many of Bunau-Varilla's friends, including the Boyds and the Obaldias, had repeatedly asked that the company bring Louis Pasteur to Panama to study the pandemia plaguing the isthmus. Conversations with Antonio Carbone, Enrique Arce, and Americo Valero. Also, Giselle Bunau-Varilla Rocco to the author, April 15, 1973.

3. Rocco to the author, May 15, 1972.

4. The Culebra cut was viewed by Bunau-Varilla as the saddle between the valleys of the Rio Grande and Obispo rivers. When the Americans took over the canal, the name *Culebra* was applied not only to this saddle proper but also to the cut in the valley of the Obispo River and the high valley of the Rio Grande. It was then nine statute miles long.

5. Philippe Bunau-Varilla, *The Creation, Destruction, and Resurrection* (New York: McBride, Nast and Co., 1914), p. 68.

6. Open letter of Ferdinand de Lesseps to the Canal Shareholders, September 15, 1883, distributed as a handbill in Paris. In the Varillana of Philip Bunau-Varilla II.

7. At this time, Philippe was convinced that small vessels could navigate the canal by December 1891.

8. Rocco to the author, April 15, 1973. A close scrutiny of Fig. 6–1 provides visual evidence for Philippe's conjectures.

9. Entirely avoiding the end of the hard volcanic hill would have meant creating a sharp and dangerous turn that would have jeopardized navigation.

10. About twenty-four miles from the waters of the Pacific Ocean.

11. For a detailed geological survey of the Isthmus of Panama, see Ralph J. Roberts, Earl M. Irving, and Frank S. Simons "Mineral Deposits of Central America," and idem., "Manganese Deposits of Panama," *Geological Survey Bulletin 1,034*, plate no. 1 (U.S. Government Printing Office, Washington, D.C., 1957). See also, P. Zurcher, "Communication preliminaire relative aux observations faites dans une mission recemment executee dans l'Isthme de Panama," *Societe Geologique Bulletin* (Paris, 1898), 3rd series, vol. 26, pp. 69–70.

Bunau-Varilla's theories were confirmed in this way, first in 1898 and again in 1957.

12. Rocco to the author, April 22, 1972. Also, Bunau-Varilla, pp. 69–70, and conversation with Antonio Anguizola, Jr.

13. Bunau-Varilla, pp. 70 ff.

14. Rocco to the author, April 22, 1972.

15. Ibid.

16. Bunau-Varilla, pp. 70–71.

17. Ibid.

18. Ibid., p. 72. Also, Rocco to the author, April 22, 1972.

19. Bunau-Varilla, pp. 72 ff.

20. John S. C. Abbott, *The History of Napoleon Bonaparte* (New York: Harper and Brothers, 1854), vol. 2, pp. 58–114.

21. Rocco to the author, May 19, 1972.

22. M. M. Alba C., *Cronologia de los Gobernantes de Panama* (Havana: n.p., 1935), p. 131. Also, conversation with Arce.

23. Alba C., p. 131. Author's translation.

24. Rocco to the author, May 19, 1972. Also, conversation between Bunau-Varilla and Santos Zelaya, as related to the author by Delores Sunley in conversation.

25. Conversations with Arce, Anguizola, and Carbone. Also, Rocco to the author, May 19, 1972.

26. Bunau-Varilla, pp. 79–80.

27. Ibid., p. 81.

28. Ibid.

29. Conversation with Diego Suarez. Archimedes used the word *eureka*, "I have found it."

30. Conversation with Suarez. Also, Rocco to the author, June 3, 1972.

31. Bunau-Varilla, p. 81. Also, Rocco to the author, June 3, 1972.

32. Bunau-Varilla, pp. 81 ff.

33. A very young messenger in twentieth century France whose job was to take messages throughout the city. The canal company dressed its messengers in gold. Conversation with Madame Guy Lathan.

34. Bunau-Varilla, pp. 81–82. Also, Rocco to the author, June 3, 1972.

35. Conversation with Arce. Also, Rocco to the author, June 3, 1972.

36. Ibid. Also, Bunau-Varilla, pp. 83, 449–50.

37. Ibid. The new corporation, named for three engineer friends of Bunau-Varilla's, was Erzinger, Delphieux, Galtier & Co.

38. Rocco to the author, July 4, 1972. Also, Bunau-Varilla, p. 74.

39. Conversation with Arce. The measures taken by the new departmental governor, General Alejandro Posada, who strictly enforced hygienic regulations, probably helped reduce epidemics in the area of the canal. See Alba C., p. 132.

40. Bunau-Varilla, p. 83.

41. Ibid.

42. Alba C., p. 132. Alba mourns the absence of Panamanians in the government house, yet he admits, by inference, that none or very few of the native heads of state were as honest as Posada.

43. Ibid.

44. The lycée is a six-year preparatory school that includes the first two years of a United States college. This lycée was staffed by French teachers who volunteered their services as their canal duties permitted. Philippe Bunau-Varilla arranged this exchange. Alba C., p. 132. Also, conversation with Arce.

45. Jacques Robichez, Le XIXe Siècle Francis (Paris: Editions Seghers, 1962), pp. 177 ff., "The Boulanger, Panama, and Dreyfus Affairs." L'affaire Dreyfus was the climax of an anti-Semitic movement which reached hysterical heights in 1895 with the conviction of Artillery Captain Alfred Dreyfus, who was falsely accused of treason. Dreyfus was eventually vindicated. See Georges Eugene Clemenceau, Contre Justice (Paris: P. V. Stock, 1900) and Vers la Reparation (Paris: P. V. Stock, 1899). Clemenceau's stand on the side of the eventual winner and of justice may have been responsible for restoring to him the popularity and influence so badly damaged by the collapse of the company.

46. London Times, March 28, 1888, p. 5. Daniel Wilson was convicted, but his sentence was reversed because there were no penalties for anyone who might sell the Legion of Honor. Now there are.

47. London Times, July 21, 1887, p. 3; November 2, 1887, p. 5; and January 21, 1888, p. 7.

48. Conversation between Bunau-Varilla and Santos Zelaya, as related by Sunley to the author in conversation. The painters mentioned by Bunau-Varilla were popular during and immediately after the Napoleonic era.

49. Adrian Dansette, Historie des Presidents de la Republique (Paris: Amiot-Dumont, 1953), pp. 91-129; idem, Le Boulangerisme (Paris: Librairie Fayard, 1946); Stanton Budington Leeds, These Ruled France (Indianapolis: Bobbs-Merrill, 1940), pp. 16 ff; and Albert Gerard, Beyond Hatred (New York: Scribner's, 1925), pp. 45 ff.

50. Rocco to the author, April 22, 1972.

51. Andre Siegfried, Suez and Panama (Oxford: Alden Press, 1940), pp. 268 ff.

52. Maron J. Simon, The Panama Affair (New York: Scribner's, 1971), pp. 76 ff.

53. La Cocarde (Paris), April 7 and 9, 1888, p. 1; La France (Paris), April 9, 1888, p. 1; and La Lanterne (Paris), April 9 and 16, 1888, p. 1.

54 L'Intransigeant (Paris), April 19, 1888, p. 1, and La Cocarde (Paris), April 21, 1888, p. 1.

55. Conversation with Arce and Anguizola, Jr.

56. Bunau-Varilla, p. 87.

57. Ibid., pp. 88–89.

58. Ibid., pp. 87–88.

59. Simon, pp. 77–78. Also, Rocco to the author, May 15, 1973.

60. Simon, pp. 77 ff.

61. Conversations with Arce, Anguizola, and Sunley.

62. *Panama Star and Herald,* December 15, 1888 and January 1, 1889, p. 1; Bunau-Varilla, p. 89; and Alba C. 132-33. Also, conversation with Arce.

63. *London Times,* December 17, 1888, p. 5.

64. Ibid., January 7, 1889, p. 5.

65. *New York Times,* January 28, 1889, p. 1.

66. *L'affaire Boulanger* was one of the most pervasive subjects in history and civic classes in Panama after the creation of the Republic. Conversation with Arce. The author personally heard this rhetoric from some of the lawyers who were part-time professors at the Instituto Nacional.

67. For insight into the dynamics of these committees and grand committees in France and the way they operated during the Third and Fourth Republics, see R. K. Gooch, *The French Parliamentary Committee System* (New York: Appleton-Century, 1935), pp. 60–144.

68. Siegfried, p. 270, and *L'Aurore* (Paris), February 5, 1889, p. 1.

69. Conversation between Zelaya and Sunley, as related by Sunley to the author in conversation.

70. Rocco to the author, August 20, 1973.

71. Edouard Drumont, *The Last Battle* (Paris, 1890), pp. 102–49, 168–69.

72. Ibid., pp. 180–83.

73. Siegfried, pp. 272–73, and Bunau-Varilla, pp. 94–101.

74. Siegfried, p. 274, and Bunau-Varilla, pp. 94–104.

75. Conversation between Zelaya and Sunley, as related to the author by Sunley in conversation. Also, Rocco to the author, May 15, 1973.

76. Bunau-Varilla, p. 104.

77. Ibid., p. 105.

78. Ibid., p. 103.

79. Siegfried, p. 279. Minister Baihaut asked for $275,000, but, not being able to keep his promise, refused the rest of the money. Conversation with Sunley.

80. Simon, p. 192.

81. Siegfried, p. 280. The details of *l'affaire Panamisme* are given in Simon, pp. 153–82 ff.

82. This statement was much quoted after World War II, when it was attributed to Winston Churchill, but it was probably well known in antiquity and certainly in the Middle Ages. Similar words were uttered by the grand constable of France, Jean de Boucicaut, in 1415 after the battle of Agincourt.

83. Bunau-Varilla, pp. 116–22; Siegfried, pp. 275–80; *New York Times,* June 20, 1893, p. 5, and June 25, 1893, p. 2; *New York Tribune,* January 31, 1893, p. 1; and Simon, p. 182.

84. Bunau-Varilla, p. 114, and Siegfried, pp. 275–76.

85. Ibid.; *New York Tribune,* June 16, 1893, p. 11; *London Times,* December 8, 1894, p. 6; and *Panama Star & Herald,* December 8, 1894, p. 1.

86. U.S. House of Representatives, 52nd Cong. 2nd Sess. Report of February 6, 1893, no. 2,615; the *New York Times,* January 30, 1893, p. 1.; and the *New York Tribune,* January 29, 1893, p. 2.

87. Conversation with Arce. The dire economic conditions in the isthmus and the death of President Nunez quashed any attempt in Panama or Colombia to expose more people for misappropriation of funds or extortion.

88. Bunau-Varilla, *Panama: Le Passé, le Present, l'Avenir* (Paris, 1892), pp. 11–91. The book appeared on the stands on March 20, 1892.

89. Conversation between Bunau-Varilla and Zelaya, as related to the author by Sunley, in conversation.

90. Bunau-Varilla, *The Creation,* pp. 124–33.

91. Ibid., pp. 126–27.

92. Ibid., p. 128.

93. Rocco to the author, August 20, 1973.

94. Bunau-Varilla, *The Creation,* pp. 132–33.

Notes 7

1. Royal Cortissoz, *The Life of Whitelaw Reid* (New York: Scribner's, 1921), vol. 1, 56–116. Also, conversation with Florence Loomis, July 23, 1973.

2. John Bigelow, *Retrospective of an Active Life* (Garden City, N.Y.: Doubleday, Page and Co., 1913), vol. 5, pp. 88-90.

3. Ibid., pp. 102-3. Bigelow helped Reid to acquire 51 percent of the stock of the Western Union Telegraph Company in 1873. Immediately after, Reid built new headquarters for his newspaper.

4. Cortissoz, pp. 71–73. Upon Arthur's accession, Reid wrote to Hay: "Arthur's antecedents do not inspire confidence. He is now, however, entitled to support, unless he forfeits it."

5. Ibid., pp. 136-52.

6. Conversation with Loomis, July 1973.

7. Ibid.

8. Giselle Bunau-Varilla Rocco to the author, August 22, 1972.

9. Ibid.

10. Lester E. Klimm, *Man's Role in Changing the Face of the Earth* (Norman: University of Oklahoma Press, 1956), p. 535. Nero and Gaius Caesar tried to cut the Corinth isthmus.

11. Rocco to the author, April 15, 1973; also, conversation between Dolores Sunley and Santos Zelaya, as related to the author by Sunley in conversation, December 1973.

12. N. Sherwin-White, ed., *The Letters of Pliny: A Historical and Social Commentary* (New York: Oxford Univ. Press, 1969), 2d ed.

13. C. G. Rockwood, Jr., "The Ischian Earthquake of July 28, 1883," *American Journal of Science* (New Haven, Conn.) no. 151 (July-December 1883), article 53, p. 473.

14. Stanley Gibbons, *Stamps of Foreign Countries: Price Catalogue* (391 Strand, London, 1914), p. 458.

15. Ibid., p. 151.

16. Ibid., p. 472. Also, conversation with Marina Sanchez Santiago, December 1973.

17. *La Libre Parole* (Paris), September 1, 2, 5, and 15, 1892, p. 1.

18. Philippe Bunau-Varilla, *The Creation, Destruction and Resurrection* (New York: McBride, Nast and Co., 1914). p. 142.

19. George J. B. Fisher, *Le Sauvetage du Canal de Panama* (Paris: Librairie Plon, 1934), p. 8, and Bunau-Varilla, pp. 146–47.

20. *Le Matin* (Paris), June 25 and November 2, 1894, p. 1, and Bunau-Varilla, p. 151.

21. Rocco to the author, June 15, 1974. Also, the *New York Tribune*, November 16, 1903, p. 1.

22. Douglas Johnson, *France and the Dreyfus Affair* (New York: Walker and Co., 1966), pp. 14-23.

23. Rocco to the author, June 15, 1974. Also, Jacques Kayser, *The Dreyfus Affair* (London: William Heinemann, 1931), pp. 95-96; and Johnson, p. 77.

24. Lee Max Friedman, *Alfred Dreyfus 1859-1935* (New York: Herbell House, 1966); Nicholas Halasz, *Captain Dreyfus: The Story of Mass Hysteria* (New York: Grove Press, 1935); Georges Maurice Paleologue, *Journal de l'Affaire Dreyfus et le Quai d'Orsay* (Paris: Librairie Plon, 1955). Two enemies of the canal, Edouard Drumond of *La Libre Parole* and Quesnay de Beaurepaire, who secured the conviction of the de Lessepses, bitterly attacked Dreyfus, contributing greatly to the anti-Semitic campaign then ravaging France.

25. Bunau-Varilla, pp. 152–53.

26. Senate Documents no. 34, 57th Cong., 2nd Sess., pp. 1–6.

27. *New York World*, December 5, 1898, and *Congressional Record*, 55th Cong., 3rd Sess., pp. 107–8. The *New York World* became the official mouthpiece of the Nicaraguan canal lobby.

28. Robaglia to Bunau-Varilla, September 28, 1898. Bunau-Varilla, p. 153.

29. Benjamin Keen, *Latin American Civilization* (Boston: Houghton Mifflin, 1974), vol. 2, p. 6.

30. Ibid. Also, Francisco Bilbao, *La American en Peligro* (Santiago: n.p., 1941), pp. 33–45.

31. Salvador de Madariaga, *Ingleses, Francesses, Espanoles* (Buenos Aires: Editorial Losada S. A., 1942), p. 57.

32. Russell W. Ramsey, "Critical Bibliography on *La Violencia* in Colombia," *Latin American Research Review* (University of Texas Printing Division), vol. 8, no. 1 (Spring 1973), pp. 3–44.

33. Orlando Fals Borda, *La Subversion en Colombia: El Compendio Social en la Historia* (Bogota: n.p., 1961).

34. M. M. Alba C., *Cronología de los Gobernantes de Panama* (Panama: n.p., 1935), p. 133.

35. Cortissoz, pp. 194–209.

36. Reid to Loomis, April 8, 1896. Loomis Collection, Stanford University, boxes 1-2, folders 1.

37. Cortissoz, p. 209.

38. Ibid., p. 214. McKinley feared senatorial opposition to Reid's appointment, especially from Reid's enemy, Thomas Platt of New York. See Margaret Leech, *In the Days of McKinley* (New York: Harper, 1959), pp. 108–9.

39. Cortissoz, p. 213.

40. Ibid., p. 214.

41. See H. Portell y Vila, *Historia de Cuba y sus relaciones con España*, 4 vols. (Madrid: publisher, 1838–1841).

42. See Valriano Weyler Nicolau, *Mi Mando en Cuba* (Madrid: n.p., 1910). General Ramon Blanco y Arenas replaced Weyler.

43. Ronald H. Spector, "The Battle of Santiago," *American History Illustrated* (Gettysburg, Penn.), vol. 9, no. 4 (July 1974), pp. 12–25, and Leech, pp. 155–293.

44. Cortissoz, p. 219.

45. Spector, p. 12 ff.

46. Cortissoz, pp. 224–27. The American commissioners were Judge William R. Day of Ohio, Senator Kushman K. Davis of Minnesota, Senator William P. Frye of Maine, Senator George Gray of Delaware, and Reid. The Spanish mission was composed of Don Eugenio Montero Rios, Don Buenaventura Arbazuza, Don Jose de Garnica, Don Wenceslao R. de Villa-Urrutia, and General Rafael Cerero. Moore's appointment as secretary to this commission boded well for the canal. John Hay had been recalled from England to become secretary of state, and he recommended Moore for the job. Also, see Margaret Clapp, *Forgotten First Citizen: John Bigelow* (Boston: Little Brown and Co., 1947), p. 309.

47. Reid's refusal to acquiesce to Spain's demands about the Cuban debt were thoroughly discussed later in his treatise, "Some Consequences of the Treaty of Paris," in which he established the principle that "a national debt incurred in efforts to subdue a colony cannot be attached in the nature of a mortgage to that territory or colony." Cortissoz, p. 234. Reid was in confidential correspondence with McKinley. Leech, p. 339.

48. Bunau-Varilla, p. 161.

49. Conversation with Diego Suarez, December 1971. Suarez was a Colombian diplomat who spent most of his adult life in the United States, but whose recollections of Colombian history were vivid. Also, Rocco to the author, May 15, 1973.

50. Jesus Maria Henao y Gerardo Arrubla, *Historia de Colombia*, 7th ed. (Bogota, 1952), pp. 781, 783.

51. Ibid., pp. 783, 784. Arrubla attributes the quotation to the liberal newspaperman Anibal Galindo.

52. Ibid., pp. 787, 781.

53. Orlando Fals Borda, *Subversion and Social Change in Colombia* (New York: Columbia University Press, 1969), pp. 114–15.

54. Gonzalo Jimenez de Quezada, Sebastian Belalcazar, and Nicolas Federman found themselves in the plateau of Bogota one day looking at each other. See R. B. Cunninhame Graham, *The Conquest of New Granada* (London: Heinemann, 1922), pp. 165–213, and German Arciniegas, *The Knight of El Dorado* (New York: Greenwood Press, 1968), pp. 186–238.

55. Arrubla, pp. 792–99. Each of these missions had a separate territory to catechize or in which to perform merciful chores and attend to the social welfare of the inhabitants.

56. Borda, p. 115.

57. Nunez first named General Eliseo Payan vice-president. But when Payan secretly conspired to overthrow Nunez' constitution, the president left his estates and deposed the usurper. The presidential term in Colombia had been set at six years. Arrubla, p. 786.

58. Conversation with Suarez, December 1971. Also, Arrubla, p. 801.

59. Ibid., p. 806. Also, conversation with Dr. Enrique Arce. Arce reported the general suspicion that Nunez was poisoned. Suarez said there was no proof because he was buried almost immediately, but that it could have been a combination of old age and a "strong medicine."

60. Arrubla, pp. 807–8.

61. Nicolas Esguerra, *Canal de Panama: Escritos* (Bogota: Imprenta de Luis M. Holguin, 1903), pp. 11, 12. Also, conversations with Suarez and Arce.

62. Esguerra, pp. 12–15, Arrubla, p. 811.

63. The battles were of *Vieja Negra* (old black woman), on June 24, 1900; *Calendonia*, June 24-26; *Pueblo Nuevo*, July 12, 1901; *El Silencio*, July 22-23; *Rio Grande*, February 8, 1901; *Aguadulce* (sweet waters), February 9, 1901; *El Picacho* (the peak), May 13, 1901; and *Aguadulce*, February 22, 1902. Alba C., pp. 136-38.

64. Rocco to the author, May 15, 1973. Also, Bunau-Varilla, p. 161.

65. Ibid. Also, conversation with Suarez, December 1971.

66. Conversation with Loomis, July 1973. A *palindrome* is a word or phrase reading the same forward and backward.

67. Bigelow to Hay, November 14, 1898, and Bigelow, November 1898. Bunau-Varilla, p. 160.

68. Conversation with Loomis, July 1973.

69. Bunau-Varilla, p. 160

70. Conversation with Loomis, July 1973.

71. Ibid., also July 1975. Also, William Elroy Curtis, *The Capitals of Spanish America* (New York: Harper and Brothers, 1888), and idem., *Venezuela: The Land Where It Is Always Summer* (New York: Harper and Brothers, 1896). Curtis traveled throughout Spanish America frequently in the late 1890s and, at one time, was correspondent for two Chicago newspapers. He became the first director of the Pan-American Union on its creation in 1890. He was a friend of Loomis and Reid, and an acquaintance of Bunau-Varilla.

72. Roosevelt to Loomis, January 4, 1898. Loomis Collection, box 4, folder 41. This letter was in reply to Loomis' request for increased naval surveillance of the southern Caribbean by American war vessels. Roosevelt did many things without consulting his superior, Navy Secretary John Davis Long of Massachusetts who, on more than one occasion, chided his impetuous under-secretary. See Karl Schriftgiesser, *The Gentleman from Massachusetts* (Boston: Little Brown 1944), pp. 169–70.

73. Conversation with Suarez, December 27, 1971.

74. Arrubla, p. 519.

75. "It was in Venezuela where the two [Bunau-Varilla and Loomis] began to plot the revolution." Conversation with Loomis, July 1973.

76. Ibid.

77. Reid to Loomis, October 13, 1898. Loomis Collection, box 4, folder 41. Reid thanked Loomis for having his writings in *Le Matin* reprinted in the Caracas press.

78. Conversation with Suarez, December 27, 1971.

79. Ibid. Also, conversation with Arce.

80. Rocco to the author, July 22, 1973.

81. The other members of the commission were Professor Peter C. Hains, Professor Lewis Haupt, Colonel Oswald Ernst, attorney Samuel Pasco, and economist Emory Johnson. Bunau-Varilla, p. 165. Also, *Report of the Isthmian Canal Commission, 1889-1902* (Sen. Doc. no. 222, 58th Cong., 2nd Sess.), (Washington, D.C.: Government Printing Office, 1904), pp. 12 ff.

82. See Christian R. De Wet, *South African War—1899-1902* (New York: Scribner's, 1902), and John A. Hobson, *The War in South Africa: Its Causes and Effects* (New York: Howard Ferling, 1969).

83. Rocco to the author, August 20, 1973.

84. Bunau-Varilla, p. 170.

85. Ibid., pp. 171–72.

86. Marcus Alonzo Hanna's ancestors were Quakers who migrated to America from northern Ireland in 1763. The basis of his wealth was his father's grocery and commission businesses. Marcus married Charlotte Augusta Rhodes, daughter of Daniel Rhodes, an iron merchant, and the two fortunes were combined in Rhodes and Company, which later became M. A. Hanna and Company. Hanna helped to organize the Union National Bank of Cleveland and bought the *Cleveland Herald* and the opera house. By 1880, he was one of the wealthiest men in the Republican Party. See H. D. Croly, *Marcus Alonzo Hanna* (New York: Macmillan, 1912); Thomas Beer, *Hanna* (New York: Knopf, 1929); and Theodore Roosevelt, *An Autobiography* (New York: Scribner's, 1931).

87. Henry Cabot Lodge, *Selections from the Correspondence of Theodore Roosevelt and Henry Cabot Lodge, 1884-1918* (New York: Scribner's, 1925), vol. 1, pp. 460–64. Roosevelt was reluctant to become vice-president for a salary of $8,000 a year, but Lodge convinced him that money was of little importance at that moment. The idea was to place him in line for the nomination to the presidency in 1903.

88. *New York Times*, July 6, 1900, p. 1. Also, conversation with Loomis. At the Republican convention of 1896, a similar statement favoring Nicaragua had been introduced by Lodge. Schriftgiesser, pp. 158–59.

89. Cortissoz, p. 276.

90. Lodge to Roosevelt, Paris, September 19, 1901. Lodge, *Selections*, vol. 1, p. 505.

91. Conversation with Loomis. Also, Leach, pp. 136–37.

92. Croly, pp. 225–32.

93. Henry Cabot Lodge, *Early Memoirs* (New York: Scribner's, 1913), and Schriftgiesser.

94. John A. Garraty, *Henry Cabot Lodge: A Biography* (New York: Knopf, 1953); *New York Times*, November 10, 1924, pp. 1, 16; and *Dallas Morning News*, November 10, 1924, p. 1.

95. Henry White to John Hay, December 22, 1898. *Diplomatic History of the Panama Canal: Correspondence . . .*, Senate Document no. 474, 63rd Cong., 2nd Sess., p. 3.

96. White to Hay, April 24, 1901. Allen Nevins, *Henry White* (New York: Harper, 1930), p. 156.

97. Lodge to Roosevelt, September 19, 1901. Lodge, *Selections*, vol. 2, p. 505. Also see Lodge to Hay, March 28, 1901. William R. Thayer, *The Life of John Hay* (New York: Houghton Mifflin, 1915), vol. 2, pp. 251–60.

98. Tyler Dennett, *John Hay: From Poetry to Politics* (New York: Dodd, Mead, 1934), p. 262.

99. Allan Nevins, *Henry White*, p. 159. Lodge did not like the first Hay-Pauncefote document, and Hay resented his opposition. See Schriftgiesser, pp. 190–91. Later, when the new treaty tacitly permitted the fortification of the canal, Lodge was satisfied. See Garraty, p. 281.

100. Bunau-Varilla, pp. 178–84.

101. Clapp, pp. 308–15. Bigelow asked George Parsons, an engineer building the New York subway system, to introduce Philippe at the Chamber of Commerce's meeting. Also see Richard M. Dorson, "American Life-Styles and Legends," *The Review:* (Indiana University Alumni Association), vol. 16, no. 2 (Winter 1974), pp. 26–27.

102. Bunau-Varilla, pp. 184–88.

103. Ibid. Also, Rocco to the author, April 15, 1972.

104. Bunau-Varilla, p. 188.

105. Bunau-Varilla, pp. 184–88.

106. Ibid. Also, Rocco to the author, April 15, 1972.

107. Bunau-Varilla, p. 188.

108. *New York American*, April 9, 1901, p. 1.

109. Bunau-Varilla, pp. 189–91.

110. *New York Herald*, Paris ed., April 13, 1901, p. 1. The headline read as follows, "The defenders of Nicaragua are alarmed. The Panama Canal project advances rapidly." Alfred Noble, a member of the canal commission who was still under Morgan's spell, warned the senator, on April 8, 1891, not to underestimate Bunau-Varilla's talent. Noble called Philippe's brochure and rhetoric a "very skillful and adroit lecture." Conversation with Suarez.

111. Ibid. Also, Rocco to the author, June 9, 1973.

112. Rafael Nunez, Jules Grevy, Sadi Carnot, Czar Alexander III, and McKinley. Grevy resigned.

113. Cortissoz, vol. 2, p. 273.

114. Ibid.

115. Lodge to Roosevelt, Paris, September 19, 1901. Lodge, *Selections*, vol. 2, pp. 504–5.

116. Conversation with Loomis.

117. Bunau-Varilla, p. 196.

118. *La Libre Parole* (Paris), April 29, and May 23, 1901, p. 1.

119. Rocco to the author, April 15, 1973.

120. Bunau-Varilla, p. 206.

121. See negotiations for the Salgar-Wise Treaty elsewhere in this book. Also see Colombia, *Anales Diplomaticos y Consulares*, vol. 1, pp. 6–18.

122. See *Report of the Isthmian Canal Commission, 1889–1901*, pp. 149 ff.

123. Ibid.

124. Conversations with Suarez and Arce.

125. Senate Document no. 54, 57th Cong., 1st Sess. Also, the *New York Journal*, November 21, 1901, p. 1.

126. Rocco to the author, April 15, 1974.

127. Ibid. Also, Bunau-Varilla, p. 207.

128. Ibid., p. 208.

129. House of Representatives, 57th Cong., 1st Sess., Document no. 15; *Congressional Record*, 57th Cong., 1st Sess., pp. 447–49.

130. *Le Matin* (Paris), December 25, 1901, p. 1.

131. Bunau-Varilla, p. 213.

132. Senate Documents, 57th Cong., 1st Sess., no. 125, pp. 2, 3.

133. Conversation with Loomis. Also, Rocco to the author, July 5, 1973.

134. *New York Herald*, editorial, January 14, 1902.

135. Conversation with Suarez. Also, Rocco to the author, July 5, 1973.

136. Senate Documents, 57th Cong., 1st Sess., no 123, pp. 9-10.

137. Rocco to the author, July 5, 1973. Also, conversations with Suarez and Kohlmeier. Dr. Kohlmeier was professor of American history at Indiana University.

138. *Congressional Record*, 57th Cong., 1st Sess., pp. 1048–49.

139. At the request of his banker, Edward Simmons, Senator Hanna asked Bunau-Varilla to have Cromwell reinstated as the new company's lawyer in the United States. Philippe had managed the change of the board's chairman and, for all practical purposes, the directorate did as he suggested. But because of Cromwell's unorthodox methods in advancing the fortunes of the new company, Philippe asked Chairman Marius Bo to warn him to be more discreet. Bunau-Varilla, pp. 214–15. Also, conversation with Suarez.

140. *Congressional Record*, 57th Cong., 1st Sess., pp. 1048–49.

141. Conversations with Suarez and Arce.

142. Bunau-Varilla, p. 219.

143. Conversations with Suarez and Arce.

144. Ibid., p. 220.

145. Alba C., pp. 137-38. Also, conversation with Arce.

146. Clapp, p. 308.

147. Bunau-Varilla, p. 221.

148. Conversations with Suarez and Arce.

149. Ibid. Also see Secretaria de Relaciones Exteriores, *Libro Azul: Documentos Diplomaticos sobre el Canal y la Rebelion del Istmo* (Bogota: n.p., 1904), pp. 91–92.

150. Ibid., pp. 136–37. Also, conversations with Suarez and Arce. The Panamanian historian M. M. Alba C. gives much credit for the formulation of the treaty project to Mutis Duran, but admits that these proposals were only *un truco diplomatico* (a diplomatic trick). See Alba C., p. 138.

151. Bunau-Varilla to "Directeur, *Star and Herald*," March 26, 1902, in Bunau-Varilla, pp. 221–22.

152. Bunau-Varilla to Concha, March 27, 1902. Ibid., p. 223.

153. Bunau-Varilla to Concha, March 27, 1902. Ibid., pp. 224–25.

154. At last, on March 31, 1902, advised by Bunau-Varilla, the Colombian minister to Washington agreed to a cash payment of $7 million and left the annuity to future negotiations. See *Diplomatic correspondence relating to the negotiation and application of an interoceanic canal, and accompanying papers* (Washington, D.C., Government Printing Office, 1914), House Document no. 611, 57th Cong., 1st Sess., exhibit 15, the *Jose Vicente Concha-John Hay Protocol, May 15, 1902.* Also see Bunau-Varilla, p. 225, and Dennett, p. 370.

155. Secretaria de Relaciones Exteriores, pp. 175 ff.

156. On September 13, 1903, Hay placed Roosevelt in a Faustian dilemma. He advised the president to take one of two courses—await the result of Bunau-Varilla's revolutionary activities or treat with Nicaragua at once. Dennett, p. 377.

NOTES 8

1. Carlos Selva,"Ultimos dias de la Administracion del Doctor Roberto Sacasa y principios del gobierno del General Jose Santos Zelaya," a series of articles published in the newspaper *Patria* of San Jose, C.R., April 2 to June 6, 1896. (Guatemala City, general edition, 1948), pp. 13–25, 29–52.

2. John Bigelow, *Breaches of Anglo-American Treaties: A Study in History and Diplomacy* (New York: Sturgis and Walton Co., 1917), pp. 107–9.

3. Ibid., pp. 103–4. Bayard to Phelps, November 23, 1888, and Gresham to Bayard, April 30 and July 19, 1894.

4. Ibid.

5. Mexican strongman, contemporary of Zelaya, who ruled until 1911.

6. Tyler Dennett, *John Hay* (New York: Dodd, Mead, 1934), pp. 273–75.

7. Ibid.

8. Conversation with Otilio Olate.

9. U.S. Department of State, *Dispatches from Central America*, vols. 69–40, nos. 652 and 654 (November 29 and December 6, 1901).

10. Dennett, p. 368.

11. Ibid., p. 369.

12. Ibid., p. 421. Also, conversation with Diego Suarez.

13. Conversation between Santo Zelaya and Delores Sunley, as related to the author by Sunley, in conversation.

14. These were the Hay-Pauncefote Treaties, the Open Door Policy with China, the Alaskan Boundary Dispute, the Venezuelan Crisis of 1902, and the problems emanating from the Treaty of Paris of 1898. See Dennett, pp. 430–33, and Royal Cortissoz, *The Life of Whitelaw Reid* (New York: Scribner's, 1921),pp. 367–68. Hay suffered from arthritis and high blood pressure.

15. André Siegfried, *Suez and Panama* (Oxford: Alden Press, 1940), pp. 323 ff.

16. Carlos J. Finlay, "Yellow Fever, Its Transmission by Means of the Culex Mosquito," *American Journal of Medical Science* vol. 92, (1886), pp. 395–409, and idem, "El Mosquito hipoteticamente considerado como agente de transmision de fiebre amarilla," *Real Academia de Ciencias* (Havana, 1881), no. 18, pp. 147–49.

17. J. D. Gullet, *The Mosquito: Its Life, Activities and Impact on Human Affairs*

(Garden City, N.Y.: Doubleday, 1922), pp. 208–9, and Folke Henschen, *The History and Geography of Diseases* (New York: Appleton, 1915), pp. 36–37. Also, conversation with Oscar Carrera, M.D.

18. Henschen, p. 36. Also, conversation with William Taliaferro, M.D.

19. William Crawford Gorgas, *Sanitation in Panama* (New York: Appleton, 1915), pp. 14, 15.

20. Ibid., p. 15, and Gullett, p. 210

21. Ibid., pp. 210–11. Also, conversation with Carrera.

22. *Chapman's Homer: The Illiad, the Odyssey and the Lesser Homerics* (New York: Pantheon Books, 1956), pp. 22 ff. Dr. Josiah Nott of Alabama and the French physician Louis Beauperthuy, who lived in Venezuela, also suspected that the mosquito had something to do with the appearance and propagation of disease.

23. Gorgas, pp. 53–55.

24. Philippe Bunau-Varilla, *The Creation, Destruction and Resurrection* (New York: McBride, Nast and Co., 1914), p. 228.

25. Conversations with Francisco Arce and Luis Ramon Salvat.

26. Giselle Bunau-Varilla Rocco to the author, September 11, 1973. Also, conversation with Suarez.

27. Herbert Croly, *Marcus Alonzo Hanna: His Life and Work* (New York; Macmillan, 1912), p. 459.

28. Ibid., p. 382. Also, conversation with Suarez.

29. Croly, p. 382. The committee voted 7 to 3 against Panama.

30. Rocco to the author, September 11, 1973.

31. Philippe Bunau-Varilla, *Comparative Characteristics of Panama and Nicaragua* (New York, n.p., 1902), and *Report of the Isthmian Canal Commission* Washington D.C., (Government Printing Office, 1902), pp. 99–132, 135–256.

32. Bunau-Varilla, *Comparative Characteristics.*

33. Ibid., p. 7.

34. *Report of the Isthmian Canal Commission* (Washington, D.C.: Government Printing Office, 1904), pp. 74, 91.

35. Rocco to the author, September 11, 1973.

36. *Congressional Record*, 57th Cong., 1st Sess., pp. 6276–77.

37. Rocco to the author, September 11, 1973.

38. Ibid., May 12, 1902.

39. Ibid., May 17, 1902.

40. *Congressional Record*, 57th Cong., 1st Sess., pp. 6276–77.

41. Croly, p. 449.

42. *New York Sun*, June 9, 1902, p. 1, and Bunau-Varilla, *The Creation*, p. 244.

43. Bunau-Varilla, *The Creation*, p. 246. One widely circulated work was written by Lindley M. Keasbey of Bryn Mawr College, who found nothing good about Panama. See his "The National Canal Policy" in *American Historical Association Report for 1902* (Washington, D.C.: Government Printing Office, 1903), p. 287.

44. Rocco to the author, October 29, 1972.

45. *Congressional Record*, 57th Cong., 1st Sess., pp. 269–70.
46. Conversation with Suarez.
47. Croly, p. 385.
48. *Le Matin* (Paris), June 20, 1902, p. 1.
49. *London Times*, April 15, 1870, p. 2.
50. Bunau-Varilla, *The Creation*, pp. 248–49.
51. Rocco to the author, April 15, 1973. Also, conversations with Suarez and Florence Loomis.
52. *Congressional Record*, 57th Cong., 1st Sess., pp. 7441–43.
53. Bunau-Varilla, *The Creation*, p. 250.
54. Ibid., p. 251.
55. Ibid., p. 253.
56. *New York Press*, editorial, June 30, 1902.
57. Dennett, pp. 370–71.
58. Conversations with Suarez and Arce.
59. *Diplomatic History of the Panama Canal*, Senate Document no 474, 63rd Cong., 2nd Sess.
60. Catalino Arrocha-Graell, *Historia de la Independencia de Panama* (Panama: Star and Herald Co., 1933), pp. 192–93. Author's translation.
61. Ibid., p. 193. The government's representatives were Generals Nicolas Perdomo, Alfredo Vasques Cobo, and Victor Salazar. Benjamin Herrera, Lucas Caballero, and Eusebio A. Morales signed the treaty for the rebels.
62. Dennett, p. 372.
63. Bunau-Varilla, *The Creation*, p. 255.
64. Arrocha-Graell, p. 193.
65. Dennett, p. 372.
66. Bunau-Varilla, *The Creation*, p. 257.
67. Ibid., p. 259.
68. See the *Congressional Record*, 58th Cong., 1st Sess., pp. 10 ff.
69. *New York Times*, December 1, 1902, p. 1. Also, conversations with Suarez.
70. Bunau-Varilla, *The Creation*, pp. 267–68.
71. Ibid., p. 269.
72. *Nuevo Tiempo* (Bogota), October 16, 1903, p. 1.
73. Arrocha-Graell, p. 215. The Colombian Senate consisted of twenty-seven members. Twenty-four voted against the treaty, two did not attend, and one left in the belief that debate was to continue the next day.
74. Ibid., pp. 217–19.
75. Ibid., pp. 219–20.
76. Nicolas Esguera, *Canal de Panama: Escritos* (Bogota: Imprenta de Luis M. Holguin, 1903), pp. xii, xiii.
77. Ibid., pp. xviii, xix. Author's translation.
78. Ibid., pp. xx-xxi.
79. Ibid., pp. vii, xix, ll.
80. Bunau-Varilla, *The Creation*, pp. 274–79.

81. Dennett, p. 376.

82. Rocco to the author, April 15, 1973.

83. Arrocha-Graell, p. 219, and Esguerra, pp. 26–27. Senator Agustin Arango of Panama did not attend the sessions of the Senate. He was convinced the treaty would be rejected.

84. Ernesto de J. Castillero, *Episodios de la Independencia de Panama* (Panama Ministerio de Educacion, 1958), p. 8. Author's translation.

85. Ibid., pp. 15–17.

86. Arrocha-Graell, p. 215.

87. Bunau-Varilla, *The Creation,* p. 280.

88. Dennett, p. 377.

89. Ibid.

90. Henry Cabot Lodge, *Selections from the Correspondence of Theodore Roosevelt and Henry Cabot Lodge: 1884–1918* (New York: Scribner's, 1935), p. 64. The senator was in Europe as a member of the Alaskan Boundary Commission.

91. Conversations with Loomis and Suarez. Also see Dwight Carroll Miner, *The Fight for the Panama Route* (New York: Columbia Univ. Press, 1940), p. 192.

92. Arrocha-Graell, p. 235.

93. *Le Matin* (Paris), September 2, 1903, p. 1.

94. Rocco to the author, May 15, 1972. Also Arrocha-Graell, p. 238, and conversation with Suarez.

95. Rocco to the author, April 15, 1972. Also, conversation with Arce.

96. Arrocha-Graell, pp. 240–41.

97. Arrocha-Graell, pp. 240–41; Miner, p. 248; and the *Washington Post,* September 1, 1903, p. 1.

98. Arrocha-Graell, on pp. 240–41, states that Duque rendered great service to the revolutionary movement by acting as he did. This author disagrees.

99. Herran to Foreign Minister Luis C. Rico. *Memoria del Ministerio de Relaciones Exteriores* (Bogota: n.p., 1904). Also, Arrocha-Graell, p. 241.

100. *Washington Post,* September 1, 1903, p. 1, and the *New York Herald,* September 10, 1903, p. 1.

101. George Cortelyou to F. B. Loomis, October 31, 1901. Loomis Collection, Stanford University, box 4, folder 2.

102. Roosevelt to Loomis, March 17, 1903. Loomis Collection, box 4, folder 2. The president was recommending a candidate for the post of secretary to the legation in Warsaw, whom he considered "a first class appointment."

103. William Loeb, Jr., secretary to the president, to Loomis, May 25, 1903. Loomis Collection, box 4, folder 2. James B. Foraker was the senior senator from Ohio whose presidential aspirations had been ruined earlier by Hanna when Hanna transferred his power and influence to McKinley. Croly, pp. 457–58.

104. Loomis had become acting secretary of state. Loomis collection, box 4, folder 2.

105. Conversation with Loomis.

106. B. F. Barnes, acting secretary to the president, to Loomis, July 21, 1903. Loomis Collection, box 4, folder 2. At this meeting, Roosevelt demanded to know all details of the Panama situation, especially the possibility of a revolt backed by the United States.

107. Roosevelt to Loomis, July 23, 1903. Loomis Collection, box 4, folder 2.

108. Conversation with Loomis. For unknown reasons, but perhaps because the word had a special flavor to it, Hay, Roosevelt, Loomis, and Bunau-Varilla all began to use this Spanish word in their correspondence. Later, when Manuel Espinosa Batista, a leading Panamanian revolutionary, appeared, they all chuckled when calling anything about Panama *espinosa*.

109. Zumeta to Loomis, January 14, 1903. Loomis Collection, box 4, folder 2.

110. *New York Times*, November 1, 1903, p. 4. Mommsen had made these statements two years earlier.

111. Ibid. Professor Mommsen was a liberal who deplored the fact that in 1848 the Germans refused to grasp the opportunity to rid themselves of the Hohenzollerns, Hapsburgs, Wittelsbachs, and other "barnacles" of little and big thrones. Bismark could not forgive him for his "disloyalty" to the reigning dynasty, his liberalism, and the fact that he openly deplored Prussia's attack on Austria in 1866.

112. Beaupré to Hay, June 15, 1903. Loomis Collection, box 4, folder 2.

113. Conversation between Jose de Obaldia and Antonio Anguizola, Sr., as related to the author by Antonio Anguizola, Jr., in conversation. Also, Castillero, "La Causa inmediate de la emanicipation de Panama," in *Boletin de la Academia Panamena de la Historia*, no. 3, pp. 341–42. By attacking the treaty, writer Caro was attempting to settle old political scores with Marroquin, while Porras bitterly resented being left in the shadow by the elite.

114. Loomis to Roosevelt, August 15, 1903. Loomis Collection, box 4, folder 2.

115. The unsuccessful American attempt to help Cuban exiles land in Cuba in 1961.

116. Bunau-Varilla, *The Creation*, pp. 39–41.

117. Rocco to the author, April 15, 1972.

118. Bunau-Varilla, *The Creation*, pp. 315–22.

119. Ibid., pp. 311–13.

120. Ibid., pp. 297–98.

121. Rocco to the author, June 14, 1972. Also, conversation with Loomis.

122. Rocco to the author, June 14, 1972.

123. Bunau-Varilla, *The Creation*, p. 315.

124. Conversation between Obaldia and Anguizola, Sr., as related to the author by Anguizola, Jr., in conversation.

125. Bunau-Varilla, *The Creation*, p. 316.

126. Loomis had scheduled Philippe's visit to his office to coincide with that of Hay. Since the offices were adjacent and the doors partly opened, the secretary had no difficulty in learning that the man "with a plan and a canal"

had arrived. Rocco to the author, July 13, 1972. Also, conversation with Loomis.

127. Rocco to the author, July 13, 1972. The book was a gift from Loomis to Hay. Also, see Bunau-Varilla, *The Creation*, p. 332.

128. Rocco to the author, July 13, 1972. On June 14, 1822, Don Manuel Torres was received by President James Monroe as the first minister of Colombia. Torres, like Bunau-Varilla, spent much of his life in the United States advancing the interest of his adopted country. See Colombian Legation in Washington, D.C., *In Honor of the Patriot Don Manuel Torres, 1764–1822* (Washington, D.C.: Colombian Embassy, 1926), pp. 8, 10, 12. Also, see Margaret Clapp, *Forgotten First Citizen: John Bigelow* (Boston: Little, Brown, 1947), pp. 132, 133.

129. Conversation with Arce.

130. In Panama, Dr. Arnulfo Arias was elected president four times and was overthrown four times because of his lack of vision and his unreal appraisal of the national and international situation. The same was true of Dr. Arturo Frondizi in Argentina in the 1950s.

131. Bunau-Varilla, *The Creation*, p. 324.

132. Philippe Bunau-Varilla, *Les 19 Documents Cles du Drame de Panama: Adoption, Revolution, Convention* (Paris: Librairie Plon, 1938) document A, p. 44.

133. Ibid., document A, p. 46.

134. Ibid., document B, pp. 48–50.

135. Ibid., document C, p. 52.

136. Conversation with Carlos Manuel Gallegos, Barcelona, September 1966.

NOTES 9

1. Henry Moody, a Massachusetts congressman, was a friend of Roosevelt's. After his tenure as secretary of the navy, Moody was made attorney general to break the great trusts that were hectoring the president. Before leaving the presidency, Roosevelt named him to the Supreme Court.

2. Loomis to Beard, October 23, 1903. Loomis Collection, Stanford University, box 4, folder 2.

3. Jose Maria Gonzalez Valencia, *Separation of Panama from Colombia: Refutation of the Misstatements and Erroneous Conception of Mr. Roosevelt in an Article Entitled "The Panama Blackmail Treaty"* (Washington, D.C.: Press of Gibson Brothers, 1916), p. 7. Senor Valencia mentions Jose Marcelino Hurtado.

4. *New York Times*, November 4, 1903, p. 1.

5. Conversations with Diego Suarez and Dr. Enrique Arce. Also, Giselle Bunau-Varilla Rocco to the author, May 13, 1972. Arce and Suarez said that one of the purchasing agents was Joshua Lindo.

6. *New York Times*, November 5, 1905, p. 2. The Colombia consul in New York, Arturo de Brigard, a nephew of President Manuel Marroquin, might have been the one duped by the would-be insurgents.

7. Valencia, p. 7.

8. Conversation between Florencio Harmodio Arosemena and Antonio Anguizola, Jr., as related by Anguizola in conversation with the author.

9. Conversations with Jose E. Lefevre, Ricardo Alfaro, and Arce.

10. Conversation with Domingo Diaz Arosemena.

11. Conversation with Ricardo A. de la Espriella.

12. Conversation with Tomas Gabriel Duque.

13. Rocco to the author, November 11, 1973. The first flag of Panama was stitched together by Mme. Bunau-Varilla with the help of Mrs. Francis Bigelow. The emblem had a gold background and two suns, instead of stars, on opposite corners, symbolizing the isthmus' attachment to Spain and Colombia. Also, conversation with Philippe Bunau-Varilla II. Also see Margaret Clapp, *The Forgotten First Citizen: John Bigelow* (Boston: Little, Brown, 1947), p. 313.

14. Bunau-Varilla, *The Creation, Destruction and Resurrection* (New York:

McBride, Nast and Co., 1914), p. 332 ff., and the *New York Times*, November 1, 1903, p. 1.

15. Conversations with Arce, Harmodio Arias, and Anguizola.

16. Rocco to the author, November 11, 1973. Also, conversation with Florence Loomis.

17. Rocco to the author, August 29, 1973. Also, conversation with Loomis.

18. Conversation with Loomis.

19. Bunau-Varilla, p. 331.

20. Ehrman to Hay, November 3, 1903. Loomis Collection, box 4, folder 2.

21. James Darling, assistant secretary of the Navy, to R. Malmros, consul at Colon. Loomis Collection, box 4, folder 2.

22. Malmros to Loomis, November 3, 1903. Loomis Collection, box 4, folder 2.

23. Amador to Hay, November 3, 1903. Loomis Collection, box 4, folder 2.

24. Ehrman to Hay, November 3, 1903. Loomis Collection, box 4, folder 2.

25. *New York Times*, November 4, 1903, p. 1. Also, conversation with Arce.

26. *New York Times*, November 4, 1903, p. 1.

27. Malmros to Hay, November 3, 1903. Loomis Collection, box 4, folder 2.

28. Bunau-Varilla, p. 335.

29. *New York Times*, November 4, 1903, p. 1.

30. Malmros to Hay, November 4, 1903. Loomis Collection, box 4, folder 2.

31. Bureau of Navigation, Navy Department, to *Nashville*, November 4, 1903. Loomis Collection, box 4, folder 2.

32. Bunau-Varilla, p. 344.

33. Ibid., pp. 344–45.

34. Colonel Torres' bravado was cooled not only by the gold but by the threat of the superintendent of the railroad that an American force of five thousand men was about to land. The emissaries of the junta who delivered the money to the colonel were Jose Edgardo Lefevre and a Colon citizen named Porfirio Melendez. The troops departed on the steamer *Orinoco* on November 5th. Conversations with Lefevre and Arce. Also, see Ernesto de J. Castillero R., *Episodios de la Independencia de Panama* (Panama: n.p., 1958), pp. 133–36.

35. Ibid., p. 131. General Gutierrez had secret orders to remove governor Obaldia and make himself civilian and military chief of Panama.

36. Ibid., p. 139. Translation by the author.

37. Ehrman to Hay, November 6, 1903. Loomis Collection, box 4, folder 2. The gunboat *Padilla* had declared itself for the revolution.

38. Bunau-Varilla, p. 346.

39. Ibid., p. 348

40. Ibid.

41. Ibid., p. 349.

42. *New York Times*, November 5, 1903, p. 1.

43. Ibid., November 6, 1903, p. 2.

44. Editorial, *New York Times*, November 6, 1903.

45. Ibid., p. 2.

46. Editorial, *London Times*, November 5, 1903.

47. *Le Temps* (Paris), November 5, 1903, p. 1, and *Le Matin*, (Paris), November 5, 1903, p. 1.

48. Editorial, *New York Herald*, November 8, 1903.

49. Editorials, *New York Tribune*, November 5–25, 1903.

50. Ibid., November 5, 1903, p. 8.

51. Ibid., November 6, 1903, p. 8.

52. Ibid., November 8, 1903, p. 8.

53. Ibid., November 15, 1903, p. 8.

54. Royal Cortissoz, *The Life of Whitelaw Reid* (New York: Scribner's, 1921), vol. 2, p. 292.

55. Bunau-Varilla, *The Creation*, pp. 354–56. Also, George Grutstuck to Bunau-Varilla, Varillana of Philippe Bunau-Varilla II.

56. *New York Times*, November 6, p. 2.

57. Ibid., November 7, p. 2.

58. Conversation with Loomis. Also, the *New York Times*, November 9, 1903, p. 1.

59. *Le Matin* (Paris), November 10, 1903, p. 1, and the *New York Times*, November 13, 1903, p. 1.

60. Pavey to Bunau-Varilla, November 11, 1903. Bunau-Varilla mss., Library of Congress.

61. *Le Galois* (Paris), November 8, 1903, p. 1.

62. Bigelow to Bunau-Varilla. Bunau-Varilla mss.

63. *New York Times*, November 11, p. 2.

64. Bunau-Varilla, p. 356.

65. Rocco to the author, August 29, 1973. Also, the *New York Times*, November 10, 1903, p. 1. There were only two Democrats on the committee. Morgan was one of them. He had been allowed to chair the committee because of his enthusiasm for interoceanic canals, especially in Nicaragua.

66. *New York Times*, November 13, 1903, p. 1.

67. Ernesto de J. Castillero Reyes, *Episodios de la Independencia de Panama* (Panama: n.p., 1957), p. 160 ff. Loomis to Bunau-Varilla, December 30, 1903, in the Varillana of Philippe Bunau-Varilla II.

68. *New York Times*, November 5, 1903, p. 2.

69. Ibid., November 10, 1903, p. 2.

70. Arthur Matthias Beaupre to Hay, November 6, 1903, *Diplomatic Correspondence Relating to the negotiation and application of an Interoceanic canal and accompanying papers*, 63rd Cong., 2nd. Sess., Senate Document no. 474. (1914), p. xii.

71. *New York Times*, November 14, 1903, p. 1. Also, Bigelow to Bunau-Varilla, November 17, 1903. Bunau-Varilla Mss.

72. The junta proposed to Philippe that he request a war vessel to intercept Reyes before he landed at Colon or Galveston. Valencia, p. 7. Also, conversations with Arce and Suarez.

73. Conversations with Arce and Suarez. Also, Rocco to the author, June 14, 1973.

74. Espriella to Bunau-Varilla, November 11, 1903. Bunau-Varilla, *The Creation*, p. 259.

75. Ibid.

76. Ehrman to Hay, November 10, 1903. Diplomatic correspondence relating to the negotiation, document no. 474.

77. Bunau-Varilla to Loomis, November 12, 1903, The Loomis Collection, box 4, folder 3.

78. *New York Tribune*, November 9, 1903, p. 2.

79. Ibid., November 13, p. 2.

80. *New York Times*, November 14, 1903, p. 2.

81. *New York Tribune*, November 14, 1903, p. 1.

82. Ibid., November 16, 1903, p. 1.

83. Bunau-Varilla to Loomis, November 12, 1903. Loomis collection, box 4, folder 3. Also, the *New York Tribune*, November 17, 1903, p. 1.

84. Ibid., November 20, 1903, p. 2.

85. Ibid.

86. Conversation with Suarez. Also, the *New York Tribune*, November 17, 1903, p. 2.

87. Ibid., November 17, 1903, p. 2. *Gil Blas, Le Petit Journal, Le Presse,* and *La Patrie* advocated this move. *L'Eclair* and *Le Temps* leaned toward the cancellation of the contract. Only *Le Matin* and *Le Galois* supported the status quo.

88. *New York Tribune*, November 17, 1903, p. 1.

89. Ibid., November 14, 1903, pp. 1, 2.

90. Ibid., Editorial, November 12, p. 8.

91. Ibid., November 13, 1903, p. 8.

92. Ibid., November 15, 1903, p. 8.

93. Ibid., November 7, 1903, p. 2.

94. Ibid., p. 1.

95. Ibid., November 17, 1903, p. 2; November 22, p. 2; November 29, p. 3; and November 30, p. 4. Senor Esteban Jaramillo, the foreign minister, addressed the communication to the Senate, while Cardinal Merry del Val, the pope's chancellor, received overtures from the Colombian envoy at the Vatican. Don Manuel Samper, financial agent of the French company, demanded cancellation of the agreement with the United States. Cipriano Castro of Venezuela rejected Colombia's appeal.

96. Ibid., November 22, 1903, p. 1.

97. Ibid., editorial, November 7, 1903.

98. Ibid., November 22, 1903, p. 2.

99. Ibid., November 10, 1903, p. 5, and editorial, *Louisville Courier Journal*, November 9, 1903.

100. *New York Tribune*, November 20, 1903, p. 1.

101. See the text of the Treaties of 1903 and 1978 in Appendix 3.

102. Bunau-Varilla, *The Creation*, p. 376.

103. Ibid., p. 378.

104. Espriella to Bunau-Varilla, November 20, 1903. Ibid., p. 379.

105. *New York Tribune*, November 21, 1903, p. 1. Also, Rocco to the author, September 18, 1974.

106. Ibid. Also the *New York Tribune*, November 18, p. 1.

107. Ibid., November 21, 1903, p. 1.

108. Ibid., and November 26, 1903, p. 1.

109. Ibid., November 19, 1903, p. 1.

110. Ibid., November 18, 1903, p. 2. Also, Rocco to the author, September 18, 1974.

111. *New York Tribune*, November 22, 1903, p. 1.

112. Rocco to the author, September 18, 1974. Also, Bunau-Varilla, *The Creation*, p. 383.

113. Editorial, *New York Tribune*, November 22, 1903.

114. Ibid.

115. *La Estrella de Panama*, November 18, 1903, p. 1; *El Cronista*, November 19, 1903, p. 1; and *El Lapiz*, November 19, 1903, p. 1. Amador's "popular choice" was engineered by his friends in the municipality of Panama City, who declared him "favorite son" to the detriment of Arango.

116. *New York Tribune*, November 18, 1903, p. 2.

117. Ibid., November 24, 1903, p. 2.

118. Loomis to Hay, December 10, 1903, Loomis Collection, box 4, folder 3. Reyes had written *in extenso* to Loomis and Roosevelt about this matter.

119. Conversations with Suarez and Arce.

120. Bunau-Varilla to Espriella, November 25, 1903. Bunau-Varilla, *The Creation*, p. 384.

121. Ibid., pp. 284–85. Also, the *New York Tribune*, November 23, 1903, p. 1, and November 27, p. 3.

122. Ibid., November 26, 1903, p. 1, and November 29, p. 1.

123. Rocco to the author, November 6, 1974. Also, Bunau-Varilla, *The Creation*, p. 388.

124. *New York Herald*, November 29, 1903, p. 1.

125. Ibid., editorial, November 27, 1903.

126. Bunau-Varilla, *The Creation*, p. 399.

127. *New York Tribune*, November 29, 1903, p. 1.

128. *New York Herald*, November 30, 1903, p. 1.

129. Bunau-Varilla, *The Creation*, pp. 405–14.

130. Ibid., p. 424. Also see U.S. Congress, House of Representatives, Committee on Foreign Affairs, *The Story of Panama: Hearings on the Rainey Resolution before the Committee on Foreign Affairs of the House of Representatives*, House Resolution no. 32, 62nd. Cong., 1st Sess. (Washington D.C.: Government Printing Office, 1913). Beers was the railroad agent at Colon, and Drake was one of the lawyers in Sullivan and Cromwell's firm.

131. Conversation with Suarez. Also, Rocco to the author, December 15, 1974. Eventually $6 million was left in the care of Cromwell to be invested in

real estate. See Ricardo J. Alfaro, "Manuel Amador Guerrero," *Loteria* (Panama City) no. 216 (1974), p. 44. High commissions paid to the investors and a bad market diminished this sum so greatly that, in 1940, the regime of Dr. Arnulfo Arias cancelled the agreement after heavy losses. Conversations with Manuel Roy.

132. Conversation with Loomis. Miss Loomis stated that "We really know nothing about Cromwell's role in these matters."

133. Espriella to Bunau-Varilla, December 2, 1903. Library of Congress, Bunau-Varilla mss.

134. The junta to Bunau-Varilla, December 2, 1903. Bunau-Varilla ms., p. 404.

135. Rocco to the author, November 10, 1973.

136. Ibid.

137. Loomis to Scrymser, November 19, 1903. Loomis Collection, box 4, folder 3.

138. Loomis to Hay, December 10, 1903. Loomis Collection, box 4, folder 3.

139. Bunau-Varilla, *The Creation*, p. 416.

140. *New York Herald*, December 6, 1903, p. 1, and December 10, p. 1.

141. Loomis to Landreth H. King, December 12, 1903. Loomis Collection, box 4, folder 3.

142. The Quill club, *Panama, November, 1903: Menu,* (New York, December 15, 1903). The dinner took place at the Hotel Manhattan and it consisted of the following: "Blue points, Petite marmite with celery and olives, Lobster à la Newburg, Saddle of lamb au jus with stuffed tomatoes and sweet potatoes, browned, Kirsch punch, Quail on toast; Macedoine salad, Biscuit glacé, Assorted cakes, and Coffee." Loomis Collection, box 4, folder 3.

143. Roosevelt to Loomis, December 17, 1903. Loomis Collection, box 4, folder 3.

144. Leo S. Rowe to Bunau-Varilla, December 19, 1903. Bunau-Varilla, *The Creation*, p. 415.

145. *New York Tribune*, December 18, 1903, p. 2, and December 20, p. 5.

146. Loomis to W. I. Buchanan, December 14, 1903, Loomis Collection, box 4, folder 3. Buchanan was still at Holland House, New York. Soon after, Morgan challenged his nomination to "a non-existent country." It was approved by the Senate, but Buchanan retired from his post a month later to become manager of Westinghouse Electric Company in Europe. He was replaced by William Worthington Russell, previously secretary to the legation in Caracas. See the *New York Tribune*, January 31, 1904, p. 2.

147. Ibid., December 30, 1903, p. 1. Also, conversation with Suarez.

148. Loomis to Bassett Moore, December 26, 1903. Loomis Collection, box 4, folder 3.

149. Snyder to Loomis, January 26, 1904, and Loomis to Herran, January 29, 1904. Loomis Collection, box 4, folder 3. John Snyder was the chargé d'affaires at Bogota.

150. Bassett Moore to Loomis, December 28, 1903. Loomis Collection, box 4, folder 3.

151. Loomis to Bassett Moore, December 31, 1903. Loomis Collection, box 4, folder 3.

152. *New York Tribune,* December 10, 1903, pp. 2, 3; and December 12, p. 1.

153. Bunau-Varilla to Hay, December 12, 1903. In correspondence, Rocco to the author, December 15, 1974.

154. *New York Tribune,* December 10, 1903, p. 2.

155. Ibid., December 8, 1903, p. 2, and December 10, p. 2.

156. Ibid., December 14, 1903, p. 1.

157. Ibid., December 15, 1903, p. 1; December 17, p. 9; and December 18, p. 1.

158. Ibid., December 19, 1903, p. 5.

159. Ibid., pp. 2, 5; December 20, 1903, p. 5; December 25, 1903; p. 2; and December 29, p. 1. Navy Secretary Moody ordered Elliott to "let Colombia take the initiative."

160. Conversations with General Esteban Huertas and Esteban Huertas Ponce. The officer entered the army as a *mochuelo* at the age of nine, and by the age of thirty-two, he had lost a hand in battle and had become a full general. Also, conversation with Alfaro and Arce. Also, the *New York Times,* March 29, 1975, p. 2, and the *Chicago Daily News,* November 9, 1903, p. 1.

161. Herbert Croly, *Marcus Alonzo Hanna: His Life and Work* (New York: Macmillan, 1912), p. 452.

162. Clapp, p. 306.

163. Rocco to the author, July 15, 1974.

164. *New York Tribune,* January 19, 1904, p. 1. Roosevelt to Bigelow, January 6, 1904, in Clapp, p. 312. The president categorically denied any collusion with Hay and Philippe, as the lawyer Mac Veagh had charged. Roosevelt said that Bunau-Varilla was a "very able fellow" whose business "was to find out what he thought the government would do . . . and to advise his people accordingly. . . . He would have been a very dull man had he been unable to make such a guess."

165. Hay to Reyes, January 5, 1904. Loomis Collection, box 4, folder 4. Also, Bunau-Varilla, *The Creation,* pp. 419–21.

166. *New York Sun,* editorial, January 28, 1904.

167. *New York World,* January 17, 1904, p. 1.

168. Seitz to Bunau-Varilla, July 2, 1909. Bunau-Varilla ms., Document G.

169. Committee on Foreign Affairs, *The Story of Panama,* pp. 6 ff.

170. Ibid., p. 71.

171. Bunau-Varilla, *The Creation,* p. 164.

172. Croly, pp. 325–26. $50,000 was returned to the Standard Oil Company in 1900, and $10,000 to some Wall Street bankers because they requested, by implication, particular services from the senator.

173. Committee on Foreign Affairs, *The Story of Panama,* p. 680.

174. Ibid., pp. 140, 365, 372–77, 680.

175. *New York Tribune,* January 21, 1904, p. 1.

176. *New York World,* October 4, 1904, p. 2.

177. Hay to Senator Cullom, January 20, 1904. Dwight C. Miner, *The Fight for the Panama Route* (New York: Columbia Univ. Press, 1940), p. 384.

178. Maryland Senator Gorman's pet scheme was the passage of a resolution offered by several of his colleagues calling for the investigation of the role of Roosevelt and Philippe in the revolution. The Committee on Foreign Relations was to be empowered to conduct hearings. Passage of the measure would have prolonged debate until the opening of the political campaign, when the House was to recess. Lodge, Platt of Connecticut, Cullom, and Foraker opposed the proposal. Conversation with Suarez.

179. At the annual meeting of the Aldin Association at Yale University on January 28, several professors including the institution's chaplain, Newman Smyth, attacked Panama. He thundered, "A treaty with Panama breaks the ten commandments. [Roosevelt made it read] 'thou shall not steal except in the interest of collective civilization.'" *New York Tribune,* January 29, 1904, p. 5.

180. Bogota purchased a steamer in New Orleans to transport troops and secure rifles from Belgium by the way of Guayaquil. Conversations with Alfaro and Arce.

181. Ibid. Also, the *New York Tribune,* January 10, 1904, p. 4, and January 31, p. 2.

182. Ibid., December 23, 1903, p. 3. However, the governor of Georgia and the national committeeman, Clark Howell, editor of the *Atlanta Constitution,* favored the treaty.

183. *New York Tribune,* p. 21, 1904, p. 1.

184. Ibid., January 28, 1904, p. 2.

185. *El Noticiero,* November 19, 1903, p. 1.

186. *El Comercio,* November 19, 1903, p.1.

187. *El Latinoamericano,* Editorial, November 15, 1903.

188. *El Telégrafo,* Editorial, November 21, 1903.

189. *El Chileno,* Editorial, November 25, 1903.

190. *La Estrella de Panama,* January 20, 1904, p. 1, and January 27, p. 1, and the *New York Tribune,* January 28, 1904, p. 2. Also, conversations with Arce, Alfaro, and Pablo Arosemena Forte.

191. Morgan attacked Philippe in the Senate, and Congressman C. Thayer of Massachusetts berated Roosevelt in the House. *New York Times,* February 2, 1904, p. 7.

192. Ibid., February 16, 1904, p. 1.

193. Ibid., February 9, 1904, p. 1, and V. C. Jones, "The Great Baltimore Fire," *American History Illustrated* (National Historical Society, Gettysburgh, Penn.), vol. 7, no. 6 (October 1972), pp. 4–9, 39–49. Only $50 million was covered by insurance.

194. *New York Times,* February 10, 1904, p. 1.

195. Croly, pp. 456–57.

196. *New York Times*, February 9, 1904, p. 9.

197. Ibid., editorial.

198. Ibid., editorial, February 15, 1904.

199. Ibid., February 19, 1904, p. 1; February 20, p. 2, and editorial; February 21, part 2, p. 2; February 22, p. 1; and February 24, p. 2.

200. Rocco to the author, November 5, 1974.

201. *New York Times*, February 23, 1904, p. 7, and February 21, part 2, p. 1.

202. Ibid.

203. Rocco to the author, April 15, 1973.

204. Conversations with Suarez. Also, the *New York Times*, February 26, 1904, p. 5.

205. Conversations with Alfaro and Arce. Also, the *New York Times*, February 27, 1904, p. 9. Amador had earlier refused the pen with which Philippe had signed the treaty on November 18, 1903, and which Philippe offered him at Union Station in Washington. It is now owned by Bunau-Varilla's heirs.

206. Amador Guerrero to Bunau-Varilla, February 24, 1904. Library of Congress, Bunau-Varilla ms.

207. Pablo Arosemena to Bunau-Varilla, February 27, 1904, in the Varillana of Philippe Bunau-Varilla II. Author's translation.

208. The franc was stabilized in those years at 4.22 per dollar. Rocco to the author, April 19, 1974.

209. John G. Walker, George W. Davis, William Barclay Parsons, Frank Hecker of Detroit, Benjamin Harrod, Edward Crusky, and William Burr finally made up the commission. Alfred Noble, of the earlier canal commission, did not accept appointment. *New York Times*, February 24, 1904, p. 1, and February 25, 1904, p. 1.

210. Rocco to the author, June 15, 1974. Also, W. J. Curtis, *Annual Address Delivered before the Alabama State Bar Association at Birmingham* (July 8, 1909), pp. 26–30.

211. Ibid.

212. Sullivan and Cromwell presented the new company with a bill for $800,000 because "Cromwell and his associates prevented a House vote in favor of the Morgan bill," and for other services to the corporation. Bunau-Varilla, *The Creation*, p. 164.

213. Conversation with Philippe Bunau-Varilla II.

214. Bunau-Varilla to Loomis, October 25, 1904. Loomis Collection, box 4, folder 3.

215. Ibid. Bunau-Varilla to Loomis, October 25, 1904. Loomis Collection, box 4, folder 3.

216. Ibid. Bunau-Varilla to Loomis, October 22, 1904. Porter was the American ambassador to France.

217. Loomis was defended in this ordeal by the evidence, by Hay, who labeled Bowen a rascal, and by Roosevelt himself. See Roosevelt to Loomis from Oyster Bay, September 27, 1905; William J. Pike to Loomis, June 24,

1905; Reid to Loomis, April 15, 1905; and Hay to Loomis, April 25, 1905. Hay considered an attack on Loomis an attack on himself. The Loomis Collection, box 4, folder 39.

218. Bunau-Varilla to Loomis, May 18, 1905. Loomis Collection, box 5, folder 3.

219. Virginia Fairweather, "The Forgotten Engineer: John Stevens and the Panama Canal," *Civil Engineering ASCE*, February 1975, p. 55.

220. Bunau-Varilla, *The Creation*, p. 81. Also, Rocco to the author, June 3, 1972.

221. Fairweather, p. 55.

222. Ibid. Also, conversations with Arce and Alfaro.

223. *Canal Record*, December 11, 1907, p. 1.

224. Ibid., July 29, 1908, p. 1.

225. Loomis Collection, box 5, folder 6. Philippe Bunau-Varilla, *The Strait of Panama* (Cincinnati: Cincinnati Publishing Co., 1924), pp. 20–21. These ideas were advanced publicly through the United States during 1924, and Philippe reappeared before the Commercial Club of Cincinnati on January 19, 1924.

226. Ibid.

227. Ibid., pp. 411–13.

228. Isthmian Canal Commission, *Report*, November 16, 1904.

229. Bunau-Varilla to Loomis, February 15, 1907. Loomis Collection, box 5, folder 6. By 1924, tonnage had reached 24 million.

230. Consulting Board, *Report*, p. 413.

231. Bunau-Varilla to Loomis, February 15, 1907. Loomis Collection, box 5, folder 6.

232. Ibid.

233. Alfred Noble, "The Strait of Panama." Speech at Stevens Technological Institute, February 15, 1909. Loomis Collection, box 5, folder 6. Also, Bunau-Varilla, *The Strait of Panama* (Cincinnati: Cincinnati Publishing Co., 1924).

Notes 10

1. Conversation with Florence Loomis.
2. Bunau-Varilla to Francis Loomis, April 11, 1907. Loomis Collection, box 5, folder 8.
3. Ibid.
4. Ibid., July 5, 1907.
5. Bunau-Varilla to Jose de Obaldia, May 3, 1909 (copy). Loomis Collection, box 5, folder 8.
6. Obaldia to Bunau-Varilla, May 13, 1909, in Bunau-Varilla to Loomis. Loomis Collection, box 5, folder 8.
7. Giselle Bunau-Varilla to the author, August 20, 1973.
8. *Encyclopedia Universal Illustrada* (Barcelona, 1924), vol. 30, p. 756.
9. Bunau-Varilla to Loomis, December 20, 1910. Loomis Collection, box 5, folder 8.
10. Bunau-Varilla to Loomis, September 1, 4, and 12, 1912. Loomis Collection, box 6, folder 8.
11. Ibid.
12. Ibid., Aug. 15, 1913.
13. November 4, 1913. Loomis Collection, box 6, folder 8.
14. Rocco to the author, August 20, 1973.
15. Bunau-Varilla to Loomis, November 4, 1913. Loomis Collection, box 6, folder 8.
16. Ibid. During their journey from Cincinnati to San Francisco, Loomis and Philippe visited the Warrengton Inn, in Warrengton, Indiana, where Lincoln and then Hay had slept during their youth.
17. Roosevelt to Loomis, July 6, 1914. Loomis Collection, box 6, folder 8.
18. Roosevelt to Loomis, July 21, 1914. Loomis Collection, box 6, folder 8.
19. *Canal Record,* vol. 7, no. 52 (August 19, 1914), p. 521, and M. M. Alba C., *Cronologia de los Gobernartes de Panama* (Panama, 1935), pp. 148–50.
20. Bunau-Varilla to Loomis, November 23, 1914. Loomis Collection, box 6, folder 8.
21. Ibid.
22. Rocco to the author, August 20, 1973.
23. Ibid.
24. Bunau-Varilla to Loomis, November 23, 1914. Loomis Collection, box 6, folder 8.

25. Bunau-Varilla to Loomis, April 15, 1915. Loomis Collection, box 6, folder 8.

26. Ibid.

27. Bunau-Varilla to Loomis, May 1, 1915. Loomis Collection, box 6, folder 8.

28. Ibid.

29. *Encyclopedia of Science and Technology*, (1966), vol. 14, p. 173. Also, conversation with Oscar Carrera, M.D.

30. *New York Times*, Editorial, February 7, 1904.

31. For a history of chlorination in the United States, see G. M. Fair, J. C. Geyer, and D. A. Okun, *Water and Wastewater Engineer* (New York: John Wiley and Sons, 1968), vol. 2.

32. Bunau-Varilla, *Les victoires éclatantes de la Verdunisation* (Paris: Librarie J. B. Balliere & Fils, 1938), pp. 25–27.

33. Ibid., p. 28. Also, Rocco to the author, August 20, 1973.

34. Bunau-Varilla, *Les Victoires*, p. 29.

35. Rocco to the author, August 20, 1973.

36. Ibid.

37. Bunau-Varilla to Loomis, from the battlefront near Verdun, January 19, 1917. Loomis Collection, box 5, folder 8.

38. Bunau-Varilla to Loomis, May 23, 1919. Loomis Collection, box 5, folder 8.

39. Rocco to the author, July 27, 1973. For an account of the Battle of Verdun, see J. B. W. Gardiner and Thomas Y. Ybarra, *How the War Was Lost and Won* (New York: Harper, 1920), pp. 182–97.

40. Henry Cabot Lodge to Bunau-Varilla, July 12, 1924. Loomis Collection, box 5, folder 8. Also, conversations with Henry Cabot Lodge II, March 1973, and with Florence Loomis.

41. Bunau-Varilla to Loomis, June 25, 1923. Loomis Collection, box 5, folder 8.

42. See Gustav Anguizola, "The Making of a Treaty, *Arlington Quarterly* (University of Texas at Arlington), vol. 2, no. 2 (Spring 1971), pp. 191–200, and Alba C., pp. 154–55.

43. Narciso Garay to the author, June 11, 1952.

44. Alba C., p. 153.

45. Conversation with Enrique Arce.

46. *Figaro*, March 22, 1923, p. 1.

47. Bunau-Varilla to Loomis, June 25, 1923. Loomis Collection, box 5, folder 8. Also, Rocco to the author, December 5, 1973.

48. Philippe Bunau-Varilla, *The Creation, Destruction and Resurrection* (New York: McBride, Nast and Co., 1914), pp. 284 ff.

49. Paul R. Leach, *That Man Dawes* (Chicago: Reilly and Lee Co., 1930), pp. 13–14, 46–57.

50. Bunau-Varilla to Loomis, September 26, 1924. Loomis Collection, box 6, folder 8. Also, Autographed Letters Signed Collection (A.L.S. Collec-

tion), Newberry Library, Price Bell ms; Virginia Butts to the author, June 5, 1975.

51. Conversation with Diego Suarez. Also, Rocco to the author, September 15, 1973.

52. To appreciate Mellon's financial reforms, see Philip H. Lowe, *Andrew W. Mellon: The Man and His Work* (Baltimore: F. H. Coggins and Co., 1929).

53. Bunau-Varilla to Loomis, September 26, 1924. Loomis Collection, box 6, folder 8.

54. Leach, pp. 196–213. For a detailed explanation of the complicated agreement known as the Dawes Plan, see League of Nations, *Monthly Bulletin of Statistics* (Geneva), January–December 1924, and December 1925, and Dennys P. Myers, *The Reparation Settlement*, World Peace Foundation Pamphlets (Boston, 1929), vol. 12, no. 5, pp. 809–17.

55. Bunau-Varilla to Loomis, September 26, 1924. Loomis Collection, box 6, folder 8.

56. *Le Figaro*, August 15, 1926, p. 1, and *Paris Herald*, August 15, 1926, p. 1.

57. Bunau-Varilla to Price Bell, August 31, 1926. Newberry Library, A.L.S. Collection, Price Bell ms.

58. Bunau-Varilla to Price Bell, September 1, 1926. A.L.S. Collection, Price Bell ms.

59. Ibid. Also, *Le Figaro*, June 5, 1926, p. 1.

60. Price Bell to William Dennis from Paris, September 2, 1926. A.L.S. Collection, Price Bell ms.

61. Bunau-Varilla to Loomis, December 18, 1926. Loomis Collection, box 6, folder 8.

62. Bunau-Varilla to Price Bell, September 4, 1926. A.L.S. Collection, Price Bell ms.

63. David Bryn-Jones, *Frank B. Kellogg* (New York: G. P. Putnam's Sons, 1937), p. 222.

64. Rocco to the author, August 20, 1974.

65. *Le Matin*, April 7, 1927, p. 1, and *La Lanterne*, April 6, 1927, p. 1.

66. Henry Cabot Lodge, *Selections from the Correspondence of Theodore Roosevelt and Henry Cabot Lodge* (New York: Scribner's, 1925), pp. 153–63, Lodge to Roosevelt, July 6, 9, 12, 1905, and Roosevelt to Lodge, July 16, 1905. Also, Lodge to Bunau-Varilla, July 12, 1924, Loomis Collection, box 5, folder 3.

67. James Thomson Shotwell, *War as an Instrument of National Policy*, (London: Constable and Co., 1929), p. 39.

68. See Allan Keller "Over the Atlantic Alone," *American History Illustrated*, vol. 9, no. 1 (April 1974), pp. 38–45.

69. After the rejection of the treaty which was to supplant the Taft Convention on January 27, 1927, Panama's National Assembly, highly emotional, recommended to future generations of Panamanians to "damn forever Philippe's name." Conversation with Arce.

70. Rocco to the author, March 22, 1973. Also, conversation between

Eusebio A. Morales and Anguizola, Jr., as related to the author by Anguizola, Jr., in conversation.

71. Shotwell, p. 67.

72. Bunau-Varilla to Loomis, August 8, 1926, Loomis Collection, box 6, folder 8. Also, Rocco to the author, June 15, 1973.

73. Dennys P. Meyers, *Origin and Conclusion of the Paris Pact*, World Peace Foundation Pamphlets, (Boston, 1929), vol. 12, no. 2, pp. 45–56. The nations were Australia, Belgium, Canada, Czechoslovakia, France, Germany, Great Britain, India, Ireland, Italy, Japan, New Zealand, Poland, South Africa, and the United States. For his work in promoting world peace, Baron Shidehara of Japan nominated Bell for the Nobel Peace Prize in 1931.

74. Bryn-Jones, pp. 248–49, 257.

75. Bunau-Varilla to Loomis, July 13, 1931. Loomis Collection, box 6, folder 8.

76. *San Francisco Chronicle*, June 29, 1914, p. 1.

77. Loomis to Bunau-Varilla, April 26, 1935, and Bunau-Varilla to Loomis, May 19, 1935. Loomis Collection, box 6, folder 8.

78. Bunau-Varilla to Loomis, December 9, 1928. Loomis Collection, box 6, folder 8.

79. Rocco to the author, June 15, 1973.

80. Southam Craivanich, "Chlorination and Ozonation of Sewage Affluents" (Master's thesis, University of Texas at Arlington, 1973), p. 8.

81. Philippe Bunau-Varilla, *Chemical Radiolisis* (Paris: Librairie J. B. Ballière et fils, 1926), p. 7, and idem, *Les Victoires*, p. 45.

82. Ibid., p. 9.

83. Ibid., p. 48.

84. Ibid., p. 43.

85. Ibid.

86. Ibid., p. 23, and *Le Matin*, May 26, 1925, p. 1.

87. Bunau-Varilla, *Chemical Radiolisis*, p. 9.

88. Ibid., pp. 62–63. Carrel, a celebrated brain surgeon, wrote *Man the Unknown*.

89. Bunau-Varilla, *L'Assainissement National: Conference de M. Philippe Bunau-Varilla au Club du Faubourg* (January 24, 1935), and idem, *Les Victoires*, pp. 33–34.

90. Ibid., p. 43.

91. Ibid., pp. 12–13.

92. Ibid., p. 31.

93. Rocco to the author, September 25, 1972. Each Italian soldier carried chlorination tablets to dilute in specific quantities of water.

94. Bunau-Varilla, *Les Victoires*, pp. 84–85. For a detailed account of Philippe's contribution to the chlorination technique, see his works: *Quelques Documents sur la Verdunisation des Eaux* (Paris: Ballière & Fils, 1938), and *Les Victoires*.

95. Bunau-Varilla to Loomis, April 14, 1929. Loomis Collection, box 6,

folder 8. Loomis was in London on his way to The Hague. From there he went to Paris.

96. Ibid., January 4, 1931. Loomis visited Philippe again in late 1930.

97. Ibid., May 19, 1935.

98. Rocco to the author, August 20, 1973.

99. Bunau-Varilla to Loomis, August 7, 1935. Loomis Collection, box 6, folder 8.

100. Bunau-Varilla, *Les Victoires*, pp. 84–85, 62–23.

101. *Le Matin*, September 11, 1936, p. 1; *Le Petit Parisien*, September 11, 1936, p. 1; and the *New York Herald*, September 11, 1936, p. 1.

102. Alexis Carrel to Bunau-Varilla, September 12, 1936. Bunau-Varilla, *Les Victoires*, p. 63.

103. Philippe Bunau-Varilla, *The Great Adventure of Panama* (London: Doubleday, Page & Co., 1920), p. 34.

104. Bunau-Varilla to Loomis, April 1, 1905. Loomis Collection, box 6, folder 8.

105. Ibid.

106. Emile Fraguet, *The Cult of Incompetence*, trans. by Beatrice Barstow (New York: E. P. Dutton & Co., 1913), pp. 1–23, 140–51; and Raymond Poincaré, *How France is Governed*, trans. by Bernard Miall (New York: McBride, Nast and Co., 1914), pp. 161-204. For an account of the quick deterioration of the Third Republic, see Sir Denis William Brogan, *France, History of the Third Republic: 1870-1940* (London: H. Hamilton, 1967); William Lawrence Shirer, *The Collapse of the Third Republic: An Inquiry Into the Fall of France* (New York: Simon & Schuster, 1969); and Hamilton Fish Armstrong, *Chronology of Failure: The Last Days of the French Third Republic* (New York: Macmillan, 1941).

107. Paul Reynaud, *In the Thick of the Fight: 1930–1945* (New York: Simon and Schuster, 1955); Robert Mengin, *No Laurels for de Gaulle*, trans. by J. Allen (New York: Farrar, Straus & Giroux, 1960); and Ives Bouthillier, *Le Drame de Vichy* (Paris: Librairie Plon, 1950–1951).

108. *Le Petit Parisien*, July 16, 1938, p. 1, and Philippe Bunau-Varilla, *Les 19 documents: Clés du Drame de Panama* (Paris: Librairie Plon, 1938), Document J, pp. 100–1. The Grand Cross was awarded to him on July 14, 1938, but the actual presentation took place on September 12.

109. Petain to Bunau-Varilla, July 13, 1938. Author's copy from Philippe Bunau-Varilla II.

110. Bunau-Varilla to Loomis, February 5, 1938. Loomis Collection, box 6, folder 8. Philippe suffered a severe attack of grippe with pulmonary congestion in the winter of 1938.

111. Ibid.

112. Bunau-Varilla to Loomis, May 16, 1939. Loomis Collection, box 6, folder 8.

113. Ibid., April 21, 1940.

114. *New York Times*, May 12, 1940, pp. 32, 34.

115. Rocco to the author, August 20, 1973.

116. *New York Times*, May 17, 1940, p. 1.

117. Ibid.

118. Conversation with André Geraud. Geraud, who wrote under the pseudonym Pertinax, was one of the most influential journalists of his time. He wrote for *L'Echo de Paris*, the *Pall Mall Gazette*, and the *Daily Telegraph* of London, and was a frequent contributor to the *New York Tribune*, the *Baltimore Sun*, and the *New York Times*. Also, Rocco to the author, August 20, 1973.

119. Ibid.

120. Bunau-Varilla to Loomis, June 25, 1923. Loomis Collection, box 5, folder 8.

121. *Loteria* (Panama City), no. 217 (March 1974), pp. 1–9; no. 218 (April), pp. 44–49; and no. 219 (May), pp. 1–23.

122. Alexander Olivier Exquemelin, *The Buccaneers of America* (London: George Allen and Unwin, 1951), pp. xx-xxi, 206–38, and Robert Carse, *The Age of Piracy* (New York: Rinehart, 1957), pp. 160–64. The Spaniards lost Panama to Morgan for three weeks in January 1671, in the same way the French lost the battle of Agincourt in 1415. Heavy rains softened the ground, and the Spanish cavalry sank into it and became easy prey to the buccaneers. Morgan withdrew to Port Royal after hearing that a fleet was approaching from Peru, cheated his followers of their share of the loot, and retired to Jamaica to become its governor.

Notes Appendix 1

1. Some of Antonio Varilla's works are *La Politique de les Maisons d'Autriche* (Paris, 1658); *Histoires du Regne de Saint Louis* (Paris, 1684); *Les Anecdotes de Florence* (Paris, 1685); *Histoire des Revolutions Arrives dans l'Europe en Matiere de Religion* (Paris, 1681–1689); *Histoire des Heresies, 1374–1589* (Paris, 1686); *Histoire de France* (from the reign of Louis XI to Henry III) (Paris, 1688); *Histoire d'Espagne* (from the reign of Ferdinand of Aragon to the beginning of the reign of Charles I) (Paris, 1689); *Histoire de Charles IX*, 2 vols. (Paris, 1685); *Histoire de Louis XII*, 3 vols. (Paris, 1688); and *Histoire d'Henry III*, 2 vols. (Paris, 1694). Conversation with Madame Guy Lathan, January 1944. She was the author's French teacher at preparatory school. Conversations with Federico Brid, March 1955; he was the author's French history teacher. Conversations with Don Carlos Manuel Gallegos, August 1965. Professor Gallegos, an educational official of Panama, retired to Barcelona, in 1954. As he was an old friend of my father's, I asked his cooperation in researching the ancestry of Bunau-Varilla and other prominent figures of his time. I was pleasantly surprised when, in the summer of 1965, he told me to return to Spain immediately. (I was engaged in an archeological excavation in Greece at the time.) At his home in Barcelona and in my room in the Hotel Barcelona, the old professor regaled me with historical information about many prominent people. Besides the information he conveyed to me about Bunau-Varilla (Senor Gallegos had visited France five times during the previous four years), he also had much data on such men as Jose Domingo de Obaldia, Manuel Amador Guerrero, Carlos Constantino Arosemena, Federico Boyd, Francisco de la Espriella, Belisario Porras, presidents Sanclemente and Marroquin, Tomas Herran, Jose Vicente Concha, and Carlos Martinez Silva. He startled me with much information about my own ancestors. Also, *Enciclopedia Ilustrada* (Madrid, Espasa-Calpe, 1958), vol. 9, p. 1403; vol. 67, p. 79.

2. Conversations with Gallegos and Lathan. Antonio Varilla probably named his son "Philippe" in gratitude for the patronage of Philippe d' Orleans. By royal consent, a French consortium established the French *Asiento* Company, which was expanded in 1703 to allow French vessels to proceed from Spanish ports to the South Seas in order to trade there. See William Spence Robertson, *History of the Latin American Nations*, 2d ed. (New York: Appleton and Co., 1932), pp. 166–82. Many of the fortunes inherited by

Latin-American revolutionary leaders such as Simon Bolivar and the Carrera brothers, heroes of the independence of Chile, have their origin in the philosophy of trade espoused by Campillo. Alexander Bunau's father was a natural son of Count Henry. The Varillas kept transliterating the first name "Felipe" or "Philippe", depending on where they lived—Spain and her empire or France and her possessions.

3. Robertson, pp. 166–82. Spain's colonial policy began to change rapidly after the arrival of the Bourbon dynasty. The intelligence behind the new order of things was the influential royal minister Campillo, who wrote the *Nuevo Sistema de gobierno económico para la América* (Madrid, 1793). Beginning in 1741, Campillo insisted on a survey of the colonial economy and of the excessive accumulation of property in mortmain by the church. He championed the identity of the Creoles as well as the Indians.

4. Conversations with Gallegos and Lathan. Also, Giselle Rocco to the author, June 7, 1972. Brabant is a province in Central Belgium, south of the Netherlands, but the name was generally applied in those days to the inhabitants of the Catholic provinces in the Low Country. The Scheldt, named by the French Escaut River, flows from northern France through western Belgium and the southwest Netherlands into the sea. Navigation of the river had been prohibited by the Treaty of Wesphalia in order to hinder the economic prosperity of the Brabants but, when the Treaty of Utrecht was signed, the provinces passed from Spain to Austria and the navigation of the waterway was permitted. The Dutch cities, through secret subsidies, kept the river closed and, after the Treaty of Fontainebleau in 1785, the river was to remain permanently closed. For an account of the complicated financial transaction involving Joseph II, see The Princess Lamballe, *Secret Memoirs of the Royal Family of France* (London: H. S. Nichols & Co., 1895).

5. Harry Damm, Sr., to the author, August 19, 1947, and Harry Damm, Jr., to the author, July 23, 1973; August 19, 20, 25, and 26, 1973. Harry Damm, Jr.'s mother was an Ebert, related to Friedrich Ebert, Socialist leader and president of the Weimar Republic. The Eberts, whose ancestors had been saddle merchants, also claim to be related to Count Henry Bunau. The American Damms were furniture merchants.

Notes Appendix 2

1. Emory Adams Allen, *Our Canal in Panama* (Cincinnati: Cincinnati Publishing Co., 1913), pp. 83–85. Also, Giselle Bunau-Varilla Rocco to the author, July 15, 1972.

2. Talleyrand believed that the opening up of the Suez route would react on England in the same fatal way that the discovery of the Cape of Good Hope ruined Genoa and Venice.

3. It was through Barras, a powerful member of the Directory, that Napoleon met Josephine, and it was through Josephine that Barras influenced the young, visionary, and seemingly unruly Bonaparte.

4. Ferdinand de Lesseps, *Souvenir de Quarante Ans*, 2 vols. (London: Chapman and Hall, 1887). He was vice-consul in Lisbon in 1825, in Tunis in 1837, in Alexandria in 1832; consul at Cairo, 1833–1837, at Rotterdam, 1837, and then at Malaga, Spain; consul-general to Barcelona, 1844–1848; and minister to Madrid, 1848–1849. He was special envoy to Rome at the time of the abortive revolution that created a short-lived democratic regime, 1849. His liberal sympathy for these volatile republicans caused his retirement from the diplomatic service in 1850.

5. Edgar G. Bonnet, *Ferdinand de Lesseps* (Paris: Librairie Plon 1951), vol. 1, pp. 33–91. Perhaps de Lesseps was the product of his age. Most people born near the Age of Reason secretly believed in their stars—among them Napoleon, Laplace, Talleyrand, Bolivar, San Martin, Francia, and Disraeli. In our own time, many notables have taken precautions in order to assure themselves of success. Churchill, Mussolini, Hitler, and Franklin Delano Roosevelt were fond of consulting the astrologers. During his visits to Panama after 1933, F.D.R. and his wife invariably consulted the Costa Rican star gazer Marco A. Fernandez. (Marco A. Fernandez to the author, August 15, 1937.) Senor Fernandez was often spirited away in the very early morning hours in a presidential limousine which punctually arrived at the Hotel Colon at 3:00 A.M. On more than two occasions, I witnessed the departure of this man in this way. My father and I used to live at this hotel while visiting Panama.

6. Bonnet, vol. 1, pp. 33–91.

7. Ibid.

8. Ibid.

9. Ibid.

10. De Lesseps was a cousin of Eugenie de Montijo, the French empress.

11. *London Times*, July 8, 1856, p. 2, and *Le Matin* (Paris), July 15, 1856, p. 2.

12. Bonnet, vol. 2, pp. 153–60. The approaching Civil War in the United States and the oncoming Austro-Prussian conflict had much to do with their abstention. As for Russia, she was still in a bad mood after signing the Peace of Paris of 1856, which for all practical purposes expelled her from the Black Sea.

13. *London Globe*, editorial, November 30, 1858. Publications such as the *Edinburg Review, Economist*, and *Saturday Review of Literature* joined the *London Times* and other periodicals in consistently attacking de Lesseps and his canal.

14. *Le Matin* (Paris), July 7, 1864, p. 1.

15. Ibid., March 20, 1866, p. 1. The English built their railroad using thousands of *fellahs* and without Turkey's approval. Not a voice was raised about "revival of slavery" then.

16. *Bulletin de la Compagnie Universalle du Canal Maritime de Suez*, Paris, 1867–1868.

17. Gustave Anguizola, "The Negro in the Building of the Panama Canal," *Phylon: Review of Race and Culture*, vol. 29, no. 4 (1970), pp. 351–60.

18. *Le Matin* (Paris), May 1, 1868, and July 19, 1868, p. 1.

19. *Le Matin* (Paris), August 15, 16, 18, 19, 1869. One speaker compared the inauguration of the canal with the dedication of the Parthenon in 437 B.C. Another prophesied that soon other seas and oceans would be joined by man. More than 6,000 official guests drank 20,000 bottles of champagne and as much liquor in ten days of celebrations. Ten tons of fireworks were used in a brilliant display of pyrotechnics, and 1,700 cooks and waiters joined a retinue of 5,000 native servants in the task of feeding and pampering the guests. Ricardo Zozaya to the author, July 19, 1940. Maestro Zozaya was a music teacher at the Lyceum in Panama. Also, conversation with Pablo Picasso, July 1966, on the occasion of a visit to France and the town of Varilla by the author.

20. *Star & Herald* (Panama City), December 31, 1879, p. 1.

21. London *Times*, April 15, 1870. Editorial. De Lesseps was not bereft of friends in England, for he enjoyed the esteem of Thomas Waghorn, who had tried unsuccessfully to enlist his countrymen in the canal project.

Bibliography

Books

Abbot, Willis John. *Panama and the Canal in Picture and Prose*. New York, 1913.

Abbott, John S. C. *The History of Napoleon Bonaparte*. New York, 1854.

Adam, C. and Tannery, P. *Oeuvres de Descartes*. Paris, 1913.

Adams, Henry. *The Education of Henry Adams*. Boston, 1918.

Aeschylus. *The Eumenides in The Complete Greek Drama*, edited by Whitney J. Oates and Eugene O'Neill, Jr. New York, 1938.

Aguilera, Fito. *Cincuenta Millas de Heroicidad*. Panama City, 1934.

Alba, Manuel Maria. *Cronología de los Gobernates de Panama*. Panama, 1935.

Alba, Manuel Maria. *Cronología de los Gobernates de Panama*. Panama, 1967.

Alfaro, Ricardo J. *Vida del General Tomás Herrera*. Panama, 1946.

Allen, Emory Adams. *Our Canal in Panama*. Cincinnati, 1913.

Ammen, Daniel. *American Isthmian Canal Routes*. Philadelphia, 1889.

Ammen, Daniel. *The Old Navy and the New*. Philadelphia, 1891.

Anderson, C. L. G. *Old Panama and Castilla del Oro*. Washington, 1911.

Angeli, Hildergarde. *Simón Bolívar*. New York, 1930.

Anghiera, Pietro Martire d'. *De Rebus Oceanicus il Orbe Novodeuxieme Decades*, edited by Paul Gaffarel. Dijon, 1895.

Anghiera, Pietro Martire d'. *Décadas del Nuevo Mundo*, edited by Edmundo O'Gorman and Agustin Millares Carlo. Mexico City, 1964.

Anguizola, Gustave. *Human Rights and Civil Liberties in Panama*. Washington D.C., 1977.

Anguizola, Gustave. *Isthmian Political Instability: 1821-1976*, Washington D.C., 1977, 1978.

Anguizola, G. *The Taft Convention*. Panama, 1955.

Arango, José Augustín. *Datos para la Historia de la Independencia del Istmo*. Panama, 1922.

Arbeláez, Enrique Pérez. *José Celestino Mútis y la Real Expedición Botánica del Nuevo Reino de Granada*. Bogota, 1967.

Arce, Enrique J. *Guia Histórica de Panama*. Panama, 1942.

Arce, Enrique J. *Historia de Panama*. Panama, 1934.

Arciniegas, German. *The Knight of El Dorado*. New York, 1968.

Arias, Harmodio. *The Panama Canal*. London, 1911.

Armstrong, Hamilton Fish. *Chronology of Failure: The Last Days of the French Third Republic*. New York, 1941.

447

Arosemena, Mariano. *Apuntamientos Históricos*. Panama, 1949.

Arosemena, Mariano. *Independencia del Istmo*. Panama, 1959.

Arosemena, Justo. *El Estado Federal de Panama*. Panama, 1855.

Arrocha, Graell Catalino. *Historia de la Independencia de Panama*. Panama, 1934.

Atkins, John. *A Voyage to Guinea, Brazil, and the West Indies*. London, 1735.

Bailey, Helen Miller and Nasatir, Abraham P. *Latin America*. New Jersey, 1960.

Barras, Jean Nicolas. *Memoires*. Translation by Charles E. Roche. London, 1895-96.

Beale, Howard K. *Theodore Roosevelt and the Rise of America to World Power*. Baltimore, 1956.

Beatty, Charles. *De Lesseps of Suez: The Man and His Times*. New York, 1956.

Belly, Felix. *L'isthme de Panama*. Paris, 1858.

Biesany, John, and Biesany, Mavis. *The People of Panama*. New York, 1955.

Bigelow, John. *Breaches of Anglo-American Treaties: A Study in History and Diplomacy*. New York, 1917.

Bigelow, John. *Report to the Chamber of Commerce of New York on His Trip of Inspection of the Panama Canal in February, 1886*. New York, 1886.

Bigelow, John. *Retrospective of an Active Life*. New York, 1913.

Bilbao, Francisco. *La America en Peligro*. Santiago, 1941.

Bishop, Farnham. *Panama, Past and Present*. New York, 1913.

Bishop, Joseph Bucklin. *The Panama Gateway*. New York, 1913.

Bishop, Joseph Bucklin. *Theodore Roosevelt and His Time*. 2 vols. New York, 1920.

Blake, Robert. *Disraeli*. New York, 1967.

Bonnet, Edgar. *Ferdinand de Lesseps*. Paris, 1951.

Borda, Orlando Fals. *La Subversión en Colombia: El Compendio Social en la Historia*. Bogota, 1961.

Borda, Orlando Fals. *La Subversión en Colombia: Vision del Cambio Social en la Historia*. Bogotá, 1968.

Bosquet, J. *Comunicación entre el Señor Carlos Biddle, Coronel de los Estados Unidos del Norte y la Sociedad Amigos del País*. Panama City, 1836.

Boyd, Federico. *Exposición Histórica Acerca de los Motivos que Causaron la Separación de Panama de la República de Colombia en 1903*. Panama, 1911.

Brinton, Crane C. *The Americans and the French*. Cambridge, 1968.

Brinton, John. *Aramaco World*. Vol. 20. 1969.

Brogan, Sir Dennis William. *France, History of the Third Republic: 1870-1940*. London, 1967.

Bruun, Geoffrey. *Clemenceau*. Cambridge, 1943.

Bryn-Jones, David. *Frank B. Kellogg*. New York, 1937.

Bunau-Varilla, Philippe. *Chemical Radiolisis*. Paris, 1926.

Bunau-Varilla, Philippe. *Comparative Characteristics of Panama and Nicaragua*. New York, 1902.

Bunau-Varilla, Philippe. *From Panama to Verdun: My Fight for France*. Philadelphia, 1940.

Bunau-Varilla, Philippe. *The Great Adventure of Panama*. London, 1920.

Bunau-Varilla, Philippe. *Panama—Le Passe, le Present, l'Avenir.* Paris, 1892.
Bunau-Varilla, Philippe. *Panama or Nicaragua?* New York, 1901.
Bunau-Varilla, Philippe. *Panama: The Creation, Destruction, and Resurrection.* New York, 1914.
Bunau-Varilla, Philippe. *Quelques Documents sur la Verdunisation des Eaux.* Paris, 1932.
Bunau-Varilla, Philippe. *The Strait of Panama.* Cincinnati, 1924.
Burr, Aaron. *Memoirs.* Edited by Mathew L. Denis. New York, 1958.
Bury, J. B. *History of the Later Roman Empire.* London, 1889.
Butler, O. F. *Studies in the life of Eliogabalus.* New York, 1908.
Caldas, Jose de. *Escritos Varios.* Bogota, 1803.
Calderon, Francisco Garcia. *Latin America, Its Rise and Progress.* London, 1911.
Callejas, B. Santander. *Resumen Político de la Administración del Dr. Manuel Amador Guerrero.* Panama, 1933.
Camacho-Leyva, Ernesto. *Quick Colombian Facts.* Bogota, 1946.
Canal Record. Ancon. C. Z. 1907-1914.
Cano, B. Sanin. *Administración Reyes, 1904-1909.* Lausane, 1909.
Capers, Gerald M. *Encyclopedia Americana.* Vol. 7. New York, 1970.
Cardenas, Raul de. *China en la Apertura del Canal de Panama.* La Habana, 1929.
Carles, Ruben D. *Historia del Canal de Panama.* Panama, 1973.
Carles, Ruben D. *A 150 Años de la Independencia de Panama de España 1821-1971.* Panama, 1960.
Carles, Ruben D. *The Centennial City of Colon.* Panama, 1952.
Carles, Ruben D. *Comunicación Interoceánica.* Panama, 1973.
Carse, Robert. *The Age of Piracy.* New York, 1957.
Casas, Fray Bartolome de las. *Brevísima Relación de la Destrucción de las Indias.* Sevilla, 1552.
Castillero, R. Ernesto de J. *Documentos Históricos acerca de la Independencia del Istmo de Panama.* Panama, 1930.
Castillero, R. Ernesto de J. *El Doctor Manuel Amador Guerrero Procer de la Independencia y Primer Presidente de la Republica de Panama.* Panama, 1933.
Castillero, R. Ernesto de J. *Episodios de la Independencia de Panama.* Panama, 1957.
Castillero, R. Ernesto de J. *Historia de la Comunicación Interocéanica y de Su Influencia en la Formación y en el Desarrollo de la Entidad Nacional Panameña.* Panama, 1941.
Castillero, R. Ernesto de J. *La Causa Immediata de la Emancipación de Panama.* Panama, 1933.
Castillero, R. Ernesto de J. *Panama: Breve Historia de la República.* Buenos Aires, 1939.
Cermoise, A. *Deux Ans a Panama.* Paris, 1886.
Chapman, Guy. *The Third Republic of France.* New York, 1962.
Chen, T. T. *Research in Protozoology.* 4 vols. New York, 1967-69.
Chevalier, Michael. *L'Isthme de Panama.* Paris, 1844.
Chincholle, G. *Le General Boulanger.* Paris, 1889.

Clapp, Margarett. *Forgotten First Citizen—John Bigelow.* Boston, 1947.

Clemenceau, Georges. *Contre la Justice.* Paris, 1902.

Clemenceau, Georges. *Vers la Reparation.* Paris, 1899.

Clifton, Francis, M.D. *Hippocrates upon Air, Water, and Sanitation.* London, 1734.

Congres International d'Etudes du Canal Interoceanique. *Compte Rendu des Seances.* Paris, 1879.

Congressional Record. (59th Cong. 2nd Sess. to 90th Cong. 2nd Sess.). Washington, D.C.

Corbitt, Duvon Clough. *A Study of the Chinese in Cuba, 1847-1947.* Wilmore, Kentucky, 1971.

Cortissoz, Royal. *The Life of Whitelaw Reid.* New York, 1921.

Croiset, M. *Essai sur la Vie et les Oeuvres de Lucien.* Paris, 1882.

Croly, Herbert. *Marcus Alonzo Hanna: His Life and Work.* New York, 1912.

Cullen, Edward. *The Isthmus of Darien Ship Canal.* London, 1852.

Curtis, William Elroy. *The Capitals of Spanish America.* New York, 1886.

Curtis, William Elroy. *The Land Where It Is Always Summer.* New York, 1891.

Dansette, A. *Histoire des Presidents de la Republique.* Paris, 1953.

Dansette, A. *Le Boulangerisme.* Paris, 1938.

Davis, Rear Admiral Charles H. *Report on Interoceanic Canals and Railroads between the Atlantic and Pacific Oceans.* Washington, 1867.

Dean, Arthur H. *William Nelson Cromwell.* New York, 1957.

Dennett, Tyler. *John Hay: From Poetry to Politics.* New York, 1934.

De Wet, Christian R. *South African War, 1899-1902.* New York, 1902.

Dozer, Donald Marquand. *Latin America: An Interpretive History.* New York, 1962.

Dreyfus, Alfred. *Five Years of My Life.* New York, 1901.

Dreyfus, Alfred, and Dreyfus, Pierre. *The Dreyfus Case.* New Haven, 1937.

Drumont, Edouard. *The Last Battle.* Paris, 1890.

DuVal, Captain Miles P., Jr. *Cadiz to Cathay: The Story of the Long Struggle for a Waterway across the American Isthmus.* Stanford University, 1940.

Edgar-Bonnet, G. *Ferdinand de Lesseps.* Paris, 1951.

Edwards, Albert. *Panama: The Canal, the Country and the People.* New York, 1913.

Esguerra, Nicolas. *Canal de Panama-Escritos.* Bogota, 1903.

Euripides. *Medea.* Edited by Mortimer Lawson Earle. New York, 1904.

Exquemelin, Alexander Olivier, *The Buccaneers of America.* London, 1951.

Finlay, Carlos E. *Carlos Finlay and Yellow Fever.* New York, 1940.

Fisher, J. B. *Le Sauvetage du Canal de Panama.* Paris, 1934.

Fombona, Rufino Blanco. *El Pensamiento Vivo de Bolívar.* Buenos Aires, 1942.

Forot, Victor. *L'Ingenieur Godin de Lepinay.* Paris, 1910.

Frank, Tanney. *Economic Survey of Ancient Rome.* New Jersey, 1959.

Friedman, Lee Max. *Alfred Dreyfus—1859–1935.* New York, 1966.

Frontinus, Sextus Julius. *The Stratagems and the Aqueducts of Rome.* Translation by Charles E. Bennett. London, 1961.

Gallegos, Manuel Modesto. *Generales Antonio Guzman Blanco y Joaquín Crespo.* Caracas, 1934.

Garay, Narciso. *Es el Nuevo Tratado entre Panama y Los Estados Unidos una Alianza Militar?* Panama, 1937.

Garraty, John A. *Henry Cabot Lodge: A Biography.* New York, 1953.

Gaulle, Charles de. *The Army of the Future.* Philadelphia, 1941.

Gaxote, Pierre. *Histoire de France.* Paris, 1960.

Gershoy, Leon. *The French Revolution and Napoleon.* New York, 1933.

Gerster, Arpad. *Recollections of a New York Surgeon.* New York, 1917.

Geyer, J. C. and Okun, D. A. *Water and Wastewater Engineer.* Vol. 2. New York, 1968.

Gibbons, Stanley. *Stamps of Foreign Countries.* London, 1914.

Gillett, J. D. *The Mosquito: Its Life, Activities, and Impact on Human Affairs.* New York, 1972.

Godechot, Jacques, *The Napoleonic Era in Europe.* New York, 1971.

Goethals, George W., ed. *The Panama Canal: An Engineering Treatise.* 2 vols. New York, 1916.

Gomara, Francisco Lopez de. *Cronica general de las Indias.* Vol. 2. Zaragosa, 1552.

Gooch, R. K. *The French Parliamentary Committee System.* New York, 1935.

Gorgas, William Crawford. *Sanitation in Panama.* New York-London, 1918.

Graell, Catalino Arrocha. *Historia de la Independencia de Panama: Sus Antecedentes y Sus Causas—1821-1903.* Panama City, 1933.

Graham, Cunninhame. *The Conquest of New Granada.* London, 1922.

Gredilla, A. F. *Biografia de Don José Celestino Mútis.* Madrid, 1911.

Greene, L. *The Filibuster: The Career of William Walker.* New York, 1937.

Griswold C. D., M.D. *The Isthmus of Panama: And What I Saw There.* New York, 1852.

Guayonges, Pascual. *Cartas y Relaciones de Hernan Cortéz al Emperador Carlos V.,* Paris, 1866.

Guerard, Albert. *Beyond Hatred.* New York, 1925.

Guiteras, P. G. *Historia de Cuba.* Havana, 1927-28.

Halasy, Nicholas. *Captain Dreyfus: The Story of Mass Hysteria.* New York, 1935.

Haskins, William C., ed. *Canal Zone Pilot.* Panama, 1908.

Haworth, P. L. *The Hayes-Tilden Disputed Presidential Election of 1876.* New York, 1906.

Hearings before the Senate Committee on Interoceanic Canals on H.R. 3110. (Sen. Doc. 253, 57th Cong., 1st Sess.). Washington, D.C., 1902.

Hearings before the Senate Committee on Interoceanic Canals on the Senate Resolution Providing for an Investigation of Matters Relating to the Panama Canal. (Sen. Doc. 401, 59th Cong. 2nd Sess.). Washington, D.C., 1907.

Henao, Jesus Maria y Arrubla, Gerardo. *Historia de Colombia.* Bogotá, 1952.

Henderson, B. W. *The Life and Principate of the Emperor Nero.* London, 1903.

Henry, O. *Cabbages and Kings.* New York, 1913.

Henschen, Folke. *The History and Geography of Diseases.* New York, 1962.

Herring, Hubert. *History of Latin America*. New York, 1968.

Hibbert, Christopher. *Agincourt*. Philadelphia, 1964.

Hippocrates. *Epidemics*. Translation by W. H. S. Jones. Cambridge, 1923.

Hobson, John A. *The War in South Africa: Its Causes and Effects*. New York, 1969.

Horace. *Odes*. Translation by Helen Rowe Henze. Norman, Oklahoma, 1961.

Horace. *Odes*. Translation by Kenneth J. Reckford. New York, 1969.

Howarth, David. *Panama, Four Hundred Years of Dreams and Cruelty*. New York, 1966.

Huertas, Ponce Estéban. *Memoria y Bosquejo Biográfico del General Estéban Huertas, etc.* Panama, 1958.

Humboldt, Alexander von. *Political Essay on the Kingdom of New Spain*. London, 1811.

Humboldt, Alexander von. *Viajes a las Regiones Equinoxiales de America*. Santiago, 1898.

Huntington, C. P. *The Nicaragua Canal*. N.p., 1900.

Icarbalceta, Joaquin Garcia. *Colección de Documentos para la Historia de Méjico*. Mexico City, 1558.

Instrucions to Rear Admiral Daniel Ammen and Civil Engineer A. G. Menocal, U.S. Navy, Delegates on the Part of the United States to the Interoceanic Canal Congress, Held at Paris May, 1879, and Reports of the Proceedings of the Congress. Washington, 1879.

Isthmian Canal Commission. *Annual Reports*. 1904-1914.

The Isthmus of Panama Inter-Oceanic Canal: M. le Comte de Lesseps at Liverpool. Exeter, England, 1880.

Jameson, J. Franklin; Learned, H. Barrett; Scott, James Brown; and Bemis, Samuel. *The American Secretaries of State and Their Diplomacy*. Vol. 5. New York, 1958.

Jessop, T. E. *The Treaty of Versailles: Was It Just?* London, 1942.

Jessup, Philip C. *Elihu Root*. Vol. 1. New York, 1938.

Johnson, Douglas, *France and the Dreyfus Affair*. New York, 1966.

Johnson, William Fletcher. *Four Centuries of the Panama Canal*. New York, 1906.

Keating, J. M. *The Yellow Fever Epidemic of 1878 in Memphis, Tennessee*. Memphis, 1879.

Keen, Benjamin. *Latin American Civilization*. Boston, 1974.

Kelly, Howard A. *Walter Reed and Yellow Fever*. Baltimore, 1906.

Kimball, Lieutenant William W. *Special Intelligence Report of the Progress of the Work on the Panama Canal during the Year 1885*. (House Misc. Doc. 395, 49th Cong., 1st Sess.). Washington, 1886.

Klimm, Lester E. *Man's role in Changing the Face of the Earth*. Norman, Oklahoma, 1956.

Kulski, Wladyslaw Wszebn. *De Gaulle and the World: The Foreign Policy of the Fifth French Republic*. Syracuse, 1966.

Labas, J. B. A. *L'Obelisque de Luxor*. Paris, 1839.

Laertius, Diogenes, *Lives of Eminent Philosophers: Diogenes of Sinope*. Translation by R. D. Hicks. Cambridge, 1928.

Lamballe, Princess. *Secret Memoirs of the Royal Family of France*. London, 1895.

Lameda, León y Rosales, Manuel Landaeta. *Historia Militar y Politica del general Joaquín Crespo*. Caracas, 1897.

Launay, Jacques de. *De Gaulle and His France*. New York, 1968.

Leach, Paul R. *That Man Dawes*. Chicago, 1930.

Leech, Margaret. *In the Days of McKinley*. New York, 1959.

Leeds, Stanton Budington. *These Ruled France*. Indianapolis, 1940.

Leon, Manuel Cano, and Arbazuza, Guillermo Brockman. *El Canal Interocéanico*. Madrid, 1879.

Levi-Strauss, Claude. *Tristes Tropiques*. Paris, 1955.

List of Books and of Articles in Periodicals Relating to Interoceanic Canal and Railway Routes. (Sen. Doc. No. 59, 56th Cong., 1st Sess.). Washington, D.C., 1900.

Lodge, Henry Cabot. *Early Memoirs*. New York, 1913.

Lodge, Henry Cabot. *Historical and Political Essays*. Boston, 1892.

Lodge, Henry Cabot. *Selections from the Correspondence of Theodore Roosevelt and Henry Cabot Lodge*. New York, 1925.

López, Hipólito Ruíz. *Quinología: O Tratado del Arbol de la Quina o Cascarilla— Con Su Descripcion y la de Otras Especies de Quinos—del Modo de Beneficiarla*. Madrid, 1792.

Lorant, Stefan. *The Life and Times of Theodore Roosevelt*. Garden City, 1959.

Mack, Gerstle. *The Land Divided*. New York, 1944.

Madariaga, Salvador de. *The Fall of the Spanish Empire in America*. New York, 1948.

Madariaga, Salvador de. *Ingleses, Franceses, Españoles*. Buenos Aires, 1942.

Mahan, Captain A. T. *From Sail to Steam, Recollections of a Naval Life*. New York, 1907.

Mahan, Captain A. T. *The Influence of Sea Power upon History*. Boston, 1890.

Manual of Information Concerning Employments for Service on the Isthmus of Panama. Washington, D.C., 1909.

Marcellinus, Ammianus. *Rerum Gestarum*. Translation by John C. Rolfe. London, 1960.

March, José Maria. *La Batalla de Lepanto y Don Luís Requesens, Lugarteniente General de la Mar. Con Nuevos Documentos Inéditos*. Madrid, 1944.

Marsh, Richard Oglesby. *White Indians of Darién*. New York, 1934.

Markham, L. *A Memoir of the Lady Ana de Osorio*. London, 1869.

Marucchi, O. *Gli Obelischi Egiziani de Roma*. Rome, 1898.

Mendez, Pereira Octavio. *Justo Arosemena*. Panama, 1949.

Mendez, Pereira Octavio. *Panama en la Gran Colombia*. Panama, 1939.

Mendez, Pereira Octavio. *Para la Historia: La Defensa de Panama*. Panama, 1926.

Mendoza, Diego. *Expedición Botánica de José Celestina Mutis por el Nuevo Reino de Granada*. Madrid, 1909.

Merrill, William C., et al. *Panama's Economic Development*. Ames, Iowa, 1975.

Miner, Dwight Carroll. *The Fight for the Panama Route*. New York, 1940.

Minter, John Easter. *The Chagres*. New York, 1948.

Momigliano, A. *Cambridge Ancient History*. Vol. 10. 1934.

Moore, John Bassett. *A Digest of International Law*. Washington, 1906.

Morales, David Turner. *Estructura Económica de Panama*. Mexico City, 1958.

Morales, Eusebio A. *Ensayos, Documentos y Discursos*. Panama, 1939.

Morison, George Abbot. *George Shattuck Morison, 1842-1903*. Peterborough, 1932.

Morison, George S. *The Isthmian Canal*. 1902.

Morison, Samuel Eliot. *Admiral of the Ocean Sea*. Boston, 1942.

Morison, Samuel Eliot. *The European Discovery of America: The Southern Voyages, 1492-1616*. New York, 1974.

Morris, Donald R. *The Washing of the Spears*. New York, 1965.

Muñoz, D. Juan Bautista. *Historia de la Conquista de America*. Madrid, 1793.

Mutis, José Celestino. *El Arcano de la Quina*. Bogotá, 1793.

Myers, Dennys P. *Origin and Conclusion of the Paris Pact*. Boston, 1929.

Myers, Dennys P. *The Reparation Settlement*. Boston, 1929.

Nevins, Allan. *Henry White: Thirty Years of American Diplomacy*. New York, n.d.

Nicolau, Valeriano Weyler. *Mi Mando en Cuba*. Madrid, 1910.

Orlando, Fals Borda. *La Subversión en Colombia*. Bogotá, 1968.

Ortiz, Scalabrini. *Política Británica en el Rio de la Plata*. Montevideo, 1910.

Otis, Fessenden Nott. *History of the Panama Railroad; and of the Pacific Mail Steamship Company. Together with a Traveller's Guide and Business Man's Hand-book for the Panama Railroad*. New York, 1867.

Oviedo, Fernandez de. *Historia Natural y General de las Indias*. Madrid, 1554.

The Panama Canal, 25th Anniversary. Canal Zone Publication, 1939.

Pelayo, J. Menendez. *Historia de la Poesía Hispano-Americana*. Bogotá and Madrid, 1913.

Pepperman, Walter Leon. *Who Built the Panama Canal?* New York, 1915.

Perez, Modesto, and Nougues, Pablo. *Los precursores Españoles del Canal Interocéanico*. Madrid, 1920.

Phoebus, G. *Die Delandre—Bouchardatschen Chinarinden*. Giessen, 1913.

Plutarch. *Lives*. Translation by John Dryden. New York, n.d.

Plutarch. *Lives*. Translation by John and William Langhorn. N.p., n.d.

Portocarrero, Carlos M. *Tratados y Convenios Comerciales de Colombia*. Bogota, 1972.

Radie, Betty. *The letters of the Younger Pliny*. Baltimore, 1962.

Report of the Isthmian Canal Commission 1889-1901. (Sen. Doc. 222, 58th Cong., 2nd Sess.). Washington, D.C., 1904.

Reports of the United States Commissioners to the Paris Universal Exposition, 1878. Washington, D.C., 1878.

República de Colombia. *Anales Diplomáticos y Consulares*. Bogotá, 1900.

República de Colombia, Academia de la Historia. *Boletín*. Bogotá, 1900.

República de Panama. *Anales de la Asamble Nacional*. Panama, 1934-1940.

República de Panama, Secretaría de Relaciones Exteriores. *Memorias*. Panama, 1910, 1930, 1940, 1950.

Reynaud, Paul. *In the Thick of the Fight: 1930-1945*. New York, 1955.

Ripoll, Emilio Castelar y. *Historia del descubrimiento de America.* Madrid, 1892.

Robertson, William Spence. *General Don Francisco de Miranda and the American Independence.* New York, 1929.

Robertson, William Spence. *History of the Latin American Nations.* New York, 1932.

Robertson, William Spence. *Life of Francisco de Miranda.* North Carolina, 1929.

Robichez, Jacques. *Le XIXe Siecle Francais.* Paris, 1962.

Rodrigues, José Carlos. *The Panama Canal: Its Political Aspects and Financial Difficulties.* New York, 1885.

Roosevelt, Nicholas. *Theodore Roosevelt: The Man as I Knew Him.* New York, 1967.

Roosevelt, Theodore. *An Autobiography.* New York, 1920.

Samper, Acosta de, M.D. *Compendio de Historia de Colombia.* Bogotá, 1909.

Sanchez, R. Guerra. *Manual de la Historia de Cuba.* Havana, 1938.

Sanchez, R. Guerra. *Historia de la Nación Cubana.* Havana, 1952.

Sanchez-Barba, Mario Hernandez de. *La Ultima Expansión Española en América.* Madrid, 1957.

Secundus, Plinius. *Natural History.* Translation by H. Rochman. Vol. 2. London, 1958.

Sherwin-White, N. *The letters of Pliny: A Historical and Social Commentary.* Oxford, 1966.

Shirer, William Lawrence. *The Collapse of the Third Republic: An Inquiry Into the Fall of France.* New York, 1969.

Sibert, William L., and John F. Stevens. *The Construction of the Panama Canal.* New York, 1915.

Siculus, Diodorus. *History.* Translation by C. H. Oldfather. London, 1933.

Siegfried, André. *Suez and Panama.* Oxford, 1940.

Simon, Maron J. *The Panama Affair.* New York, 1971.

Sloane, William Milligan. *Napoleon Bonaparte.* London, 1896.

Smith, Philip. *Ancient History of the East.* New York, 1899.

Society of the Chagres. *Yearbook, 1913.* Culebra, C.Z.

Starr, Chester. *The Roman Imperial Navy.* New York, 1941.

Stein, H. *Herodoti Historiae.* Paris, 1869-71.

Stephens, John Lloyd. *Incidents of Travel in Central America, Chiapas, and Yucatan.* New York, 1841.

Sullivan, Lieutenant John T. *Report of Historical and Technical Information Relating to the Problem of Interoceanic Communication by Way of the American Isthmus.* Washington, 1883.

Susto, Juan Antonio. *Homenaje al Doctor Manuel Amador Guerrero en el Centenario de su nacimiento. 1833-Junio-1933.* Panama, 1933.

Tacitus. *History.* Harvard, 1927.

Tacitus. *Tacitus Complete Works.* Edited by Moses Hadas. New York, 1942.

Taylor, Alfred Edward. *Thomas Hobbes.* London, 1908.

Taylor, Charles Carlisle. *The Life of Admiral Mahan.* London, 1920.

Testimony Taken before the Select Committee on the Interoceanic Ship Canal. Washington, 1880.

Thayer, W. R. *Life and Letters of John Hay.* 2 vol. New York, 1916.

The Story of Panama: Hearings on the Rainey Resolution before the Committee on Foreign Affairs of the House of Representatives. Washington, D.C., 1913.

Tomes, Robert. Panama in 1855: An account of the Panama Rail-road. New York, 1855.

Tordesillas, Antonio de Herrera y. Historia General de los Hechos de los Castellanos en las Islas y Tierra Firme del Mar Oceano Indico. Madrid, 1615.

Tranquillus, C. Suetonius. Lives of the Caesars. Translation by J. C. Rolfe. n.p., 1959.

Velarde, Fabian. Analisis del Nuevo Tratado. Panama, 1926.

Vizetelly, Ernest A. Court Life of the Second French Empire. New York, 1907.

Vizetelly, Ernest A. Republican France, 1870-1912. Boston, 1912.

Wedell, H. A. Histoire Naturelle des Quinquinas. Paris, 1849.

Weill, B. Grandeur et Decadence du General Boulanger. Paris, 1931.

Weinberg, Albert K. Manifest Destiny, a Study of National Expansion in American History. Baltimore, 1935.

Welk, W. H. The Monroe Doctrine and the Control of the Isthmus. New York, 1881.

Williams, Wythe. The Tiger of France. New York, 1949.

Wyse, Lucien Napolean-Bonaparte. Canal Interoceanique 1876-77. Rapport Sur les Etudes de la Commission Internationale d'Exploration de l'Isthme du Darien. Paris, 1877.

Wyse, Lucien Napoleon-Bonaparte. Le Canal de Panama, l'Isthme Americain. Explorations, Comparison des Traces Etudies; Negociations; Etat des Travaux. . . . Paris, 1886.

Newspapers and Magazines

American History Illustrated
American Historical Review
American Journal of Science
American Journal of Tropical Medicine
American Society of Civil Engineers, Proceedings
American Society of Civil Engineers, Transactions
Armco World
The Arlington Daily News, Arlington, Texas.
The Arlington Quarterly, University of Texas in Arlington.
Atlanta Constitution, Atlanta, Georgia.
L'Aurore (Paris)
Baltimore Sun
Boletin de la Academia Panameña de la Historia, Panama City, Panama
Bulletin de la Societé de Geographie, Paris, France.
Bulletin du Canal Interoceanique, Paris, France.
Bulletin of the Pan-American Union, Washington, D.C.
Chicago Tribune
El Chileno, Santiago, Chile.
El Comercio, Lima, Peru.
El Cronista, Guayaquil, Ecuador.
Current Medical Digest

Daily Telegraph (London)
Dallas Morning News
Dallas Times Herald
El Derecho (Bogota)
L' Echo de Paris
La Estrella de Panama
Le Figaro (France)
Fort Worth Press
Le Galois (Paris)
Iranian Oil Journal
Journal of Inter-American Studies and World Affairs
Journal of Modern History
El Lapiz, Bogota, Colombia.
Latin American Research Review
El Latinoamericano, Mexico City, Mexico.
La Libre Parole (France)
Lippincott's Magazine
London Daily News
London Globe
London Times
Loteria (Panama)
Louisville Courier-Journal (Kentucky)
Le Matin (France)
Monthly Bulletin of Statistics
Nation
National Enquirer
National Geographic Magazine (Washington, D.C.)
New York Herald
New York Press
New York Sun
New York Times
New York Times Magazine
North American Review
El Noticiero, Caracas, Venezuela.
Outlook
Pacific Historical Review, San Francisco, Calif.
Pall Mall Gazette
Panama Canal Spillway
Panama Star & Herald
Paris Herald
Patria (San Jose, C.R.)
Patrimonio Histórico, Panama City, Panama.
La Prensa, Buenos Aires, Argentina.
El Relator (Bogotá)
The Review: Indiana University Alumni Association

Review of Reviews
San Francisco Chronicle
San Francisco Examiner
Saturday Evening Post
Scientific American
The States-Item (New Orleans, Louisiana)
El Telégrapho, Guayaquil, Ecuador.
Le Temps
U.S. News and World Report
Washington Post
Washington Star

Documentary Collections

Varillana, Philippe Bunau-Varilla II and Madame Giselle Bunau-Varilla.

The Loomis Papers, Miss Florence Loomis and the Loomis Collection, Stanford University, California.

Price Bell Collection, Newberry Library, Chicago, Ill.

The George Goethals, William Gorgas, John Hay, Theodore Roosevelt, John Stevens, William Howard Taft collections, Library of Congress.

The Records of the Compagnie Universalle du Canal Interoceanique and of the Compagnie Nouvelle du Canal de Panama, Isthmian Canal Commission.

The Latin American Collection, University of Tulane, New Orleans, La.

The Enrique Arce, Octavio Mendez Pereira and Santiago Anguizola libraries.

The Antonio Anguizola Lastra and Antonio Anguizola Palma papers.

Documentos Pertinentes al Periodo Colonial, la historia del ferrocarril de Panama, el Canal de Panama y la Independencia del Istmo, Archivo Nacional, Panama City, Panama.

Index

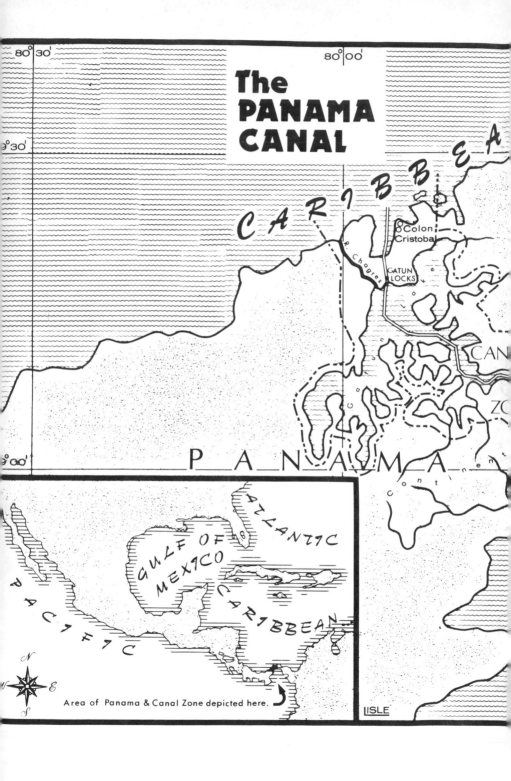

The PANAMA CANAL

80° 30'
80° 00'

9°30'

CARIBBEA

R Chagres

oColon
Cristobal

GATUN
LOCKS

CAN

ZO

9°00'

PANAMA

Continent

ATLANTIC

GULF OF MEXICO

CARIBBEAN

PACIFIC

N
W   E
S

Area of Panama & Canal Zone depicted here.

ISLE